THE ARCHEOLOGY
OF THE NEW TESTAMENT

About the Book and Author

The Archeology of the New Testament:
The Mediterranean World of the Early Christian Apostles
Jack Finegan

This book, a companion volume to Dr. Finegan's *The Archeology of the New Testament: The Life of Jesus and the Beginning of the Early Church* (Princeton University Press), provides an introduction to the Mediterranean world in which the early Christian apostles moved. Drawing on the geographic setting and available archeological materials to create a sense of the contemporary environment, the book traces the 15,000-mile travels of Paul, whose world was also the world of Peter, John, and many other early Christians.

Dr. Finegan presents a consistent chronology for the major apostles based on his integration of existing histories, literary accounts, and archeological information with recent discoveries and new theories on dating New Testament events and documents. He illustrates his text lavishly with photographs of archeological sites and museum artifacts, providing maps and site plans as well. There is also a detailed essay on ancient sources that supplements the biblical references included throughout.

Jack Finegan is professor emeritus of New Testament history and archeology at the Pacific School of Religion and has been a frequent visitor to the Mediterranean and Middle East. In addition to his first volume on the New Testament, he has written *Archaeological History of the Ancient Middle East* (Westview, 1979).

THE ARCHEOLOGY
OF THE NEW TESTAMENT

The Mediterranean World of
the Early Christian Apostles

Jack Finegan

Westview Press • Boulder, Colorado

Croom Helm • London, England

Copyright © 1981 by Westview Press, Inc.

Published in 1981 in the United States of America by
   Westview Press, Inc.
   5500 Central Avenue
   Boulder, Colorado 80301
   Frederick A. Praeger, Publisher

Published in 1981 in Great Britain by
   Croom Helm Ltd.
   2-10 St. John's Road
   London, S.W. 11

Library of Congress Cataloging in Publication Data
Finegan, Jack, 1908–
   The archeology of the New Testament.
   Includes bibliographical references and indexes.
   Vol. 2 published by Westview Press, Boulder, Colo.
   CONTENTS: [v.1.] The life of Jesus and the beginning of the early church.–[v.2.] The Mediterranean world of the early Christian apostles.
   1. Bible. N.T.–Antiquities. I. Title.
BS 2375.F5   225.9'3   69-18057
ISBN (U.S.): 0-86531-064-5 (Westview: v.2)
ISBN (U.K.): 0-7099-1006-1

Printed and bound in the United States of America

CONTENTS

MAPS AND PLANS

Maps

Plans

ILLUSTRATIONS

ILLUSTRATION CREDITS

With the exception of Figures 13, 74, 76, 102, 114, and 115, I have taken all of the photographs for this volume, and the black-and-white prints have been made by William J. Petzel. Photographs taken in museums were with the museums' permission, and I would like also to acknowledge their permission to reproduce those photographs in this book:

Figures 9, 10, and 11, the Archaeological Museum, Antioch, Turkey.

Figures 18, 20, and 23, the Archaeological Museum, Antalya, Turkey, and Professor Dr. Jale Inan, the excavator of Perga.

Figure 22, the Archaeological Museum, Side, Turkey.

Figures 25, 119, and 120, the Greco-Roman Museum, Alexandria, Egypt.

Figure 39, the Crypt Museum of Agios Dimitrios, Thessaloniki, Greece.

Figures 41, 42, and 43, the Archaeological Museum, Thessaloniki, Greece.

Figures 48, 51, 63, 64, 65, 66, and 68, the National Archaeological Museum, Athens, Greece.

Figures 54, 55, 56, 57, and 58, the Agora Museum in the Stoa of Attalos, Athens, Greece.

> (For the foregoing photographs from the National Archaeological Museum in Athens and the Agora Museum in the Stoa of Attalos in Athens, permission is also acknowledged from the Greek Archaeological Service—TAPA, Athens).

Figures 67 and 75, the Byzantine Museum, Athens, Greece.

Figures 86, 87, 88, and 89, the Ephesus (Selçuk) Museum, Ephesus, Turkey.

Figures 107, 108, and 109, the Archaeological Museum, Kos, Greece.

All of the maps and plans were prepared by me and drawn for publication by Adrienne Morgan. Plans 4, 21, and 22 are reproduced from my *Light from the Ancient Past* by permission of Princeton University Press.

PREFACE

My book *The Archeology of the New Testament: The Life of Jesus and the Beginning of the Early Church* was published by Princeton University Press in 1969, with a second hardcover printing in 1972, and as a Princeton Paperback in 1978. This was intended as the first volume of a two-volume work, and the original expectation was that the second volume, on the latter part of the New Testament, would be written by another author. Since this has not been done I have now myself—after too long a delay for the foregoing reason—written this second volume, *The Archeology of the New Testament: The Mediterranean World of the Early Christian Apostles*, for Westview Press. Together the two volumes are intended to provide an archeological guide to New Testament sites and to make available archeological materials relevant to the study of New Testament history.

After the Gospels the largest part of what is written in the New Testament is associated with the name of the apostle Paul, and accordingly, the record of his travels provides the most convenient outline to follow in moving out across the Mediterranean world. On just the journeys described so carefully in the Book of Acts the apostle Paul may be reckoned to have traveled not less than 12,000 miles (20,000 kilometers), and on the later trip to Spain referred to by Clement of Rome and the further journeys in the East presupposed by the pastoral letters, he must have gone an additional 3,000 miles (5,000 kilometers) or more, in all a tremendous total in excess of 15,000 miles (25,000 kilometers). On land most of this travel was probably on foot for, like Jesus, who is only once described as riding a donkey into Jerusalem, Paul is only once spoken of as riding horseback, and that was when a detachment of Roman cavalry was taking him to prison in Caesarea (Ac 23:24). His passages at sea were hardly less arduous—he was only partway through his career when we learn that he had already been shipwrecked three times (II Cor 11:25).

To follow the apostle in these travels—whether in imaginative study, in actual journeying on the routes he traversed, or both—is an exciting and amazing experience. There is excitement because one goes—in imagination or in actuality—to what were the chief centers of life in the ancient Mediterranean world, these being exactly the strategic points toward which Paul directed his efforts. The experience brings amazement because one derives a fresh and vivid realization of the sheer magnitude of the physical accomplishment of the apostle, alongside the more generally recognized towering intellectual achievement of his theology.

In fact, those who are concerned with any or all aspects of Paul's work may find illumination in the study of his life in its original setting. There is a notable example in the work of Adolf Deissmann. After many years of academic study of the ancient records of Paul and their modern interpreters, Deissmann felt that he found a new teacher—in no sense academic—when he went into the bright sunshine and open air of the world of the East, and the world of Paul. In his preface to *Paul, A Study in Social and Religious History*, he summed up the effect of his travels:

I may say that the good germs of an historical appreciation of Paul, which I owed to my teachers and my own studies, underwent new growth in the apostle's own field and beneath the rays of his sun, but that many rank shoots that had sprung up in the shade of the school walls withered under the same beams. . . .

Therefore beside the Paul who has been turned into a western scholastic philosopher, beside the aristocratised, conventionalised, and modernised Paul, now suffering his eighth imprisonment in the paper bondage of "Paulinism," I would fain set the Paul whom I think to have seen at Tarsus, Jerusalem and Damascus, in Antioch, Lycaonia, Galatia, Ephesus, and Corinth, and whose words became alive to me at night on the decks of Levant shipping, and to the sound of birds of passage winging their flight towards the Taurus—alive in their passionate emotion, the force of their popular appeal, and their prophetic depth. I mean Paul the Jew, who in the days of the Caesars breathed the air of the Mediterranean and ate the bread which he had earned by the labour of his own hands; the missionary whose dark shadow fell on the glittering marble pavement of the great city in the blinding glare of noon; the mystic devotee of Christ who, so far as he can be comprehended historically at all, will be understood not as the incarnation of a system but as a living complex of inner polarities which refuse to be parcelled out.[1]

The world of Paul was also the world of Peter, John, Timothy, Titus, and other leaders of the early Christian church, and several of these persons will be dealt with in what follows. This is particularly true in my consideration of the chronology of Paul, where his death and that of Peter are closely connected in early Christian tradition. Also, at the respective archeological sites there are remembrances of both Paul and Peter at Rome; of Paul, John, and Timothy at Ephesus; and of Titus as well as Paul on Crete.

Serious study of the subject calls for an examination of literary sources and chronological history as well as of archeological sites, and the first two of these topics are taken up in some detail in the first two chapters of this volume. For the sites, however, one may, if it is wished, proceed immediately to the third and following chapters. Thirty-five maps and plans outline the places, and my own photographs—except where otherwise indicated—provide illustration.[2]

Jack Finegan

NOTES

1. Adolf Deissmann, *Paul, A Study in Social and Religious History* (London: Hodder and Stoughton, 2d ed., 1926), pp. ix–x.

2. In general for all the sites discussed see Pauly-Wissowa, *Realencyclopädie der classischen Altertumswissenschaft*, 1894 and continuing (abbreviated pwre); *Dictionnaire d'archéologie chrétienne et de liturgie*, 1924–53 (abbreviated dacl); *The Interpreter's Dictionary of the Bible*, 1962 (abbreviated idb, many of the relevant articles by the present author, with references and bibliographies); and *Supplementary Volume*, 1976 (abbreviated idb-s); *The Princeton Encyclopedia of Classical Sites*, 1976 (abbreviated pecs). Also four volumes, *In the Footsteps of the Saints*, by Otto F. A. Meinardus, *St. Paul in Greece, St. Paul in Ephesus and the Cities of Galatia and Cyprus, St. Paul's Last Journey*, and *St. John of Patmos and the Seven Churches of the Apocalypse*, first published by the Lycabettus Press in Athens, have now been published in North America by Caratzas Brothers, Publishers, New Rochelle, New York, 1979.

ALPHABETICAL LIST OF ANCIENT SOURCES

Aeschylus (525–456 B.C.). The Greek tragic dramatist was born at Eleusis, Attica, and served in the Athenian armies in the Persian wars. Of his many plays, seven have survived, among them the *Eumenides*, which was produced in 458.

Aetheria (Eucheria or Egeria). The nun and pilgrim probably came from the south of France, made a journey to the Holy Land in A.D. 385–388, and wrote a detailed account of her travels, which is called *Peregrinatio ad loca sancta*.

Ammianus Marcellinus (A.D. c. 330–395). The last great Roman historian was born in Antioch of a Greek family, served in the Roman army in Gaul and Persia, and also visited Egypt and Greece. After 378 he settled in Rome and there wrote, in Latin, his *History* of the Roman Empire, a continuation of the historical works of Tacitus. Of an original thirty-one books, eighteen are extant, covering the years 353 to 378.

Apocryphal New Testament. The books commonly grouped under this heading are ones that in title or content resemble the four literary forms of the canonical New Testament, i.e., they are Gospels, Acts, Epistles, or Apocalypses, and they often purport to be works of New Testament personages. Although often obviously legendary or imaginative in character, they may sometimes contain a historical core.

Apollonius (second century A.D.). The anti-Montanist writer was the author (probably A.D. c. 196–197) of a refutation of the ascetic, charismatic heresy that took its name from the prophet Montanus (c. 156), flourished in Phrygia, and was adopted by Tertullian. Eusebius (*Ch. Hist.* v 18, 1–14) tells about Apollonius and quotes from his work.

Apollonius of Tyana (first century A.D.). The Neopythagorean sage was born at Tyana in Cappadocia about the beginning of the Christian era and died at Ephesus probably in 98. He lived as a wandering teacher and visited distant lands, including India. Letters of Apollonius and a travel diary of his companion, the Assyrian Damis, were utilized by Flavius Philostratus to write the *Life of Apollonius*. Little of Apollonius's own writings survives.

Appian (second century A.D.). The Roman historian was probably born under Domitian (81–96) and held office in Alexandria, but after gaining Roman citizenship he moved to Rome. Under Antoninus Pius (138–161) he wrote, in Greek, his *Roman History*. Of the original twenty-four books, eleven survive in full, some are in fragments, and some are lost. The arrangement is ethnographic, and the work treats the various Roman conquests in turn as well as the civil wars.

Arculf (seventh century A.D.). The Frankish bishop and pilgrim visited the Near East and stayed in Jerusalem for nine months, being the first Christian traveler of note to go there after the rise of Islam. On his return journey Arculf went to Britain and related his experiences to Adamnan, the abbot of Iona (679–704). The latter wrote down the narrative in three books, concerning Jerusalem, the Holy Land, and Constantinople, respectively.

Aristides (A.D. c. 125). The Greek Christian apologist was the author of an *Apology* of which a complete manuscript in Syriac was found by J. Rendel Harris at Mt. Sinai in 1891.

Aristides, Aelius (A.D. 117 or 129–189). The public speaker and man of letters was born in Mysia, studied in Athens, and became an admired Greek rhetorician. After suffering illness in Rome he spent much time as a patient in the Asklepieion at Pergamum. He made his later home in Smyrna and occupied his time in writing and lecturing. His *Sacred Teachings* record the revelations he received in dreams from Asklepios. His other works are addresses, polemical essays, and prose hymns to various gods.

Aristotle (384–322 B.C.). The Greek philosopher was born at Stagira in Chalcidice, studied under Plato (c. 429–347) in the Academy at Athens (367–347), tutored Alexander the Great (c. 342–335), and taught in Athens as the head of the Peripatetic school (335–322). His numerous works deal with logic, metaphysics, natural science, ethics, politics, rhetoric, and poetics.

Athenaeus (end of second century A.D.). The Greek scholar was from Naucratis, Egypt. His only extant work is the *Deipnosophists* ("the learned banquet"), probably completed after the death of Commodus in 192. Now in fifteen books (perhaps thirty originally), the work cites a very large number of authors, plays, and poems.

Athenagoras (second century A.D.). The Christian philosopher and apologist was from Athens. His apology called *Supplication for the Christians* is addressed to Marcus Aurelius (161–180) and his son Commodus (180–192) in c. 177, and it defends the Christians against the three charges of atheism, cannibalism, and incest. At the end of the apology Athenagoras promises to write about the Resurrection, and this work is his *On the Resurrection of the Dead*, composed in twenty-five chapters, considered the best early Christian treatise on the subject.

Athenodorus of Tarsus (c. 74 B.C.–A.D. 7). The Stoic philosopher was a friend of Cicero and Strabo and a tutor of Augustus. In his old age he was sent by Augustus on a mission to Tarsus, where he became the chief citizen. Among his writings were an account of Tarsus, a work against the categories of Aristotle, and various ethical writings. Use has been made of the ethical writings by Seneca.

Augustine, Aurelius Augustinus (A.D. 354–430). The Christian theologian was born at Thagaste in Numidia, and he taught rhetoric at Carthage, Rome, and Milan. Originally a Manichaean, he came under the influence of Bishop Ambrose of Milan, was converted to Christianity, and accepted Catholicism as the "divine philosophy." As bishop of Hippo in proconsular Africa (396–430) Augustine stood forth as the champion of orthodoxy against the Manichaeans, Donatists, and Pelagians. His most famous works are *The City of God* and his autobiography, *Confessions*, but he also wrote many other treatises, sermons, and letters. He died at Hippo in 430 while the city was under siege by the Vandals.

Chronography of 354. This is a calendar and directory for the city of Rome that was edited in the year A.D. 354 by Furius Dionysius Filocalus, the later secretary and calligrapher of Pope Damasus I (366–384). The work contains a state calendar; consular fasts; Easter tables; a list of prefects of the city and a description of the fourteen districts of the city; a chronicle of the world, the *Chronica Horosii*, which is a Latin version and continuation to 334 of the chronicle of Hippolytus; a chronicle of the city of Rome; a list of the anniversaries of the Roman bishops and martyrs, known as the *Depositio episcoporum* and the *Depositio martyrum*; and a list of popes down to Liberius (352–366), the *Catalogus Liberianus*.

Chrysostom, John (A.D. c. 354–407). The eloquent preacher (*chrysostom*, "golden mouthed") was born in Antioch of Syria, practiced asceticism in the nearby desert, was ordained a deacon and a priest, and became patriarch of Constantinople in 398. In 403 he was banished by the empress Eudoxia and Theophilus, bishop of Alexandria (385–412), and recalled, banished again in 404 to Armenia, and died in exile. He was the author of homilies, commentaries, and letters.

Cicero, Marcus Tullius (106–43 B.C.). The Roman orator, statesman, and philosopher was educated in rhetoric and philosophy in Rome and later in Greece and became the leading figure of his time at the Roman bar. In 70 he secured the condemnation of C. Verres for extortion in Sicily; in 62 he gathered decisive evidence against the Cataline conspirators. In 51/50 he governed Cilicia as proconsul for a year. He wrote orations, works on rhetoric, philosophy, theology, and ethics, and many letters.

Clement of Alexandria (died before A.D. 215). The Greek theologian was born c. 150, probably at Athens, of pagan parents. He was converted to Christianity and traveled extensively to study with various Christian teachers, finally with Pantaenus, head of the catechetical school at Alexandria. Upon the death of Pantaenus (probably before 200), Clement became head of the school and continued in that position until c. 202 when, during the persecution under Septimius Severus, he went to Asia Minor. His preserved works are *Exhortation to the Gentiles, Pedagogue, Stromata, What Rich Man Shall be Saved?* and *Excerpts from Theodotus,* plus fragments.

Clement of Rome (A.D. c. 96). The bishop of Rome is identified by Eusebius (*Ch. Hist.* III 15, 1) with the associate of Paul mentioned in Phil 4:3. Irenaeus (*Against Heresies* III 3, 3) names Clement as the third successor of Peter in the headship of the church at Rome; Tertullian (*On Prescription Against Heretics* 32) says that Clement was consecrated by Peter himself. The *First Epistle* of Clement was addressed to the church at Corinth. Other works later attributed to Clement include a *Second Epistle* to the Corinthians and *Homilies* and *Recognitions.*

Constantine VII Porphyrogenitus (A.D. 905–959). The Byzantine emperor was the son of the emperor Leo VI (886–912), and his appellation means "born in the purple." He was himself emperor 912–959, at first under the regency of Alexander (912–913), the brother of Leo VI, and of his own mother Zoë (913–919). He was a patron of arts and literature and the author of a number of political treatises.

Cyprian (died A.D. 258). The Christian bishop and martyr was probably born at Carthage between 200 and 210, as the son of wealthy pagan parents. By c. 246 he was converted to Christianity, and in 248/249 he became bishop of Carthage. During the persecution under Decius in 250 he went into hiding in the vicinity of the city but kept in touch with the church, and he was afterward involved in the question of terms for the readmission to the church of the lapsed, of whom he expected severe penance. During the persecution under Valerian he was beheaded near Carthage on September 14, 258. He wrote, in Latin, many tracts and letters, and from his numerous quotations much of the Old Latin Bible can be reconstructed.

Dio Cassius (A.D. c. 155–235). The Roman politician and historian wrote, in Greek, a *Roman History,* which covered Roman history from the beginning to A.D. 229, in which year Dio was consul for the second time with Alexander Serverus. The work is in eighty books, some fully preserved, some preserved only in part.

Diodorus (first century B.C.). The Greek historian Diodorus Siculus was so surnamed because he was born at Agyrium in Sicily. He was the author of a world history known as the *Historical Library,* composed in forty books, of which books 1–5 and 11–20 are fully preserved, and the others are fragmentary.

Dionysius of Corinth (second century A.D.). As the bishop of Corinth, Dionysius was a contemporary of Soter of Rome (A.D. c. 166–174), and he was outstanding among non-Roman bishops. Eusebius (*Ch. Hist.* II 25, 8; IV 23) gives some information concerning seven general epistles and one private letter that Dionysius wrote, and from among these Eusebius quotes from the *Letter to the Romans.*

Dionysius of Halikarnassos (first century B.C.). The Greek scholar lived and taught at Rome for many years from c. 30 B.C. onward, and he devoted himself to writing the history of Rome. This work, his *Roman Antiquities,* began to appear in 7 B.C., and of its twenty books the first ten survive. His other works are chiefly on rhetoric.

Epiphanius (A.D. c. 315–403). The Eastern Church leader and writer was born near Eleutheropolis in Palestine and, after a stay with Egyptian monks, he founded a monastery at Eleutheropolis, of which he was the head for some thirty years. In 367 he became bishop of Constantia (Salamis), Cyprus. He was opposed to Greek learning, attacked the use of images in churches, and contended against the followers of both Origen and Arius. His largest work, written in 374–377, is the *Panarion haereses* ("medicine chest for curing heresies"), in which he deals with no fewer than eighty heresies, including pagan philosophies and Jewish sects. The *Ancoratus* is on the doctrines of the church. *De mensuris et ponderibus* deals not only with measures and weights occurring in the Bible, but also with the books and versions of the Old Testament and with the geography of Palestine.

Eratosthenes (c. 275–194 B.C.). The Greek astronomer, geographer, and chronographer was born in Cyrene and was called to Alexandria by Ptolemy III Euergetes I (246–222) to head the library there. His *Chronographies* are the first scientific attempt to fix the dates of political and literary history. In his *On the Measurement of the Earth* (probably a part of his *Geography*) Eratosthenes calculated the circumference of the earth, with a high degree of accuracy, and the magnitude and distance of the sun and moon, with much less accuracy.

Eudoxus (c. 390–340 B.C.). The Greek scholar of Knidos studied at Athens under Plato and in Egypt with the priests at Heliopolis. He did work of importance in mathematics, astronomy, and geography.

Eusebius of Caesarea (A.D. c. 260–340). The theologian and church historian was born in Palestine, was educated under Pamphilus in the school at Caesarea founded by Origen, and was made bishop of Caesarea c. 314. His *Chronicle* provides synchronistic chronological tables beginning with the birth of Abraham (2016/2015 B.C.). His *Church History* was completed soon after 324, after the fall of Licinius, and the work quotes from many earlier authorities and documents. The *Onomasticon* is the surviving part of a large work on biblical geography written c. 330. Other works are *Martyrs of Palestine*, *Praeparatio Evangelica*, *Demonstratio Evangelica*, *On the Theophany*, and panegyrical writings in honor of Constantine.

Gregory of Nazianzus (A.D. 329–389). The Eastern Church ecclesiastic was born near Nazianzus in Cappadocia, where his father, Gregory the Elder, was bishop. He was educated at Caesarea in Cappadocia, Caesarea in Palestine, Alexandria, and Athens. He was a lifelong friend of Basil of Caesarea, Cappadocia (A.D. c. 330–379), who organized monastic communities in Asia Minor and composed rules for them. Gregory was involved in church administration and was even briefly (381) bishop of Constantinople. After that, however, he devoted himself to the practice of asceticism and to literary works, and he was later surnamed Theologus (the theologian). His writings are *Orations*, *Letters*, and *Poems*.

Gregory of Tours (A.D. 538–594). The real name of the Frankish ecclesiastic and historian was Georgius Florentius. In 573 he became bishop of Tours, the religious center of Gaul. His *Historia Francorum* is a work of national history. His *Miraculorum libri VIII*, of which Book I is *In gloria martyrum*, tells of the lives and miracles of many saints and martyrs.

Herodotus (fifth century B.C.). The Greek historian was born at Halikarnassos in Asia Minor. In the course of his studies he traveled over most of the then known world. He lived for a time in Samos, later in Athens, and finally in Thurii in Italy. His great work is a *History* of the Greco-Persian wars from 500 to 479 B.C.

Hesiod (c. 700 B.C.). The writer is one of the oldest known Greek poets, and there is a story of his meeting and contest with Homer, although Homer may actually have lived somewhat earlier. The *Theogony* of Hesiod is an account of the beginnings of the world and the origin and genealogies of the gods. The *Works and Days* recommends a life of honest work and gives practical information on agriculture, seafaring, and social and religious conduct.

Hippolytus (A.D. c. 170–236). The ecclesiastic was a native of the Greek East and wrote in Greek, although he lived and worked in Rome as a presbyter and probably as a rival pope to Callistus (217–222). During the persecution under Maximinus Thrax (235–238) both heads of the church, Pontianus (230–235) and Hippolytus, were exiled to Sardinia where both died and both were buried on the same day (August 13), Pontianus in the Crypt of the Popes in the Catacomb of Callistus and Hippolytus in the cemetery that was named for him on the Via Tiburtina. It was probably in his burial vault that his followers erected the famous statue of Hippolytus (rediscovered in 1551 and placed in the Lateran Museum), on which are engraved his Easter table and a partial list of his writings. The known writings of Hippolytus include works against various heresies (*Syntagma*, *Philosophoumena*), exegetical and dogmatic works, and a *Chronicle*, which begins with the creation of the world and ends with the year 234.

Homer (probably before 700 B.C.). The famous Greek poet was variously thought to have been from either Chios or Smyrna. According to tradition he was blind. The major works attributed to Homer are the *Iliad* and the *Odyssey*, which are epics on the Trojan War and the subsequent wanderings of Odysseus (Ulysses). The so-called *Homeric Hymns* are probably the work of others.

Horace (65–8 B.C.). Quintus Horatius Flaccus was a Roman lyric poet and satirist. He was educated at Rome and Athens, and in Rome he enjoyed the favor of the emperor Augustus. Among the works of Horace are satires, poems, odes, and epistles.

Ignatius (died A.D. c. 110). The bishop of Antioch was taken to Rome during the reign of Trajan (98–117) and thrown to the the beasts in the arena. On the way he wrote seven letters, which we still have. From Smyrna he wrote to Ephesus, Magnesia, and Tralles to thank the churches for having sent legates to greet him on his way and to the Romans to ask them not to try to keep him from martyrdom. At Troas he learned that the persecution in Antioch had ceased, and he wrote to Philadelphia and Smyrna and also to Polycarp, bishop of Smyrna, asking them to send delegates to congratulate the church at Antioch on reaching peace.

Ignatius. The medieval monk was the author of an account of the conversion of Theodora, daughter of the emperor Galerius (A.D. 305–311), and of a description of the mosaic in the church of Hosios David in Thessalonica. The Greek text of Ignatius has been published by S. Pelekanides, ΠΑΛΑΙΟΧΡΙΣΤΙΑΝΙΚΑ ΜΝΗΜΕΙΑ ΘΕΣΣΑΛΟΝΙΚΗΣ (Thessalonica, 1949), and it has been translated by R. F. Hoddinott, *Early Byzantine Churches in Macedonia and Southern Serbia* (London: Macmillan, 1963), pp. 68f., 178f.

Irenaeus (A.D. c. 180). The Greek church writer came from Asia Minor, and in his youth he listened to Polycarp, bishop of Smyrna (Eusebius, *Ch. Hist.* v 20, 5–6). In 177/178 Irenaeus became bishop of Lyons. Of his writings we have the *Unmasking and Refutation of the False Gnosis*, usually called *Adversus haereses (Against Heresies)*, and the *Presentation of the Apostolic Preaching*, as well as fragments of other works.

Jerome (A.D. c. 348–420). The scholar Eusebius Hieronymus, as he is known in Latin, was born in Dalmatia, studied in Rome, and lived as a hermit in the desert of Chalcis east of Antioch. He was in Rome again, 382–385, where he was friend and secretary of Pope Damasus (died 384), and Jerome was charged with making a revision of Latin texts of the Bible, later known as the Vulgate. He was also associated with several ladies of the Roman aristocracy, the widows Marcella and Paula, and the latter's daughter Eustochium. Jerome left Rome in 385 and soon settled in Bethlehem, where he lived for the last thirty-four years of his life. Paula and Eustochium followed him to Bethlehem where Paula built three convents for women, of which she was the head, and one monastery for men, with Jerome as the head. He revised the *Chronicle* of Eusebius in 380/381, and in *Lives of Illustrious Men* (392) Jerome wrote short notices of 135 Christian writers. He also wrote commentaries, homilies, some polemical works, and many personal letters.

John I. The bishop of Thessalonica in 610–649, John composed the first book of legends about St. Demetrius, called *Miracula sancti Demetrii*, and also wrote a number of homilies.

Josephus (first century A.D.). The Jewish historian Flavius Josephus was born in Jerusalem in A.D. 37/38, and he was a priest and a Pharisee. In the war of the Jews against Rome he was a commander in Galilee, but he was captured and saved his life by prophesying that Vespasian would become emperor,

as he did. Josephus then remained with Titus until the fall of Jerusalem (70) and thereafter settled in Rome where he received Roman citizenship. He published his account of *The Jewish War* (c. 75) and his *Jewish Antiquities* (93/94), which recounts Jewish history from the Creation to immediately before the outbreak of the war. His last works were his own *Life* (written after the death of Herod Agrippa II, probably after 95) and a defense of Judaism called *Against Apion*. The date of the death of Josephus is unknown.

Julius Africanus (A.D. 170–240). Sextus Julius Africanus, the Christian traveler and historian, was born in Aelia Capitolina (Jerusalem), and in Alexandria he attended the lectures of Heraclas and was a friend of Origen. He later lived in Emmaus-Nicopolis in Palestine. He wrote *Chronographies* in five books, giving synchronistic chronological tables from the creation of Adam to A.D. 221 and placing the birth of Jesus in the year 5500 from Adam. These tables were the basis of the *Chronicle* of Eusebius. Julius Africanus also dedicated a work called *Embroideries* to the emperor Alexander Severus (222–235).

Justin Martyr (A.D. 100–165). The Christian philosopher and martyr was born of pagan parents at Flavia Neapolis (ancient Shechem, modern Nablus) in Palestine, and he studied under Stoic, Peripatetic, Pythagorean, and Platonic teachers. At Ephesus he had a chance contact with an aged Christian and was converted to Christianity. Still wearing the cloak of a Greek philosopher, he went from place to place as an itinerant teacher, and he founded a school at Rome. At Ephesus he debated with a Jewish opponent named Trypho; at Rome the Cynic philosopher Crescens opposed him strongly. Eusebius (*Ch. Hist.* IV 18) names eight treatises written by Justin, but of those only three survive—the *Dialogue with Trypho* and two *Apologies Against the Gentiles*, the longer addressed to Antoninus Pius (138–161), the shorter addressed to the Roman Senate.

Juvenal (A.D. c. 60–140). The Roman lawyer and satirist was a friend of Martial. Five books of his *Satires* are extant, containing sixteen individual satires. He is very critical of Domitian (81–96) and of Roman society of his time, and he may have been exiled by Domitian, to return after Domitian was murdered. On the other hand, he compliments Hadrian (117–138) as a friend of literature. In all his works he exposes the follies and vices of contemporary humanity with biting accuracy.

Ktesias (fifth century B.C.). The Greek physician and historian came from Knidos and served at the court of Artaxerxes II Mnemon (404–359) in Persia. He wrote on the history of Persia and of India.

Libanius (A.D. c. 314–393). The Greek rhetorician was born at Antioch in Syria, was educated there and at Athens, taught at Constantinople and Nicomedia, and in 354 accepted an official chair of rhetoric in Antioch where he spent the rest of his life. His works chiefly consist of a very large number of orations and letters.

Liber Pontificalis or *Book of the Popes*. This is a collection of lives of popes, all arranged according to much the same pattern. The oldest part is based on the *Catalogus Liberianus* of the *Chronography of 354*. It begins with Peter and comes down to Felix III (526–530), and it was probably compiled under Boniface II (530–532). An excerpt is known as the *Catalogus Felicianus*. Later additions continue the record to Hadrian II (died 872), Stephen V (died 891), and Martin V (died 1431).

Livy (59 B.C.–A.D. 17). The Roman historian Titus Livius was born in Padua, and at Rome he enjoyed the patronage of the emperor Augustus. Livy wrote a history of Rome from its foundation down to 9 B.C. The work, known as *Ab urbe condita*, was composed in 142 books, of which only 35 are extant, together with some fragments, excerpts, and epitomes.

Lucian (A.D. c. 102–after 180). The Greek satirist and wit was born at Samosata in Syria, became a traveling lecturer, at about the age of forty moved to Athens, and still later held a post under the Roman administration in Egypt. He is most notable for the development in his many writings of a distinctive form of satiric dialogue. Objects of his satire were popular religious ideas, human vanity, and philosophic pretensions.

Malalas (A.D. c. 491–578). The Greek monk, rhetorician, and historian lived in Antioch. His *Chronicle* is a history of the world from the Creation to A.D. 565.

Marcion (mid second century A.D.). The Christian Gnostic was given a friendly reception by the Roman community c. 139, then excommunicated by c. 144. Marcion was opposed to Judaism, rejected the Old Testament, and made his own New Testament consisting of the Gospel according to Luke and ten Pauline Epistles, with excisions even in those. His followers, the Marcionites, had churches in North Africa, Gaul, Asia Minor, and Egypt.

Martial (A.D. c. 40–102). Marcus Valerius Martialis was born and educated in Spain but was long a resident in Rome, although he finally returned to Spain. In Rome he was a friend to Juvenal and Pliny the Younger, and he enjoyed the patronage of Titus (79–81) and Domitian (81–96). Fourteen books of his *Epigrams* are extant. In them he gives compact expression to his keen observations of all aspects of Roman society—high and low, good and bad.

Martyrs' Records. Records concerning the Early Christian martyrs consist of *Acts*, for which the official minutes of the trial and condemnation of martyrs were sometimes used; *Martyrologies*, based on descriptions given by eyewitnesses or other contemporaries; and later legends. Examples are the *Martyrdom of Peter* (fourth century), the *Martyrdom of Peter and Paul* (fourth century), the *Martyrology of James* (fifth century), and the *Martyrology of Jerome* (fifth or sixth century).

Melito of Sardis (A.D. c. 140–190). The bishop of Sardis in Asia Minor was the author of a number of works, which are named by Eusebius (*Ch. Hist.* IV 26). Of these the last Eusebius mentions is an *Apology*, which was addressed to Marcus Aurelius c. 170. In the preface of another work called *Extracts*, from which Eusebius quotes, Melito tells of his pilgrimage to the Holy Land, making him the first Christian pilgrim to the East of whom we are informed.

Muratorian Fragment (mid second century A.D.). The oldest known list of New Testament books, with brief statements about their origins, this document was published at Milan in 1780 by L. A. Muratori from an eighth-century manuscript in the Ambrosian Library. The text is in Latin, but there may have been a Greek original.

Origen (A.D. c. 185–254). The Christian writer and teacher was probably born at Alexandria, where he was educated by his father Leonides (a martyr in 202 during the persecution under Septimius Severus) and in the catechetical school by Pantaenus and Clement. After the departure of Clement (c. 202) Origen was appointed head of the school. He chose his friend Heraclas as his assistant for teaching grammar, and Origen himself taught philosophy, theology, and scripture. In 231 he moved to Caesarea in Palestine and founded a school there similar to the one in Alexandria. Under Decius he was imprisoned and tortured, and he died at Tyre in his sixty-ninth year. He wrote *Against Celsus, On the Principal Doctrines, On Prayer, Exhortation to Martyrdom*, many commentaries, and the *Hexapla* with Hebrew and Greek versions of the Old Testament in parallel columns.

Orosius (fifth century A.D.). Paulus Orosius, a Spanish priest, was born in northern Portugal. He fled from the Vandals to North Africa in A.D. 414 and became a pupil of Augustine, to whom he presented a work on the errors of the Priscillianists and Origenists. In 415 he went to Palestine, visited Jerome at Bethlehem, and wrote a work against Pelagius. In 417–418 he wrote *Seven Books of History Against the Pagans* at the suggestion of Augustine, and the work was intended to supplement Augustine's *City of God* by demonstrating that the pre-Christian world suffered even more from wars and troubles than did the contemporary world, hence, Christianity was not to be blamed for the unfortunate happenings of the time. The history of the world is summarized from Adam to A.D. 417, and it is divided into four periods on the basis of Dan 7. The chronology follows Eusebius and Jerome.

Pausanias (A.D. c. 150). The Greek traveler and geographer was acquainted with Palestine, Egypt, Italy, and Rome, and especially with Greece, with which he dealt in detail in his *Description of Greece*. Pausanias generally outlines the history and then the topography of important places, giving special attention to artistic monuments.

Petronius, Gaius (first century A.D.). The Roman writer was active at the court of Nero and was known as *arbiter elegantiae* ("judge of elegance"). Only fragments of his work are extant.

Philo (c. 20 B.C.–A.D. 54). Philo Judaeus or Philo of Alexandria was a Hellenistic Jewish philosopher of Alexandria. In his very numerous writings he endeavored to harmonize the doctrines of the Pentateuch with the thought of Plato, Aristotle, and other Greek philosophers. In A.D. c. 40 he headed an embassy of five Jews who went to Rome to plead with the emperor Gaius Caligula (37–41) not to require divine honors from the Jews, and this mission is recorded in Philo's *Embassy to Gaius*.

Philostratus (born A.D. c. 170). Flavius Philostratus studied at Athens, was one of the philosophers patronized by Septimius Severus (193–211) and his wife Julia Domna, and died in the reign of Philip the Arab (244–249). At the instance of Julia Domna, Philostratus wrote the *Life of Apollonius of Tyana* (published after the death of Julia Domna in 217).

Pliny the Elder (A.D. 23–79). Known in Latin as Gaius Plinius Secundus, the Roman scholar was probably educated at Rome and then spent a dozen years in military service. In later life he was a counselor of Vespasian and then of Titus, and he was appointed commander of the fleet at Misenum. On August 24, 79, he sailed from Misenum to observe the eruption of Vesuvius and perished from the fumes of the volcano. His nephew, Pliny the Younger (A.D. c. 61–112), names many of his uncle's writings; of them his *Natural History*, composed in thirty-seven books, survives.

Plutarch (before A.D. 50 to after 120). The Greek philosopher and biographer was born at Chaeronea in Boeotia, was educated in Athens, traveled widely, lectured in Rome, and in later life returned to Chaeronea. Among his works are the *Moralia*, a collection of more than sixty essays on a variety of questions, and the *Parallel Lives*, in which he presents character studies of distinguished Greeks and Romans, in pairs, from the time of Theseus and Romulus down to his own time.

Polybius (c. 205–125 B.C.). The Greek politican was active in the Achaian League, was taken as a prisoner to Rome (168), and remained in exile for about seventeen years. He became a friend of Scipio the Younger (185–129 B.C.) and through him an associate of leading literary figures in Rome, and he was with Scipio at the destruction of Carthage (146). Thereafter he occupied himself with the writing of his *Histories*, an account of Rome and nearby countries from 266 to 146 B.C. Of an original forty books, the first five are extant, as well as fragments and excerpts.

Procopius (born A.D. c. 500). The Byzantine historian was born in Caesarea in Palestine, served under the emperor Justinian (527–565) on military campaigns in Persia, Africa, and Italy, and was back in Constantinople by 540–542 where, in 562, he became prefect of the city. He wrote a *History of the Wars of Justinian* in eight books, and in 553–555 at the emperor's command, he composed a work *On Justinian's Buildings* (commonly known as *Buildings*), with detailed architectural descriptions.

Prologues to the Gospels and the Pauline Epistles. Many Latin manuscripts of the Vulgate and some Greek manuscripts contain introductions or prologues to individual books of the Bible. The so-called anti-Marcionite prologues of Mark, Luke, and John are believed to have originated c. 160–180. The prologues to the Pauline Epistles are probably of partly Marcionite origin. The Monarchian prologues are believed to date from the late fourth or early fifth century.

Prudentius (A.D. 348–410). Aurelius Clemens Prudentius, the Latin Christian poet, was a native of Spain and held an official position under Theodosius I (379–395). Eventually Prudentius gave up public life, retired to a monastery, and dedicated himself to Christian poetry. In 402/403 he made a pilgrimage to Rome and visited the tombs of the martyrs. His works include *Cathemerinon* (Book of Daily Songs), *Peristephanon* (Crowns of Martyrdom), *Apotheosis* (Divinity of Christ), *Hamartigenia* (Origin of Sin), *Psychomachia* (Battle of the Soul), *Contra Symmachum* (Against Quintus Aurelius Symmachus, prefect of Rome in 384 and the most prominent pagan opponent of Christianity in his time), and *Dittochaeon* (Twofold Food, an explanation of biblical scenes).

Seneca (c. 4 B.C.–A.D. 65). The Roman rhetorician and philosopher Lucius Annaeus Seneca was born at Cordoba, Spain, studied in Rome, and entered the legal profession. He was tutor to the young Nero, and in the early years of Nero's reign he was a political adviser and minister of the emperor. In later years Seneca retired from public life and devoted himself to philosophy, and Nero turned against him and in 65 forced him to commit suicide for alleged participation in an unsuccessful conspiracy. Seneca wrote moral and philosophic essays and letters, tragedies, and epigrams.

Socrates (A.D. c. 380–450). The church historian was a lawyer in Constantinople, and he wrote a *Church History* in seven books, continuing the work of Eusebius and covering the years between 305 and 439. This work was a principal source for the church histories of Sozomen and Theodoret.

Sozomen (died A.D. c. 450). The church historian was a lawyer in Constantinople, and his *Church History*, in nine books, covers the years 324 to 439. The work draws upon the *Church History* of Socrates and other documentary material.

Statius (A.D. 45–96). Publius Papinius Statius, the Roman poet, was born at Naples, where his father was a poet and a schoolmaster. Statius settled in Rome, where he recited his works to fashionable audiences and became a member of the court of the emperor Domitian (81–96). His works include the epics *Thebais* and *Achilleis* and the *Silvae*, a collection in five books of thirty-two occasional poems addressed to his friends.

Stephanos of Byzantium (sixth century A.D.). The Greek grammarian was probably a contemporary of Justinian I (527–565) and a teacher in the imperial university in Constantinople. He compiled a geo-graphical dictionary called the *Ethnika*, of which only fragments are extant. It is essentially an alphabetical list of place names, together with the adjectives derived from them.

Strabo (c. 63 B.C.–after A.D. 21). The Greek geographer was born in Pontus, lived in Rome at least intermittently from 44 B.C. until his death, and traveled widely, collecting geographical material. His *Geography* is extant in seventeen books, and it describes Europe, Asia, Egypt, and North Africa. His forty-seven books of *Historical Sketches* are lost.

Suetonius (born A.D. c. 69). The Roman historian and biographer probably accompanied Pliny the Younger to Bithynia about 111, for from that province Pliny wrote to Trajan (98–117) about him. In c. 119–121 Suetonius served as private secretary to Hadrian (117–138). The chief work of Suetonius is his *Lives of the Caesars*, which contains twelve biographies from Julius Caesar to Domitian. Another work on *Illustrious Men*, giving biographies of Roman literary men arranged by classes, is only partly preserved.

Sulpicius Severus (A.D. c. 360–420). The Latin lawyer and Christian writer came from a noble Aquitanian family, and in about 389 he was converted to Christianity together with his friend Paulinus of Nola. After the early death of his wife, and under the influence of his friend Bishop Martin of Tours, he organized a sort of monastic life on his own estates for himself and his friends. His writings include two works on the life of St. Martin (who died in 397) and most importantly a *Sacred History* or *Chronicle of the World*. The last work, composed in two books, gives the history of the world from the Creation down to A.D. 400, and it draws upon other Christian chronographers, especially Jerome, and also pagan writers.

Tacitus (A.D. c. 55–117). The Roman orator, politician, and historian held several official positions, including serving as proconsul of Asia, probably in 112/113. He is best known for his two long works that recount Roman history from A.D. 14 to 96 and are commonly known as the *Histories* and the *Annals*.

Tertullian (A.D. c. 160–240). The Latin ecclesiastical writer Quintus Septimius Florens Tertullianus was born at Carthage, was trained in law and rhetoric, and was a lawyer at Rome. He returned to Carthage as a Christian about 195 and there began a long literary career on behalf of the church. In approximately 207 he joined the Montanist movement, in which he soon became the head of a party of his own. Thirty-one of his works survive, and they are chiefly apologetic, dogmatic, polemical, practical, and ascetical.

Theodoret (A.D. c. 393–466). The Greek Christian theologian of the Antioch school was born in Antioch of Syria and educated in the monastic schools of that city. In 423 he became bishop of Cyrrhus, a small town east of Antioch. In the Christological controversies of the time he was a friend and supporter of Nestorius, the patriarch of Constantinople (428–431), and an opponent of Cyril, the bishop of Alexandria (412–444). In 431 the Council of Ephesus, under Cyril, condemned Nestorius as a heretic; in 449 the Council of Ephesus deposed Theodoret; in 451 the Council of Chalcedon reinstated Theodoret as an "orthodox teacher"; and in 553, long after the death of Theodoret, the Council of Constantinople condemned Theodoret and his writings. He wrote exegetical works and commentaries, sermons and letters, and dogmatical, polemical, apologetical, and historical works. In the last category are twelve books called *Graecorum affectionum curatio* (Cure of the Pagan Diseases), and a *Church History* from Constantine to 428.

Theodosius (A.D. c. 530). The pilgrim to the Holy Land is known only from the itinerary of his travels. Known as *Theodosius de situ terrae sanctae*, the work is of value for its concise notations on the holy places as they were known in the early sixth century.

Thucydides (c. 460–400 B.C.). The Greek historian was born at Athens and was a commander in the Peloponnesian War. When he failed to prevent the capture of Amphipolis by Brasidas, he went into exile (423–403), and during that time he wrote his *History of the War Between Athens and Sparta*, covering in eight books the years 431–404.

Varro (116–27 B.C.). The Roman scholar Marcus Terentius Varro was educated in Rome and Athens. In 49 he fought in Spain as a partisan of Pompey; in 47 he was appointed by Caesar as director of the library Caesar planned to found; in 43 he was outlawed by Antony but escaped death and thereafter devoted himself to his studies. He wrote on many subjects including languages, religion, law, customs, political institutions, philosophy, geography, and biography. The titles of fifty-five of his works are known, although of those only two have survived substantially—namely, *On the Latin Language* and *On Agriculture*.

Vergil (70–19 B.C.). The Roman poet Publius Vergilius Maro was born near Mantua in Cisalpine Gaul, studied in Rome, was a friend of Horace, and enjoyed the patronage of Augustus. His *Eclogues* and *Georgics* are pastoral poems; his *Aeneid* is the story of Aeneas and his wanderings after the fall of Troy and his settling in Latium.

Vitruvius (first century B.C.). The Roman architect and engineer was appointed a military engineer by Augustus. His main work is *On Architecture*, and it was dedicated to Augustus. In ten books it treats town planning, building materials, civic and domestic buildings, pavements and decorations, water supplies, and many other topics.

Xenophon (c. 428–354 B.C.). The Greek historian was born at Athens and was a disciple of Socrates. Xenophon joined the expedition of Cyrus the Younger against his brother Artaxerxes II of Persia (404–359), and after the death of Cyrus in the Battle of Cunaxa (401) and the murder by the Persians of the Greek commanders Xenophon himself became the leader and guided the Greek soldiers back to the Black Sea. The *Anabasis* of Xenophon recounts the expedition of Cyrus and the Greek retreat. The *Hellenica* is a history of Greece from 411 to 362. The *Memorabilia* tells of the life and teachings of Socrates. The *Symposium* is a dialogue with Socrates as the chief figure. The *Cyropaedia* is a historical novel based on the life of Cyrus the Great (559–529).

REFERENCES

Webster's Biographical Dictionary (Springfield, Mass.: G. and C. Merriam, 1956); F. L. Cross, ed., *The Oxford Dictionary of the Christian Church* (London: Oxford University Press, 1957); Johannes Quasten, *Patrology*, 3 vols. (Utrecht: Spectrum, 1950–60); Berthold Altaner, *Patrology* (New York: Herder and Herder, 1960); N.G.L. Hammond and H. H. Scullard, *The Oxford Classical Dictionary* (Oxford: Clarendon Press, 2d ed., 1970); Jerald C. Brauer, ed., *The Westminster Dictionary of Church History* (Philadelphia: Westminister Press, 1971).

For texts and translations of the classical sources see especially the respective volumes of the *Loeb Classical Library*. For the Christian writers see *Die griechischen christlichen Schriftsteller der ersten Jahrhunderte; Corpus scriptorum ecclesiasticorum latinorum; Corpus Christianorum, Series Latina; The Fathers of the Church; The Ante-Nicene Fathers;* and *A*

Select Library of Nicene and Post-Nicene Fathers of the Christian Church. For the Talmud see I. Epstein, ed., *The Babylonian Talmud*, 34 vols. (London: Soncino Press, 1935–48). For the Apocrypha of the New Testament see Montague Rhodes James, *The Apocryphal New Testament* (Oxford: Clarendon Press, 1924); Edgar Hennecke, Wilhelm Schneemelcher, and R. McL. Wilson, eds., *New Testament Apocrypha*, 2 vols. (London: Lutterworth Press, 1963–65). In addition see other works specifically cited in the text and notes of the present book.

ABBREVIATIONS

AJA   *American Journal of Archaeology.*

ANF   *Ante-Nicene Fathers*, ed. Alexander Roberts, James Donaldson, and A. Cleveland Coxe, 1925.

BA   *Biblical Archaeologist.*

BASOR   *Bulletin of the American Schools of Oriental Research.*

BCH   *Bulletin de correspondance hellénique.*

CAH   *Cambridge Ancient History.*

CCSL   *Corpus Christianorum, Series Latina.*

CSEL   *Corpus scriptorum ecclesiasticorum latinorum.*

DACL   *Dictionnaire d'archéologie chrétienne et de liturgie*, 1924–53.

GCS   *Die griechischen christlichen Schriftsteller der ersten Jahrhunderte.*

IDB   *Interpreter's Dictionary of the Bible*, 1962.

IDB-S   *Interpreter's Dictionary of the Bible, Supplementary Volume*, 1976.

JBL   *Journal of Biblical Literature.*

JTS   *Journal of Theological Studies.*

KJV   *King James Version.*

KLT   *Kleine Texte für theologische und philologische Vorlesungen und Übungen.*

NEB   *New English Bible.*

NPNFSS   *Select Library of Nicene and Post-Nicene Fathers of the Christian Church*, Second Series, ed. Philip Schaff and Henry Wace.

NTS   *New Testament Studies.*

PECS   *Princeton Encyclopedia of Classical Sites*, 1976.

PWRE   Pauly-Wissowa, *Realencyclopädie der classischen Altertumswissenschaft.*

RSR   *Recherches de science religieuse.*

RSV   *Revised Standard Version.*

ZNW   *Zeitschrift für die neutestamentliche Wissenschaft und die Kunde der älteren Kirche.*

ZWT   *Zeitschrift für wissenschaftliche Theologie.*

1
SOURCES

The chief source of information concerning the travels of Paul is the Book of Acts in the canonical New Testament. In the New Testament the Third Gospel (in the usual order of the Four Gospels) is directed to a certain Theophilus (Lk 1:3), and the Book of Acts begins with a reference to a previous book addressed to Theophilus (Ac 1:1). Therefore, both of these books (although now separated in the New Testament order) were originally two volumes of one work and probably both by the same author. In the earliest manuscripts the Third Gospel has the heading "according to Luke," and that is the traditional name of the author of both volumes.

In the letters collected in the New Testament under the name of Paul, we meet a man who is named Luke. In Col 4:14 this Luke is called "the beloved physician"; therefore, he was a person of the medical profession. In the same chapter several companions are named who are "men of the circumcision" (i.e., Jews) and then several others, who are evidently not Jews but Gentiles, and Luke appears in the latter group, so he was presumably a Gentile too. In Phm 24 Paul calls Luke a fellow worker; in II Tim 4:11 Luke is said to be the only person with Paul at that time.

This is the man—Luke the physician and companion of Paul—whom the early church writers name as the author of the Book of Acts. In the Muratorian Fragment (lines 2, 8) Luke is said to have written both the Third Gospel and the Acts of the Apostles. It is fur-

ther stated that in respect to the Gospel, he had not himself seen the Lord, but in the Acts he showed that several things were done in his own presence by leaving out the passion of Peter and also the departure of Paul from the city (i.e., from Rome) on his journey to Spain. Irenaeus (*Against Heresies* III 14, 1) emphasizes the passages in the Book of Acts in which Luke writes in the first person plural, such as "we came to Troas" and "we sailed from Philippi," and then comments, "As Luke was present at all these occurrences, he carefully noted them down in writing." Clement of Alexandria (*Stromata* V 12) introduces a quotation from Paul's address at Athens with the words "as Luke in the Acts of the Apostles relates." Origen (quoted by Eusebius, *Ch. Hist.* VI 25) speaks of "Luke, the author of the Gospel and the Acts." Such was the apparently unanimous opinion in the early church as to the authorship of the Third Gospel and the Book of Acts.

In this connection the texts in the Book of Acts to which Irenaeus calls attention—the so-called we passages—are of special interest. Although it is not always possible to know exactly where these sections begin and end, at least the following portions are composed in the first person plural, and in them, the writer says that "we" did so-and-so.

16:10–17	Journey from Troas to Philippi
20:5–16	Journey from Philippi to Miletus
21:1–18	Journey from Miletus to Jerusalem
27:1–28:16	Journey from Caesarea to Rome

Before and after and in between these passages the text is composed in the third person and says that "he" or "they" did so-and-so; thus the "we" passages stand out plainly as narrating events in which their author took part personally, in contrast with the other passages in which the writer tells what other persons did. On the other hand the "we" passages do not differ in style or vocabulary from the surrounding sections, so it appears that one and the same author wrote the "we" accounts and composed the entire book. Accordingly the simplest explanation of the state of affairs is that this author was a personal companion of Paul on at least those portions of his journeys where the narrative is couched in the first person plural, and that at least in those sections the author is drawing upon personal reminiscences or even upon personal notes written at the time. This, then, is entirely in harmony with the early tradition that the author of Acts was Paul's companion, Luke the physician.

Interestingly enough, there is also a "we" passage in the so-called Western text of Ac 11:28. In the context at this point it is explained that certain prophets came from Jerusalem to Antioch and then, in the text found in most of the most ancient manuscripts, it is stated, "And one of them named Agabus stood up and foretold by the Spirit that there would be a great famine over all the world." But in a sixth-century manuscript that once belonged to Theodore Beza and is now in the Cambridge University Library (a manuscript designated as D), and in a few other ancient sources that are considered to represent "Western" texts, the statement begins, "And there was much rejoicing, and when we were gathered together one of them named Agabus spoke." If this reading is correct, the same person who was with Paul on several of his journeys and who speaks of events on those journeys in the first person plural was already a member of the Christian community at Antioch at this earlier time. This, again, is in harmony with a remark by Eusebius (*Ch. Hist.* III 4, 7) that Luke, the author of the Gospel and the Acts, was an An-tiochian by race as well as a physician by profession.

The same relationship of Luke to Antioch is also stated in an old prologue to the Gospel according to Luke, in which some additional personal information about the author of Luke/Acts is provided. This prologue is found in several Greek and Latin manuscripts, and it is believed to have been composed in its present form in the third century, incorporating earlier and valuable biographical material. The biographical data are largely in the first paragraph, which reads as follows: "Luke is a Syrian of Antioch, a doctor by profession, who was a disciple of apostles, and later followed Paul until his martyrdom. He served the Lord without distraction, unmarried, childless, and fell asleep at the age of 84 in Boeotia, full of the Holy Spirit."[1] Boeotia, where this prologue says Luke died, is a district in Greece north of Athens. In his *Lives of Illustrious Men* (7) Jerome also describes Luke as a physician of Antioch, but Jerome says that in the twentieth year of Constantius (A.D. 357) Luke's bones were transferred to Constantinople for final burial.

In spite of all this early evidence to the effect that the Book of Acts was written by Luke, the companion of Paul, the belief was advanced in the nineteenth century by members of the so-called Tübingen school of New Testament study that this was not the case. Ferdinand Christian Baur (1792-1860), professor of theology at Tübingen, thought that Acts was a tendentious and subjective work aimed at reconciling the supposedly antithetical Petrine (Jewish-Christian) and Pauline (Gentile) parties in the early church and, as such, must have been composed at a time far along in the second century A.D.[2] The successors of Baur carried this line of analysis further: Albert Schwegler (1819-1857) spoke of the "unhistorical, arbitrary" procedure of the author of Acts,[3] and Eduard Zeller (1814-1908) dated the book in the second or third decade of the second century A.D. and saw in it much that was invented in order to commend Gentile Christianity to Jewish

Christians.[4] By the end of the nineteenth century Adolf Jülicher (1857–1938) represented rather widely prevailing views along much the same line when he dated Acts just after the beginning of the second century and argued that its picture of the apostolic age was an idealization that represented the nebulous conceptions of a later generation and showed that only meager information was still available to the author at that later time.[5]

In the twentieth century similar assessments of the character of the Book of Acts have been set forth by not a few scholars, each of course shaping his presentation in his own individual way. In his *Chapters in a Life of Paul*, John Knox argues that the picture of Paul's career in terms of three great missionary journeys, as narrated in Acts, is very different from what one would deduce from Paul's own letters and, since the latter are unquestionably the primary sources, the letters are to be used in preference to Acts whenever there is any question of conflict between them. As an example of such conflict, Knox's reconstruction of the chronology of Paul's life and work leads him to suggest that Luke may have been entirely mistaken in having Paul appear before the Roman proconsul Gallio on Paul's first visit to Corinth (Ac 18:12) or that, if the incident did occur, it may have been on a later visit by Paul to Corinth than is represented in Acts.[6]

In his life of Paul, Günther Bornkamm expresses grave doubts about the early church tradition concerning Luke and Acts, he dates the Book of Acts at the earliest toward the end of the first century, and he states that from this later standpoint the book gives a simplified and an idealized picture of Paul. At the same time, in contrast with John Knox, Bornkamm believes that the appearance of Paul before Gallio, as recorded in Ac 18:12, provides the one absolute datum for the establishment of the chronology of Paul.[7]

Again, in this same tradition, deriving ultimately from F. C. Baur, Ernst Haenchen in his commentary on Acts states that the picture of Paul—and indeed the entire picture of the missionary situation in the Book of Acts—

shows that no co-worker of Paul is speaking here, but rather a person of a later generation who is trying to set forth things on which he no longer possesses the true perspective.[8]

In the 1800s an event of an entirely different sort took place in respect to the evaluation of the Book of Acts. The famous story has often been told.[9] In 1876 a young man named William Ramsay, in his last year at Oxford University, was ordered to travel for his health, and in 1880 he received a scholarship for research in Greek lands. He wished to work in Athens, but he landed in Izmir (ancient Smyrna) and was persuaded by Charles Wilson to proceed instead to Phrygia in the interior of Asia Minor. No trustworthy map was available of the region, so William Ramsay undertook to make one and to trace the history of Roman institutions in Asia. At the time he was not interested in the bearing of his discoveries on the New Testament, and he accepted the opinion of German scholars who held that the Book of Acts was a tendentious and largely imaginary reconstruction formulated in the second century A.D. As a result of his discoveries and further studies, however, he was led to a complete change of opinion. He described the course of his research and the conclusion to which it led him in these words:

I may fairly claim to have entered on this investigation without any prejudice in favour of the conclusion which I shall now attempt to justify to the reader. On the contrary, I began with a mind unfavourable to it, for the ingenuity and apparent completeness of the Tübingen theory had at one time quite convinced me. It did not lie then in my line of life to investigate the subject minutely; but more recently I found myself often brought in contact with the book of *Acts* as an authority for the topography, antiquities, and society of Asia Minor. It was gradually borne in upon me that in various details the narrative showed marvellous truth. In fact, beginning with the fixed idea that the work was essentially a second-century composition, and never relying on its evidence as trustworthy for first-century conditions, I gradually came to find it a useful ally in some obscure and difficult investigations. . . .

I know the difficulties of this attempt to understand rightly a book so difficult, so familiar, and so much misunderstood as *Acts*. It is probable that I have missed the right turn or not grasped the full meaning in some cases. I am well aware that I leave some difficulties unexplained, sometimes from inability, sometimes from mere omission. But I am sustained by the firm belief that I am on the right path, and by the hope that enough of difficulties have been cleared away to justify a dispassionate historical criticism in placing this great writer on the high pedestal that belongs to him. . . .

Our hypothesis is that *Acts* was written by a great historian, a writer who set himself to record the facts as they occurred, a strong partisan indeed, but raised above partiality by his perfect confidence that he had only to describe the facts as they occurred, in order to make the truth of Christianity and the honour of Paul apparent. . . . It is not my object to assume or to prove that there was no prejudice in the mind of Luke, no fault on the part of Paul; but only to examine whether the facts stated are trustworthy, and leave them to speak for themselves (as the author does). I shall argue that the book was composed by a personal friend and disciple of Paul, and if this be once established there will be no hesitation in accepting the primitive tradition that Luke was the author."[10]

Again Ramsay expressed the view that "Luke's history is unsurpassed in respect of its trustworthiness," and he wrote that "Further study of Acts XIII–XXI showed that the book could bear the most minute scrutiny as an authority for the facts of the Aegean world, and that it was written with such judgment, skill, art and perception of truth as to be a model of historical statement. It is marvellously concise and yet marvellously lucid."[11]

As we have seen, there are not a few present-day scholars who continue the type of analysis begun by F. C. Baur and, like him, find in the Book of Acts relatively late materials of at least questionable historical value—a view that has come to be a part of what may be called "critical orthodoxy" in New Testament studies.

But there are also not a few works of contemporary research that reach conclusions more like those of Ramsay; that is, they find in Acts an essentially reliable historical document.

In his detailed commentary on the Greek text of Acts, F. F. Bruce studies the book as one would study other Greek historical literature and finds that the author's insistence on accuracy (Lk 1:3) in the recording of important events is shown by the precision of his historical and geographical references to have been a characteristic of his work. As is the case when any independently written ancient documents are compared with each other, some questions arise when Acts is compared with Paul's letters, but there are many affirmative points of correspondence and many places where Acts provides the historical background for a letter or where a letter provides complementary details that would otherwise be lacking. The traditional attribution of the Book of Acts to Luke, the companion of Paul, is therefore acceptable according to Bruce.[12]

In an extensive analysis of the Book of Acts and its historical worth (1921) and in a subsequent commentary on the entire book (1961), Alfred Wikenhauser tests against secular witnesses a very large number of the most varied details in Acts about persons, happenings, institutions, matters of cultural and religious history, Jewish history, Roman officers, cities, provinces, etc., and concludes that in most cases what the book says is brilliantly confirmed by those witnesses. In only a few cases, he remarks, are there differences between Acts and the secular sources, and in no case can the statements of Acts be proved incorrect.[13]

In a study of Roman society and law in the New Testament (1963), A. N. Sherwin-White reaches the following conclusions about the Book of Acts: Acts gives detailed narratives concerning the relationship of Paul to the municipal authorities at Philippi, Thessalonica, and Ephesus, and the picture that is drawn corresponds with the civic situation that was otherwise known to have existed in the first and early second centuries and, in particular, falls into place in the earlier rather than the later phase of development. Acts states that Paul enjoyed Roman citizenship (22:25–28; 23:27) and reflects the alarmed reaction of officials who found that they had unwittingly mistreated a Roman citizen (16:38; 22:29). In the early period and in the East there were not many Roman citizens, and such citizenship was valued for the political rights it conferred. Later, after the end of the reign of Claudius (A.D. 54), Roman privileges were more widely extended in the provinces, and the nature of the advantages citizenship conferred began to change and to lessen, so what Acts reports in connection with Paul fits the early period. Paul's appeal to Caesar (Ac 25:11) fits the known circumstances of the first century when such an appeal was made before the judge gave his verdict; the procedure was later changed so that an appeal was made after a sentence was pronounced. These and other points suggest an author who is accurately informed concerning the circumstances about which he writes, not a later writer who might easily have misrepresented matters of such detail.[14]

The remarkable accuracy of Acts is also documented by R.P.C. Hanson in his commentary on the book (1967). He points out that the titles of officials used in Acts are confirmed by inscriptions for the civic authorities (πολιτάρχης) of Thessalonica (Ac 17:6) and for the town clerk (γραμματεύς) and the religious authorities (Ἀσιάρχης) at Ephesus (Ac 19:31, 35). In addition, the title of proconsul (ἀνθύπατος) is correctly assigned to the two governors of senatorial provinces named in Acts, Sergius Paulus in Cyprus (13:7) and Gallio in Achaia (18:12). From these and many other such points we can conclude that the Book of Acts was indeed written by an author who was personally familiar with Christianity and its environment around the middle of the first century A.D.[15] In a comprehensive survey of the criticism of the Book of Acts from Baur to Haenchen, on the one hand, and from Ramsay to Hanson, on the other hand, Ward Gasque (1976) concludes that the critics who

assess the author of Acts as a dependable historian of early Christianity are essentially correct and that "there is no reason to doubt the essential reliability of the narrative of Acts."[16]

Biblical study continues, and new discoveries are made from time to time that cast fresh light on previously unsolved problems. For example, the statement in the Gospel according to Luke that Jesus was born at the time of a census conducted in Palestine when Quirinius was governor of Syria (Lk 2:2) has long been considered incorrect. The reason is that Josephus (Ant. xviii i, 1 §§1–4) states that Quirinius was sent to Syria as governor at the same time that Coponius was sent to Judea as procurator, and thereupon conducted a census that caused an attempted revolt by some of the Jews. Coponius came to replace Archelaus, who was deposed in A.D. 6, and the census took place "in the thirty-seventh year of Caesar's victory over Antony at Actium" (Josephus, Ant. xviii ii, 1 §26), which was also the year 6. But according to Mt 2:1, Jesus was born while Herod the Great was still king of the Jews, and according to data also provided by Josephus, Herod died in 4 B.C. (or perhaps in 1 B.C., with appropriate adjustment of other dates in his life). Thus, there appears to be a large discrepancy between the date given for Jesus's birth and the date of the known census under Quirinius. Now, however, E. Jerry Vardaman has discovered "micrographic" lettering on coins and inscriptions of the time that show that Quirinius was proconsul of Syria and Cilicia from 11 B.C. until after the death of Herod the Great. Quirinius also served during this period as procurator of numerous colonies and provinces, including Judea. This new evidence removes doubt as to the accuracy of the statement of Lk 2:2 that Quirinius ruled Syria at the time that Jesus was born in Bethlehem.[17] Similar "micrographic" evidence for the important date of the accession of Festus (Ac 24:27) will be discussed later on in connection with the chronology of Paul.

This conclusion that the Book of Acts—studied in the same way in which other books of ancient history and literature are studied—is an essentially reliable source obviously bears upon the questions of the date and the authorship of the book. The accuracy of the book, particularly with respect to conditions around the middle of the first century, appears to preclude its being written at a late time, say far down in the second century, as was held by various nineteenth-century scholars, and to make it improbable that the book was written at the end of the first century, as is held by some contemporary scholars who believe that Acts presents an idealized and unhistorical picture of the early church. The book's same character of accuracy also appears to allow acceptance of the early tradition that attributes it to Luke, the companion of Paul.

As to a more exact determination of date, even many of those scholars who accept Acts as an essentially reliable work, and perhaps also accept the traditional attribution of the book to Luke, suggest dates of composition after the death of Paul (Wikenhauser) and perhaps in the 70s or 80s (Hanson). There is, however, one very interesting consideration, noted and discussed by Adolf Harnack, that points to an even earlier date. The Book of Acts closes with Paul awaiting trial having been in custody in Rome for two years (Ac 28:30–31). Why are we not informed as to the outcome? Although various theories have been advanced to account for the conclusion of the book at this point, the most natural and simplest explanation may be that it was written at that very time. In his thorough investigation of the problem Harnack came to the conclusion that "We are accordingly left with the result: that the concluding verses of the Acts of the Apostles, taken in conjunction with the absence of any reference in the book to the result of the trial of St. Paul and to his martyrdom, make it in the highest degree probable that the work was written at a time when St. Paul's trial in Rome had not yet come to an end."[18] Several contemporary scholars, F. F. Bruce, for example, judge it probable that Acts was written in Rome toward the end of the two years of Paul's imprisonment there,[19]

and this author shares that opinion.

The fact that there are letters of the apostles in the New Testament makes those letters sources of obvious importance, but the letters do not contain as many historical and geographical references as the Book of Acts. Thirteen letters in the canonical New Testament bear Paul's name, and all are listed as his in the Muratorian Fragment. Of these letters the Tübingen school allowed that only four were genuine—namely, Romans, Galatians, and I and II Corinthians. Along the same general line of criticism, Bornkamm more moderately accepts all the letters as genuine except the "deutero-Pauline" Ephesians, Colossians, and II Thessalonians and the "pastorals," I and II Timothy and Titus. However, except for possible "post-Pauline additions" to I and II Timothy and Titus, Adolf Deissmann feels that all thirteen letters are from Paul:

> The chief evidence for the essential genuineness of the letters of Paul that have come down to us is the circumstance, impossible to invention, that each letter portrays him as the same character, each time in a new light and giving a new impression, or even with great changes of impression in the same letter. It is no unalterable cold marble statue of "Paulinism" that we see each time; rather it is ever the living man, Paul, whose very speech and gesture we hear and see, here smiling gentle as a father and tenderly coaxing to win the hearts of his foolish children—then, thundering and lightening in passionate anger, like Luther, with biting irony and sharp sarcasm on his lips. Another time his eye shines with experience of the seer and his mouth overflows as he witnesses to the grace he has known, or his thought loses itself in the tortuous maze of a religious problem, and his soul trembles under a load of trouble, or he draws from the harp of David a gracious psalm of thanksgiving. It is ever the same Paul in ever new attitude, and where apparent contradictions can be noticed, even there it is the same man, Paul.[20]

In the case of Peter there are two letters under his name in the canonical New Testament. The Muratorian Fragment does not name any letter by Peter, but this omission could be because the text of this important list is only partially preserved. Eusebius (*Ch. Hist.* III 3, 1) states that one letter of Peter, the first, is acknowledged as genuine and was used freely by the earlier fathers of the church—the "ancient elders" as he calls them—as an undisputed work, but the second letter does not belong to the canon, although many have thought it profitable and have used it along with the other Scriptures. In 1 Pet the author seems to speak with the authority of an apostle (1:1) and with the memories of an eyewitness to the life of Jesus (5:1). The references to the dangers to which Christians might at any time be exposed (1:6; 3:14; 4:12) reflect the situation in Rome and elsewhere in which hostility to the Christians was building up to Nero's outright persecution in which Peter himself undoubtedly perished (A.D. 65).[21] Not only three letters but also the Fourth Gospel and the Book of Revelation are associated with the name of John in the canonical New Testament (these writings are discussed in Chapter 2).

In addition to the writings collected in the canonical New Testament there are many other relatively early documents that, in title, form, or content, are like the canonical works. In analogy to the more definitely grouped Apocrypha of the Old Testament, it is customary to collectively describe these documents as the apocryphal New Testament. Among these books there are some letters under the names of apostles, and a considerable number of works bear the title of Acts of various apostles. Thus Eusebius (*Ch. Hist.* III 3, 2 and 5) mentions "the so-called Acts of Peter" and "the so-called Acts of Paul" but says that these works have not been universally accepted, nor has he found them among the undisputed writings. In fact, even if in title, form, and content these Acts bear some similarity to the canonical Book of Acts, their character is markedly different. As to their date, the evidence of when they are first mentioned and the evidence of the type of thought they represent point to the second and third and even later centuries for their composition. As to their content, they largely give the impression of popular stories, and much of their material seems obviously legendary. Even so, there conceivably may be historical elements in these documents too. In the apocryphal *Acts of Paul and Thecla*, for example, the knowledge displayed of the local road from Pisidian Antioch to Iconium and of a certain queen Tryphaena, who actually did exist, and the personal description given of Paul lead William Ramsay to hold that the work contains a historically reliable nucleus of fact.[22] Yet it is usually difficult to know how far the historically reliable record of any actual event extends, how far later traditions have been incorporated, and to what extent the author has made individual additions.[23] Thus much care must be exercised in any attempt to evaluate the apocryphal material fairly.[24]

Finally, the writers of the early church, commonly known as the church fathers, preserved information and traditions known to them concerning the apostles and other leaders of the early church, and this material also is to be evaluated and utilized.[25]

2
CHRONOLOGICAL HISTORY

An investigation of chronological questions in the time of Paul and the other leaders of the early church must deal with Jewish, Roman, and Christian sources. With respect to Jewish chronology, the later Jewish calendar begins the years with "the first month, which is the month of Nisan" (Est 3:7) and can, therefore, be recognized as deriving from the Babylonian calendar, which began the year with the month of Nisanu, in the spring. From cuneiform tablets and astronomical data, Babylonian chronology has been reconstructed from 626 B.C. to A.D. 75 with such accuracy that in the chronological tables that are now available for those years, probably only a certain number of dates may be wrong by at most one day.[1] However, because it remains uncertain whether the corresponding Jewish observations of the moon and the intercalations of the months coincided with the Babylonian determinations, the Jewish dates have a larger margin of uncertainty. In Roman history the dates of the emperors' reigns are in general known with accuracy, and there are available compilations showing the times when the emperors received certain honors and lists of the consuls by whose time in office calendar years were identified.[2]

As to early Christian sources, it was as a basis for his own *Church History*—and probably by making use of the earlier *Chronographies* of Julius Africanus (A.D. 170–240), now extant only in fragments[3]—that Eusebius prepared his "Chronological Canons" (*Ch. Hist.* I 1, 6). The Greek text of this work, commonly called the *Chronicle* of Eusebius, is lost, but a Latin version made by Jerome, probably in 381,[4] and an Armenian version[5] are extant. Since the figures in the Latin version are usually closer to those in the Greek text of the *Church History* than are the figures in the Armenian version, the Latin is usually preferred to the Armenian for the dates.

For convenient reference Table 1 outlines the years of Roman emperors for the time with which we are concerned as they appear in the Latin *Chronicle*. As a continuous frame of reference Eusebius cites the Olympiads and lists the successive years of the emperors' reigns within this framework. In Table 1 the dates signified by the Olympiads are supplied, and the dates of the factual years of the emperors' reigns are given. Eusebius's statement of the years, months, and days of a reign is also included for each emperor.

According to all four canonical Gospels the death of Jesus took place at or near the Jewish Feast of Passover, therefore in the spring of the year. Clement of Alexandria (*Stromata* I 21) states that the followers of Basilides (the famous Gnostic teacher who flourished at Alexandria about A.D. 117–138) put the death of Jesus in the sixteenth year of Tiberius (A.D. 29/30); if the reference is to the factual years of Tiberius's reign, the date refers to the spring of the year 30. In his *Chronographies* Julius Africanus appears to have put the death of Jesus in Olympiad 202, 1 (A.D. 29/30), also in

TABLE 1. Roman Emperors, Tiberius to Nero.

	Olympiad Year July 1–June 30		Reign	Years
TIBERIUS, born Nov. 16,	198, 2	Year 1	Aug. 19, 14–Aug. 18, 15	A.D. 14–15
42 B.C., began to govern the	3	2	Aug. 19, 15–Aug. 18, 16	15–16
provinces jointly with Au-	4	3	Aug. 19, 16–Aug. 18, 17	16–17
gustus in A.D. 13 (CAH 10	199, 1	4	Aug. 19, 17–Aug. 18, 18	17–18
[1934], p. 158).[a] Augustus	2	5	Aug. 19, 18–Aug. 18, 19	18–19
died on Aug. 19, A.D. 14,	3	6	Aug. 19, 19–Aug. 18, 20	19–20
Tiberius confirmed as his	4	7	Aug. 19, 20–Aug. 18, 21	20–21
successor by the Senate on	200, 1	8	Aug. 19, 21–Aug. 18, 22	21–22
Sept. 17, reigned twenty-	2	9	Aug. 19, 22–Aug. 18, 23	22–23
three years, died Mar. 16,	3	10	Aug. 19, 23–Aug. 18, 24	23–24
37. Factual years of sole	4	11	Aug. 19, 24–Aug. 18, 25	24–25
reign are shown, but it is	201, 1	12	Aug. 19, 25–Aug. 18, 26	25–26
possible that upon occasion	2	13	Aug. 19, 26–Aug. 18, 27	26–27
years were also counted	3	14	Aug. 19, 27–Aug. 18, 28	27–28
from the time when Tiber-	4	15	Aug. 19, 28–Aug. 18, 29	28–29
ius began to govern the	202, 1	16	Aug. 19, 29–Aug. 18, 30	29–30
provinces jointly with Au-	2	17	Aug. 19, 30–Aug. 18, 31	30–31
gustus.	3	18	Aug. 19, 31–Aug. 18, 32	31–32
	4	19	Aug. 19, 32–Aug. 18, 33	32–33
	203, 1	20	Aug. 19, 33–Aug. 18, 34	33–34
	2	21	Aug. 19, 34–Aug. 18, 35	34–35
	3	22	Aug. 19, 35–Aug. 18, 36	35–36
	4	23	Aug. 19, 36–Mar. 16, 37	36–37
GAIUS (CALIGULA),	204, 1	Year 1	Mar. 16, 37–Mar. 15, 38	37–38
born Aug. 31, 12, suc-	2	2	Mar. 16, 38–Mar. 15, 39	38–39
ceeded Tiberius Mar. 16,	3	3	Mar. 16, 39–Mar. 15, 40	39–40
37, reigned three years,	4	4	Mar. 16, 40–Jan. 24, 41	40–41
ten months, assassinated				
Jan. 24, 41.				
CLAUDIUS, born Aug.	205, 1	Year 1	Jan. 24, 41–Jan. 23, 42	41–42
1, 10 B.C., proclaimed	2	2	Jan. 24, 42–Jan. 23, 43	42–43
emperor in succession to	3	3	Jan. 24, 43–Jan. 23, 44	43–44
Caligula on Jan. 25, 41,	4	4	Jan. 24, 44–Jan. 23, 45	44–45
reigned thirteen years,	206, 1	5	Jan. 24, 45–Jan. 23, 46	45–46
eight months, twenty-	2	6	Jan. 24, 46–Jan. 23, 47	46–47
eight days, poisoned to	3	7	Jan. 24, 47–Jan. 23, 48	47–48
death on Oct. 13, 54.	4	8	Jan. 24, 48–Jan. 23, 49	48–49
	207, 1	9	Jan. 24, 49–Jan. 23, 50	49–50
	2	10	Jan. 24, 50–Jan. 23, 51	50–51
	3	11	Jan. 24, 51–Jan. 23, 52	51–52
	4	12	Jan. 24, 52–Jan. 23, 53	52–53
	208, 1	13	Jan. 24, 53–Jan. 23, 54	53–54
	2	14	Jan. 24, 54–Oct. 13, 54	54

TABLE 1. (continued)

	Olympiad Year July 1–June 30		Reign	Years
NERO, born Dec. 15,	3	Year 1	Oct. 13, 54–Oct. 12, 55	54–55
37, succeeded Claudius	4	2	Oct. 13, 55–Oct. 12, 56	55–56
Oct. 13, 54, reigned	209, 1	3	Oct. 13, 56–Oct. 12, 57	56–57
thirteen years, seven	2	4	Oct. 13, 57–Oct. 12, 58	57–58
months, twenty-eight	3	5	Oct. 13, 58–Oct. 12, 59	58–59
days, died by suicide	4	6	Oct. 13, 59–Oct. 12, 60	59–60
June 9, 68.	210, 1	7	Oct. 13, 60–Oct. 12, 61	60–61
	2	8	Oct. 13, 61–Oct. 12, 62	61–62
	3	9	Oct. 13, 62–Oct. 12, 63	62–63
	4	10	Oct. 13, 63–Oct. 12, 64	63–64
	211, 1	11	Oct. 13, 64–Oct. 12, 65	64–65
	2	12	Oct. 13, 65–Oct. 12, 66	65–66
	3	13	Oct. 13, 66–Oct. 12, 67	66–67
	4	14	Oct. 13, 67–June 9, 68	67–68

[a]Suetonius (*Tiberius* 20–21) and Dio (*Rom. Hist.* LVI 28, 1) tell of the appointment of Tiberius to govern the provinces jointly with Augustus, and Tacitus (*Annals* I 3) calls him "colleague in the empire"; the date, however, given above as in the year 13, has also been placed in 12 and in 11 (George Ogg, *The Chronology of the Public Ministry of Jesus* [1940], pp. 173 f.; Louis Dupraz, "De l'association de Tibère au principat à la naissance du Christ," *Studia Friburgensis* New Series 43 [1966]).

the spring of the year 30.[6] Tertullian (*Answer to the Jews* 8) gives the date as being in the consulate of Rubellius Geminus and Fufius Geminus, which designates the calendar year 29.[7] In the *Chronicle* of Eusebius the date is in the eighteenth year of Tiberius (31/32) in the Latin version,[8] the spring of 32, and in the nineteenth year of Tiberius (32/33) in the Armenian version,[9] the spring of 33.

According to the Fourth Gospel Jesus was crucified on "the day of Preparation for the Passover" (Jn 19:14), and the Babylonian Talmud (*Sanhedrin* 43a) also places the event "on the eve of Passover." This means that Jesus was put to death on the day when the Passover lambs were slain (cf. 1 Cor 5:7), and in terms of the Jewish calendar, this was Nisan 14 (Ex 12:6). The sequence of events in all four Gospels indicates that the day was Friday. Calendrical and astronomical information show that in the years that come into question on or around the dates given by the ancient sources, Nisan 14 probably fell on a Friday only in the years 30 (Apr 7) and 33 (Apr 3). The weight of the most ancient sources is on the side of an earlier date, and the spring of the year 30 may be considered probable.[10] A possible argument for the other and later date (A.D. 33) is that in October of the year 31 Tiberius deposed and allowed the killing of his previously powerful anti-Semitic minister Sejanus and thereafter instructed his provincial governors to treat the Jews with more consideration.[11] This instruction, it is held, could explain the vacillation of Pilate during the trial of Jesus if the date were after that time, as 33 would be.[12] Yet surely at any time a Roman governor might waver as to his duty with respect to an otherwise apparently innocent prisoner charged with making himself a king (Jn 19:12), so that argument for the later date is not necessarily conclusive.[13]

PAUL

After the death of Jesus, how long was it until the conversion of Saul/Paul? In Ac 7–9 the conversion of the future apostle follows the stoning of Stephen. Stoning was a Jewish method of execution (e.g., Ex 19:13), but in connection with the trial of Jesus, the Jews told Pilate that it was not lawful for them to put anyone to death (Jn 18:31), and this probably was the situation under strict Roman administration and under Pilate, who generally dealt strictly and even harshly with the Jews. However, in the shift of Tiberius's policy to greater leniency toward the Jews, of which his deposition of Sejanus was a part, Tiberius appointed Vitellius imperial legate in Syria (A.D. 35–37), and in the year 36, Vitellius deposed Pilate to gain favor with the Jews and sent his own protégé Marcellus to Caesarea. Marcellus is often listed as one of the procurators (A.D. 36–37), but in fact he possessed no direct imperial authority. Vitellius also replaced Caiaphas (A.D. 18–36) with Jonathan as high priest and, in a gesture of recognition, gave Jonathan possession of the high-priestly vestments, which earlier procurators had kept locked up in the Antonia except for special festivals (Josephus, *Ant.* XVIII 4, 3 §§90–95). It was during this time of permissiveness in Roman administration that the opportunity arose for actions such as that of the Jewish authorities in the stoning of Stephen, and the high priest who presided over this action (Ac 7:1) was presumably none other than Jonathan. For this event a date in A.D. 36 may therefore be accepted as probable, and the ensuing conversion of Saul may probably be placed in the same year.[14]

After referring to the revelation that came to him during his conversion Paul says in Gal 1:18 that "after three years" he went to Jerusalem to visit Cephas; counted inclusively, the three years were A.D. 36, 37, and 38. In the year 37 Vitellius replaced Jonathan as high priest with Jonathan's brother Theophilus (37–41). This change probably meant a cessation of the persecution that Jonathan had headed and provided an opportunity for Paul to come back to Jerusalem the next year (38) without encountering in office the high priest who had given him letters of authority for his own mission of persecution to Damascus (Ac 9:2).[15]

"After fourteen years" (Gal 2:1), doubtless counted inclusively from his conversion in A.D. 36 and therefore in the year 49, Paul again visited Jerusalem, this time for a consultation about his mission to the Gentiles (probably the conference recorded in Ac 15). Since Paul's first missionary journey (Ac 13–14) preceded the Jerusalem conference, that journey may have taken place in approximately A.D. 47–48.[16]

After the conference Paul was again in Antioch, then "after some days" departed on his second missionary journey (Ac 15:36–18:22). Because he and his companions were first of all engaged in delivering the decisions from the Jerusalem meeting (Ac 16:4), it is probable that Paul started out soon after the conference and proceeded rapidly on at least the first part of this journey.[17] If the conference were in the first months of the year 49, he could have left in the spring of that year. Cicero (*Letters to Atticus* v 21, last paragraph) says that "the snows prevent passage of the Taurus until June," but modern travelers have gone through in the latter part of April, so Paul might have passed that way in late spring or early summer. From the Cilician Gates it was 800 mi (1,300 km) to Troas, a journey of perhaps two months since no stops of great length are indicated.[18] With work thereafter in Macedonia and a brief stay in Athens, Paul could have reached Corinth by the end of the year 49.

The time just indicated as a reasonable probability for the arrival of Paul in Corinth is, in fact, the time required by the Gallio inscription from Delphi. The inscription was found on several pieces of broken stone at Delphi, and it consists of the fragmentary text of a letter from the emperor Claudius (A.D. 41–54) to that city. Although the text is broken, it is almost certain that it mentions the twenty-sixth acclamation of Claudia as *imperator*, an honor accorded the emperor in his twelfth year (Jan. 24, 52–Jan. 23, 53).[19] The emperor's twenty-seventh acclamation is recorded on his aqueduct at Rome, which was dedicated on Aug. 1, 52, so the date of the communication to Delphi is between Jan. 24 and Aug. 1 in the year 52. In the text Claudius also unmistakably mentions "Gallio my friend and proconsul." This is none other than Lucius Junius Gallio Annaeus, older brother of the philosopher. Seneca and the proconsul of Achaia before whom Paul was brought in Corinth (Ac 18:12). At the time Claudius's letter was written, Gallio had evidently been in office in Achaia long enough to have sent a message to the emperor pertaining to circumstances in Delphi, thereby occasioning Claudius's communication with Delphi. According to Pliny (*Nat. Hist.* II 47) the sailing season on the Mediterranean ended on Nov. 11 and began again on Feb. 8, and Dio Cassius (LX 17, 3) tells us that Claudius required provincial governors to set out from Rome for their posts not later than the middle of April. Assuming four or five weeks in passage from the latter date, Gallio was presumably in Corinth by the month of May. Dio also says (LX 25, 6) that Claudius allowed some governors to hold office for two years, but this statement appears to describe exceptional cases and allows the assumption that the normal term of office was for one year; the conclusion is that Gallio probably held office in Corinth for only one year. In that year Gallio sent word of some kind to Claudius about Delphi, and Claudius sent his communication to Delphi in the first seven months of A.D. 52, so the term of Gallio in Corinth was probably in 51/52, and Gallio must have arrived in Corinth to begin his year as proconsul in May 51.[20]

From Ac 18:12 it appears that the Jews in Corinth took the opportunity of the new governor's arrival to bring Paul before him, and the date of the appearance of Paul before Gallio was probably in May of 51. At that time Paul had already been in Corinth for one year and six months (Ac 18:11), so he must have ar-

rived in Corinth about the month of December in the year 49. This determination of the time when Paul was before Gallio thus provides an important anchor point for the entire chronology of Paul.[21]

Paul's arrival in Corinth at the end of 49 is also confirmed by the fact that he found there a Jew named Aquila, with his wife Priscilla, "lately come from Italy . . . because Claudius had commanded all the Jews to leave Rome" (Ac 18:2). This must be the same event described by Suetonius (*Claudius* 25), who says that Claudius expelled the Jews from Rome because they "constantly made disturbances at the instigation of Chrestus," and by Orosius (*Seven Books of History Against the Pagans*, tr. Irving W. Raymond [New York: Columbia University Press, 1936], p. 332), who speaks of the same occurrence and dates it as in the ninth year of Claudius (Jan. 24, 49–Jan. 23, 50).[22]

After his appearance before Gallio, probably in May 51, Ac 18:18 states that Paul stayed in Corinth "many days" (RSV) or "some time" (NEB). Although the Greek adjective (ἱκανός) is often used with the sense of "much" or "many," its literal meaning is "enough" or "sufficient," and this literal meaning seems appropriate in the present passage, which may be understood to say that Paul only stayed on in Corinth "enough" or "sufficient" time to show that he was not being forced to leave; he then departed, perhaps in June of 51. En route back to Antioch he stopped at Ephesus and was asked to stay "for a longer period" (Ac 18:20), but he declined and therefore was evidently traveling rapidly. Presumably he could have reached Antioch in July A.D. 51.

At Antioch Paul now remained only "some time" (Ac 18:23), and in view of his promise to return to Ephesus (Ac 18:21), it is probable that he started out again soon, say in the late summer or early fall of 51.[23] This was the third missionary journey (Ac 18:23–21:16), and on it, Paul traveled through Galatia and Phrygia to Ephesus (Ac 18:23; 19:1). We are explicitly told that he stayed in Ephesus for a relatively long period, speaking in the synagogue for three months (Ac 19:8) and lecturing in the hall of Tyrannus for two years (Ac 19:10), a total period of time called three years in Ac 20:31. If the journey from Antioch to Ephesus were in Aug.–Sept., the three months in the synagogue could be Oct.–Nov.–Dec., and the two years in the hall of Tyrannus could be substantially the two full years of 52 and 53. Thereafter Paul went by way of Macedonia to Greece and spent three months there (Ac 20:1–3), probably from early January to early April in 54. To conclude this journey, Paul and his party went up to Philippi, sailed away from there after Passover (Ac 20:6), and hastened to be at Jerusalem, if possible, by Pentecost (Ac 20:16). In the year 54 the Passover date of Nisan 14 probably fell on Apr. 12, and Pentecost, fifty days later, was on May 31.

Paul was now placed in prison in Caesarea (Ac 23:35), say in June 54 according to the foregoing reckoning, and he remained there for two years (Ac 24:27), probably until May 56. At that point the procurator Felix was succeeded by Porcius Festus. Felix had been appointed at the suggestion of the former high priest, Jonathan,[24] probably the ecclesiastic who had killed Stephen, and it is not surprising that Felix went out of office leaving Paul in prison in order to do the Jews a favor (Ac 24:27). Festus, however, was evidently a more conscientious administrator, since he heard Paul's case promptly (Ac 25:6), but he also wished to favor the Jews (Ac 25:9) and thereby provoked Paul's appeal to Caesar (Ac 25:11). Because it was a Jewish question Festus also laid the case before King Agrippa II (Ac 25:14), but although both of them judged Paul undeserving of either imprisonment or death (Ac 26:31), they agreed that it was necessary to send him to Rome because of his appeal.

For chronology, the crucial question is obviously that of the date Festus succeeded Felix. With respect to this question, there is a bronze coin from Palestine with a main inscription in Greek reading "Year 5 of Caesar Nero."[25] The first part of the inscription, with the date (L as the abbreviation for "Year,"[26] and E as the numeral "5") and the title "Caesar," is written

on the reverse, around a palm branch; the second part, with the name of Nero, is inscribed on the obverse within a wreath. On this coin E. Jerry Vardaman has found, written in graffiti-like "micrographics," a number of additional names.[27] Four of the persons so named are Valerius Messalla Corvinus, Fonteius Agrippa, Paconius Sabinus, and Petronius Lurco. They were the consuls in 58,[28] and that year overlapped the fourth (57/58) and fifth (58/59) years of Nero. Furthermore the name of Marcus Porcius Festus and his date of Year 3 are written on the coin a number of times. Accordingly, if the year 58 was the third year of Festus, his first year was the year 56, which overlapped the second (55/56) and third (56/57) years of Nero. In the *Chronicle* of Eusebius (in the Latin version of Jerome), the succession of Festus to Felix is noted at the point of Year 2 of Nero, and in the running sequence of years, this is the year 56.[29] Considering the sailing season and the usual time when governors went out to their posts, and assuming five or six weeks for the passage to Palestine, we may presume that Festus arrived in Caesarea toward the end of May in the year 56. This date agrees with the supposition that that month rounded out Paul's two years in custody in Caesarea.

The famous shipwreck journey of Paul to Italy (Ac 27:1–28:14) must have begun, then, in the summer of 56. Taking a ship of Adramyttium to Myra in Lycia and, from there, a ship of Alexandria bound for Italy, they made slow progress and were only in Fair Havens on the south coast of Crete when "the fast had already gone by" (Ac 27:9). The fast was the Day of Atonement, observed on the tenth day of the seventh month, Tishri (Lev 16:29). In the year 56 the first day of Tishri was probably on Sept. 30 and the tenth day on Oct. 9. When that date had already gone by, not too much time remained before the end of the sailing season on the Mediterranean (Nov. 11). Undertaking at least to get along the coast to the better harbor at Phoenix, they were caught and driven out to sea by the east-north-east wind called Eurakylon (Greek Εὖρος, east wind, and Latin *aquilo*, north-by-east wind). They managed to run under the lee of the small island Cauda to undergird the ship, but then they drifted helplessly and were storm tossed across the sea of Adria until, on the fourteenth night, they approached what they later found to be the island of Malta (Ac 27:27). The distance from Cauda to St. Paul's Bay on Malta is 476.4 nautical miles, and an experienced Mediterranean navigator estimates that a ship hove to and drifting before the wind would make about 36 nautical miles in twenty-four hours; thus it would travel 477 nautical miles in thirteen and one-quarter days.[30]

Shipwrecked on Malta, the party spent the three months (Ac 28:11) of the winter nonsailing season (approximately Nov.-Dec.-Jan.) on the island and then, presumably with the opening of navigation on Feb. 8, proceeded to Italy. With only brief stops en route at Syracuse, Rhegium, and Puteoli, arrival in Rome might have been at about the end of February in the year 57. There Paul remained in custody for two years (Ac 28:30), until approximately February of 59.

The statement of Ac 28:30 that Paul remained two whole years in his own rented place (as the Greek μίσϑωμα may most literally be translated) is couched in the aorist tense (ἐνέμεινεν) and pictures that period as completed. The first impression may still be—as Adolf Harnack thinks—that these words were written immediately after the expiration of the two years and before Paul's presumed trial had come to an end.[31] Although we are not told what happened thereafter, it is surely indicated that the situation changed. Perhaps two years were the maximum legal time of detention, like the two years at Caesarea, at the end of which time Felix evidently should have resolved Paul's case but chose instead to leave him in prison to do the Jews a favor, a state of affairs promptly remedied by Festus.[32] A trial at the end of this imprisonment is no doubt presupposed in II Tim 4:16, because Paul's first "apology" (ἀπολογία) is not some single speech concerning his present situation but an entire

legal defense on an earlier occasion.[33] That the outcome of the trial was favorable to Paul is also surely indicated in II Tim 4:17, which speaks of rescue "from the lion's mouth." This statement at least means rescue from danger (e.g., as in Ps 22:21), or possibly it more specifically means, as Jerome (*Illustrious Men* 5) thought, rescue from Nero, called a lion on account of his cruelty (cf. Josephus *Ant.* XVIII 6, 10 §228, where Tiberius is also called a lion).

Factors that probably were conducive to a favorable outcome were that Paul's opponents in Jerusalem evidently did not follow him to Rome with condemnatory letters, nor did any of them come in person to speak against him (Ac 28:21). At the same time, Festus and King Agrippa II presumably sent favorable reports, since they had already agreed upon Paul's innocence (Ac 26:32). Also the trial would have taken place in the earlier and better part of Nero's reign. As a boy of eleven the future emperor had had the philosopher Seneca as his tutor, and when Nero took the throne, Seneca and Afranius Burrus were his most influential advisers. This situation continued until the death of Burrus in A.D. 62 and Seneca's ensuing virtual retirement into private life, a life the philosopher was finally ordered by Nero to end by his own hand in 65, even as Nero also commanded Seneca's older brother Gallio to commit suicide in 66.[34] It has therefore been surmised that Seneca, still influential at the time and the younger brother of Gallio who, as proconsul at Corinth, had refused to make any judgment against Paul, was instrumental in the release of Paul. It has even been speculated that the famous philosopher was the "friend of God" (Theophilus) to whom the work (Lk/Ac) was dedicated, a work that concludes so dramatically at this very point and may even have been written at this very time (A.D. 59).[35]

Assuming Paul's release from Roman imprisonment in the spring of 59, did he go on to Spain? It was certainly his previously expressed intention and desire to do so (Rom 15:24, 28), and it may be judged that so far-reaching a project would not be lightly abandoned but

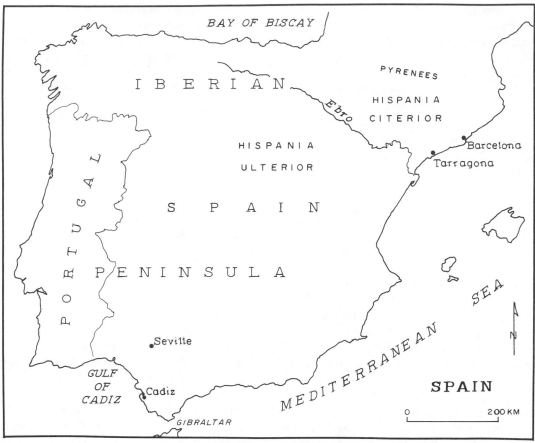

MAP 1.

would be undertaken forthwith if and when the opportunity arose.

Already in the second century B.C. Spain was divided into two Roman provinces, Hispania Citerior ("nearer") and Hispania Ulterior ("farther"—beyond the Ebro River, the ancient Iberus, from which the Iberian Peninsula derives its name; see Map 1, which shows the river's course and these divisions). In the first century B.C. Augustus divided Hispania Ulterior into two provinces, and thus there were three provinces altogether. By the first century A.D. there was a veritable network of Roman civilization over the whole peninsula, and many natives of Spain regarded themselves as first of all Romans. Among these were Seneca himself and also the later

emperors Trajan and Hadrian. Communications were also good between Italy and Spain, both by the military roads that Pompey had constructed over the Pyrenees and by vessels sailing to Tarragona and other Spanish ports.

So the apostle, who long since had preached the gospel from Jerusalem to Illyricum and had no more room for work in the East (Rom 15:19, 23), wanted to encompass the West too, and Rome was by no means the end of the West nor his final goal. Indeed, it is possible to understand the statement in II Tim 4:17 that at the time of his earlier trial and deliverance he was given strength "to proclaim the word fully, that all the Gentiles might hear it" as meaning that the purpose and result of his rescue were that he might go on to further work in regions previously untouched by himself or any other missionaries, and this could mean the farther West and Spain.[36]

That Paul actually did go to Spain is plainly implied in the *First Letter to the Corinthians* written by Clement of Rome in about A.D 95–96. Clement was the head of the church in Rome (approximately 92–101) and, according to Irenaeus (*Against Heresies* III 33), had conversed with both Peter and Paul, as would have been easily possible in view of the dates involved. Concerning Paul, Clement writes: "After he had been seven times in bonds, had been driven into exile, had been stoned, had been a preacher in the East and in the West, he received the noble reward of his faith; having taught righteousness unto the whole world, and having come to the boundary of the West, and having borne witness before rulers, he thus departed from the world and went unto the holy place, having become a notable pattern of patient endurance" (5 f).

From the point of view of Clement in Rome the "boundary" (τέρμα) of the West was surely the point or line not where the West begins, but where it ends. In his *Roman History* Appian tells how Octavian and Antony made a fresh partition of the whole Roman Empire between themselves. The dividing line was at Scodra, a city of Illyria about midway up the Adriatic Gulf; all to the east as far as the Euphrates was to belong to Antony, "and all west of it to the ocean to Octavian" (*Civil Wars* v 65). Appian (Preface 3) describes the Roman Empire as extending to Spain, to the western ocean, and to the Pillars of Hercules (Gibraltar and an eminence across from it on the African coast). For Clement, in Rome, the West could not be less than those regions, and he affirms that Paul went thither. Also the Muratorian Fragment, which probably represents Roman opinion in the middle or second half of the second century, speaks of "the departure of Paul from the city [i.e., Rome] on his journey to Spain." And the apocryphal *Acts of Peter* (*Actus Vercellenses*), also probably later second century in date, begins with a short account of how the Lord commanded Paul to "arise and

be a physician to those who are in Spain" and how the people in Rome lamented at his going and asked him not to stay away longer than a year.[37] Thus these sources, which are beyond the limits of the canonical New Testament but are dated relatively early, strongly attest Paul's visit to Spain.[38]

After the journey to Spain, which we may assume was Paul's major concern after his release from Roman imprisonment, and even if that journey lasted considerably longer than the one year to which the people of Rome were supposed to have asked him to limit it, there would no doubt have been time for further travels, and according to the indications preserved in the so-called pastoral letters, these travels were in the East.[39] At least several places are explicitly noted. In Crete Paul left Titus (Titus 1:5), and at Ephesus he left Timothy and went to Macedonia (I Tim 1:3) and Nicopolis (Titus 3:12) — the last was probably the "city of victory" founded by Octavian in Epirus in northwestern Achaia, at the place where he had camped before his victory over Mark Antony at Actium in 31 B.C. Later Paul was at Miletus, where he left Trophimus ill (II Tim 4:20), and at Troas, where he left a cloak and papyrus and parchment scrolls (II Tim 4:13); then he was once again in prison in Rome (II Tim 1:16-17). Was it because he had been arrested at Troas that he had left there the cloak and books that he now, in prison, wanted to have?

At any rate, in his new imprisonment — in contrast to what happened at the time of his "first defense" (II Tim 4:16) — he expected that the outcome of the matter would be his death (II Tim 4:6). For further information about the death of Paul we must turn to records beyond the canonical New Testament, and in most of these, the martyrdom of Paul is associated with that of Peter.

PETER

In the first eleven chapters of Acts Peter appears as the leader of the early church in

Jerusalem, working there and in the immediately surrounding regions, including Samaria where he controverted Simon Magus (8:9ff.) and Caesarea where he baptized Cornelius the Roman centurion (10:1ff.). In Ac 12:1-5 Herod the king kills James the brother of John and puts Peter in prison, intending after Passover "to bring him out to the people"—evidently a euphemism meaning to execute him.

This Herod was a grandson of Herod the Great and Mariamme I (the second of Herod's ten wives) and the son of Aristobulus and Berenice, so he was one-quarter Jewish and three-quarters Idumean.[40] He was born in the year 10 B.C. When he was three his father was executed by Herod the Great, and at the age of about five he went with his mother to Rome where he grew up in close association with the imperial family, under Augustus and Tiberius. For a Roman name he was called Agrippa —after Marcus Vipsanius Agrippa, the minister of Augustus—and he is now commonly designated as Agrippa I, since his own son was also named Agrippa (II). When Tiberius was in his old age Agrippa I incautiously remarked to his friend Gaius (a member of the imperial family better known as Caligula, "Little Boots," from his early life in the army camps) that he hoped the emperor would soon leave the stage and leave the government to Caligula. When told of the remark, Tiberius put Agrippa in jail with a heavy iron chain over his purple robe. There Agrippa was standing under a tree in the courtyard, with other prisoners, when an owl settled on a branch overhead. A fellow prisoner, who was a German tribal chief, declared it a sign of forthcoming release and advancement to high position (for in the West the owl was a sign of good fortune). But the German also said that when Agrippa should again see the bird (which was an omen of ill in the East), he would have but five days to live. In fact Tiberius was soon dead (Mar. 16, A.D. 37), under unclear circumstances, and Caligula was the new emperor (37–41). Caligula promptly freed Agrippa, gave him a gold chain equal in weight to the iron one he had worn in prison, and bestowed upon him a kingdom in the north of Palestine. When Caligula himself was assassinated (Jan. 24, 41), Agrippa helped his royal friend Claudius, born like himself in the year 10 B.C., obtain the throne. Claudius was proclaimed emperor on Jan. 25, 41, and "forthwith," Josephus says, gave Agrippa additional territories, especially including Judea and Samaria, so that his entire realm was as extensive as that of his grandfather. He went "forthwith" to take over his kingdom (*War* II 11, 5 §215; *Ant.* XIX 5, 1 §§274ff.; 6, 1 §§292ff.).

In Rome Agrippa had lived as a Roman and, indeed, had lived so extravagantly as to incur enormous debts; now, with such notably improved fortunes, he "turned quickly homewards," and at home began to comport himself as a pious Jew. In Jerusalem, which he made his capital rather than Caesarea, he offered sacrifices of thanksgiving according to the strict ritual of the law, hung up his golden chain in the Temple treasury, and began to build another wall on the north side of the city. Agrippa's grandmother, Mariamme, was of royal Maccabean lineage, and Agrippa himself was in many ways the last acceptable male heir of that line, since the descendants of Alexander, his uncle (brother of his father, Aristobulus), gave up all claims of Jewishness (*Ant.* XVIII 5, 4 §141). So the Jews welcomed him and said, "You are truly our brother."[41]

With the Roman procurators gone and a king of their own once again upon the throne, the Jewish leaders who were opposed to early Christianity plainly had an opportunity to instigate hostile action, and Agrippa I obviously agreed with such action. Other Jewish authorities acted against early Christianity in times when Roman control slackened—for example, in the stoning of Stephen and also in the later execution of James the brother of the Lord when the procurator Festus was dead and his successor Albinus was still on the way (Josephus, *Ant.* XX 9, 1 §200)— and the present situation was extremely favorable for similar attacks. Therefore the execution of James the brother of John and the imprisonment of Peter

were probably accomplished soon after Agrippa's arrival.[42] Since Claudius gave Agrippa his
enlarged kingdom very shortly after Claudius's
own accession on Jan. 25, 41, and since
Agrippa went very quickly to Jerusalem, he
probably sailed from Rome as soon as navigation opened on Feb. 8 and arrived in Palestine
in the customary time of five or six weeks, at
least by the middle of March. In that year the
first day of Nisan was probably on Mar. 22 (if
there were no intercalary month at the end of
the preceding year; on Apr. 21 if there were
such an intercalation), and Passover on Nisan
14 was on Apr. 4 (or May 4). This Passover of
the spring of 41 was therefore probably the
Passover of Ac 12:2–4, around which the killing of James the brother of John and the in-
carceration of Peter revolved.

Ac 12:19–23 continues immediately with an
account of the death of Herod Agrippa at
Caesarea, but for the exact date of the death of
Agrippa I, the presently available evidence is
apparently contradictory. Josephus (*War* II 11,
6 §219; *Ant.* XIX 8, 2 §343) states that Agrippa
died at the end of three years of reign, which
would presumably mean in the year 44. At
that time, Josephus relates, Agrippa went to
Caesarea to preside at "spectacles in honor of
Caesar." The building of Caesarea—named for
Caesar—was completed by Herod the Great in
the twenty-eighth year of his reign (10/9 B.C.)
and games, which were to be repeated every
five years, were instituted to commemorate the
occasion (Josephus, *Ant.* XIV 16, 4 §487 for the
beginning of the reign of Herod the Great with
the taking of Jerusalem in the fall of 37 B.C.;
XVI 5, 1 §137 for the institution of the games).
The games were accounted a birthday
celebration of the city, and we learn from
Eusebius (*Martyrs of Palestine* [appended to bk.
VIII of his *Ch. Hist.*] XI 30) that the date of the
birthday festival was Mar. 5. Beginning in 10/9
B.C. and counting the last year of the preceding
five-year cycle as the first year of the next, the
sequence of the quinquennial games comes to
A.D. 43/44, and therefore the birthday celebration of the city fell on Mar. 5, 44. On the second day of the spectacles (Mar. 6), as Josephus

continues to narrate (*Ant.* XIX 8, 2 §§343ff.),
Agrippa came into the theater at Caesarea at
daybreak, dressed in a garment woven of silver
and radiant in the first rays of the sun so that
the people called him a god (a point noted also
in Ac 12:22). Shortly thereafter, however, he
looked up and saw an owl perched on a rope
over his head, recalled the earlier prediction of
his death to be associated with such an appari-
tion, was seized with sudden pain, and after
five straight days of unremitting agony, died.
Thus the date of his demise can be calculated
as falling on Mar. 10, 44.

In that year the first day of Nisan was probably on Mar. 20 (if there were no intercalary
month at the end of the preceding year; on
Apr. 18 if there were such an intercalation),
and Passover on Nisan 14 was on Apr. 2 (or
May 1). According to the foregoing argument,
therefore, the death of Agrippa I was prior to
Passover in the year 44, and it would not be
possible to place his Passover-time execution of
James the brother of John and imprisonment
of Peter in that year.[43] If this is the case, the
fact that Acts narrates the attack upon the
apostles and the death of Agrippa in immediate sequence may be explained by the fact
that it seems to be characteristic of Luke/Acts
to complete a topic at the time that it is introduced. For example, Lk 3 not only describes
the public work of John the Baptist as do Mt 3
and Mk 1, but also includes immediately the
fact of his imprisonment (Lk 3:19–20), which
took place at a later time and is recorded in Mt
14 and Mk 6. Thus in such an instance a subject is handled most compactly in Luke/Acts
and is not only introduced but also concluded
in the same sequence.

On the other hand, there is an ostracon (an
inscribed fragment of pottery) bearing the name
of Marcus Julius Alexander and the date "the
fourth year of Claudius" (Jan. 24, 44–Jan. 23,
45). Marcus Alexander was the son-in-law of
Agrippa I, and Alexander died before Agrippa
I by a considerable period—at least enough
time for Agrippa to give his daughter Berenice,
who had been Alexander's bride, to Herod of
Chalcis after Marcus Alexander's death

(Josephus, *Ant.* XIX 5, 1 §§276–277). E. J. Vardaman also reads at the end of the text of the ostracon the name of the Egyptian month Pauni (approximately our June), and he concludes that Agrippa I must have died not earlier than late A.D. 44, and perhaps as late as early A.D. 45.[44] On this basis, if Agrippa's action against the apostles was followed rather closely by his own death (as the sequence in Ac 12 can suggest), the death of James the brother of John and the imprisonment of Peter could have taken place at Passover in A.D. 44.

From his imprisonment at Passover in either the year 41 or 44, Peter was wonderfully delivered, went to the house of Mary the mother of John Mark, directed those there to tell the event to James and the brethren, and then "departed and went to another place" (Ac 12:6–17). The reference to James must be to James the brother of the Lord and may imply a handing over of leadership to him. In Ac 1:14 Mary, the mother of Jesus, and his brothers are with the apostles in the upper room; in Gal 1:18–19 Paul sees James the Lord's brother along with Cephas in Jerusalem; in Gal 2:9 James is mentioned first, along with Cephas and John; and in Ac 15:13ff. it is James who states the judgment of the Jerusalem conference. Thus he was plainly, at least in these later times, the leader of the Jerusalem church, as Clement of Alexandria and Hegesippus (quoted by Eusebius, *Ch. Hist.* II 1, 23), calling him James the Just, also tell us he was. If Peter's departure were at Passover in 41, it would correspond with the tradition—attested by the second-century *Kerygma of Peter* (quoted by Clement of Alexandria, *Stromata* VI 5, 43) and by Apollonius (quoted by Eusebius, *Ch. Hist.* V 18, 14)—that the apostles were to stay first in Jerusalem and work in Israel and then, after twelve years, go out into the world, for the twelve years would be 30 to 41, counted inclusively.

In the *Chronicle* of Eusebius according to the version of Jerome, however, the death of Jesus is placed in the eighteenth year of Tiberius (Aug. 19, 31–Aug 18, 32), and the twelve years, counted inclusively, would come to the second year of Claudius (Jan. 24, 42–Jan. 23, 43).[45] It is at this point in the *Chronicle* that it is noted that the apostle Peter, after founding the church at Antioch, went to Rome and continued for twenty-five years as bishop of that city. In his own *Illustrious Men* (1) Jerome says that "Simon Peter . . . after having been bishop of the church of Antioch and having preached to the Dispersion—the believers in circumcision, in Pontus, Galatia, Cappadocia, Asia, and Bithynia—pushed on to Rome in the second year of Claudius to overthrow Simon Magus, and held the sacerdotal chair there for twenty-five years until the last, that is the fourteenth, year of Nero."

According to both Eusebius and Jerome, then, Peter went first to Antioch when he departed from Jerusalem and "went to another place" (Ac 12:17). As to the several provinces in Asia Minor named by Jerome, the list is identical with the list in I Pet 1:1, and the list was evidently taken by Jerome as meaning that Peter preached in those regions. It is also possible to think that Peter passed through Corinth, for Paul later (I Cor 1:12) refers to Cephas adherents there, and Dionysius, bishop of Corinth in the latter half of the second century, says in his *Letter to the Romans* (quoted by Eusebius, *Ch. Hist.* II 25, 8): "You have thus by such an admonition bound together the planting of Peter and of Paul at Rome and Corinth. For both of them planted and likewise taught us in our Corinth. And they taught together in like manner in Italy, and suffered martyrdom at the same time."

The notation in the *Chronicle* of Eusebius supposes that Peter went to Rome in the year 42, or at any rate at the latest by Jan. 23, 43, the end of the second full year of Claudius, and this date is compatible with the supposition that Peter departed from Jerusalem around Passover time in the spring of 41.[46] In the next two years of Claudius the *Chronicle* also notes that Mark, the evangelist and interpreter of Peter, "preached Christ" in Egypt and Alexandria (Claudius Year 3) and that Evodius was ordained as bishop of Antioch (Claudius Year 4). Jerome (*Illustrious Men* 8) says that Mark, the disciple and interpreter of Peter, wrote a short gospel at Rome and then went to Egypt, so Mark may have accompanied Peter to Rome.

Regarding the twenty-five years of Peter as head of the Roman church, this could be made up of thirteen years under Claudius (his Year 2, Jan. 24, 42–Jan. 23, 43, to his Year 14, beginning on Jan. 24, 54, and ending with his death by poisoning on Oct. 13, 54) plus twelve years of the reign of Nero (his Year 1, Oct. 13, 54–Oct. 12, 55, to his Year 12, Oct. 13, 65–Oct. 12, 66). Jerome, however, brings the twenty-five years down to the fourteenth and last year of Nero (which extended from Oct. 13, 67 to his death by suicide on June 9, 68) and places the deaths of both Peter and Paul in that year and indeed on the same day (*Illustrious Men* 1 and 5). Here it may be noted that if Peter did not leave Jerusalem until A.D. 44, the period of time to A.D. 68 would be twenty-five years, counted inclusively.

That Peter is considered to have been the head of the Roman church for this period of twenty-five years does not require that he had to stay in Rome continuously for all that time. After the death of Herod Agrippa I in 44 or early 45 and the appointment by Claudius of a new procurator, Cuspius Fadus, there was a new situation in which Peter presumably could have returned to Jerusalem.[47] John Mark was there (Ac 12:25) in order to go with Paul and Barnabas (Ac 13:5) on their first missionary journey (A.D. 47–48), and Peter, at all events, was present and spoke at the Jerusalem conference in 49 (Ac 15:7) and also visited Antioch afterward (Gal 2:11).

Although the Christian message may well have been brought to Rome before either Peter or Paul were there, perhaps by the "visitors from Rome" who were at Jerusalem on the day of Pentecost (Ac 2:10), it is clearly indicated that both of these notable apostles went to Rome and were thereafter considered as founders and heads of the Roman church. In the canonical New Testament the Book of Acts tells us that Paul was there, and the reference to Babylon in 1 Pet 5:13 most prob-

ably implies Peter's presence in Rome.

In a literal sense Babylon was, of course, the famous ancient city in Mesopotamia, but by this time that place was probably largely deserted. Strabo (XVI 1, 5), who visited Babylon during the reign of Augustus (27 B.C.–A.D. 14), says that the greater part of the city was so deserted that one might appropriately quote concerning it the poetic saying, "The Great City is a great desert." Pliny (A.D. 23–79) stated that in Babylon the Temple of Marduk was still standing but "in all other respects the place has gone back to a desert" (*Nat. Hist.* VI 121f.). Trajan was in Babylon in A.D. 116, and Dio Cassius says that "he saw nothing but mounds and stones and ruins." In the second half of the second century Lucian illustrated the vanity of human endeavors by writing, "Nineveh has already perished, and not a trace of it now remains. As for Babylon, the city of the magnificent towers and the great circuit-walls, soon it too will be like Nineveh, and men will look for it in vain" (*Charon* 23). It seems unlikely, therefore, that 1 Pet 5:13 refers to the Mesopotamian city. Babylon was also the name of a Roman fort in Egypt (the ruins of which are in Old Cairo), but other evidence is lacking to indicate that Peter was in Egypt, although Mark surely was. In Revelation (16:19; 18:2ff.), however, the name of Babylon is almost certainly used in a metaphoric sense for Rome, and it is this usage that is most probable in 1 Pet 5:13. Since some Roman officials and especially the members of the Herodian family were no doubt antagonistic to Peter, it may have been desirable to keep his whereabouts relatively secret, which can help explain the use of this symbolic language.

When Ignatius, bishop of Antioch in succession to Evodius (Eusebius, *Chronicle*;[48] Jerome, *Illustrious Men* 16), was on his way to Rome and martyrdom, he wrote in his *Letter to the Romans* (IV 3): "I do not, as Peter and Paul, issue commandments to you. They were apostles; I am but a condemned man." Ignatius, himself head of a leading church in the East, recognized the two apostles as the authorities of the Roman church, no longer living, of course, but greatly honored in remembrance. That both of the apostles died in Rome is attested early, widely, and without contradiction.

DEATHS OF PETER AND PAUL

In the canonical New Testament the death of Peter is foreshadowed (Jn 21:18-19) in Jesus saying to him, "'when you are old, you will stretch out your hands, and another will gird you and carry you where you do not wish to go.' (This he said to show by what death he was to glorify God.)" To "stretch out the hands" is doubtless a euphemism for crucifixion (cf. Irenaeus, *Against Heresies* v 17, 3). In II Pet 1:14 there is also an anticipation of Peter's death, as indicated formerly by Jesus. As for Paul, in II Tim the apostle is aware of imminent death and that the time of his departure has come (4:6).

Beyond the canonical New Testament, Clement of Rome, first of all, speaks of the deaths of the two apostles in his *First Letter to the Corinthians* (5f.). In the context of a warning to the Corinthians against contentions in the church, he illustrates the ill effects of jealousy and envy. The passage begins, "Let us set before our eyes the good apostles [or, perhaps, our good apostles]."[49] Then Clement continues with this statement about Peter: "Peter, who on account of unrighteous jealousy endured not one nor two, but many sufferings, and so, having borne his testimony, went to his deserved place of glory."

Continuing, Clement says about Paul, "On account of jealousy and strife Paul pointed out the prize of endurance," and then Clement makes the further statement concerning Paul, his preaching, and his death quoted earlier. In conclusion, Clement describes a whole multitude of Christians who shared the same fate of martyrdom with the two great apostles.

> Unto these men who lived lives of holiness was gathered a vast multitude of the elect, who by many indignities and tortures, being the victims of jealousy, set the finest examples among us. On account of jealousy women, when they had been persecuted as Danaids [the daughters of Danaüs suffered in the underworld] and Dircae [Dirce was tied by the hair to a wild bull and dragged], and had suffered cruel and unholy insults, safely reached the goal in the race of faith and received a noble reward, feeble though they were in body.

This description by Clement of the cruel insults, indignities, and tortures experienced by a multitude of Christians agrees quite unmistakably with what we know the emperor Nero did in the latter part of his reign. Suetonius (*Nero* 16) refers to the matter in general terms when he says that "many abuses were severely punished and put down" by Nero, and Suetonius then includes among these abuses the fact that "punishment was inflicted on the Christians, a class of men given to a new and mischievous superstition." Tacitus (*Annals* xv 38-44) tells in detail what happened. In the tenth year of Nero (63/64), on the nineteenth of July, fire broke out in the Circus Maximus by the Palatine and Caelian hills. Tacitus says it was not known whether this was by chance or whether the fire was set by Nero; Suetonius states that the city was set on fire openly by Nero, who pretended to be disgusted with the ugliness of the old buildings and the narrow and crooked streets. For the homeless and fugitive populace, Tacitus continues, Nero opened the Campus Martius and even his own gardens, put up emergency shelters, and brought food from Ostia. The fire burned for six days, stopped at the foot of the Esquiline Hill, then started up again in other parts of the city, and burned longer. When finally it was at an end only four of Rome's fourteen districts (as organized by Augustus) were intact. After that, Nero set forth guidelines and took steps for a major rebuilding of the city with broad thoroughfares, buildings of restricted height, open spaces, and colonnades. Some of the expenses Nero paid himself, and he offered rewards for rebuilding. Prayers and sacrifices were also made to the gods. Then Tacitus writes:

But neither human help, nor imperial munificence, nor all the modes of placating Heaven, could stifle scandal or dispel the belief that the fire had taken place by order. Therefore, to scotch the rumor, Nero substituted as culprits, and punished with the utmost refinements of cruelty, a class of men, loathed for their vices, whom the crowed styled Christians. Christus, the founder of the name, had undergone the death penalty in the reign of Tiberius, by sentence of the procurator Pontius Pilatus, and the pernicious superstition was checked for a moment, only to break out once more, not merely in Judea, the home of the disease, but in the capital itself, where all things horrible or shameful in the world collect and find a vogue. First, then, the confessed members of the sect were arrested; next, on their disclosures, vast numbers were convicted, not so much on the count of arson as for hatred of the human race. And derision accompanied their end: they were covered with wild beasts' skins and torn to death by dogs; or they were fastened on crosses, and, when daylight failed were burned to serve as lamps by night. Nero had offered his Gardens for the spectacle, and gave an exhibition in his Circus, mixing with the crowd in the habit of a charioteer, or mounted on his car. Hence, in spite of a guilt which had earned the most exemplary punishment, there arose a sentiment of pity, due to the impression that they were being sacrificed not for the welfare of the state but to the ferocity of a single man.

Since the death of Peter, the death of Paul, and the deaths of a large number of Christians are grouped together in one passage in Clement's *First Letter to the Corinthians*, and since the "indignities and tortures" of the "vast multitude" sound exactly like what Tacitus tells of Nero's persecution of the Christians after the fire of July 64, it is possible to conclude that all these events happened about the same time and that therefore both Peter and Paul died in 64.[50] But looked at more closely and in detail, even the Tacitus narrative describes a rather long sequence of events, making it likely that the persecution of the Christians occurred, at the earliest, considerably later than the month of July 64, and

very possibly not until early in the year 65.[51] Furthermore, there is additional information in the *Sacred History* or *Chronicle of the World* (II 29) by Sulpicius Severus (A.D. 363–420), a highly educated contemporary of Jerome and, in his own career, first of all a lawyer. Sulpicius Severus gives the same familiar facts about the fire and the persecution of the Christians, in which "many were crucified or slain by fire," and then goes on to say that "Afterwards, too, their religion was prohibited by laws which were enacted; and by edicts openly set forth it was proclaimed unlawful to be a Christian. At that time Paul and Peter were condemned to death, the former being beheaded with a sword, while Peter suffered crucifixion."

In the promulgation of such anti-Christian laws we may surmise that Nero wanted to establish legal grounds for what he had already done as an act of outright violence—at any rate it may be assumed that the inauguration of these laws and their application to accomplish legal condemnations and executions required some length of time. Since Severus speaks as if Paul and Peter were condemned at the same time and on the basis of these laws, and since his contemporary Jerome says that Peter and Paul died in the fourteenth year of Nero (67/68) and on the same day, it is possible to conclude that both apostles died as a result of legal action and perhaps in the year 67/68.[52]

But, in fact, the manner of death and the places of death and burial were different for Peter and for Paul, and it must therefore be asked whether or not the dates of their deaths were also different. For Peter the manner of death was by crucifixion. Tertullian (*On Prescription Against Heretics* 36) compares Peter's passion to that of his Lord's, i.e., he was crucified. Origen (cited by Eusebius, *Ch. Hist.* III 1) says Peter "was crucified head-downwards, for he had requested that he might suffer in this way." Jerome (*Illustrious Men* 1) related that he was "nailed to the cross with his head towards the ground and his feet raised on high, asserting that he was unworthy to be crucified in the same manner as his Lord." The second-century apocryphal *Acts of Peter* gives the well-known *Quo vadis, Domine?* story and follows it with Peter's statement to those who put him to death, "I request you therefore, executioners, to crucify me head-downwards." The apocryphal *Acts* goes on to say that afterward Peter's friend, a senator named Marcellus, put the body in his own burial vault (a story possibly patterned after the burial of Jesus by Joseph of Arimathea).[53]

For Paul, however, as a Roman citizen (Ac 16:37; 22:27–29; 23:27), it would be expected that a death penalty would be carried out, after condemnation in a legal trial, by the method usual for a citizen, i.e., decapitation by the sword. This is, in fact, the way in which the death of Paul is represented as having taken place. Tertullian, who compared the passion of Peter with that of Jesus in that both were crucified, says in the same passage that Paul won his crown in a death like John's, i.e., like John the Baptist, who was beheaded (Mt 14:10; Mk 6:27; Lk 9:9). In the second-century apocryphal *Acts of Paul* it is stated that the executioner struck off Paul's head, and it is also fancifully related that milk spurted upon the soldier's clothing.[54]

As to the places associated with the death and burial of each of the two apostles, there is the important and early evidence of Gaius, who was a presbyter in the church at Rome under Pope Zephyrinus (A.D. 199–217). At that time, a leader of the Montanists, in Asia Minor, a certain Proclus, supported his position in that prophetic movement by appealing to the existence at Hierapolis of the tombs of Philip the evangelist (Ac 6:5; 8; 21:8–9) and his four daughters, who were prophetesses (Eusebius, *Ch. Hist.* III 31). In answer to Proclus and in behalf of the church at Rome, Gaius made a counterbalancing affirmation in a published disputation (Eusebius, *Ch. Hist.* II 25). Gaius declared: "But I can show the trophies of the apostles. For if you will go to the Vatican or to the Ostian Way, you will find the trophies of those who laid the foundations of this church."

A "trophy" in Greek and in Latin (τρόπαιον, *tropaeum*) is a token of the turning around (τροπή), hence of the rout of an enemy, and thus is a sign or memorial of victory that is often raised on the field of battle. Since Proclus appealed to the tombs of Philip and his daughters, the trophies cited by Gaius must have been the grave monuments of Peter and Paul. These are memorials of triumph, because they mark the last resting places of the apostles who died as heroic witnesses. At the Vatican and on the Ostian Way, respectively, these trophies of Peter and of Paul were well-known Christian landmarks at the time of Gaius, i.e., around the year 200.

In addition to what Gaius says about Peter's trophy or grave monument at the Vatican, other references speak of either the place of his burial or the place of his execution or both as being at the Vatican. The fourth-century apocryphal *Martyrdom of Peter* (falsely attributed to Linus, Peter's disciple and successor) states that Peter was taken "to a place which is called Naumachia, near Nero's obelisk, on the hill."[55] The fourth-century apocryphal *Martyrdom of Peter and Paul* (falsely attributed to the senator Marcellus) and the fourth-century *Acts of Peter and Paul* state in identical language that Peter was buried "under the terebinth near the Naumachia, in a place called Vatican."[56] The *Liber Pontificalis* or *Book of the Popes*, compiled in the sixth century but containing earlier information, records that Peter was buried "on the Via Aurelia, in the shrine of Apollo, near the place where he was crucified, near the palace of Nero, in the Vatican, near the triumphal district, on June 29."[57] In addition to Gaius, who speaks of the grave monument (trophy) of Paul on the Ostian Way, the *Acts of Peter and Paul* states that Paul was beheaded at a place called Aquae Salviae, under a pine tree,[58] and later legend affirms that at each of the three places touched by Paul's rolling head after it was cut off, a spring burst forth (now Tre Fontane).[59]

As to the obtaining and the interment of the bodies of the two apostles, so that their last resting places could indeed be known and remembered, an executed criminal had no legal right to burial, but the laws evidently allowed friends or relatives to claim a body for burial. Such a claim was made for Jesus by Joseph of Arimathea, and the same probably was made for Peter and for Paul and, no doubt, for other victims of persecution also.[60]

Vatican

The Vatican, where according to the foregoing, the death and burial of Peter took place, was the last of the fourteen administrative districts into which Rome was divided by Augustus. The name (adjective *Vaticanus*, substantive *Vaticanum*) may have been derived from an early Etruscan settlement.[61] The whole area, called the Ager ("field" or "district") Vaticanus, was across from the Campus Martius on the west side of the Tiber River and north of Janiculum Hill. To the northwest was a conspicuous hill, the Mons Vaticanus, one of several *Montes Vaticani* extending from the Janiculum to Monte Mario. On the south side of Mons Vaticanus was a valley, the Vallis Vaticana, and to the east was a flat, open ground extending to the river, the Campus ("flat place," "plain") Vaticanus. The district was rural or suburban, considered unhealthy (Tacitus, *Hist.* II 93, 2), infested by large snakes (Pliny, *Nat. Hist.* VIII 37), known for its clay from which bricks, tiles, and earthenware vessels ("brittle dishes," according to Juvenal, *Satires* VI 344) were made, and also known for its vineyards from which poor wine (according

PLAN 1.

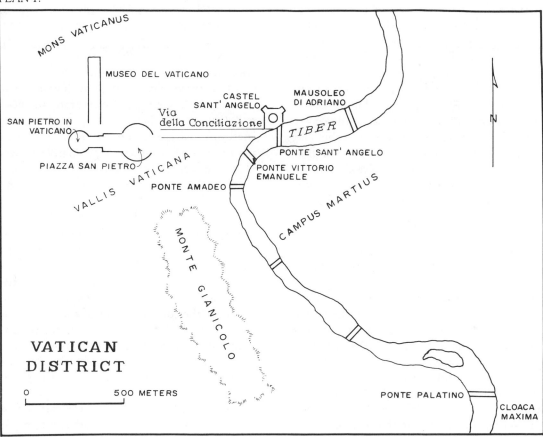

to Martial, *Epigrams* v 45, 5; vi 92, 3) was produced.

In the district, however, several properties belonged to the imperial family, and these properties were improved in the form of gardens.[62] The Horti Agrippinae belonged to Agrippina and her husband Germanicus (15 B.C–A.D. 19), and these gardens passed later to their youngest son, Gaius or Caligula. Thus Philo, for example, tells of coming with a delegation to Rome (*Embassy to Gaius* 181) and speaks of the emperor Gaius as "receiving us first of all on the level ground beside the Tiber, for he happened to be coming out of his mother's garden." The Horti Domitiae were probably owned first by Domitia Lepida, an aunt of Nero, and these gardens included the land on which the Mausoleum of Hadrian (Castel Sant' Angelo) was later built. All of these gardens came eventually into the possession of Nero and were the Horti Neronis, the Gardens of Nero. In the Gardens of Agrippina and in the Vallis Vaticana a circus was built by Gaius that later belonged to Nero, the Circus Gai et Neronis. Pliny (*Nat. Hist.* xxxvi 14–15) tells of three Egyptian obelisks that were brought to Rome and set up, one in the Campus Martius, one on the *spina* (the "backbone" or low wall running lengthwise in the center) of the Circus Maximus, and one "in the Vatican Circus (in *Vaticano . . . circo*) that was built by the emperors Gaius and Nero." Like the obelisk in the Circus Maximus, the obelisk in the Vatican Circus was presumably set up on the *spina* of the racecourse, although *in circo* could possibly have the broader meaning of in the vicinity of the circus.

From other references and representations it is also known that there were in the Vatican district two *naumachiae* or places for simulated naval battles, a Temple of Cybele, the Magna Mater from Asia, a pyramidal tomb of the first century A.D. later taken for the Tomb of Romulus and called the Meta Romuli, and another tomb called the Terebinthus from *Tiburtinus* (the stone of Tivoli used in its construction).[63] To cross the Tiber from the Campus Martius on the east to the Vatican district

on the west there was a bridge, later known as the Pons Neronianus, the piers of which can still be seen at low water today, near the modern Ponte Vittorio Emanuele. Also in the Vatican district there were roads named Via Aurelia, Via Triumphalis, and Via Cornelia, the last perhaps following a route more or less like that of the modern Via della Conciliazione.[64]

Underneath the Church of St. Peter in the Vatican (San Pietro in Vaticano) excavations were conducted in 1940–49, with further investigations in 1953 and later,[65] and it was found that simple early burials were made on the Vatican hillside in the first century A.D. One tomb, for example, was covered with tiles on one of which was a manufacturer's mark datable in the reign of Vespasian (A.D. 69–79), and close by was a clay lamp with the name of a potter known elsewhere on lamps datable about A.D. 70.[66] Then in the period from approximately 130 to 300 a double row, running from east to west, of more magnificent mausoleums was built, and they partly obliterated the earlier cemetery. These mausoleums were rectangular structures of concrete faced with brick, much like small houses, with exterior decoration in *opus reticulatum* (small diamond-shaped stones in a "network" pattern) and terra cotta, with *titulus* inscriptions of the owners on marble tablets above the entrances, and with reliefs, mosaics, and paintings in the interior. In the inner walls there were niches for the cremation urns, but provision was made for burials too as the Roman custom changed gradually to inhumation in the second and third centuries. The decorations generally exhibit the themes of pagan religion, but there were some Christian burials too. One small mausoleum (the Tomb of the Julii, first half of the third century, labeled "M" on the excavators' plan) is entirely Christian, and on its ceiling is an adaptation of pagan symbolism in which Christ is shown ascending in a chariot like Helios, the sun.

In the *titulus* of tomb "A" at the east end of the north row of the mausoleums, a tomb of

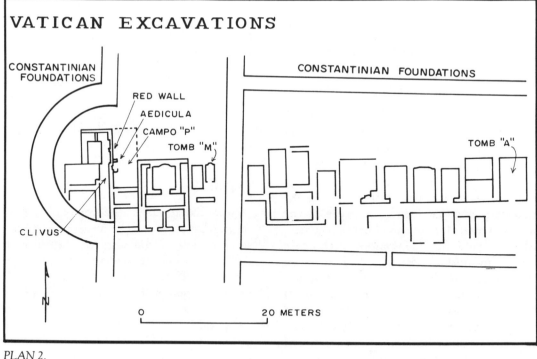

VATICAN EXCAVATIONS

CONSTANTINIAN
FOUNDATIONS

CONSTANTINIAN FOUNDATIONS

RED WALL

AEDICULA

CAMPO "P"

TOMB "M"

TOMB "A"

CLIVUS

N

0   20 METERS

PLAN 2.

the first half of the second century, the owner, a certain Gaius Popilius Heracla, states that he has directed his heirs to bury him *in Vatic(ano) ad circum* ("in the Vatican near the circus"). This is proof that the cemetery is in the vicinity of the famous Circus of Gaius and Nero, although that circus has not yet been found. The Egyptian obelisk that stands now in the center of Piazza San Pietro, and was formerly on the south side of San Pietro in Vaticano, is presumably the obelisk that Pliny says was *in circo*, either on the *spina* or at least in the vicinity of the circus. For tombs to line the roads on the outskirts of a Roman city, and also to be built in proximity to places of amusement, is of course familiar; for example, there are tombs on the Via Appia Antica and near the Circus of Maxentius (A.D 303–312).

Near the west end of the double row of mausoleums are an open court (Campo "P") and a steep narrow street (the Clivus). Beneath the Clivus is a drain, partly built of tiles, five of

which bear an identical stamp datable in A.D. 146–161. On the east side of the Clivus is a wall, the purpose of which was to fix the boundaries of the street and of the adjacent tombs. Set into the east side of this wall, facing the open court, is a two-story niche or shrine (the Aedicula). The wall was plastered and colored red (hence it is called the Red Wall), and the Aedicula was constructed at the same time as the wall into which it is recessed, about A.D. 160. Some early burials extend under the Red Wall, and there are traces of an ancient grave under the Aedicula.[67] On the Red Wall, probably dating not much later than the wall and the Aedicula, was a graffito with the name of Peter and a word possibly meaning "is within," thus a scratched notation by some worker or visitor that "Peter is buried inside."[68] This notation attests the belief that the Aedicula marked the last resting place of Peter, and this shrine may accordingly be recognized, as it is by most scholars, as the trophy of Peter at the

Vatican to which Gaius made reference around 200.[69]

At the exact place believed to have this significance the emperor Constantine built a large church. To put the church precisely on the spot involved a project of extraordinary difficulty. The preexisting cemetery was invaded (surely a moral if not also a legal problem), and a large building area was leveled (involving the moving of more than one million cubic feet [28,000 cubic meters] of earth.[70] In most cases the roofs of the mausoleums were removed, earth was packed into the exposed chambers, and the foundation walls of the church were set into the midst of the cemetery. Like several other Constantinian churches (San Giovanni in Laterano in Rome, the Church of the Nativity in Bethlehem, the Church of the Holy Sepulcher in Jerusalem) this church was a basilica, a Roman type of building used for various purposes, and known from at least the second century B.C., in which a hall is subdivided by colonnades. The Constantinian church in question is known from some remaining portions of it found in the excavations under the present San Pietro in Vaticano and from drawings and plans of it made before or during its demolition to make way for the present church. It was a five-aisled basilica, 279 ft (85 m) long and 210 ft (64 m) wide, with a single projecting apse at the west end and a narrow transept.[71] The apse was oriented precisely to the Aedicula, and over the tomb believed to be that of Peter were set spiral columns, which the *Liber Pontificalis* says were brought from Greece.[72]

In the fifteenth century it was decided to demolish the Constantinian basilica because of its dilapidated condition, and in the sixteenth and seventeenth centuries it was replaced by the present church, designed by Bramante. The first stone was laid in 1506, Bramante's work was continued by Raphael (1514) and others, the great dome was designed by Michelangelo (1546), the dedication was in 1626, and Bernini designed the bronze canopy over the altar (1633) and later the colonnades around the elliptical piazza to which the Egyp-

tian obelisk had been moved in 1586. Six of the spiral columns that Constantine had put above the tomb survive, and they were placed by Bernini in galleries in the dome of the present church. Under the present altar, built at the behest of Clement VIII (1592–1605), are the altars of Callistus II (1119–24) and Gregory the Great (590–604), and beneath them all, in direct line, are the Red Wall and the Aedicula, the trophy of Peter.

Ostian Way

According to Gaius, the trophy of Paul was on the Ostian Way. The ancient Via Ostiensis—the modern Via Ostiense—began at the Porta Ostiensis—the modern Porta San Paolo—and ran 12.5 mi (20 km) to Ostia at the mouth (*ostium*) of the Tiber. One monument, which was erected even before the time of Paul, still stands at the Porta San Paolo, namely, the pyramid tomb of Gaius Cestius, a praetor who died in the year 12 B.C. At a later time this monument was thought to be the Tomb of Remus, and it was called the Meta Remi, even as the pyramid tomb at the Vatican was thought to be the Tomb of Romulus and was called the Meta Romuli. In some accounts of the death of Peter it is stated that the place where he perished was *inter duas metas*. The *meta* was the turning post at each end of the *spina* in a circus, so this phrase meant that Peter was crucified midway between the two turning posts, i.e., at the middle of the *spina*. *Meta* also means pyramid, however, and the reference can also be taken to signify a point midway between the two conspicuous pyramids, the Meta Romuli and the Meta Remi. Such a point is to be found on the Janiculum Hill, and it is marked by the Tempietto, a small circular temple built by Bramante about 1500, and the adjacent church of San Pietro in Montorio, rebuilt in the fifteenth century and restored in the nineteenth century.[73]

At a distance of 1.25 mi (2 km) from the Porta San Paolo is the Church of St. Paul Outside the Walls (San Paolo Fuori le Mura), and, at a like distance further on out the Via Os-

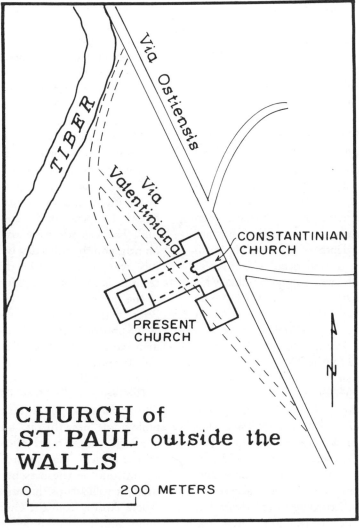

TIBER

Via Ostiensis

Via Valentiniana

CONSTANTINIAN CHURCH

PRESENT CHURCH

N

CHURCH of
ST. PAUL outside the
WALLS

0   200 METERS

PLAN 3.

tiense and to the east on the Via Laurentina is the Abbey of the Three Fountains (Abbadia della Tre Fontane). At the end of the abbey garden in the Church of St. Paul of the Three Fountains (San Paolo alle Tre Fontane). This church was built in the fifth century (and reconstructed in 1599) over the three springs believed to be in the place where Paul was executed.[74] The abbey was virtually abandoned for a long time, owing to its swampy and malarial situation, but it was given to the Trappists around 1867. In digging in connection

with one of their buildings in 1875 the Trappists unearthed a mass of coins of Nero, together with several fossilized pinecones.[75]

As the Via Ostiense approaches the church of San Paolo Fuori le Mura from the city, the road passes a pagan necropolis, the excavation of which has revealed tombs of the same type (with *opus reticulatum*) as at the Vatican but, on the whole, older and poorer. At the church itself no scientific excavation has been conducted, but the site is surely where Constantine built a basilica over the traditional trophy of Paul. In some work around the altar, portions of an early apse were found, no doubt that of the Constantinian church, oriented toward the west and the Tiber River. When the present church was being constructed a marble slab was seen under the altar, and it is preserved under the present altar, with an inscription to Paul, apostle and martyr (PAULO APOSTOLO MART[YRI]) in letters of the time of Constantine.[76] The Constantinian church was small, was entered from the Via Ostiensis to the east, and the west end practically abutted upon a side road, the Via Valentiniana, remains of which have been found immediately to the west of the Constantinian apse at a depth of about 13 ft (4 m) below the present ground level.[77] Again, as at the Vatican, the site was extremely unlikely for a church unless there were a very special reason for building it there; it was in a pagan cemetery, it was in a constricted space between two roads, and it was in a low-lying, swampy area often flooded by the Tiber.

To remedy the situation of the Constantinian church the three emperors Valentinian II (375–392), Theodosius I the Great (379–395), and his son Arcadius (383–402) addressed a letter in A.D. 384 (or 386) to Sallust, the urban prefect of Rome, ordering that the old side road be moved to provide room for a new church, which would be larger and also set on higher ground.[78] According to an inscription in the mosaics on the triumphal arch, the church was begun by Theodosius, but it was completed by Honorius, who was the younger son of Theodosius and himself emperor in 395–423. This great basilica stood until the night of July 15, 1823, when it was almost completely destroyed by fire. The present church, of impressive plan and dimensions like its predecessor, was begun immediately afterward and dedicated in 1854.

Catacumbas

Confirming the special remembrances of Peter and Paul at the Vatican and on the Ostian Way, but also introducing an additional problem, is the *Chronography of 354*, a calendar for the city of Rome, edited in that year by Furius Dionysius Filocalus, later secretary and calligrapher for Pope Damasus (366–384). In this calendar the section called "Depositio martyrum" lists the feasts celebrated in honor of martyrs, supposedly on the day each martyr was placed in the grave. For Peter and Paul the text[79] is apparently defective, but it is supplemented by a corresponding item, which is longer and evidently more correct, in the so-called *Martyrology of James*, a work of about the beginning of the fifth century.[80] The item in question appears under the date of "III. kal. Iul." The calends were the first day of the month, and the third day before the calends of July was June 29. On that day, the text records, is the "birthday" (i.e., the celebration of the day of entry into the heavenly life) "of Peter in the Vatican, of Paul on the Ostian Way, and of both *in Catacumbas*." Then the item closes with a date "in the consulate of Bassus and Tuscus," which is the designation for the year 258.[81]

The term *catacumbas* (equivalent to the Greek κατὰ κύμβας) may mean "by the hollow," or "near the pit," and it was the name of a region at the third milestone from the city on the ancient Via Appia. There, about 3 mi (5 km) outside the present Porta San Sebastiano, a valley runs diagonally across the Via Appia Antica from the church of San Sebastiano, which is on the right side of the road as one goes away from the city, to the ruins of the Circus of Maxentius and the Tomb of Cecilia Metella, which are on the left side of the road. The Circus of Maxentius was erected in A.D. 309 (with a Roman obelisk in it, which is now on Bernini's fountain in Piazza Navona, the site of the stadium of Domitian), and a biographical notice of Maxentius in the *Chronography of 354* states that is was this emperor who built the circus in Catacumbas. The Tomb of Cecilia Metella, a huge cylindrical tower, was the burial place of the wife of one of Caesar's generals in Gaul, and at the tomb there was also an imperial police station.

Excavations begun in 1892 and continued in

1915 and afterward under the present church of San Sebastiano[82] have revealed architectural remains on three main levels; namely, (1) a pagan necropolis, (2) memorial rooms associated with Peter and Paul, and (3) a basilica of the time of Constantine. In the vicinity there is a pozzolana quarry of the first century A.D., if not even earlier, and if the word *catacumbas* did not refer to the whole natural valley in the region, it may have originated as a reference to the "pit" of this quarry. Near the quarry is the pagan cemetery. The first tombs in this cemetery belong to the first century A.D. and the first half of the second century, and they include a number of columbaria. In the columbaria are the usual niches for the cremation urns, but as the custom changed, there were also burials in the floor. In the course of the second century some assembly rooms were added, probably intended for meals held in honor of the deceased.[83] By the end of the second century and the beginning of the third, there were also at least three large mausoleums, one for cremation and two for inhumation, and in construction and decoration these mausoleums were more or less like those discovered under the church of San Pietro in Vaticano. The tombs built up to the middle of the second century reveal only the themes of paganism, but in those tombs built from the end of the second and the beginning of the third centuries there are some indications of Christianity.[84]

About the middle of the third century, and in a place almost exactly under the center of the later church, the pagan necropolis was filled in, and some places of Christian assembly were constructed; namely, several rooms and a brick-paved, walled courtyard with masonry benches along the sides. In one corner of this courtyard is a small well, in the drain of which were found the bones of fish, chicken, and hare. This discovery suggests that meals were eaten here, and the courtyard is accordingly called the *triclia*, a Latin word for an eating room (from *triclinium*, a couch extending around three sides of a table). Near the entrance of the *triclia* is a sort of little shrine, with marble and mosaic decoration.[85] On the painted walls of the *triclia* are many graffiti, some still in their original place, others fallen to the ground in fragments. These are written in both capital letters and cursive script, and in both Latin and Greek. One inscription is also accompanied by a consular date equivalent to the year 260.[86] For the most part the graffiti contain appeals to the apostles Peter and Paul, and also references to the holding of *refrigeria*. Typical examples follow:

Paul and Peter pray for Victor

Peter and Paul pray for Leontius

Paul and Peter pray for us all

Peter and Paul, have Antonius in mind

To Peter and Paul, I, Tomius Coelius, made a *refrigerium*

Near Paul and Peter, I made a *refrigerium*[87]

In Latin the word *refrigerium* means a "cooling," and hence a consolation or refreshment; accordingly in Christian usage it signified the rewards and comforts of heaven, but here it evidently also refers to a meal held in honor of the deceased. It is known that funeral banquets and meals were held in honor of and for the benefit of the dead in ancient paganism, as attested in inscriptions where the same word *refrigerium* (or related forms) appears,[88] and such meals were apparently provided for in the assembly rooms of the pagan necropolis on this particular site. The existence of this custom among the Christians, probably for only a limited time, is also indicated by an inscription in the Catacomb of Priscilla, in which a wife speaks of a *refrigerium* "for Antisthenes, her sweetest husband."[89] So, in the middle of the third century, this *triclia* on the Via Appia, above the older pagan cemetery, was evidently a gathering place for Christians who wrote appeals to Paul and Peter on the walls and ate meals in honor of the two apostles.

The famous martyr Sebastian, who died in

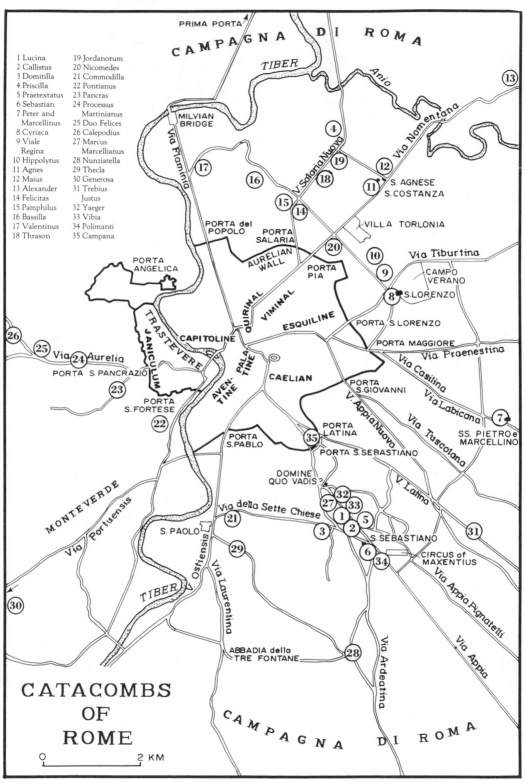

PRIMA PORTA

CAMPAGNA DI ROMA

TIBER

Anio

1 Lucina
2 Callistus
3 Domitilla
4 Priscilla
5 Praetextatus
6 Sebastian
7 Peter and
   Marcellinus
8 Cyriaca
9 Viale
   Regina
10 Hippolytus
11 Agnes
12 Maius
13 Alexander
14 Felicitas
15 Pamphilus
16 Bassilla
17 Valentinus
18 Thrason

19 Jordanorum
20 Nicomedes
21 Commodilla
22 Pontianus
23 Pancras
24 Processus
   Martinianus
25 Duo Felices
26 Calepodius
27 Marcus
   Marcellianus
28 Nunziatella
29 Thecla
30 Generosa
31 Trebius
   Justus
32 Yaeger
33 Vibia
34 Polimanti
35 Campana

MILVIAN
BRIDGE

Via Flaminia

⑬

④
Via Nomentana
⑫
⑲
⑪ S. AGNESE
S. COSTANZA
⑰
⑯
⑱
V. Salaria Nuova
⑮
⑭
VILLA TORLONIA

Via Tiburtina
⑩
⑨
CAMPO
VERANO
⑧ S. LORENZO

PORTA del
POPOLO
PORTA
SALARIA
AURELIAN
WALL
PORTA
PIA
⑳

PORTA
ANGELICA

QUIRINAL
VIMINAL
ESQUILINE

PORTA S. LORENZO

PORTA MAGGIORE

Via Praenestina

Via Casilina

TRASTEVERE
JANICULUM
CAPITOLINE

AVEN-
TINE
PALA-
TINE

CAELIAN

PORTA
S. GIOVANNI
Via Appia Nuova
Via Labicana

Via Tuscolana

⑦ SS. PIETRO e
MARCELLINO

㉖
㉕ Via ㉔ Aurelia
PORTA S. PANCRAZIO
㉓
PORTA
S. FORTESE
㉒

PORTA
S. PABLO

PORTA
LATINA
㉟

PORTA S. SEBASTIANO

V. Latina

DOMINE
QUO VADIS?
㉜
㉗ ① ㉝
③ ② ⑤
S. SEBASTIANO
⑥
㉞
CIRCUS of
MAXENTIUS

Via della Sette Chiese
㉑
S. PAOLO
㉙

MONTEVERDE

Via Portuensis

Ostiensis

TIBER

Via Laurentina

Via Ardeatina

Via Appia

Via Appia Pignatelli

㉛

㉚

ABBADIA della
TRE FONTANE

㉘

CAMPAGNA DI ROMA

CATACOMBS
OF
ROME

0   2 KM

the persecution by Diocletian (A.D. 284–305), was also buried here, and the *Chronography of 354* lists his memorial feast as celebrated on "XIII. kal. Feb. [Jan. 20] *in Catacumbas.*"[90] No doubt it was because of the remembrance of Peter and Paul, and also of Sebastian, that many other Christians wished to be interred nearby, and thus there came into being in the vicinity a very extensive network of underground corridors and burial places, the Catacomb of St. Sebastian. It was from this large cemetery at Catacumbas that the name "catacombs" came into use for all such subterranean burial areas.

The Christian meeting rooms with the graffiti calling upon Peter and Paul were in turn buried beneath a church that was built directly above, with its foundations extending downward as much as 33 ft (10 m) into the assembly rooms and the surrounding catacomb. The structure was a basilica with three aisles, the construction of its walls is similar to that of the Circus of Maxentius (A.D. 309), and it was doubtless built in the Constantinian period.[91] Continuing to honor the memory of both Peter and Paul, it was known as the Basilica of the Apostles. At the beginning of the fifth century the crypt of Sebastian, under the church, was elaborately rebuilt,[92] and by the ninth century, the church itself was known as the Basilica of St. Sebastian (San Sebastiano).[93] This church was rebuilt in its present form in 1612.

Regarding the connection of Peter and Paul with this memorial place at Catacumbas, there is also to be noted one of the poetic inscriptions composed by Pope Damasus (A.D. 366–384), lettered by Filocalus, and set up at various burial places—for example, at the Crypt of the Popes in the nearby Catacomb of Callistus, where the inscription was found in more than one hundred fragments. Of these inscriptions the one relating to Peter and Paul is found in a partial thirteenth-century copy on a stone in the crypt of San Sebastiano, and it is also preserved in several manuscripts of the Middle Ages.[94] The text addresses itself to those people who ask after the names of Peter

and Paul, states that it should be known that "the saints dwell here" or "formerly dwelt here" (the manuscripts vary between *habitare* and *habitasse*), then declares that these saints came indeed from the Orient as disciples of Christ but, on account of their martyrdom, Rome has won the right to claim them as citizens. Also in the fifth-century *Acts of St. Sebastian* it is stated that that martyr was buried "at *Catacumbas* in the entrance to the crypt near the vestiges of the apostles."[95] Yet again in the *Liber Pontificalis*[96] it is said that under Pope Cornelius (A.D. 251–253) the bodies of Paul and Peter were taken up from Catacumbas and buried on the Via Ostiensis and at the Vatican, respectively.

The information provided by the foregoing references, which link Peter and Paul to some extent with Catacumbas, is not wholly consistent nor unambiguous, and several theories have been advanced to explain the circumstances. One theory is that the two apostles were buried originally at Catacumbas on the Via Appia,[97] but it is difficult to see why, if that were the case, it would be only in the middle of the third century that they were tangibly memorialized there when there were already trophies of their martyrdom at the Vatican and on the Ostian Way in the second century. Also the *Liber Pontificalis* itself, which speaks of the taking of the bodies from Catacumbas in the time of Pope Cornelius, states that Peter was buried (presumably first) in the Vatican.[98]

Another theory supposes that the bodies of Peter and Paul were buried originally at the Vatican and on the Ostian Way, respectively, and that both were transferred to Catacumbas in A.D. 258. The reason given for the transfer at that particular time is that it was the year of a persecution of the Christians by the emperor Valerian (253–260) and the remains were taken there for safety.[99] This theory makes it possible to understand Damasus's statement that the apostles "formerly dwelt here" in the sense that their bodies were actually in Catacumbas for a time. However, the earlier texts of the *Chronography of 354* and the *Mar-*

tyrology of Jerome, a work of the fifth or sixth century, say nothing about such a translation of the bodies but speak only of a memorial remembrance of the two apostles at Catacumbas on June 29, 258. Furthermore it would hardly seem likely that the Christians would be free to disturb the earlier burials and bring the bodies here, especially in a time of persecution, and the more so because the place was not far from the imperial police station at the Tomb of Cecilia Metella.[100]

Yet another theory therefore supposes that it was only some relics of the two apostles, possibly only simple objects that had touched their tombs, that were put at Catacumbas, possibly in the little marble-and-mosaic-decorated shrine near the entrance to the triclia.[101] Perhaps these were the "vestiges" or traces of the apostles mentioned in the Acts of St. Sebastian, and perhaps Damasus's statement that the apostles "dwell" or "formerly dwelt" there refers to their spiritual presence rather than to the literal presence of their bodies.

At any rate the earliest evidence—namely, the information in the Chronography of 354 and the Martyrology of James about the remembrance of Peter and Paul at Catacumbas on June 29, 258, and the graffiti in the triclia under the church of San Sebastiano with a consular date of 260—shows that at that time Catacumbas was a center for the veneration of the two apostles. The date of 258 must have something to do with the persecution of Valerian, which was unleashed in that year. In the preceding year an edict had been issued forbidding the Christians to hold assemblies in their cemeteries (Eusebius, Ch. Hist. VII 11, 4 and 11, quoting Dionysius, bishop of Rome 259-268), but in 258, in defiance of the edict, Pope Sixtus II (257-258) and four deacons went into the cemetary of Callistus where preceding popes, beginning with Zephyrinus (died in 217), had been buried. All five men were martyred on Aug. 6 (Cyprian, Epistle 81; Liber Pontificalis),[102] and Sixtus was buried in the Crypt of the Popes in the same cemetery. The triclia under the church of San Sebastiano is not far away from the Catacomb of Callistus and

must have been in Christian hands by this time. Perhaps the triclia was chosen as a place for the veneration of Peter and Paul, the first heads of the church, because it was near the burial place—then inaccessible for purposes of assembly—of many of the later popes including the noble martyr Sixtus II.[103] June 29 was observed in a Roman festival as the day of the foundation of the city by Romulus, and perhaps it was for this reason that June 29 also became the day of the memorial feast of Peter and Paul as the two founders of the Roman church.[104] Later it was readily supposed that June 29 was also the day of the deaths of the two apostles (both on the same day according to Jerome, Illustrious Men 5; that day, June 29, according to Liber Pontificalis),[105] and in the Roman Church June 29 is still the date of the Feast of Peter and Paul.[106]

Dates of the Deaths

The evidence seems unmistakable, therefore, that Peter was crucified and Paul executed by the sword, that the place of death and burial for Peter was at the Vatican, and that the place of death and burial for Paul was on the way to Ostia (the Via Laurentina and the Via Ostiensis). As to when the two apostles died, we have seen that Dionysius of Corinth says that they suffered martyrdom at the same time; Jerome puts their death on the same day in the same year, the fourteenth year of Nero; and Sulpicius Severus speaks of the enactment of laws that made it unlawful to be a Christian and says that Paul and Peter were condemned to death at that time. Assuming that Peter and Paul did indeed die "at the same time," as Dionysius says, the date could be placed in 64/65 if they were a part of the multitude killed by Nero in the aftermath of the famous fire, but if it were a matter of formal execution on the basis of the laws Sulpicius Severus speaks of, the date might have been as late as Jerome's date of the fourteenth year of Nero, i.e., in 67/68. But from the very different manner of death of the two apostles and the very different places of their executions and burials, it would appear very likely that they were put to death separately and therefore very possibly at different times rather than both at the same time.[107]

With respect to Peter, the facts that his death was by crucifixion and that the remembrance of the place of his death and burial is at the Vatican in the vicinity of the Gardens and Circus of Nero make it probable that his death was indeed in connection with the persecution of the Christians subsequent to the fire of July 64, in which Tacitus says that Christians were crucified in Nero's gardens and circus. Since that persecution probably took place some considerable time after the fire itself, i.e., later in 64 or in 65, it would appear that 64/65 is the probable date of the death of Peter, with a reasonable allowance of time pointing to the year 65.

With respect to Paul, the fact of his Roman citizenship must be taken into account. The laws passed by Nero prohibiting Christianity, as described by Sulpicius Severus, could have provided the legal basis for proceeding against Paul, and the time involved for legal action and eventual execution by the sword, as prescribed for Roman citizens, would point to a date for the death of Paul later than the date for the death of Peter but at a time, of course, still within the reign of Nero. Allowing for these factors, Jerome's date of the fourteenth year of Nero (67/68) might be not unreasonable, and the year of 67 might be taken as probable for the death of Paul. In agreement with this date and even possibly confirming it, it can be surmised[108] that Paul was arrested in the East (where he had to leave behind his cloak and books at Troas, II Tim 4:13) during the time of Nero's travels in Greece, which took place from the end of September 66 to about January 68.[109]

In the sequential tabulation of the years here in question, the *Chronicle* of Eusebius, in the Latin version by Jerome,[110] notes at the point of Nero's Year 10 (63/64) that the emperor burned the larger part of Rome, and at the point of his Year 14 (67/68) there is the notation that "Above all of his evil doings Nero is the first to make a persecution of Christians, in which Peter and Paul gloriously entered into rest in Rome." In the Armenian version of the *Chronicle*,[111] however, the corresponding notation is found at the point of Year 13 of Nero (66/67), and it states that "Above all of his crimes Nero was the first to provoke persecutions of Christians, under whom Peter and Paul suffered martyrdom in Rome."

In the Armenian version, in contrast with the Latin, the "persecutions" (plural) could be more extended than a single event confined to a definite year, and it is Nero "under whom" the two apostles died rather than a single persecution "in which" they perished. Phrased in this way, it is possible to think that Eusebius has placed his remark about the slaying of the Christians near the end of the reign of Nero (along with a mention of the Jewish war, which provides a transition to the ensuing reign of Vespasian) because the slaughter of the Christians was the climax of all of Nero's atrocities; and under the heading, as it were, of "Nero the persecutor of the Christians," Eusebius has noted that Peter and Paul suffered martyrdom under this emperor.[112] According to this interpretation, Eusebius has not given us a definite date, nor an indication that the date was in one and the same year, for the deaths of the two apostles. Also, perhaps even the statement of Dionysius of Corinth that Peter and Paul suffered martyrdom at the same time might be interpreted in some such broader sense.

In comparison with the foregoing understanding of the Armenian version of the *Chronicle*, the Latin version by Jerome appears to contain a later change of wording because it speaks of a "persecution" (singular) "in which" Peter and Paul laid down their lives. The development then goes a step further in Jerome's own *Illustrious Men* (1 and 5), in which he states that Peter and Paul died not only in the same fourteenth year (67/68) of Nero, but also on the same day. A further development is the identification of that day as specifically the twenty-ninth day of June, and a later legend goes further still in stating that the two apostles met on the way to their respective places of execution and gave each other an embrace in token of forgiveness of the rivalry of their lives.[113]

In spite of this tendency in the tradition to bring together the deaths of the two apostles, the earlier view of the matter, according to which the two martyrdoms occurred at separate times, as the preceding investigation has found to have been likely, is still discernible. In a passage on Paul and Peter in his *Crowns of Martyrdom* (12) the Latin Christian Prudentius (A.D. 348–410) describes the annual celebration in Rome in memory of the two apostles.

> Today we have the festival of the apostles' triumph coming round again, a day made famous by the blood of Paul and Peter. The same day, but recurring after a full year, saw each of them win the laurel by a splendid death. The marshland of Tiber, washed by the nearby river, knows that its turf was hallowed by two victories, for it was witness both of cross and sword. . . . First the sentence of doom carried off Peter, when under the orders of Nero it was commanded that he should hang on a high tree. . . . When the round wheel of the turning year had run full circle and the rising sun brought again the same day, Nero disgorged his burning rage on the neck of Paul, ordering the teacher of the Gentiles to be beheaded. . . . Tiber separates the bones of the two and both its banks are consecrated as it flows between the hallowed tombs. The quarter on the right bank took Peter into its charge and keeps him in a golden dwelling. Elsewhere the Ostian Road keeps the memorial church of Paul, where the river grazes the land on its left bank. . . . There you have two dowers of the faith, the gift of the Father supreme, which he has given to the city of the toga to reverence.

It is plain that the single date of June 29 is accepted by Prudentius, but combined with the tradition of a considerable interval between the two martyrdoms by the supposition that the deaths fell on the same day exactly one year apart. Since the date of June 29 is probably arrived at artificially, it is the tradition of a relatively long interval between the two deaths that is more likely to have a basis in fact. Since the interval of exactly one year corresponds with the double use of the June 29 date, the earlier tradition might have called for a different and less exact length of intervening time—perhaps a longer time but also perhaps something less than two years so that it could be rounded off to a year.

So the outer limits, chronologically speaking, for the deaths of Peter and Paul would seem to be plain, namely, between the fire of July 64 in the tenth year of Nero (63/64) and the death of the emperor himself on June 9, 68, in his fourteenth year (67/68). Furthermore, within these limits it seems probable that the crucifixion of Peter was connected with the general persecution following the fire, and perhaps should be placed in 65; and that the execution of Paul followed the promulgation of the laws prohibiting Christianity and was at the end of a legal process, and therefore came at a later time, perhaps in 67. Between the two deaths the intervening time could have been a little less than two years—i.e., a year (66) and a number of months on either side (in 65 and in 67)—which in round numbers could be called a year. On the basis of the preceding considerations the entire series of probable dates connected with Paul and Peter is set forth in Table 2.

JOHN

In the early chapters of the Book of Acts the apostle John appears prominently along with Peter (3:1, etc.), but after John's brother James is killed by Agrippa I (Ac 12:2) and Peter departs (12:17), Peter is mentioned only once more in Acts (15:7) and John is not mentioned again at all. In the early Christian tradition subsequent to the canonical New Testament, however, much is said concerning John. In general in that tradition it was supposed that the apostle John the son of Zebedee of the first three Gospels, the beloved disciple of the Fourth Gospel, and the author of the Fourth Gospel, the letters of John, and the Book of Revelation were one and the same person and that, after his earlier life in Palestine and

TABLE 2. Dates in the Lives of Paul and Peter

Date A.D.	General History	Paul	Peter
14–37	Reign of Tiberius		
26/27	Tiberius "retires" to Capri		
30 or 33	Crucifixion of Jesus		
31	Tiberius deposes Sejanus		
35	Tiberius appoints Vitellius legate in Syria		
36	Vitellius deposes Pilate, sends Marcellus to Caesarea, replaces Caiaphas with Jonathan as high priest		
		Stoning of Stephen and conversion of Saul/Paul (Ac 7–9)	
37	Vitellius replaces Jonathan with Theophilus as high priest		
37–41	Reign of Caligula		
38		Paul visits Jerusalem "after three years" (Gal 1:18)	
41–54	Reign of Claudius		
Jan./Feb. 41	Claudius gives Agrippa I his kingdom		
Mar. 41	Agrippa I arrives in Jerusalem		
Passover, 41 or 44			Agrippa I kills James the brother of John and puts Peter in prison (Ac 12:2)
			Peter is delivered from prison and departs to another place (Ac 12:17)
41 or 44			Peter founds the church at Antioch, goes through Asia Minor and Corinth, and comes to Rome

(TABLE 2 continues on p. 38)

TABLE 2. (continued)

Date A.D.	General History	Paul	Peter
Jan. 24, 42–Jan. 23, 43	Year 2 of Claudius		
44–45	Death of Agrippa I		
47–48		First missionary journey (Ac 13–14)	
Early 49		Visit to Jerusalem "after fourteen years" (Gal 2:1) and "conference" (Ac 15)	Peter at Jerusalem "conference" (Ac 15:7)
Spring 49		Paul leaves Antioch on second missionary journey (Ac 15:40)	
June 49		Paul passes through the Cilician Gates	
Dec. 49		Paul arrives in Corinth (Ac 18:1)	
51	Claudius appoints Gallio proconsul of Achaia		
		Paul stays one year and six months in Corinth (Ac 18:11)	
May 51	Gallio arrives in Corinth	Paul is brought before Gallio (Ac 18:12)	
June 51		Paul leaves Corinth (Ac 18:18)	
July 51		Paul returns to Antioch (Ac 18:22)	
Aug.–Sept. 51		Paul goes from Antioch to Ephesus (Ac 18:23; 19:1) on third missionary journey	
Oct.-Nov.-Dec. 51		Paul at Ephesus, three months in the synagogue (Ac 19:8)	
Jan. 52–Dec. 53		Paul at Ephesus, two years in the hall of Tyrannus (Ac 19:10)	
Early Jan.–early Apr. 54		Paul three months at Corinth (Ac 20:3)	

TABLE 2. (continued)

Date A.D.	General History	Paul	Peter
Passover, Apr. 12, 54		Paul sails from Philippi after Passover (Ac 20:6)	
Pentecost, May 31, 54		Paul arrives at Jerusalem by Pentecost (Ac 20:16)	
June 54–May 56		Two years of imprisonment at Caesarea (Ac 24:27)	
54–68	Reign of Nero		
56	Year 1 of Festus, in succession to Felix, as procurator of Judea		
May 56		Festus proceeds promptly with the trial of Paul (Ac 25:6)	
Summer 56		Paul sails for Italy (Ac 27:2) on shipwreck journey	
Day of Atonement, Oct. 9, 56		The fast already gone by, and the ship only as far as Fair Havens (Ac 27:9)	
Nov. 11, 56–Feb. 8, 57		Paul on Malta during the three months of the non-sailing season (Ac 28:11)	
Feb. 57–Feb. 59		Paul in custody in Rome for two years (Ac 28:30) Paul travels in Spain and in the East	
Oct. 13, 63–Oct. 12, 64	Year 10 of Nero		
July 64	Fire in Rome		
65	Persecution of Christians by Nero		Crucifixion of Peter
Sept. 66–Jan. 68	Nero travels in Greece		
Oct. 13, 67–June 9, 68	Year 14 of Nero		
67		Execution of Paul	

Jerusalem, he later lived and worked in Asia Minor and Ephesus and finally died and was buried at Ephesus. Among the many witnesses to this tradition it is possible to discern a remarkable sequence of connections in the case of Irenaeus (A.D. 180), who reports information concerning John that Irenaeus had heard from Polycarp (a martyr at Smyrna in A.D. 156 after having served Christ for eighty-six years, therefore having been born in A.D. 69), who himself had seen and listened to John (Irenaeus, quoted by Eusebius, *Ch. Hist.* v 20) and had been appointed bishop of Smyrna by John (Tertullian, A.D. 200, *On Prescription Against Heretics* 32). Also there is eyewitness testimony from Justin (a martyr in Rome in A.D. 165), who lived for some time in Ephesus and says, undoubtedly with respect to that time, "there was a certain man with us, whose name was John, one of the apostles of Christ" (*Dialogue with Trypho* 81). Other such witnesses will be cited in what follows, and of them all it is possible to say that "the universal testimony of antiquity assigns John's later life to Ephesus."[114]

As to when John went from Palestine to Asia Minor, the early tradition was that the apostles went out into the world after twelve years, and it is probable that Peter left Jerusalem at that time (A.D. 41) and went to Antioch, Corinth, and Rome. It may well be that John departed from Jerusalem at that time too, which was just after the killing of his brother James by Agrippa I (Ac 12:2). Both Peter and John were in Jerusalem (again, according to the present theory) at the consultation recorded in Gal 2:1-10 (probably in A.D. 49 and probably the same conference as the one recorded in Ac 15). At this conference it was agreed (Gal 2:9) that Paul and Barnabas should go to the Gentiles (which they were already doing) and James, Cephas, and John should go to the Jews. This James was the Lord's brother (Gal 1:19), and he worked as the head of the church in Jerusalem (Ac 12:17) until he was martyred there in A.D. 62, but the work of Peter (Cephas) among the Jews had already taken him out into the Diaspora (An-

tioch, Corinth, Rome), and it is possible that John was already out in the Diaspora (Ephesus) too. Noticeably, Ac 21:18 suggests that when Paul is in Jerusalem (probably A.D. 54), of the three great leaders only James appears to be in the city and Peter and John are apparently not there.

As to the writings of John, Irenaeus, in his work *Against Heresies,* says that Matthew issued a written Gospel among the Hebrews in their own dialect while Peter and Paul were preaching at Rome; Mark handed down in writing what had been preached by Peter; Luke, the companion of Paul, wrote a Gospel; and "afterward, John, the disciple of the Lord, who also had leaned upon his breast [Jn 13:25], did himself publish a Gospel during his residence at Ephesus in Asia" (III 1, 1). Irenaeus also quotes not only from the Fourth Gospel but also from the first two letters of John (III 16, 5 and 8) and from the Revelation (IV 20, 11) and says that all of these works were by John, the disciple of the Lord. So, many scholars agree that "The tradition of the Church is unanimous in representing the evangelist John as at the same time the author of Revelation and the Johannine Epistles—and as none other than the apostle John, the son of Zebedee. . . . Until after the death of Origen, all the Johannine writings in the New Testament were assigned by all the Fathers of the Church to the same author without question."[115]

Indeed, after Origen's death, his pupil Dionysius (head of the catechetical school in Alexandria in A.D. 231/232, bishop of Alexandria in 247/248, died 264/265, quoted by Eusebius, *Ch. Hist.* VII 25) thought that the ideas and words of the Book of Revelation were so different from those of the Fourth Gospel and the First Letter of John that the Revelation must have been written by some John other than the apostle John, and for the existence of such a hypothetical person Dionysius referred to hearsay evidence that there were two memorials (μνήματα) in Ephesus, each bearing the name of John. The argument of Dionysius is based essentially on what is now called literary criticism, and on similar grounds, many modern critics have also concluded that the Gospel and the three letters, on the one hand, and the Revelation, on the other hand, must be by different authors. There are, however, decided affinities as well as contrasts between the respective works, and it has been suggested that one man writing as a prophet and modeling his visions in the literary form of the prophetic writings of the Old Testament would necessarily use language that differed from the language he would employ in pastoral communications to churches under his care or in writing an account of the deeds and sayings of Jesus.[116] Thus one modern commentator even says "that his earlier conviction of the impossibility of maintaining a unity of authorship has been much weakened by a study of the two books prolonged through the years."[117]

Eusebius also, probably influenced by Dionysius, is unsure about the matter but thinks that Revelation might possibly have been written by a John other than the apostle, and Eusebius quotes a passage from Papias to show that there was a second "elder John" in Asia (Ch. Hist. III 39). Papias (bishop of Hierapolis around 125–130) is an ancient authority for he was a companion of Polycarp and, like him, a hearer of John (Irenaeus, Against Heresies v 33, 4), but the passage Eusebius quotes is obscure in its language. Papias said, "If, then, any one came, who had been a follower of the elders, I questioned him in regard to the words of the elders—what Andrew or what Peter said, or what was said by Philip, or by Thomas, or by James, or by John, or by Matthew, or by any other of the disciples of the Lord, and what things Aristion and the elder John, the disciples of the Lord, say." And Eusebius comments:

> It is worth while observing here that the name John is twice enumerated by him. The first one he mentions in connection with Peter and James and Matthew and the rest of the apostles, clearly meaning the evangelist; but the other John he mentions after an interval, and places him among the others outside of the number of the apostles, putting Aristion before him, and he distinctly calls him an elder. This shows that the statement of those is true, who say that there were two persons in Asia that bore the same name, and there were two memorials (μνήματα) in Ephesus, each of which, even to the present day, is called John's.

In spite of this explanation, Eusebius has probably misunderstood Papias, and the correct understanding is more probably as follows. In his investigations in earlier years into the Christian faith Papias would ask questions of any who came along who could give him information derived from either of two sources. Some of his informants had lived in Palestine and could tell him what the apostles had said (εἶπεν, aorist past tense). In this first group Papias names seven of the twelve closest followers of Jesus, including John, and calls them "disciples," because that term describes their personal relationship to Jesus, and also "elders," because they were older teachers in relation to himself and his generation. But some of his informants could tell him what certain authorities were even then still continuing to say (λέγουσιν, present tense). In this second group Papias names Aristion and John. He calls both of them "disciples," and he calls John "elder." Of Aristion we know nothing more, but John is described by exactly the same two terms when the name occurs in the first group, and Eusebius is under a misapprehension in supposing that the elder John in the second group is a different person from the apostle in the first group.[118] So the tradition, understood in this way, probably affirms that there was just one great teacher named John at Ephesus, namely, the son of Zebedee who had been a disciple of Jesus and was also known as the elder. That there were two memorials to John at Ephesus need be no more remarkable than the fact that in Rome Peter and Paul were remembered both at their respective places at the Vatican and on the Ostian Way and also together at Catacumbas.[119]

Concerning the dates of John's experiences and the dates of his writings, Irenaeus (Against

Heresies v 30, 3) states that the visions of the Revelation were seen by John "no very long time since, but almost in our day, towards the end of Domitian's reign." Tertullian (*Apology* 5) describes Domitian (A.D. 81–96) as "a man of Nero's type in cruelty" and says that "he tried his hand at persecution; but as he had something of the human in him, he soon put an end to what he had begun, even restoring again those whom he had banished." Eusebius (*Ch. Hist.* III 18–20) quotes both of the foregoing passages by Irenaeus and Tertullian and gives a few instances of Domitian's persecution—e.g., that in his fifteenth year (A.D. 95/96) he banished Flavia Domitilla (wife of the consul Flavius Clemens, whom Domitian killed, according to Dio [*Rom. Hist.* LXVII 14, 1f.]) and others to the island of Pontia (Pandateria, according to Dio) because of testimony borne to Christ. Eusebius also reports that "It is said that in this persecution the apostle and evangelist John, who was still alive, was condemned to dwell on the island of Patmos in consequence of his testimony to the divine word." Also in Eusebius's *Chronicle* (in Jerome's Latin version) it is stated that John was sent to Patmos and saw the Revelation in the fourteenth year of Domitian (A.D. 94/95), but in the first year of Nerva (A.D. 96/97) the Senate reversed the decrees of Domitian, many returned from exile, and John came back to Ephesus where he had a place of hospitality (*hospitiolum*) and beloved friends.[120]

In his own *Illustrious Men* (9) Jerome summarizes the same tradition. John, he says, wrote the Gospel at the request of the bishops of Asia, against Cerinthus (a Gnostic teacher described by Polycarp and Irenaeus [*Against Heresies* I 26, 1; III 3, 4 and 11, 1]) and the Ebionites (a Jewish Christian sect described by Irenaeus [*Against Heresies* I 26, 2; III 21, 1; v 1, 3]). Also Matthew, Mark, and Luke give the history of only one year in the life of Jesus (from the imprisonment of John the Baptist to the Crucifixion), and John wished to relate the events of the earlier period before John the

FIGURE 1. Skala Harbor on the Island of Patmos.

Baptist was imprisoned. John wrote one letter, and the other two are said to be by John the elder, "to the memory of whom another tomb (*sepulcrum*) is shown at Ephesus to the present day, though some think that there are two memorials (*memoriae*) of this same John the evangelist." Under Domitian, Jerome goes on to say, John was banished to Patmos where he wrote the Book of Revelation. Then Jerome concludes his account:

> But Domitian having been put to death and his acts, on account of his excessive cruelty having been annulled by the Senate, he [i.e., John] returned to Ephesus under Pertinax [i.e., Nerva Pertinax, A.D. 96–98] and continuing there until the time of the emperor Trajan [98–117], founded and built churches throughout all Asia, and, worn out by old age, died in the sixty-eighth year after our Lord's passion [since in Jerome's version of the Chronicle the death of Jesus is placed in the eighteenth year of Tiberius (Aug. 19, 31–Aug. 18, 32), this statement appears to give a date of A.D. 100 for the death of John] and was buried near the same city.

Although the foregoing represents the tradition that has prevailed, which places the exile of John under Domitian, there is some evidence that suggests that the persecution of John could have been under Nero rather than under Domitian, and indeed, from all the information available, Nero was a much more fearsome enemy of early Christianity than Domitian. Clement of Alexandria, writing probably before A.D. 200, says that the apostle John came back to Ephesus from the island of Patmos after "the tyrant" died. He does not give the name of the emperor in question, so it could have been either Nero or Domitian—among the likeliest candidates—and the epithet is perhaps more appropriate to Nero than to Domitian (*Who Is the Rich Man That Shall Be Saved?* 42; also quoted by Eusebius, *Ch. Hist.* III 23, who of course thought that it was Domitian). Clement also continues with narratives about the ensuing strenuous activities of John in overseeing the churches in the surrounding regions, which may be

FIGURE 2. Court of the Monastery of St. John on Patmos.

thought to fit better at an earlier point in John's life than in very old age.

Tertullian (*On Prescription against Heretics* 36), writing around A.D. 200, makes a statement in which he links what happened to John directly with the deaths of Peter and Paul. As far as this presentation goes, it would sound as if John's experience were also in Rome and under Nero. "You have Rome," Tertullian writes, "How happy is its church, on which apostles poured forth all their doctrine along with their blood! where Peter endures a passion like his Lord's! where Paul wins his crown in a death like John's! where the apostle John was first plunged, unhurt, into boiling oil, and thence remitted to his island-exile!"

The Syriac *History of John* (written perhaps in the fourth century and preserved in two manuscripts of the sixth and ninth centuries) explicitly relates that when the gospel was in-

FIGURE 3. Painting on the Facade of the Church of the Monastery of St. John on Patmos. Christ is on the throne (ΙΣ ΧΣ Ο ΩΝ); at his right, Mary the Mother of God (ΜΡ ΘΥ); at his left, John the Evangelist and Theologian (Ο ΕΥΑΓΓΕΛΙΣΤΗΣ Ο ΘΕΟΛΟΓΟΣ) and St. Christodoulos (Ο ΑΓΙΟΣ ΧΡΙΣΤΟΔΟΥΛΟΣ), to whom the Byzantine emperor Alexis Commenos ceded the island in A.D. 1088.

creasing in Ephesus by the hands of the apostles, the wicked king Nero, who also slew Paul and Peter, sent and laid hold on John and drove him into exile, then later ordered him freed and returned to Ephesus.[121]

In the Greek *Acts of John* (purportedly written by Prochorus, one of the seven at Jerusalem in Ac 6:5 and the disciple and secretary of John, but probably actually written in the fifth century) John and Prochorus are exiled to Patmos by Trajan and released by an unnamed different emperor, but a chronological summary states: "We spent 26 years in Ephesus after we came back from exile; in Patmos we spent 15 years; before the exile we were in Ephesus 9 years. John was 50 years and 7 months old when we came from Jerusalem to Ephesus, but I Prochorus, the disciple of John, was 30 years and 3 months old." According to this representation John's total age was 100

years and 7 months, and if his death occurred around A.D. 100, he would have gone to Patmos in 59 under Nero (54-68) and returned in 74 under Vespasian (69-79).[122]

There is also reason to think that the writings associated with the name of John should be dated relatively early. Many factors, including knowledge of Palestine, similarities of ideas and language with the Dead Sea Scrolls, and agreement with the concerns of the early church, suggest that the Fourth Gospel was written perhaps in the late 50s or early 60s, and the letters were presumably written at more or less the same time because they are very similar.[123] In tradition the Muratorian Fragment states that John's fellow disciples, including the apostle Andrew, urged John to write the Gospel, and the Syriac *History of John* relates that Peter and Paul came to Ephesus and asked John to write the Gospel;[124] these

FIGURE 4. In the Cave of the Apocalypse. Within the railing is the place where John received his vision. The icon on the wall shows Christ giving messages to the angels of the seven churches, John fallen at his feet.

stories, for whatever they are worth, at least agree with an early date of composition.

In the Book of Revelation, in 17:10–11 there is an apparently unmistakable sequence of seven kings of Rome. Of the seven, "five . . . have fallen" (Augustus, Tiberius, Caligula, Claudius, Nero), "one is" (Galba, June 68–Jan. 69), another is expected for only a little while (Otho, Jan.–Apr. 69), and there is an eighth who belongs to the seven, himself a beast with the number 666 or 616 (according to the variant textual readings of Rev 13:18). The last is surely Nero, who committed suicide on June 9, 68 (Suetonius, Nero 49), but because of circumstances there were varied reports about his death, and it was rumored that he was still alive and would return (Tacitus, Hist. II 8). Written in Hebrew characters the name and title Nero(n) Caesar have the arithmetical value indicated in Rev 13:18.[125]

Nun	50	50
Resh	200	200
Waw	6	6
Nun	50	
Qoph	100	100
Samekh	60	60
Resh	200	200
	666	616

Therefore, it is most probable that the Book of Revelation should be dated in A.D. 68, soon after the death of Nero,[126] and the Johannine writings, like probably all the other books of the canonical New Testament, appear to have been written before A.D. 70.[127] But even if both the experience on Patmos and the writings do belong before 70, John himself could perfectly well have lived on to old age in Ephesus, as the tradition generally supposes.

As to where in Ephesus John lived, died, and was buried, we have seen that according to the *Chronicle* of Eusebius/Jerome, John had a place of hospitality (*hospitiolum*) in the city, evidently a home in which he was welcome as a guest. In the narrative in the Greek *Acts of John* attributed to Leucius (a disciple of John, according to Epiphanius [*Panarion haereses* LI 5, 9, P427]), a work probably written in the second or third century, the home in which John stayed was that of Andronicus, a leading citizen of Ephesus, and his wife Drusiana. Andronicus appears first as an unbeliever (*Acts of John* 31) but was evidently converted (as probably recorded in a lost section of the text—37), and John is afterward described as staying at his house (62) and as meeting the brethren there (86). Therefore the house of Andronicus was the meeting place of the early Christian community in Ephesus. Finally (106–115) it was evidently in this same house that John broke bread with the assembled brethren on a Sunday and afterward told Verus, the brother who served him as a deacon (Βήρῳ τῷ διακονοῦντι αὐτῷ ἀδελφῷ, 30), to bring some men with baskets and shovels and follow him. John then "walked outside the gates," had them dig his grave, lay down in it, and gave up his spirit rejoicing.[128] In a parallel Syriac version of this Greek text, the name of Verus (Greek Βῆρος) appears as Birrus (Byrrhus),[129] and he is probably to be identified with a deacon of the same name (Burrhus) in the church at Ephesus, mentioned several times in the letters of Ignatius (*To the Ephesians* 2, etc.), so Andronicus and Drusiana may well be historical persons too.[130] In the Greek *Acts of John* supposedly written by Prochorus, it is Prochorus himself and six other disciples who prepare John's grave, but otherwise the account of John's death and burial is similar, and as in the Leucian *Acts*, the grave is outside the city.[131]

According to the Syriac *History of John*, John also had his own modest dwelling at Ephesus. In this narrative John goes with the procurator of the city (whom he has converted) and his nobles, to see where it would be fitting for John to dwell. They come to the Temple of Artemis, and John sees an elevated place and expresses the wish to dwell there. The procurator and nobles propose to build a palace for him, but he desires nothing more than a hut, which is constructed for him straightaway. In it he dwells and teaches, and from it he looks down upon the Temple of Artemis, over whose pagan cult the gospel is finally victorious. Afterward John is exiled to Patmos by Nero, but John returns to Ephesus later and writes the Fourth Gospel at the behest of Peter and Paul. "And the holy [man] sat in the hut summer and winter, until he was a hundred and twenty years of age, and there his Master buried him in that place, as Moses was buried on Mount Nebo."[132]

According to the foregoing traditions, then, there were three places in Ephesus especially associated with John: (1) the house of Andronicus and Drusiana, where John stayed at one time, where the believers assembled, and where John for the last time broke bread with them; (2) the hut of John on the hill overlooking the Temple of Artemis, where John lived to old age; and (3) the grave of John on the same hill outside the city. Along with the grave, either the house of Andronicus or the hut of John might explain why Dionysius, Eusebius, and Jerome all mention two memorials to John at Ephesus. The house of Andronicus was evidently in the city, and for the possibility of its being remembered there are many parallels, including the house of Peter at Capernaum for the remembrance of which there is archeological evidence;[133] the house of Cornelius at Caesarea, which Jerome (*Letter* CVIII 8) says was turned into a Christian church; the house of Philemon (Phm 1:2), which was still to be seen at Colossae in the time of Theodoret (A.D. 450), who says (*Commentary on the Fourteen Epistles of St. Paul*, on Philemon), "For indeed his house remains until today"; and the houses of Clement and of Pudens and others at Rome.

John's very simple dwelling place and burial place were both on the hill overlooking the Temple of Artemis. In his *In gloria martyrum* (I 30) Gregory of Tours (A.D. 538–594) refers to both when he speaks of the place (*locus*) "in the height of the hill" (*in summitate montis*) where John wrote his Gospel and, separately, of the Tomb (*sepulcrum*) of John.

Ayasoluk

The hill in question, overlooking the Temple of Artemis, is the hill about 2 mi (3 km) to the northeast from the main ruins at Ephesus, across the plain that contains the ruins of the Artemis temple. The hill is now known as Ayasoluk, a name probably derived from Hagios Theologos (ἅγιος θεολόγος, "holy theologian"), which was the customary designation of John in the Eastern Church.

On the highest summit of the hill, with a very extensive view over the surrounding landscape, are the ruins of a small church. Only the apse part of the church is preserved, but it was a building constructed of stone and brick, slightly less than 30 ft (9 m) long, with the apse to the east and small side rooms to the north and south. In Seljuk times this building was roofed over to create a stone-built tunnel vault that was made into a cistern. Architectural fragments recovered from the masonry of the cistern derive from the church and suggest a date, at the earliest, in the time of Justinian (A.D. 527–565). In light of the statement by Gregory of Tours that the place where John wrote his Gospel was "in the height of the hill," it is highly probable that this church, which is located on the highest summit of the Ayasoluk Hill, was built to mark the place believed to be the simple dwelling where John composed the Gospel.[134]

Whether or not the house of Andronicus or the hut of John was one of the two Johannine memorials Dionysius mentioned in the second century, John's tomb was certainly a well-known memorial at least in the second century and probably earlier. Having spoken of the burial places of Paul and Peter, Eusebius (*Ch. Hist.* III 31; V 24) remarks that the burial place of John is indicated by a letter of Polycrates, bishop of Ephesus (A.D. c. 190), to Victor, bishop of Rome (A.D. c. 189–198), and Eusebius quotes from the letter. In a dispute over the proper date of Easter, the letter reports, it was the decision of the bishops of Asia to continue to observe Nisan 14, which was the custom handed down from the great authorities of the past. Polycrates writes: "We observe the exact day, neither adding nor taking away. For in Asia also great luminaries have fallen asleep, which shall rise again on the day of the Lord's coming." Polycrates then names Philip (probably the evangelist rather than the apostle, although the two are evidently confused), "who sleeps in Hierapolis," and then John, "who was both a witness [μάρτυς, literally a martyr] and a teacher, who reclined upon the bosom of the Lord, and being a priest wore the sacerdotal plate. He also sleeps at Ephesus."

In his own *Theophany* (IV 7), a work preserved only in Syriac, Eusebius also deals with the burial places of the three apostles. He quotes the saying of Jesus to the fishermen from Galilee, "You are the light of the world" (Mt 5:14), and then cites the work of Peter, John, and Paul as illustrating the saying. Peter, Eusebius declares, brought the light of the knowledge of God to many and is so remembered by the Romans that there is a splendid burial place in Rome that bears his name, to which multitudes of people hasten as to a great sanctuary. Likewise the writings of Paul spread enlightenment in the world, and the place of his grave is greatly praised in Rome. And of John, whom he names between Peter and Paul, Eusebius writes: "So shines also the name of John, the son of Zebedee, . . . and his words enlighten the souls of people through the Gospel which he wrote, which is translated into many languages Greek and barbarian. . . . And especially the place of his death and burial at Ephesus in Asia is gloriously honored and proves that the remembrance of the light of his preeminence will not be forgotten forever."

As in the case of the graves of Peter and Paul at Rome, the grave of John at Ephesus was undoubtedly marked first by some kind of memorial marker or structure and later by a church or succession of churches. Such a memorial or church of John is mentioned by the pilgrim Aetheria (A.D. 384). As her itinerary records, she went from Antioch to Constantinople and, on the way, visited the martyrium of St. Thecla at Seleucia (the Latin *martyrium* corresponds to the Greek μαϱτύϱιον, meaning a place of testimony or witness, and is used by Aetheria as a title for various churches) and the martyrium of St. Euphemia in Chalcedon (this saint was martyred at Chalcedon in 303/304, and the Council of Chalcedon met in 451 in the basilica dedicated in her name). Then at Constantinople Aetheria formed the plan—which, as far as our information extends, she was not able to carry out—"to travel to Asia, . . . to make a pilgrimage to Ephesus, and the Martyrium of the holy and blessed Apostle John."[135]

The first church at John's burial place was replaced by a second and larger church under Justinian (A.D. 527–565). Of the sequence of events Procopius (*Buildings* v 1, 4–6) says:

> There chanced to be a certain place before the city of Ephesus, lying on a steep slope hilly and bare of soil and incapable of producing crops, even should one attempt to cultivate them, but altogether hard and rough. On that site the natives had set up a church in early times to the Apostle John; this Apostle had been named "the Theologian," because the nature of God was described by him in a manner beyond the unaided power of man. This church, which was small and in a ruined condition because of its great age, the Emperor Justinian tore down to the ground and replaced by a church so large and beautiful that, to speak briefly, it resembles very closely in all respects, and is a rival to, the shrine which he dedicated to All the Apostles in the imperial city."[136]

This great Church of St. John the Theologian at Ephesus was visited and described by many pilgrims down into the fourteenth century. Among them was Willibald, who made a pilgrimage to the East in A.D. 722. At Ephesus he visited the Catacomb of the Seven Sleepers on the northeastern slope of Mt. Pion and then went on to the splendid place of John, plainly on the Ayasoluk Hill.[137]

In A.D. 1330 the Church of St. John became a mosque, then a trading hall, and finally sank into ruins under debris many meters deep, from which it was only recovered by modern excavation. The site is on a plateau about one third of the way down the slope of the Ayasoluk Hill to the south, with the hill dropping off steeply to the west and the east. The excavations were begun by the Greek Archaeological Society in 1921/22 and continued by the Austrian Archaeological Institute in Vienna in 1926 and following.[138]

As the excavations have revealed, there is a system of subterranean chambers, of which the main one is presumably the one that was understood to be the grave of John. The additional and later chambers were perhaps the graves of other prominent Christians. In the chambers were found a coin of Constantine of around A.D. 320 and certain sarcophagus fragments that suggest a date between A.D. 155 and 160; so the underground layout was in existence at least from the second century on, surely too close to the time of John for his last resting place to have been forgotten.[139]

Over the tomb, and presumably still at a

relatively early date, a memorial building or mausoleum was constructed, a central quadrangular structure.[140] Afterward, apparently in the first decades of the fourth century, this building was enlarged by the addition of an apse to the east and thus made into a small chapel.[141] Then the central structure was made the kernel of a relatively large cross-shaped, wooden-roofed church, about 265 ft (80 m) in length.[142] The nave extending to the west and the cross arms of the transept were divided by columns into three aisles, and the part extending eastward to a new apse was divided into five aisles. The altar was in the central area, and a shaft led down to the main grave. The church in this form may date around A.D. 400.

Finally the church just described was replaced by the great Basilica of Justinian.[143] This vast structure was 427 ft (130 m) long and 213 ft (65m) wide. An atrium and a narthex gave access to the nave, which was divided by massive pillars into five aisles, still oriented to the grave of John. Over the nave and transept probably rose six domes, with the central dome over the tomb. On the north side was a baptistery room, which had a baptismal pool with steps down into it at each end. For the adornment of the church, marbles were taken from the Temple of Artemis—as was also done for Justinian's church of Hagia Sophia in Constantinople.

With respect to Paul, Peter, John, and the other apostles of the early church, it is about Paul that the Book of Acts provides the most detailed information, and it is the travels of Paul as outlined in that source that may be followed in traversing the Mediterranean world and noting the chief sites associated with his work and the work of the others. To that task we now turn in the chapters that follow.

3
BEGINNINGS

TARSUS

Saul/Paul was "a man of Tarsus" (Ac 9:11), "a Jew, born at Tarsus in Cilicia" (Ac 22:3), and therefore "a citizen of no mean city" (Ac 21:39). As to why he came to be from Tarsus, Paul was in origin a Jew of the Dispersion (Diaspora). For many reasons—war, exile, trade, business—Jews were scattered in most of the cities of the Roman Empire. The Jews of this Dispersion were of the same faith in the one God as the Jews of Judea, but in many ways they were different. They normally spoke Greek, the common language of the Roman Empire, whereas the Jews in Judea normally spoke Hebrew or Aramaic, although Greek was widely known there too. As Greek-speaking Jews, the Jews of the Dispersion read the Scriptures regularly in the Greek translation known as the Septuagint rather than in the Hebrew. Also they were naturally influenced in much of their thinking and many of their activities by living in a predominantly non-Jewish environment, although at the same time they remained aloof from pagan idolatry and immorality.

In particular Jerome (*Illustrious Men* 5) says that Paul was of the tribe of Benjamin (as Paul himself says in Rom 11:1; Phil 3:5) and from the town of Gischala in Judea (el-Jish in northern Galilee, 7 mi [11 km] west of Hazor). "When this was taken by the Romans," Jerome explains, "he removed with his parents to Tar-

sus in Cilicia." That statement hardly seems correct, since Paul says in Ac 22:3 that he was born at Tarsus, but perhaps the family went there from Gischala.

The father evidently had Roman citizenship—perhaps for some service rendered to the Romans in Palestine or at Tarsus—for Paul says, "I was born a citizen" (Ac 22:28). Perhaps this fact makes his double name especially meaningful: as a Jew he bore the famous old Jewish name of Saul; as a Roman citizen he was called by the similar sounding Roman name of Paul, Latin in origin but also used by Greeks. Appropriately, the latter name is used in Acts from the point at which Paul steps forward as the spokesman of his party in the Roman world in the presence of the Roman governor, Sergius Paulus, of Cyprus (Ac 13:9).

Concerning how long Paul lived in Tarsus, we know that at some point he went to Jerusalem—where he had a sister (Ac 23:16)—and that he studied there with the famous moderate Pharisaic teacher of the law, Gamaliel (Ac 5:34). The statement of this subject in Ac 22:3 strictly follows a traditional scheme of three stages of life (cf. Ac 7:20–22), and it can be understood to say that Paul was born in Tarsus, brought up (beginning in infancy) in Jerusalem, and (in due time) educated at the feet of Gamaliel.[1] The Hellenistic influence that seems so evident in his life, however, and his apparently lifelong familiarity with the Septuagint seem more consonant with the supposition that he spent a longer boyhood in Tarsus.[2] He was indeed "a Hebrew of the Hebrews" (Phil 3:5), and he addressed the people in Jerusalem in Hebrew or Aramaic (Ac 22:2; cf. 26:14). But he wrote in Greek, quoted the Scriptures in Greek, and was a man at home in the wider world beyond the bounds of Palestine. As to his trade—presumably learned in Tarsus in his youth—Paul was a tentmaker (Ac 18:3), which is still a trade in that city, where goats from the rugged mountains of Cilicia provide hair and skins for unusually durable fabrics and tents.

In addition to his early life in Tarsus, Paul was evidently there again between the time when the brethren "sent him off to Tarsus" from Jerusalem (Ac 9:30) and the time when "Barnabas went to Tarsus to look for" him (Ac 11:25), i.e., between his conversion and his work in the church at Antioch. Also he must have passed through Tarsus and gone through the Cilician Gates on his second missionary journey, when he went "through Syria and Cilicia" (Ac 15:41), and again on this third missionary journey, when he departed from Antioch and went "through the region of Galatia and Phrygia" (Ac 18:23).

Tarsus was in Cilicia, which was situated on the eastern part of the southern coast of Asia Minor. As a whole Cilicia was divided into two parts, "rugged Cilicia" (Cilicia Tracheia), which was the mountainous western part where the coast projects toward Cyprus, and "level Cilicia" (Cilicia Campestris), which was the fertile eastern plain, and Tarsus was in the latter part.

On the north the Taurus Mountains separated Cilicia from Cappadocia. These mountains averate 7,000 ft (2,000 m) in elevation, and some summits are more than 10,000 ft (3,000 m) high. On the east the Amansus Mountains separated Cilicia from Syria. The highest point of this range is 6,500 ft (1,981 m) in elevation. Between the Taurus and the Amanus (sometimes considered a branch of the Taurus) is the deep valley of the Jihun and its continuation, the Gulf of Alexandretta or Iskenderun.

Coming from the east the pass through the Amanus Mountains was anciently known as the Syrian Gates and is now called the Belen Pass (from Belen village 2,395 ft [730 m] high in the Hatay Vilayet of Turkey, 8 mi [6 km] south of Iskenderun), a place that also figured in modern history when the Egyptians defeated the Turks there in 1832. Going to the north the pass through the Taurus Mountains is the Cilician Gates. Here the Cakit River flows through a narrow gorge, at its most constricted point only 60 ft (18 m) wide, that has rock walls rising steeply on either side to a height of 400–500 ft (120–150 m). Anciently, perhaps as early as the eighth century B.C., a level path was cut along the east wall of this gorge, and in modern times a road was blasted in the west wall. Through this famous pass marched Darius I the Great of Persia, Alexander the Great, the armies of the Byzantine emperors and of the Crusaders, and finally, at the end of World War I, the allied Turks and Germans in retreat from the Suez Canal. In the winter the Cilician Gates and other mountain passes in inner Asia Minor are deeply snowed in and scarcely passable. In the spring passage becomes possible at least in June and perhaps in May or even late April.

In the Cilician plain there are now three main cities, Tarsus, Mersin, and Adana. Tarsus, which is the middle of the three, is the Turkish Tersous, a place of 65,000 inhabitants; Mersin, 17 mi (27 km) to the west, is the main modern port, with 51,000 inhabitants; and Adana, the largest city with a population of 172,000, is 23 mi (37 km) to the east. Tarsus itself is 79 ft (24 m) above sea level, 10 mi (16 km) inland from the sea, and 30 mi (48 km) from the Taurus Mountains to the north.

The Cydnus River flowed through the middle of the ancient city. Strabo explains in his *Geography* (xiv 5, 10–12) that the source of the river was not very far away. From its source the river passed through a deep ravine, then emptied immediately into the city, so its discharge was both cold and swift. Hence both people and cattle that were suffering from swollen sinews were helped if they immersed themselves in its waters. Below the city the river flowed into the Rhegma, a lake that was also the naval station of Tarsus. This lake was some 5 mi (8 km) away, where now there are uninhabited marshes, but at one time ships could use the lake as a harbor and smaller craft could continue up the river to the city center—as Cleopatra did on her barge on a famous occasion. In the city, however, damage was caused by the floods on the river, so in the sixth century Justinian changed the channel to the east of the town, and today only minor branches go through the city.

From Tarsus, then, one may look up the river valley and see the falls of the river in the distance and, far beyond, the foothills of the mighty Taurus range. Far away to the east, one may see the ridge of the Syrian Amanus Mountains coming from the south to meet the Taurus. So, looking toward the Amanus range and the peaks of the Taurus, in most of the year covered with snow, one may reflect that this was the very landscape upon which Paul looked in his youthful days and that it was through the passes in these mountains that he made his way on more than one of his journeys.

The history of Tarsus began at an early date. At an archeological site in the southeastern part of the town known as the Gözlü Kule, excavations could not reach the very earliest levels, which are now beneath the groundwater level, but they did explore levels that date from the Neolithic period and all the way up to Hellenistic and Roman times. Neolithic Age (c. 5000 B.C.) stone tools and two types of pottery have been found, and in the Bronze Age (c. 3000–1200) there were several cities here, one after the other. Around 1400 the Hittites invaded Cilicia and founded a state called Kizzuwatna in which Tarsus was an important city, perhaps the capital. For the Iron Age and later (c. 1200 B.C. and onward), in historical times, there are more detailed records. Greek legend says that the city was founded by Sardanapallus, a mythical Assyrian royal name sometimes used for Ashurbanipal. From Assyrian records we learn that Tarsus was captured by Shalmaneser III in

the middle of the ninth century, and when the city rebelled, it was destroyed by Sennacherib in 696. Then the Persians ruled through a puppet king named Syennesis, and his palace is described by Xenophon in the *Anabasis*. In 333 B.C. Alexander the Great arrived. The retreating Persians had planned to burn the city, but Alexander's General Parmenion came in time to occupy it instead. Alexander himself spent several months in Tarsus and became severely ill—Plutarch tells us—from bathing in the icy cold Cydnus. Afterward Alexander went on to fight one of his decisive battles against Darius III in the plain of Issus to the east.

Under the Seleucids, Antiochus IV Epiphanes called the city Antioch on the Cydnus, but the name did not continue for there were too many Antiochs. Then the Romans took the whole area. In 64 B.C., after conquests by Pompey, Cilicia was organized as a Roman province, and Tarsus was its capital. In 50 B.C. Cicero served as governor. In 38 B.C. Mark Antony was there, and Cleopatra came from Egypt to see him and sailed up the Cydnus in a splendid barge. Under Augustus, Tarsus reached the height of its prosperity and was a center of intellectual life.

Writing about Tarsus as it was at about the time of Paul, Strabo (c. 63 B.C.–after A.D. 21) says (*Geography* XIV 5, 131), "The people at Tarsus have devoted themselves so eagerly, not only to philosophy, but also to the whole round of education in general, that they have surpassed Athens, Alexandria, or any other place that can be named where there have been schools and lectures of philosophers." Strabo goes on to say that at Tarsus the schools are full of local students rather than strangers from afar, that the city has all kinds of schools of rhetoric, and that the people have the facility to "speak offhand and unceasingly on any given subject."

Tarsus was especially renowned as a center of Stoic philosophy. The founder of Stoicism in the fourth century B.C. was Zeno of Kition in Cyprus, but the third-century Chrysippus is considered the second founder of the movement, and he was born at the ancient town of Soli on the coast of Cilicia not far from Tarsus, and went from there to teach at Athens. The third-century poet Aratus was also born at Soli, and the people of Tarsus were no doubt proud of these famous persons from their region. Stoicism then continued to be a strong influence in the intellectual life of Tarsus. In the second century B.C. the two chief leaders of the movement were from Tarsus, namely, a second teacher named Zeno, who was the successor of Chrysippus, and a certain Antipater. Two other famous Stoic philosophers lived at Tarsus, and both are mentioned by Strabo. Athenodorus (74 B.C.–A.D. 7) was distinguished for his lectures and writing. He moved to Rome, where Augustus was his pupil, but returned to Tarsus in later years, and he was also governor there. As he took leave of Augustus to go back to Tarsus, he gave as his last piece of advice, "When you are angry, Caesar, say nothing and do nothing until you have repeated to yourself the letters of the alphabet." Seneca (*Epistulae Morales* x 5) also quotes Athenodorus as saying, "Know that you are set free from all passions, when you have reached such a point that you ask nothing of God that you cannot ask openly," and Seneca goes on in the same spirit to state as a rule of life, "So live with people as if God saw; so speak with God as if people were listening." Athenodorus in turn was succeeded by Nestor, also an academic philosopher and a governor of Tarsus. Nestor was still living when Strabo wrote about him in about A.D. 19, and he attained the age of ninety-two, so it has been thought that Paul himself might have heard him.

It is the fundamental tenet of Stoicism that virtue is the only good and that, through it, the wise person is fortified against all vicissitudes of external circumstances, and Paul himself speaks much like the Stoics when he says (Phil 4:11–12) that he has learned to be content in whatever state he is in, he knows how to be abased and how to abound, and in any and all circumstances he has learned the secret of facing plenty and hunger, abundance and want.

In its later history Tarsus was visited by several of the Roman emperors, there were one or two temples of emperor worship in the city, and the emperor Julian the Apostate was buried there. It was probably in the fourth century A.D. that the first Christian church buildings were erected in Tarsus. In the fifth century we hear of a Church of St. Peter outside the city, in which Leontius was proclaimed emperor in A.D. 485. In the sixth century there was a Church of St. Paul in the city, built by the emperor Maurice in A.D. 583–602. In the seventh century Tarsus was conquered by the Arabs, and the "great church" of Tarsus, probably the Church of St. Peter, was destroyed in A.D. 885. In the eleventh century the city was captured by the Crusaders, and in the sixteenth century it was taken by the Ottoman Turks.

The Hellenistic and Roman city of Tarsus, which was the city of Paul, is for the most part buried beneath the present town, 20 ft (6 m) below the surface, and largely inaccessible because of habitation above. Anciently the city was entered through three main gateways —the Valley, the Mountain, and the Sea gates—and the last of them is still to be seen, a monumental arch known as Cleopatra's Gate. In the heart of the city there is a mass of ancient masonry known locally as the Tomb of Sardanapallus (the reputed Assyrian founder of the city), but it is more probably the foundation of a Greco-Roman temple. The foundations of a Roman building with some mosaics still in place were discovered when excavation was done for a modern courthouse in the center of town. In the central area of the city is an arch known as St. Paul's Arch, but it is perhaps of only Byzantine date. Not far from this arch is St. Paul's Well, a deep well or spring from which, according to local tradition, Paul drank as a boy.

At the already mentioned archeological site of Gözlü Kule, which was a small outpost of the main city, the finds from the Hellenistic and Roman periods include a large number of terra-cotta figurines. Many of them represent deities and mythological characters, including Aphrodite, Apollo, Artemis, Athena, Dionysos, Harpokrates, Isis, and Serapis. Others are figures of animals, bears, lions, dogs, horses, birds, and fish. There are also many small portraits of people, actors, orators, warriors, and children and mother-and-child plaques. Some are very realistic, even grotesque, and show truculence, depravity, and the ravages of old age. The excavator, Hetty Goldman, thinks that these figurines exhibit something more than a primitive and cruel humor. As the Greeks settled in the crowded cities of Asia Minor, many of them mingled for the first time with natives of eastern lands and came in contact with strange forms of disease and deformity. Their response was hardly that of modern science, humanitarianism, or desire for social reform, but it was not devoid of compassion

and charity, and it contained at least the faint stirrings of something fraught with hope. The world stood upon the threshold of Christianity, and there in the eastern Mediterranean, where Christianity arose, there was at least an awareness of the sufferings and the tragic fate not only of people in the mass but also of persons as individuals.

Paul, who also knew that in our earthly life we "groan inwardly" but who believed that we are at the same time waiting "for adoption as sons, the redemption of our bodies" (Rom 8:23), came from here, from Tarsus with all of its intellectual atmosphere but at the same time with all of its burdened humanity.

DAMASCUS

When Paul refers in Gal 1:15f. to the time when it pleased God to reveal his Son to him,

FIGURE 5. Cleopatra's Gate in Tarsus.

Paul is no doubt speaking about his experience on the road to Damascus, which is described three times (Ac 9:3ff.; 22:6ff.; 26:12ff.). At Damascus a disciple named Ananias was sent to him in the house of Judas in the street called Straight (Ac 9:10ff.), and afterward Paul was with the disciples at Damascus for some time (Ac 9:19). Apparently at this point, although it is not mentioned in Acts, Paul went away into Arabia, then again returned to Damascus (Gal 1:17). In Damascus he engaged in proving to the Jews who lived there that Jesus was the Christ, and when the Jews plotted to kill him, his disciples lowered him over the wall at night in a basket (Ac 9:25), and he thereby also escaped the governor who, under King Aretas, guarded the city (II Cor 11:32f.).

Damascus, a crowded present-day city that still bears its ancient biblical name, is located in Syria at the foot of the eastern slopes of the Anti-Lebanon range, with Mount Hermon off to the southwest. The site is on a large plain called Ghuta, 2,300 ft (700 m) in elevation and 30 mi (48 km) in diameter, on the easternmost edge of the fertile regions before one comes to the desert. George Adam Smith has said that in order to understand Damascus, one should look toward the desert, for the city was a harbor of refuge upon the earliest sea people ever learned to navigate, which was the sea of the desert. "Standing upon the utmost edge of fertility, on the shore of the much-voyaged desert, Damascus is indispensable alike to civilization and to the nomads."[3] In fact, located as it was at the northwestern gate of Arabia, three great routes ran out from ancient Damascus: one south to Mecca; one east to Baghdad; and one west and southwest to the Mediterranean, Palestine, and Egypt.

The plain on which Damascus is situated is watered at this point by two rivers. The Nahr el-Barada, probably the Abana of the Old Testament, descends from the Anti-Lebanon Mountains and runs directly through Damascus from west to east. The Nahr el-Awaj, probably the biblical Pharpar, comes down from springs on Mount Hermon and passes through the plain 10 mi (16 km) south

of the city. Both rivers soon disappear in the arid country to the east, but they first make the Damascus area a luxuriant oasis. Especially to those people who came to it from the desert, Damascus seemed a most beautiful place, a veritable pearl in an emerald girdle of gardens. Muhammad is supposed to have hesitated to go into Damascus because he wished to enter paradise only once, and Yaqut, an early thirteenth-century geographer, concluded a glowing account of the city with the words, "To sum up, nothing attributed by way of description to the heavenly paradise is not found in Damascus."[4]

The name Damascus (Dimashq in Arabic) is not considered to be Semitic, and it is thought that the name shows that the city must have existed even before the Semitic Amorites settled in the region in the middle of the third millennium B.C. In the time of Abraham, the patriarch went "north of Damascus" on his expedition to recover Lot (Gen 14:15), and a servant of Abraham was Eliezer of Damascus (Gen 15:2). The city is mentioned in the tablets from Tell Mardikh, ancient Ebla (2600–2300 B.C.),[5] in the inscriptions of Thutmose III of Egypt in the fifteenth century B.C., and in the records of the Hittites. After the fall of the Hittite kingdom in 1200 B.C., Damascus was conquered by the Aramaic-speaking Aramaeans, a Semitic people much like the Amorites. With Damascus as the center of Aramaean power and the capital of Syria, the Aramaeans were neighbors and warring rivals of Israel until Assyria destroyed Damascus first and then Israel too.

Among the many happenings in this period, two are of special interest. One is the story, related in II K 5, in which Naaman, commander of the army of the king of Syria and a leper, came to the prophet Elisha in Israel for healing. When Elisha told him to go and wash seven times in the Jordan he protested, "Are not Abana and Pharpar, the rivers of Damascus, better than all the waters of Israel?" He also explained that when he was again in Damascus he would be required to go with his master and bow in the house of Rimmon. This name means "the thunderer" and was a title of the Aramaean and Canaanite storm god Hadad, sometimes called Hadad-Rimmon.

The other account to be noticed is in II K 16. Rezin, king of Syria, and Pekah, king of Israel, made war on Ahaz, king in Jerusalem, to force him to join them against Assyria. The prophet Isaiah (Is 7:4) advised Ahaz to be quiet and not fear, but Ahaz asked Tiglath-pileser III, king of Assyria, to rescue him. Thereupon Tiglath-pileser III came and conquered Damascus (733/732 B.C.), and Ahaz obediently went up to Damascus to meet him. An inscription of Tiglath-pileser III tells us that he took tribute from Ahaz, and the Bible (II K 16:10 f.) tells us that in Damascus Ahaz saw an altar that so fascinated him he had a duplicate made for Jerusalem.

After that, Damascus lost its position as the capital of a flourishing kingdom and was merely the center of a province under foreign rulers, the Assyrians, the Chaldeans, and the Persians. Then it was taken by Alexander the Great and held by his successors—first the Ptolemies, then the Seleucids—until it was conquered by the Romans in 65/64 B.C. Thereafter, although still under the Romans, Damascus appears in lists of the cities of the Decapolis, so it must have enjoyed some autonomy. In the meantime, however, it was also involved with the Nabataeans, a neighboring Arab people who had their capital at Petra. Several of the Nabataean kings were named Aretas, and when Paul escaped from Damascus, being lowered in a basket through a window in the wall, "the governor under King Aretas guarded the city" (II Cor 11:32). This would be Aretas IV (11 B.C.–A.D. 40), the king otherwise known for his defeat of Herod Antipas in revenge for the divorce of his daughter by the latter (Josephus, *Ant.* XVIII 5, 1f.). As to the control of Damascus by Aretas IV, known Roman coins from Damascus extend to A.D. 34 in the reign of Tiberius and resume again in 62 in the Reign of Nero, so in between there was probably something less than direct administration by the Romans. In fact it is known that Tiberius had bad relations with

Aretas IV, but Caligula (37–41) wished to have the Nabataeans on his side against the always dangerous Parthians, so he gave the rights to Damascus to Aretas IV for several years.[6] Caligula began to reign on Mar. 16, 37, and Aretas IV probably sent his governor to Damascus soon afterward. This was the situation, then, when Paul made his escape from Damascus three years (Gal 1:18) after his conversion in 36, therefore in 38, counting inclusively.

Later Trajan (A.D. 98–117) joined Damascus to the Roman province of Syria, Hadrian (117–138) made it a metropolis, Alexander Severus (222–235) gave the city colonial rights, and Diocletian (in 313) made it the site of an imperial armament factory—the city always has been famous for the forging of arms. As a city of Syria Damascus was a part of the Byzantine Empire until A.D. 611–614 when Syria was invaded and taken by the Persians under Chosroes II. However, Syria was soon recovered (in 628) by Heraclius, whose ancestral home was at Edessa. Nevertheless Damascus was soon captured again, this time by the followers of Muhammad. Within a few years after the death of the prophet (A.D. 632) the Muslims swept over Palestine, Syria, Iraq, Iran, and Egypt, and Khalid ibn-al-Walid took Damascus in 635. The terms of surrender read as follows.

> In the name of Allah, the compassionate, the merciful. This is what Khalid ibn-al-Walid would grant to the inhabitants of Damascus if he enters therein: he promises to give them security for their lives, property, and churches. Their city wall shall not be demolished, neither shall any Muslim be quartered in their houses. Thereunto we give to them the pact of Allah and the protection of his prophet, the caliphs, and the believers. So long as they pay the poll tax, nothing but good shall befall them.[7]

In A.D. 640 Mu'awiyah became governor of Syria and established the dynasty of the Umayyad caliphs of Damascus (661–750), named for his father Umayyah. Of these rulers Abd al-Malik (685–705) built the Dome of the

Rock at Jerusalem, and his son al-Walid (705–715) built the Aqsa Mosque at Jerusalem and the Great Mosque at Damascus. For one hundred years Damascus was the world capital of a Muslim Empire that extended from Spain to the Indus Valley and from the edge of China to the cataracts of the Nile. In 1516 the Ottoman Turks took Damascus, after World War I it fell under French mandate, and after World War II it shared in the independence of Syria.

In local tradition Damascus is associated with various Old Testament events. The oasis itself is often equated with the Garden of Eden. West of the city some 12 mi (20 km), on a barren promontory overlooking the Barada River, a domed stone building is known as the Tomb of Abel, and the name of the ancient Greek city of Abila at the foot of the mountain bears witness to the antiquity of the tradition. According to the tradition Cain wandered in the oasis for days with his dead brother on his shoulders, then he buried Abel here. Especially to the Druzes, in whose theology doctrines of Islam are mingled with mysteries known only to their own initiates, Abel is a saint, and they feast and dance at the tomb every Friday. Nearer at hand, Jebel Kasyun just north of the city, 4,300 ft (1,310 m) high, is in Muslim tradition the mountain on which it was revealed to Abraham that there is but one omnipotent God.

When Paul went to Damascus from Jerusalem he would presumably have passed north of the Sea of Galilee or moved up through Transjordan, a journey of 130–150 mi (200–240 km) requiring perhaps six days. Beside the present road from Quneitra, 6 mi (10 km) south of Damascus, a Christian shrine atop a hill called Kaukab (Celestial Light) marks the traditional site where Paul fell to the ground before the heavenly light that shone upon him.

In Damascus itself the river Barada runs through the city from west to east, and the most ancient part of the city is on the south side of the river, in the southeastern corner of modern Damascus. In the northwestern corner of this ancient area, now the Inner City of Damascus, are the Citadel and the Great Mosque. The Great Mosque provides a major point of orientation.

The approach to the Great Mosque is through the Suq Hamidiyeh, the city's most famous bazaar, built some seventy-five years ago by Sultan Abdul Hamid II. The site of the Great Mosque was originally that of an Aramaean Temple of Hadad, probably the very house of Rimmon referred to by Naaman (II K 5:18) and probably also where Ahaz saw the altar that he had duplicated for Jerusalem. Under the courtyard of the mosque are some remains of the ancient temple, and a few of the ancient finds are in the National Museum in Damascus. In their time the Romans identified Hadad-Rimmon with Jupiter (and his consort Atargatis with Venus or Juno) and rebuilt the temple as the Temple of Jupiter Damascenus. The work was done under Septimius Severus (A.D. 193–211), Gallienus (260–268), and Diocletian (284–305), and it was finished by Constantius II (337–361), who also built the Gamma, a covered bazaar to the west and north.

The temple was turned into a church under Theodosius I the Great (379–395), and it was dedicated to John the Baptist, who is often called the Prodromos, i.e., the Forerunner, in the Greek Orthodox Church. The relics of John the Baptist were supposed to have been taken to various places, and his head was said to have been enshrined here. Almost at the center of the great hall of the mosque there is a rectangular chapel with a cupola, and this is where, in a marble sarcophagus, the head of John is supposed to have been preserved ever since the time of Theodosius. The church was completed by Arcadius (395–408) and later enlarged and beautified by Justinian (527–565).

On the occasion of the dedication of the church Arcadius placed three inscriptions above the main entrance, which at that time consisted of three gates in the south wall. These gates were closed and walled up when the church was transformed into a mosque, and there is at present a very crowded bazaar

FIGURE 6. Colonnade of the Temple of Jupiter in Damascus.

close against this south wall, so the inscriptions are difficult to see. They are written in Greek and quote the Scripture in the Septuagint translation. Over the western gate are the words of Ps 89:7, "God is glorified in the council of the saints; great and terrible toward all that are round about him." Over the middle portal is Ps 145:13, with the addition of the name of Christ, "Thy kingdom, O Christ, is a kingdom of all the ages, and thy dominion endures in all generations." Perhaps there was also an inscription to the Holy Spirit over the eastern gate, so that there was reference to the entire Trinity.

The church was damaged by earthquake in A.D. 602 and by the Persians in 613, and it was probably repaired by Heraclius in 629 after he drove out the Persians. After the Muslims took Damascus (635), the church was shared with the followers of Muhammad; the Muslims used the east portion, the Christians the west. Seventy years later, however, the entire structure was taken over by the Muslims, and the Umayyad caliph al-Walid (705–715), himself a poet, musician, and composer, converted the church into the Great Mosque of Damascus, which it has been ever since.

As one approaches the Great Mosque from the west and the Suq Hamidiyeh, one passes beside a colonnade with Corinthian capitals

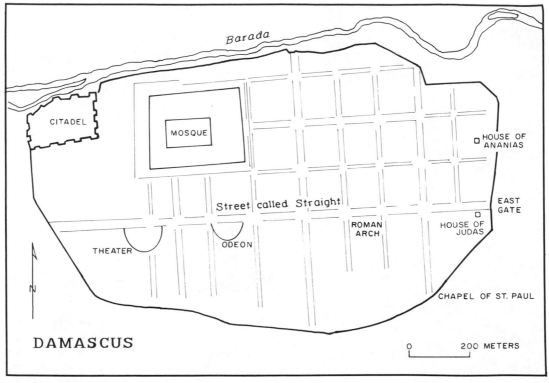

PLAN 5.

supporting high arches, and this colonnade is the remaining portion of the western propylaea of the Roman temple. Inside the mosque there is a vast marble-paved courtyard, 450 ft (137 m) long from east to west and 120 ft (37 m) wide from north to south. At three sides of the courtyard are lofty minarets, and these were built on Roman towers. The oldest minaret is that on the north side, a square tower known as the Minaret of the Bride. The one on the west side is an Egyptian minaret. The highest minaret is the slender one at the southeast corner, and it is called the Medinet Isa (Minaret of Jesus) because of the Muslim belief that this is the spot where Jesus the prophet will enter the world again when the Last Judgment begins. In the courtyard there is a stone fountain for ablutions before prayer, and opposite the fountain there is a treasure house built on twelve columns from the Roman temple. Colonnades 50 ft (15 m) high surround the

courtyard on three sides, and the main prayer hall occupies almost the entire southern side of the area. In the portico at the west end of the courtyard the stone blocks of the Roman outer wall are preserved, and on the wall there is a large section (112 ft. [34 m] long and 26 ft [8 m] high) of early Arab mosaics from the eighth century. Landscapes, houses, and tall buildings are depicted in colors of green, blue, and gold. Other mosaics in the porticos and on the facade of the prayer hall are being reconstructed after the early patterns.

The main prayer hall consists of a tall, rectangular central part amounting to a transept, flanked by two rectangular wings to the east and the west. In the hall two rows of Corinthian columns, linked by tall arches, run the entire length of the building. Parts of the ceiling are still inlaid with gold, and the floor is covered with carpets, said to be 3,000 in number. In the east end are a marble font and two short pillars, remnants from the Christian church, and in the center is the shrine with the supposed head of John the Baptist. The niche (*mihrab*) indicating the direction of prayer toward Mecca and the pulpit (*minbar*) are against the south wall, and behind them is the walled-up ancient triple entrance to the church.

Outside the entire mosque but not far away to the northwest is the mausoleum of Saladin, who defeated the Crusaders in Palestine in 1189 and died in 1193. Farther to the northwest, behind the bazaars, is the Citadel, a vast quadrangular building nearly 1,000 ft (280 m) long and 660 ft (200 m) wide, surrounded by a moat. This structure is for the most part from the thirteenth century, but the foundations are Roman, and the place was originally a Roman fort.

Because Damascus was built on fairly level ground it was relatively easy to transform the ancient city into a Hellenistic and Roman city, with colonnaded streets running straight through it from east to west and north to south, and in the eastern part of the Inner City, the grid plan of these streets is still recognizable. The streets running east and west are spaced more than 300 ft (100 m) apart, those running north and south about 150 ft (45 m) apart. The main east-west street, the Roman *decumanus maximus* and the "street called Straight" of Ac 9:11, is plainly recognizable in the present Midhat Pasha and Bab Sharqi streets, which run directly through the Inner City, parallel to the Barada River, for a distance of nearly 1 mi (1,600 m). In Roman times this street was 50 ft (15 m) wide and bordered with colonnades, consisting of two rows of Corinthian columns on either side. Some of these columns have been found by excavation or are hidden in the bazaar shops on either side of the present street, which is only one-quarter the original width. Also on the south side of the street are traces of two Roman buildings, one a theater and one perhaps a palace.[8]

Midway along this street there is a monumental Roman arch, which was discovered in 1947 at a depth of 15 ft (5 m) below the surface and rebuilt above. This arch was probably erected in 65/64 B.C. as an arch of victory to celebrate the conquest by Pompey. Farther east—2,000 ft (600 m)—the street ends at the Bab Sharqi or East Gate. This is a Roman gate with three arches, known as the Gate of the Sun and dating probably from the second century of the Christian era, and it is the only one of seven Roman gates to survive. At least the locations of the other gates are known from their modern counterparts, the Gate of Mercury (Bab al-Faradisse), the Gate of the Moon (Bab as-Salam), and the Gate of Venus (Bab Touma) in the north wall; the Gate of Jupiter (Bab al-Jabiyah) in the west; and the Gate of Mars (Bab as-Saghir) and the Gate of Saturn (Bab Kaysan) in the south and southeast stretches of the wall. On either side of the East

FIGURE 7. The East Gate of Damascus.

Gate (Bab Sharqi) the present city wall, although often rebuilt, is perpendicular to the axis of the street called Straight, and it corresponds to the ancient wall. In the course of time houses and shops were built into the gate itself, and it was partially walled up—with a tall minaret above—so that only the north arch remained open for traffic, but more of the structure has now been cleared and restored.

In the crowded Christian quarter of the city to the north of the eastern end of the street called Straight is the traditional place of the house of Ananias (Ac 9:10–18). Some 15 ft (5 m) below ground, at the level of the Roman street, is a rock-hewn chamber about 35 ft (11 m) long with a small antechamber to one side. Excavations in 1921 found the remains of a classical temple, with an altar to Jupiter-Hadad as "celestial god, national and supreme." From the style of the Greek letters in the inscription the altar is probably to be dated at least two centuries after Christ. It is possible, therefore,

that a pagan temple was deliberately built on a Christian holy place. Later, probably in the fifth or sixth century, a church was established on the site, and then, in turn, Saladin replaced the church with a mosque. The underground chamber and antechamber that are seen today were preserved as the subterranean crypt of these later structures. Near the eastern end of the street called Straight is also the traditional place of the house of Judas. The site is in a lane only a short distance off the street to the south, in what was the Jewish quarter. A small mosque stands there now, behind a projecting balcony, and if there are the remains of a house at the site they must be far underground.

In the southeastern stretch of the city wall, about 1,000 ft (300 m) from the East Gate (Bab Sharqi), is the traditional place where Paul escaped over the wall in a basket (Ac 9:25). This was the location of the Roman Gate of Saturn, probably built in the second century A.D. on the site of an earlier gate, and the

FIGURE 8. St. Paul's Chapel and Window in Damascus.

modern gate is called Bab Kaysan. Believing that this was the place of Paul's escape the early Christians built a church near the gate, and in turn, the Arabs replaced the church with a mosque, but both the church and the mosque have disappeared. Under the present Ottoman gateway, however, the Greek Catholics have built a small chapel in honor of St. Paul, and, in it, some of the lower parts of the Roman city wall are still to be seen, as well as a single column of the early church. Above, on the exterior wall of the Turkish gateway, are Christian monograms and a stonework projection called St. Paul's Window.[9]

ANTIOCH ON THE ORONTES

After Jerusalem, Antioch in Syria was the most important center of earliest Christianity. Both Peter and Paul were there, and there the disciples were for the first time called Christians, in Greek Χριστιανοί (Ac 11:26). Their contemporaries were quite familiar with terms such as the Latin *Caesarianus* for a "follower of Caesar," and to them the new name would immediately and unmistakably signify "followers of Christ."

In the ancient world there were no less than sixteen Antiochs, all established by one man, namely Seleucus I Nicator (312–281 B.C.), founder of the Seleucid dynasty. It was often the custom in ancient times for the same name to be used in alternate generations of a family, and the name Antiochus was borne both by Seleucus's father (who was one of Alexander the Great's generals) and by Seleucus's son and successor, Antiochus I Soter. So Seleucus named each of the sixteen cities Antioch, but even in antiquity it was debated whether he gave the name in honor of his father (which would probably be more likely) or in honor of his son.

Of these many Antiochs the one we are concerned with is commonly called Antioch in Syria (although with the present border it is now actually in Turkey), and with reference to the New Testament, this designation distin-guishes it from Antioch of Pisidia (Ac 13:14). In ancient times it was also known as Antioch on the Orontes, from the river that flowed through the city, or Antioch near Daphne, from the famous suburb of that name 5 mi (8 km) to the south.

Looked at on a large scale, Antioch was almost at the center of the Fertile Crescent, and on a great caravan route from the Euphrates to the Mediterranean. It was also almost opposite the island of Cyprus to the west, and this fact directed attention toward the Mediterranean world as well. In biblical relationships, Antioch was 300 mi (480 km) north of Jerusalem. Looking at its more immediate setting the site was on the southwestern corner of the large Amuk Plain, dominated by the peaks of the Amanus range, and it was between Mt. Silpius (1,800 ft [550 m] high) and the Orontes River. This river rises in the east side of the Beqa Valley (between the Lebanon and Anti-Lebanon mountains), flows north, then turns from northeast to southwest and enters the Mediterranean at a point 38 mi (61 km) south of Iskenderun. Although the mountains surrounding Antioch protected the site from attacks from the desert or the sea, the river valley still offered good communication with the coast. There, 11 mi (17 km) distant, at the mouth of the Orontes and on a bay bordered by Mt. Casius (Musa Dagh) to the south, was the seaport of Seleucia Pieria (Ac 13:4).

Considering the strategic location of the area, there must have been travel through the region and settlement there from early times. Early sites that have been excavated in the Amuk Plain are at Tell Atchana, Tell Judeideh, and Tell Tainat. Tell Tainat, for example, is just east of the village of Jisr al-Hadid, where the Antioch-Aleppo highway crosses the Orontes. At this site virgin soil lies 8 ft (2.5 m) beneath the present water table, but even so, the excavations have penetrated a span of time extending from the Neolithic Age to the Christian period, and both Assyrian and Hittite sculptures were found. In the first half of the first millennium B.C. the territory was occupied by the Syro-Hittite kingdom of Hattina, which was then offering strong resistance to the expanding power of Assyria, and two Hittite royal buildings of around 800 B.C. have been found. In the porch of one a double-lion column base of basalt was still in place, and it is now in the Archaeological Museum in Antioch.

Archeological evidence also shows that goods were brought in from Mycenae, Crete, and Cyprus, no doubt by Greek traders, and legend has it that three Greek settlements were established in the region of the future Antioch. Two of these, named Iopolis and Kasiotis, were on Mt. Silpius, and one, called Herakleia, was near the site of Daphne.

The city of Antioch itself and its neighbors Daphne and Seleucia date only from Hellenistic times. In 333 B.C. Alexander the Great won an important battle against the Persians in the Plain of Issus at the northeastern corner of the Mediterranean. In the vicinity he founded a town to commemorate the victory, and the present Turkish Iskenderun, earlier called Alexandretta (Little Alexandria), preserves the name if not the exact site. After the battle Alexander proceeded toward Phoenicia and would naturally have come through the vicinity of the future Antioch. To the east of that site he is supposed to have found a spring of especially good water. He desired to build a city there and at least made a beginning by founding a temple of Zeus Bottiaios (named for the Bottiaei, the inhabitants of Emathia, his own homeland in Thrace). In the same connection there are reports of a citadel called Emathia and a village named Bottia, the latter on the level ground beside the Orontes.

After Alexander's death (323) his generals divided his empire, Antigonus held Syria, and in 307/306 he built a capital for himself on the Orontes 5 mi (8 km) northeast of the site of Antioch, which he called Antigonia. But Seleucus I Nicator (Conqueror) soon emerged as the master. He took Babylon and began his official rule there, and thus he inaugurated the Seleucid Era, which was reckoned in the Macedonian calendar (which began the year in the fall) from Oct. 7, 312, and in the Babylo-

nian calendar (which began the year in the spring) from Apr. 3, 311. Then in 301 in the Battle of Ipsus in Asia Minor, together with Ptolemy I of Egypt and others, Seleucus defeated Antigonus and established his own rule in Syria. In the next year (300), Seleucus I Nicator founded his own cities in the valley of the Orontes to commemorate his victory.

The first city was Seleucia Pieria, founded in April and named by Seleucus for himself. The story is that Seleucus went up on Mt. Casius, which was sacred to Zeus, made a sacrifice, and inquired where he should establish his capital. An eagle, the bird of Zeus, seized the offering and carried it to the site of Seleucia, and Seleucus founded his city on the spot so indicated.

In the next month, May, Seleucus also made a sacrifice in the city of Antigonia and asked whether he should occupy that city or build another in its place. Again an eagle carried away a portion of the sacrifice and deposited it on the altar of Zeus Bottiaios, which Alexander the Great had erected, so Seleucus founded Antioch there at Bottia beside the Orontes. Antigonia, bearing the name of his defeated rival, he destroyed, and he moved its whole population to his own newly established city.

Like Damascus in the Hellenistic and Roman periods, Antioch was laid out on the gridiron plan, and it occupied an oblong area on the flat ground between the river and a road that, in Roman times, became the colonnaded main avenue of the city. Two separate quarters were marked out, each with its own wall; the larger quarter was for the European settlers, the smaller for the native Syrians.

Antiochus I Soter (281–261 B.C.) wished to make Antioch the intellectual rival of Alexandria in Egypt, and invited scholars, poets, and scientists to his court. Among these was the famous poet Aratus of Soli, who was at the Seleucid court for several years (274–272). Seleucus II Callinicus (246–225) built a third quarter of the city on a large island in the Orontes. A wall was built around the island, and the streets were again laid out on the

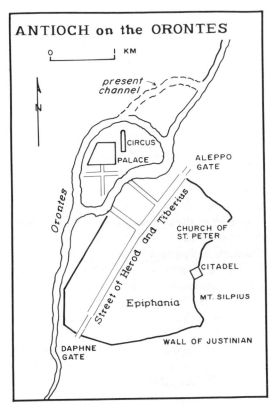

ANTIOCH on the ORONTES

0 ___ 1 KM

N

present channel →

CIRCUS

PALACE

ALEPPO GATE

Orontes

Street of Herod and Tiberius

CHURCH OF ST. PETER

CITADEL

Epiphania

MT. SILPIUS

WALL OF JUSTINIAN

DAPHNE GATE

PLAN 6.

66, the date of the surrender of Tigranes. Julius Caesar went to Antioch in 47 B.C., built various public buildings, and introduced yet another era, reckoned from Oct. 1, 49 B.C., which eventually became known as the Era of Antioch.

In 27 B.C. Augustus reorganized the Roman Empire and divided the provinces into three classes: (1) senatorial, under the jurisdiction of the Senate and governed by a proconsul, normally appointed for one year; (2) imperial, under the direct control of the emperor and administered by a legate of indefinite tenure, appointed by the emperor; and (3) procuratorial, a more exceptional category in which the governor was also of indefinite tenure and appointed by the emperor, but was known by the titles of prefect and procurator. Because of its strategic importance Syria was made an imperial province, and Augustus himself visited Antioch in 30 and 20 B.C. and did more building there.

Herod the Great also took an interest in Antioch, and Josephus says that he paved the main street of the city with marble. Tiberius completed the Temple of Zeus (Jupiter), which Antiochus IV had built, and later Roman emperors did further building in Antioch, so that it is not always possible to distinguish their works separately.

Daphne, the suburb 5 mi (8 km) south of Antioch, was an area of many springs, a great waterfall, and many oak, cypress, and laurel trees. In mythology it was here that Apollo pursued the nymph Daphne who, to escape him, was changed into a laurel tree. Accordingly Seleucus I built a temple in this place to Apollo, and there were also other temples to Aphrodite, Artemis, Isis, and Zeus. The Temple of Apollo was an asylum for fugitives from justice. A stadium was provided for local games, which were instituted under Augustus and under Claudius (A.D. 41–54) were recognized as Olympic Games and came to rival those of Greece. Titus went to Antioch after the fall of Jerusalem (A.D. 70) and built a theater in Daphne, destroying, it was said, a Jewish synagogue to make room for it. A statue

gridiron pattern, with two main streets intersecting each other at right angles in the center of the island.

Antiochus IV Epiphanes (175–164) laid out the fourth quarter, called Epiphania after himself, on the slopes of Mt. Silpius, and he erected a temple to the Olympian Zeus on the same mountain. With this expansion of the city the Hellenistic road that had run beside the settlement of Seleucus I now passed through the middle of Antioch and became the colonnaded main street of Roman times.

Tigranes of Armenia took Antioch in 83 B.C., but the Roman general Pompey defeated him in 66 and went to Antioch in 64. Pompey gave Antioch and Seleucia Pieria the status of free cities, established Antioch as the capital of the Roman province of Syria, and in Antioch replaced the Seleucid Era with his own Pompeian Era—reckoned from the autumn of of Vespasian was placed in the theater, and it was marked with a Latin inscription reading EX PRAEDA IVDAEA ("from the spoils of Judea"). Because of the attractions of the area Daphne was favored as a dwelling place by rich Syrian merchants and Roman officials, and there were many fine residences there. The Roman commander Germanicus went there for rest; the emperor Julian the Apostate spent a winter there and wrote a treatise against Christianity.

Several ancient writers describe Antioch. Strabo (XVI 2, 4) calls it a *tetrapolis*, since it consisted of four parts, each part fortified both by a common wall and by a wall of its own. Josephus (*War* III 2, 4 §29) says Antioch was the third city of the Roman Empire (after Rome and Alexandria). The population was estimated at 500,000, including Syrians, Greeks, Romans, and a large Jewish community. Josephus also speaks of the Greeks in Antioch being interested in Judaism, and we may suppose that Nicolaus of Antioch, a proselyte and one of the seven in Ac 6:5, was one of those. Juvenal (A.D. 60–140) characterizes the people of Antioch as restless, covetous, proud, turbulent, and inclined to satire. He also pictures the flooding of Rome with the superstition and immorality of the East as a flowing of the Orontes into the Tiber (*Satire* III 62). Athenaeus (end of second cent. A.D.), however, calls Antioch "the beautiful" (*Deipnosophists* I 20); Libanius, a native and famous teacher of Antioch, wrote for delivery at the local Olympic Games in A.D. 356 or 360 an enthusiastic oration in praise of the city (the *Antiochikos*, *Oration* XI); and Ammianus Marcellinus (XXII 9, 14), another native of Antioch writing in the latter part of the fourth century, calls his city the "fair crown of the Orient."

In its later secular history Antioch suffered various disasters. In A.D. 37 there was a severe earthquake, and the emperor Caligula (A.D. 37–41) provided assistance for rebuilding. Under Claudius (41–54) there was another earthquake, which damaged Ephesus, Smyrna, and many other cities of Asia Minor as well as Antioch, and a famine, caused by crop failures in Syria, Palestine, and Egypt, in which the Christians in Antioch sent relief to the brethren in Judea (Ac 11:28–30). In A.D. 115 a severe earthquake again caused much destruction, and Trajan, who was in the city, suffered at least slight injuries. In the middle of the third century the Sassanian king of Persia, Shapur I (A.D. 241–272), undertook the conquest of Syria and Asia Minor. In 256 Shapur I captured Dura-Europos, and in 260 he took prisoner the Roman emperor Valerian (253–260), captured Antioch, and deported a large part of the population to Susiana. Under the next emperor Gallienus (260–268), Prince Odenath of Palmyra helped to drive back the Persians and became in effect the ruler of the East, a position in which his wife Zenobia continued after his assassination in 266. Antioch was thus under the control of Palmyra until Aurelian (270–275) took the city and captured the fleeing queen at the Euphrates, bringing her back for exhibition as a captive at Antioch and Rome. Probus (276–282) assisted Antioch toward recovery; Diocletian (284–305) visited the city several times, bestowed various benefactions on it, and built an imperial palace on the island adjacent to the hippodrome.

In the sixth century both the recurrence of seismic disturbances and the resumption of hostilities with the Persians contributed to the decline of Antioch. In 526 a very terrible earthquake destroyed almost the entire city and killed a reported 250,000 people. Aftershocks continued and culminated in a second major quake in 528, when nearly 5,000 more were killed. The emperor Justinian I (527–565) sent help, and a gesture of propiation of the divine will, the name of the city was changed to Theoupolis (City of God). Then in 540 the Sassanian king Chosroes I captured and burned the city and again carried off a large number of the inhabitants to Mesopotamia. Although Justinian was soon able to reclaim and rebuild the city it was now much smaller than it had been, the course of the Orontes was changed, and the island was abandoned as a part of the city.

As a city of the Greco-Roman world Antioch reached its end in A.D. 637/638 when the forces of the Arab Muslims overran all of northwestern Syria. Thereafter Antioch was held by the Arabs for 300 years and then by the Seljuk Turks, by the Crusaders, and by the Ottoman Turks. Until after World War I Antioch remained a part of the Turkish Empire, but after the war it was transferred to Syria, which was placed under French mandate. In 1939, after a plebiscite, Antioch passed to Turkey, and the ancient city is now represented by the Turkish town of Antakya.[10]

In Christian history the church at Antioch, associated with the memory of Peter and Barnabas and Paul, continued strong and important, although persecuted. After Peter, as Eusebius tells us (Ch. Hist. III 22, 1), the first bishop of Antioch was Evodius, the second was Ignatius, and both were martyrs — Ignatius being taken to Rome for his death in the year 107. Further persecutions were experienced under the emperors Decius (A.D. 250) and Diocletian (303). Yet between the middle of the third century and the beginning of the sixth, thirty church synods were held at Antioch, and the Council of Nicea called Antioch the center and eye of Christianity. Indeed, in the early times the church at Antioch was considered second only to Rome.

Antioch was a place of Christian learning and theological thought. The "school of Antioch" was not an institution like the catechetical school at Alexandria, but rather a movement in theology associated with a number of prominent teachers — Lucian, Dorotheus, Eustathius, Diodorus, Theodore, and Theodoret. The school at Alexandria was inclined to the allegorical and mythological, but in contrast Antioch took the lead in historical and ·grammatical studies and in exegesis of the Bible — as Adolf von Harnack has said, the school made "remarkable strides toward true biblical criticism."

A pupil of Diodorus was the famous preacher John Chrysostom, "the golden-mouthed." He was born in Antioch around A.D. 345 and lived there until 398 when he became the patriarch of Constantinople. Harnack has said that "the thoughtful, practically edifying expositions" of Chrysostom were the fairest fruit of the school of Antioch, and Erwin Preuschen has called him "a master of the art of developing practical truths for everyday life from the Scriptures." "What made his preaching so powerful was not only the native rhetorical force which he undoubtedly possessed, but his skill in illuminating the questions of daily life from the Scriptures, in guiding people in their path through the world."[11] Incidentally the sermons of Chrysostom also give a picture of the life of Antioch at the time of his life there, and they are used as a source of information by modern archeologists. Also of great value in this regard are the writings, especially the Chronicle, .of John Malalas, a Byzantine monk (A.D. 491–578) who was born and spent most of his life in Antioch.

In view of the terrible vicissitudes of ancient Antioch — shattered by earthquakes, flooded from time to time because of heavy storms, and sacked by the Sassanian invaders from Persia — it cannot be expected that much of the ancient and splendid city has survived until now. On the other hand modern Antakya occupies no more than one-fourth of the area of the large ancient city, so there is opportunity for archeological work, and some excavations have been conducted by Princeton University expeditions. Yet this work is made difficult by the great depth of the ancient strata, for on the main axis of the city the ground has risen no less than 35 ft (11 m).[12]

The main courses of the city walls have been established; walls of the third century B.C. built by Seleucus I, of the first century of the Christian era by Tiberius, of the fifth century by Theodosius II, and of the sixth century by Justinian — these last high up on Mt. Silpius. On Mt. Silpius there was a citadel and, on the northern part of the same mountain called Mt. Staurin (for a vision of the Cross seen there after the disastrous earthquake of A.D. 526), an acropolis. A winter torrent named Parmenius

FIGURE 9. Oceanus, Mosaic, from Daphne, in the Archaeological Museum in Antioch.

flowed between Mt. Silpius and Mt. Staurin, and the so-called Iron Gate was constructed in the wall of Justinian to prevent the stream from flooding the city.

The Hellenistic city was laid out on the gridiron plan, which was associated with the name of Hippodamus of Miletus (fifth century B.C.) and was characteristic of many cities founded at the time. In aerial photographs of modern Antakya the gridiron outline of the ancient city is still discernible. The main street, which constituted the main axis of the city, ran from the Aleppo Gate on the northeast to the Daphne Gate on the south, a distance of some 2 mi (3 km). In the third century B.C. this street was only paved with stones and 50 ft (15 m) wide, but at about the beginning of the Christian era, it underwent major reconstruction, to which both Herod the Great and the emperor Tiberius are reported to have contributed. At that time the street was provided with broad sidewalks and lined with colonnades and shops. With further reconstruction by Trajan and Justinian, it must have been a truly magnificent thoroughfare, with a total width of nearly 130 ft (40 m). Other prominent features of the city were the marketplace, previously laid out in Seleucid times, a theater and an amphitheater, and on the no longer recognizable island in the river, a palace and a circus. Also the main bridge over the Orontes, although often repaired, dates back to Roman times, and several gates of the Crusader period are well preserved.

At Daphne the theater has been explored, and a number of the houses excavated, from which have come some fine floor mosaics, mostly dating from the second to the sixth centuries A.D. One of these mosaics came from a villa in Yakto, a modern part of Daphne, and dates from the latter part of the fifth century. A medallion in the center, with a woman personifying Greatness of Soul (Μεγαλοψυχία), is surrounded by hunting scenes, and scenes of buildings and people form a topographical border of the mosaic, illustrating a tour of Antioch and Daphne just like the one Libanius imagined in his oration in praise of Antioch in the preceding century. Beginning in the lower left-hand corner and going clockwise, the scenes portray the Aleppo Gate, the main colonnaded street, the island, and Daphne, depicting many aspects of daily life.[13]

At Seleucia Pieria there was a lower town on the plain to the southwest and an upper town rising in tiers on the Amanus slopes, with a long line of city walls for protection. Here too fine mosaic pavings have been recovered from the luxurious Roman villas of the upper town. The city also has a temple of Hellenistic date and a Roman theater. A rock-cut canal more than 4,000 ft (1,200 m) long, sometimes a tunnel and sometimes open to the sky, is dated by inscriptions to the time of Vespasian and Titus.[14] It was probably intended for the diversion of floodwaters, and with a large dam, it also served as a reservoir. As for the ancient harbor, it is almost entirely silted up (as are the harbors at Tarsus, Ephesus, Salamis, Perga, and many other places), and only a small port called al-Mina remains.

Concerning specific Christian traditions at Antioch, Chrysostom and Theodoret indicate that a cave was pointed out on the slope of Mt. Silpius where Paul was supposed to have lived and taught.[15] John Malalas (*Chronicle* 242, 11) also says that Paul and Barnabas preached in a street near the Pantheon, which was called Singon (Σίγγων or Σίγγων). In the Slavonic version of Malalas's work the name was apparently taken to be the similar Greek word Siagon (Σιαγών), which means "jawbone," for the text says that the place was named after a jawbone; if this were true, the name could have been derived from the shape of the street. The Pantheon, mentioned in the text, is known to have been rebuilt by Julius Caesar, but its location is not known, so the location of Singon Street is also not known.

According to the *Recognitions of Clement* (x 71), a work probably of the early third century, while Peter was in Antioch a very prominent citizen named Theophilus donated his huge house for a church, with a chair for Peter, and the multitude of believers assembled there. Later (A.D. 448) in a letter (LXXXVI) written to the bishop of Constantinople, Theodoret mentions the throne of Peter as being in the possession of the Antiochene metropolis, and he bases the precedence of Antioch over Alexandria (the see of Mark) on the association of Antioch with Peter the teacher of Mark (by this time the sequence in terms of relative importance was thought to be Rome, Constantinople, Antioch).

According to local tradition Peter also preached and baptized, and the Christians found refuge, in the so-called Grotto or Church of St. Peter. This is a natural cavern (approximately 30 ft [9 m] wide, 40 ft [12 m] deep, and 25 ft [7 m] high) in the rocky escarpment of Mt. Staurin, near where the Parmenius winter torrent descends between Mt. Staurin and Mt. Silpius. The grotto is inside the ancient city walls and perhaps 1,500 ft (450 m) from the site of the ancient theater. Inside the cavern there is a small spring, and a tunnel at the back is supposed to have provided a way of escape in time of danger. On the floor a few fragments of mosaic still remain, perhaps from the fourth or fifth century. The facade is from the time of the Crusaders in the twelfth and thirteenth centuries, and it has recently been

FIGURE 10. Tethys, Wife of Oceanus, Mosaic, from Daphne, in the Archaeological Museum in Antioch.

FIGURE 11. Sleeping Shepherd Boy, from Daphne (Second Century A.D.), in the Archaeological Museum in Antioch.

restored so that it stands out in white against the background of reddish rock. In the thirteenth century the grotto came into the hands of the Armenians, and there are remains of a fresco on the interior, upper back wall with part of the name of Peter in Armenian (Bedros). In the seventeenth to the nineteenth centuries the grotto was in the possession of the Greek Orthodox Church, but it was turned over to the French consul in Antioch in 1855. More recently it has been in the hands of the Capuchin missionary friars in Antioch, and they have made studies hoping to find proof of the association of the place with Peter, but without completely assured results. In the grotto the Feast of St. Peter is celebrated on June 29.[16]

In the literary sources many Christian church buildings at Antioch are mentioned.[17] Of them the oldest was the one Chrysostom and Theodoret call the Old Church and the Apostolic Church. It stood in the Palaea, or ancient part of Antioch, and was supposed to have been founded by the apostles. When Theodoret (*Ch. Hist.* I 2) speaks of it, the church had been restored by Vitalis, who became bishop of Antioch about A.D. 314, and the work of restoration had been completed by his successor Philogonius (319–324); therefore, the preceding building must have dated to the third century, and perhaps it had been destroyed in the persecution under Diocletian (303). As for the original church, presumably founded by the apostles, it might conceivably have been related to the tradition preserved by Malalas of the preaching of Paul and Barnabas in Singon Street.[18]

In contrast with the "old" church, a church built by the emperor Constantine and completed by his son Constantius was the "new" church in Antioch. It was begun in A.D. 327 and dedicated in 341, at which time ninety bishops were present and a church council was held. Eusebius (*Life of Constantine* III 50) describes the church as being of unparalleled size and beauty and says that "The entire building was encompassed by an enclosure of great extent, within which the church itself rose to a vast elevation, being of an octagonal form, and surrounded on all sides by many chambers, courts, and upper and lower apartments; the whole richly adorned with a profusion of gold, brass, and other materials of the most costly kind."

Known also as the Golden Church and the Great Church, this building was on the island near the imperial palace. As an octagon it evidently provided a prototype for the octagonal central part of the famous fifth-century Church of St. Simeon Stylites at Qalat Siman. In the aftermath of the terrible earthquake of A.D. 526 the Great Church burned to the ground. It was rebuilt and rededicated in 537/538, plundered by Chosroes I and the Persians in 540, and destroyed again in another severe earthquake in 588. The remains of the Great Church have not been found, but there is a representation of the church in the topographical border of the Daphne mosaic.

In the vicinity of Antioch excavations have

FIGURE 12. Facade of the Church of St. Peter in Antioch.

brought to light the ruins of two other early Christian churches. North of Antioch, on the way to the village of Kaoussie on the right bank of the Orontes, are the foundations of a cross-shaped church with mosaic floors. This was probably built around A.D. 380 by Bishop Meletius of Antioch (the man who baptized Chrysostom) as the final burial place for St. Babylas, a bishop of Antioch who was mar- tyred under Decius in 250, and in 381 Meletius himself was buried in the same church. At Seleucia Pieria are the ruins of a circular memorial church, and it probably dates to the last quarter of the fifth century. A famous object reportedly found at or near Antioch is the Chalice of Antioch, probably a piece of early Christian silver from the fourth or fifth century.[19]

4
FIRST MISSIONARY JOURNEY
(A.D. 47–48)

CYPRUS

On Paul's first missionary journey he and Barnabas, with John to assist them, sailed from Seleucia to Cyprus, landed at Salamis, and went through the whole island as far as Paphos (Ac 13:4–6). The island of Cyprus is at the crossroads of the eastern Mediterranean, and it is a meeting place of the sea routes from Syria, Asia Minor, and Egypt—and on to the West. The distance from Asia Minor to the north is only 50 mi (80 km), from Syria to the east 70 mi (113 km), and from Egypt to the south 240 mi (386 km). The main part of the island is 90 mi (145 km) from east to west and, at the most, 50 mi (80 km) from north to south, plus there is a long, narrow peninsula that points northeast toward the Gulf of Iskenderun. In his *Geography* Ptolemy calls the long peninsula the Ox Tail or Cape Cleides. Compared to other islands in the Mediterranean, Cyprus is slightly larger than Crete and Corsica and smaller than only Sicily and Sardinia.

There are two ranges of mountains on Cyprus, the northern range called Kyrenia, which rises to over 3,000 ft (900 m) in elevation, and the western range named Troödos, with Mt. Troödos 6,404 ft (1,952 m) high. A central plain is called Mesaoria ("between the mountains"), and two rivers, the Pedias and Yalias, run through the plain and join to enter the sea at Salamis on the east coast. The climate is much like that of Palestine, with the rains normally beginning at the end of October or a little later, the crops ripening and harvest coming in April and May, and a long, hot, dry summer.

In raw materials Cyprus is especially rich in copper. In the cuneiform sources, in which the island is called Alashiya, there is frequent reference to its export of copper; such references are found in texts from Ebla (twenty-fourth century B.C.), Mari (eighteenth century B.C.), and Amarna (fourteenth century B.C.). In Greek the name of the island and the word for the metal are the same, and it is from the Greek *cyprus* (κύπρος) that the English word "copper" is derived. The copper of Cyprus is not yet exhausted, and at a mine in the northwest part of the island it is said that even now more than one million tons of raw copper are extracted annually from veins that were being mined 3,000 years ago.

In the Old Testament (e.g., Ezk 27:6) the island is referred to as Kittim. Josephus (*Ant.* I vi, 1 §128) explains that Kittim (Chetima) was the old name and that one of the cities preserved the old appellation in the Hellenized form of Kition. Furthermore, Josephus says, the Hebrews gave the same name of Kittim to all the islands and most maritime countries. This explains the fact that in 1 Macc 1:1 Alexander the Great is said to have come from the land of Kittim and in the Dead Sea Scrolls the Kittim are probably the Romans (cf. Dan 11:30).

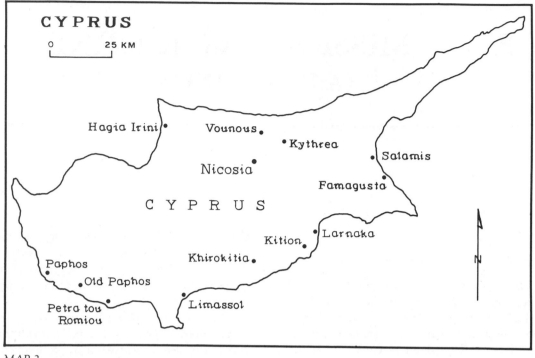

MAP 2.

Archeological excavations by the Cyprus Department of Antiquities, the Swedish Cyprus Expedition, and the American Schools of Oriental Research have revealed something of the earliest history of Cyprus. In the Neolithic Age there was a settlement, for example, at Khirokitia, near the south coast east of Limassol. Round houses were constructed with rough stone walls 1 ft (0.3 m) high, with timbers and clay above that. A sacred precinct contained an offering place with two large stone tables. Another settlement was at Kythrea, in the plain northeast of Nicosia. There too there were circular houses and also vessels and statuettes made of clay and of stone.

In the Bronze Age there was trade with Syria/Palestine and Egypt, and Cypriote pottery has been found, for example, at Lachish in Palestine and Amarna in Egypt. By the end of the Bronze Age, around 1200 B.C., Greeks began to come from the Aegean and settle on Cyprus. Much Mycenaean pottery (of

the type made at the famous site of Mycenae south of Corinth) has been found on the island, and there were Greek colonies at Salamis, Paphos, and other places.

In the Iron Age, around 1000 B.C., the Phoenicians came too, and they established colonies at various places, including Kition. Kition is the city mentioned by Josephus, and it was near the modern Larnaka on the southeast coast. It is also known that Hiram I (970–936 B.C.), the king of Tyre and friend of Solomon, and Hiram II (741–738), a later king of Tyre, had governors on Cyprus, and Is 23:1 refers to Kittim (i.e., Cyprus) in connection with Tyre. In that passage there is an oracle of doom on Tyre and Sidon, and Phoenician seamen arriving at Cyprus, homeward bound, hear the news of the disaster that has befallen their land.

In the eighth and seventh centuries B.C. the Assyrians controlled most of Cyprus. A stela of Sargon II, found at Larnaka, records tribute received by him from seven kings, and a prism of Esarhaddon lists ten cities of Cyprus —Salamis, Paphos, and other places—and their kings. In the sixth century Egypt took control of Cyprus. Although some of the great warriors of earlier times—such as Thutmose III and Ramses II—may have made brief conquests there, Herodotus (II 182) says that it was Amasis (569–527) of the twentieth dynasty, a contemporary of Cyrus II the Persian, who was the first conqueror of Cyprus and made the island tributary to himself.

When Cambyses II (529–522 B.C.), son of Cyrus II, fought against Egypt, however, Cyprus surrendered to the Persians, assisted them against Egypt, and became a province of the Persian Empire. In the empire Cyprus was in the fifth satrapy, named "across the river," but the island had its own kings instead of a Persian governor.

When Alexander the Great won the Battle of Issus (333 B.C.) against the Persians, Cyprus took Alexander's side and sent 120 ships to help him in his ensuing seven-month siege of Tyre (332). Now Cyprus became a part of the Hellenistic world and came under the sway of the Ptolemies of Egypt. They ruled for nearly two and a half centuries (294–58 B.C.) and called themselves kings of Egypt and Cyprus. During this period the island was divided into four districts, of which the two most important were those of Salamis in the east and Paphos in the west. The governor of Cyprus—who was also a general, an admiral, and a high priest—resided first at Salamis and later at Paphos. Cyprus supplied Egypt with metal, wood for shipbuilding, and grain and enjoyed a long period of relative peace and prosperity. In 58 B.C. Cyprus was annexed by Rome, and in 52 B.C. Cicero was its governor. In 22 B.C. Cyprus became a senatorial province, so when Barnabas and Paul came to Cyprus the ruling official was a proconsul, Sergius Paulus, who resided at Paphos. According to Pliny the Elder there were in his time (first century A.D.) no fewer than fifteen cities of importance on the island.

In its later history Cyprus was a part of the Byzantine Empire and was fought over by Muslims and Byzantines until it was taken by the Crusaders. Richard the Lion-Hearted sold Cyprus to the Templars, and they sold the island to Guy de Lusignan, whose family ruled there until A.D. 1475. Venice took over next, and during the Venetian period (1489–1571) vast fortifications and castles were built. The Turkish period (1571–1878) saw heavy taxation and frequent revolts. Thereafter there was the period of British administration until the Republic of Cyprus was established in 1960.

As a result of its history and its involvement in almost everything that happened in the eastern Mediterranean, there are many strata of ancient remains on Cyprus, and it has been said, not inappropriately, that the island is "in fact one huge archeological site."[1] Scattered archeological materials of the Bronze Age attest there being prehistoric cults on Cyprus, centering on a mother goddess, a serpent god, and a sacred bull. The so-called Vounous Ritual in the Cyprus Museum in Nicosia is probably older than 2000 B.C. and is a large clay model of a circular cult place, with some kind of sacred ceremony in progress. The Hagia Irini Sanctuary is a walled enclosure with a low altar and 2,000 clay statues, miniature to life-size. One is a great idol with a strange helmet, and there are many Minotaurs (half man and half bull).

Cyprus was especially important in Greek mythology, as we learn from Homer, Hesiod, and other ancient writers. Perhaps because Cyprus was already the place of worship of the mother goddess of prehistoric times, and also of Astarte (the Semitic Ishtar, probably brought in by the Phoenicians), the Greeks made Cyprus the island of Aphrodite (Venus). To the Greeks Aphrodite was the goddess of love and they called her "fair," "golden," and "beautiful." Hesiod (Theogony 199) names her "Cyprus-born," and in lyrical words a Homeric hymn (v "To Aphrodite") alludes to the legend that she came forth from the foam of the sea: "The moist breeze of Zephyr brought her there on the waves of the sea with a noise of thunder amid the soft foam, and the gold-clad Hours received her with joy. They decked her with precious jewels and set on her immortal head a beautiful crown of gold and in her ear rings of copper and gold."

The traditional birthplace of Aphrodite was on the south coast, halfway between Limassol and Paphos, and it is called Petra tou Romiou (Rocks of the Roman) from a local legend concerning a hero who picked up boulders from the mountains and threw them down on Muslim ships. There, especially, masses of sea foam are driven onshore, and it is out of those that Aphrodite arose. About 5 mi (8 km) farther west, at Old Paphos, was her famous sanctuary.

In philosophy, Kition, originally a Phoenician colony near the modern city of Larnaka, was the birthplace of Zeno, himself of Phoenician descent and the famed founder of Stoicism. An Italian-American, General di Cesnola, who served in the Civil War and was appointed by Abraham Lincoln as the U.S. consul to Cyprus, had his residence at Larnaka and found there a finely sculptured Greek head. It has the individuality of a portrait and manifests such intellectual features that it is thought to be probably the head of Zeno.

From the Ptolemaic period onward, if not earlier, there were many Jews on Cyprus. In Ac 4:36 Joseph Barnabas ("son of encouragement") is described as a Levite and a native of Cyprus; therefore, he was a Hellenistic Jew of the island. Accordingly, when Barnabas and Saul arrived in Salamis, they naturally proclaimed the Word in the synagogues of the Jews. But under Trajan (A.D. 117) the Jews of Cyprus participated in widespread uprisings against the Romans and Greeks and, as a consequence, were banished from the island. In spite of the banishment, there were at least a few there again in later centuries.

Salamis

Salamis was the city where Barnabas and Saul arrived (Ac 13:5). The site is 5 mi (8 km) north of modern Famagusta, in the curve of the great Famagusta Bay. Islands formed there in the sandy delta of the Pedius River and

allowed the development of a well-protected harbor, so Salamis was the main port and principal city of Cyprus at the time. On several occasions, however, the city was destroyed by earthquakes and was rebuilt by the Romans; then it was finally destroyed by the Arabs in A.D. 647. At that time the Christian survivors moved to nearby Arsinoe Ammochostas ("choked with sand"). This city was originally built by Ptolemy II Philadelphus in 274 B.C., and eventually it became the modern Famagusta. It was an important city in medieval times, and the citadel at the mouth of the harbor is the supposed scene of Shakespeare's *Othello*.

At Salamis the surviving ruins are mostly late Roman and Byzantine. They include a theater from the end of the first century B.C., which seated 15,000 spectators; a gymnasium and an agora, both of which were restored by Augustus; the Basilica of St. Epiphanius (bishop of Salamis in A.D. 357 and author of the *Panarion haereses* and other works); and— 1.3 mi (2 km) to the west—the Monastery of St

PLAN 7.

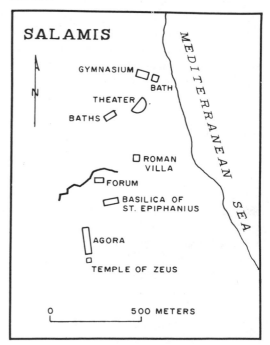

FIGURE 13. Gymnasium at Salamis. *(Published by Permission of the Director of Antiquities and the Cyprus Museum)*

Barnabas, built in the fifth century and later restored.

From Salamis Barnabas and Saul went across Cyprus all the way to Paphos. The Greek statement about this in Ac 13:6 may be translated to say that they "made a missionary progress through the whole island." The route they took is not known. They could have followed the Pedius River through the central plain and over the mountains to the west, or perhaps it is more likely that they went along the south coast, which would have taken them through Kition and other important cities.

Paphos

Some 20 mi (32 km) west of the present city of Limassol (now the chief port of Cyprus) and 5 mi (8 km) west of Petra tou Romiou was Old Paphos (Palaipaphos), the site of the sanctuary of Aphrodite. Referring to this place, the *Odyssey* (VIII 362–363) tells how "the laughter-loving Aphrodite went to Cyprus, to Paphos,

where are her sacred precinct and altar, smoking with incense," so it was a very ancient temple. Titus visited the temple on his way to Palestine shortly before the fall of Jerusalem (A.D. 70), and Tacitus, telling about this visit (*Histories* II 2–4), reports different traditions as to the founder of the temple. Tacitus also records the legend that the altar was never wet by any rain, even though it was in the open air. He says that blood was not allowed to be shed on the altar and that offering was made only with prayers and pure fire. The representation of the goddess was also not in human form but was apparently a conical object.

The modern village of Kouklia occupies part of the site of Old Paphos. Excavations have uncovered part of the fortifications of the ancient city, and they have recovered many sculptures as early as the sixth century B.C. The ruins of the Temple of Aphrodite, on a hill at the southwestern corner of the city, date from Greco-Roman times, but relatively little survives, although it can be seen that there was a great rectangular enclosure and a whole series of buildings. In the Cyprus Museum, however, there is a large conical stone that came from the temple area, and perhaps it once stood in the central shrine of the temple as the aniconic representation of the goddess. Whether Barnabas and Saul came into Old Paphos or whether they experienced any confrontation with the worshipers of Aphrodite—as Paul later did with the worshipers of Artemis at Ephesus—we do not know. Perhaps as Jews they avoided the place altogether.

New Paphos (Nea Paphos) was 10 mi (16 km) farther along on a harbor on the southwest point of the island. This city was founded in the fourth century B.C., and it became the capital of Cyprus in the time of the Ptolemies, a position it retained until the fourth century of the Christian era when the capital was moved back to Salamis.

The ruins of New Paphos are mostly unexcavated and cover a large area, only part of which is occupied by the present village called Kato Paphos. The ancient city walls can still be traced, and the breakwaters of the ancient harbor are still there. In the city a large house of Dionysos with fine floor mosaics (probably third century A.D.) has been uncovered. Outside the city to the east there was a subterranean rock-hewn sanctuary of Apollo, and to the north there was a necropolis (the Tombs of the Kings) in which it was probably the Ptolemaic rulers of the island who were buried. Strabo tells how a great crowd of men and women would assemble at Paphos (i.e., New Paphos) and make an annual procession to Old Paphos, 60 stadia (7 mi [11 km]) away on the land road. Plainly this was on the occasion of a great yearly festival of Aphrodite.

As the capital of Cyprus New Paphos was the residence of the Roman proconsul. At the time when Barnabas and Saul came, the proconsul was Sergius Paulus, and a certain Magus, a Jewish false prophet named Bar-Jesus, was associated with him. It was here that Saul stepped forward as the leader of his small company and was the spokesman in the confrontation with the false prophet. Earlier in the Book of Acts he has been a Jew among Jews, and he has been called by his Jewish name, Saul. Now he stands before a high official of the Roman Empire as a citizen of that empire, and it is at this psychologically appropriate moment that the Book of Acts explains that he is "Saul, who is also called Paul" (13:9), and from this point on he is referred to by the latter name, which is his Roman name.

When Paul went on his second missionary journey Barnabas and John Mark, who was Barnabas's cousin (Col 4:10), returned to Cyprus (Ac 15:39). The apocryphal *Acts of Barnabus* (fifth–sixth century) relates that Barnabas found a certain Heracleides, who had formerly been with Paul at Kition, and ordained him bishop of Cyprus. Barnabas himself, it is said, was carrying a copy of the Gospel, which he had received from the apostle Matthew. On the island there was again a confrontation of the missionaries with Bar-Jesus. This time Bar-Jesus stirred up the Jews, and Barnabas was dragged to the hippodrome and burned to death, while John Mark went on to Alexandria.

In A.D. 478, tradition has it, Bishop Anthemius of Cyprus had a dream that led to his discovery of the Tomb of Barnabas, who was found still holding the Gospel of Matthew in his hand. Ten years later the Monastery of St. Barnabas was founded near Salamis. Because it owes its origin to Barnabas, the Orthodox Church of Cyprus claims the position of an independent branch of the Eastern Orthodox Church and elects its own archbishop.

CENTRAL ASIA MINOR

From Cyprus Paul and his party sailed to Perga in Pamphylia (where John left them and returned to Jerusalem), proceeded to Pisidian Antioch (where a persecution was stirred up against them), went on to Iconium (where an attempt was made to stone them), fled to Lystra and Derbe, cities of Lycaonia (where at Lystra Paul was stoned), and then went back

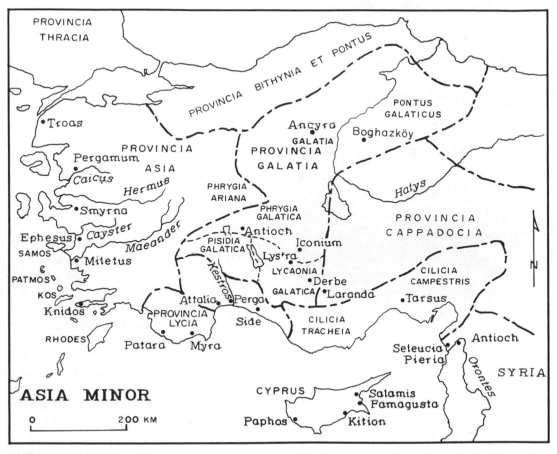

MAP 3.

the way they had come and sailed from Attalia for Antioch in Syria (Ac 13:13–14:26).

These cities and geographical regions were in what is now known as Asia Minor, the great peninsula that juts west some 500 mi (800 km) from the main mass of Asia between the Black Sea and the Mediterranean. The Romans gave the name of Asia to the province they established at the west end of the peninsula. The name Asia Minor was not used by the classical geographers, and it occurs first in Orosius in the fifth century A.D. (Irving Woodworth Raymond, *Seven Books of History Against the Pagans, The Apology of Paulus Orosius* [New York: Columbia University Press, 1936], p. 37). Another name for most of the peninsula, sometimes only for the part west of the Halys

River but sometimes for the whole area west of a line from the Gulf of Iskenderun to the Black Sea, is Anatolia (from the Greek ἀνατολή, "sunrise," i.e., eastern land), which occurs first in the literature of Constantine VII Porphyrogenitus in the tenth century. The main mass of the peninsula is a great plateau, 3,000–5,000 ft (915–1,525 m) above sea level, with low-lying coastland on the south side and deeply indented bays on the west.

As to the history of Asia Minor in general, some of the oldest known settlements and cities of the world have been discovered there. Especially notable is Catal Hüyük, a site 25 mi (40 km) south of modern Konya (ancient Iconium), where pottery and mural paintings are found dating from before 6000 B.C.[2] In the

FIGURE 14. Hittite God in the Rock Sanctuary (Thirteenth Century B.C.) at Yazilikaya at Boghazköy (Ancient Hattusas).

second millennium B.C. much of the area was in the possession of the Hittites, who had their main capital at Boghazköy (ancient Hattusas), with a remarkable rock sanctuary nearby at Yazilikaya. Then with the fall of the Hittite Empire about 1200 B.C., the Phrygians established themselves in much of northern and central Asia Minor. According to Greek tradition the Phrygians came from Thrace or Macedonia, and their language was Indo-European. In the first millennium the Assyrians, Babylonians, and Persians extended their conquests into Asia Minor, but then Alexander the Great pushed the Persians back, and he and his successors founded many Hellenistic cities. Of Alexander's successors it was chiefly the Seleucids who ruled in central Asia Minor. In the third century (beginning in 278 B.C.) a branch of the Indo-European tribe of the Celts, known in the area as Gauls or Galatians, invaded from the northwest and established themselves in the central highlands in the region of Ancyra (modern Ankara), and from them, that region was known as Galatia.

Then came the Romans. In the west in 133 B.C. the Hellenistic kingdom of Pergamum was bequeathed to the Romans by its last king, Attalus III, and the Romans organized the area as the province of Asia. Moving east in 121 B.C the Romans made Galatia a part of their empire. From 88 to 64 B.C. they had to fight the Pontic wars, in which their most formidable opponents were Mithradates VI of Pontus and his son-in-law Tigranes of Armenia. In 66 B.C. Pompey assumed command of all the Roman forces in the east and accomplished the final victory, and also cleared the eastern Mediterranean of the pirates that had infested its waters for a long while. For a time the Romans allowed the various local kings to rule but finally organized everything in Roman administered provinces, and they also proceeded to lay out a network of Roman roads.

In its later history Asia Minor belonged to the Byzantine Empire and was ruled from Constantinople. During this period the Persian king Chosroes II invaded (A.D. 616–626), and soon after, the Arabs entered Asia Minor and also besieged Constantinople (A.D. 668); for the next three centuries there was warfare between Byzantium and the Baghdad caliphs. In the eleventh and twelfth centuries came the Seljuk Turks, and there was also an invasion by the Mongols in the thirteenth century and another by Timur around A.D. 1400. In A.D. 1453 the Ottoman Turks captured Constantinople, and the history of Asia Minor became that of the Ottoman Empire until Turkey became a republic in 1923, with its capital at Ankara and Asia Minor constituting the largest part of the country.

Returning to the Roman period and to the central part of Asia Minor we are concerned with in connection with Paul, in 40 B.C. there were still three local kingdoms wth their capitals at Ancyra in Galatia proper, at Antioch in Pisidia, and at Iconium, which was variously spoken of as being in Phrygia or in Lycaonia. In 37/36 B.C. the Romans gave Galatia and Lycaonia to Amyntas, king of Galatia and Pisidia, and he added Pamphylia in the west and Cilicia in the east to his kingdom. Then, when Amyntas was killed in 25 B.C. while on an expedition against the

FIGURE 15. Colossal Head of Antiochos I of Commagene (69–34 B.C.), on the West Terrace at Nemrud Dagh.

tribes of the mountains of Pisidia, the Romans created the province of Galatia. Broadly speaking, the Roman province of Galatia was bounded by the mountains of Paphlagonia on the north, the Taurus Mountains on the south, the province of Asia on the west, and the province of Cappadocia on the east.

Cappadocia

Western Asia Minor and the province of Asia will be dealt with again later. As for Cappadocia, this region extended eastward to the upper Euphrates and abutted on the small but remarkable kingdom of Commagene to the southeast. The capital of Cappadocia was Caesarea (Mazaca), the modern Kayseri, at the northern foot of Mt. Argeus, now Erciyas Dagi, a volcanic mountain of 13,000 ft (3,960 m) in elevation. To the west of Erciyas Dagi and notably in the region of the present towns of Ürgüp and Goreme the ancient volcano laid down a vast plateau of tuff or tufa, in which intense erosion has resulted in a fantastic landscape of cones, towers, and other strange formations.

Visitors from Cappadocia were in Jerusalem at Pentecost (Ac 2:9), Peter addressed converts of the Dispersion in Cappadocia (I Pet 1:1), Jerome supposed that Peter preached in Cappadocia, and Christianity was no doubt established there early. Particularly in the Ürgüp/Goreme region, where the soft rock was easy to hollow out into caves and cells, hermits and monks probably settled from very early times. From the time of the Arab invasions in the seventh and eighth centuries and onward, underground dwellings and even whole cities provided refuge. Churches were also cut out in the rock, most often with a single vaulted nave and apse. At least from the eighth century these churches were decorated with geometrical designs and painted or carved crosses; from the ninth century and the

FIGURE 16. Rock Cone and Cell in Uchisar, Cappadocia.

restitution of icons there are many wall paintings of saints and holy scenes.[3] Cappadocia was also notable as the place where Saint Gregory the Illuminator (A.D. 240–322) was instructed in the Christian faith, to which he later won his own Armenian nation at the end of the third century. Likewise the famous fourth-century theologians Basil of Caesarea, his brother Gregory of Nyssa, and his friend Gregory of Nazianzus were all Cappadocians.

Cities of Galatia

Within the province of Galatia there were a number of regions (Latin *regiones*, Greek Χῶραι), and it was customary to designate a region (*regio*, Χῶρα) after the province of which it was a part. Thus the province of Galatia included the region of Galatia proper in the north and the regions of "Galatian" Pisidia, Phrygia, and Lycaonia in the south. In terms of these regions, Antioch was in the border zone of Phrygia, Pisidia, and Lycaonia; Strabo (XII 6, 4; 8, 14) speaks of it as a Phrygian city "toward Pisidia," and Ac 13:14 simply calls it Pisidian Antioch. Likewise Iconium was in the border zone between Phrygia and Lycaonia, with the mountains of Phrygia behind it to the west and the broad plain of Lycaonia before it to the south and east. Geographically, therefore, Iconium could be spoken of as being in Lycaonia—as Cicero does in a passage in *Letters to His Friends* (XV 4, 2) when he tells how he ordered one of his officers "to pitch his camp at Iconium in Lycaonia." Administratively, however, Iconium appears to have belonged to Galatian Phrygia, for in his *Anabasis* (I 2, 19) Xenophon relates that Cyrus came "to Iconium, the last city of Phrygia; thence he pursued his route through Lycaonia" and in the *Acts of Justin Martyr*, when Justin and several other Christians were tried in Rome (A.D. 165) one of them, a slave named Hierax, when asked who his parents were replied, "My earthly parents are dead; and I have been brought here (a slave) torn away from Iconium of Phrygia." Lystra and

FIGURE 17. Wall Painting of St. George in Cave Church in Goreme Valley, Cappadocia.

Derbe were both in the region of Lycaonia. In addition to the regions noted, Pamphylia on the south coast, between Cilicia to the east and Lycia to the west, was at times included in the province of Galatia. In A.D. 43 Pamphylia was combined with Lycia (Dio Cassius LX 17, 3), but afterward it was again joined with Galatia.[4]

The cities of Pisidian Antioch, Iconium, Lystra, and Derbe, in which Paul and Barnabas won believers on the first missionary journey, were therefore in the Roman province of Galatia. It is probable that when Paul wrote to "the churches of Galatia" (Gal 1:2) he had the Roman province in mind and was addressing the Christians in those same cities.

As to what Roman administration meant and what the people were like, the Romans evidently knew how to adapt their rule to the people of the area. Although Latin and Greek became the languages of government and of literature, the mass of the people still spoke their native languages—Phrygian, Galatian, and Lycaonian. The people also continued to believe in their own gods, and even if they were identified with the gods of Greece and Rome and called by Greek or Roman names, they still maintained much of the character of the Asiatic deities. Even when Christianity conquered the land, Anatolia remained the home of old types of religion, which expressed themselves in emotional and enthusiastic movements that were considered heresies by the orthodox church.[5]

In Pamphylia there were two cities connected with Paul, namely, Attalia and Perga. Attalia was the main port, but it is not mentioned in Acts until Paul and Barnabas go back there to get a ship for the return to Antioch (Ac 14:25). The city was founded by and named after Attalus III (159–138 B.C.), one of the three kings of Pergamum of that name. Attalia was the main point of entrance for those coming from Syria and Egypt and continuing into the interior of Asia Minor. Called Satalia in the Middle Ages and Adalia in Ottoman times, it is now Antalya and still possesses a good harbor.

The location of the city is on a flat limestone terrace 120 ft (37 m) above the seashore, to which the cliffs rise steeply. From the harbor, stairs lead up to the town, but they are Venetian and were not used by Paul; another approach through a cutting in the rock could be from his time. The town wall begins on the left and right sides of the harbor and encloses the city. Often restored, parts of the wall date from Hellenistic, Roman, Byzantine, Seljuk, and more recent times. On the south side the harbor is dominated by the Tower of Hidirlik, which was built in the second century A.D. and may have supported a lighthouse. On the east side of the city the Gate of Hadrian, built in honor of his visit in A.D. 130, has three arches and carved decorations. In the south part of the city the Kesik Minaret is a truncated minaret built on the remnants of an ancient Roman temple, which was converted into a Christian basilica in the Byzantine period and then into a mosque in the time of the Seljuks. In the north part of the city a Byzantine church was transformed into a mosque, and it is surmounted by a fluted minaret of the thirteenth century. A beautiful new museum in Antalya contains numerous Roman sculptures, including some finds from Perga.

From Attalia the Roman road ran 11 mi (18 km) northeastward to Perga and on to Side on the coast, the latter city being 40 mi (65 km) east of Attalia. If Paul landed at Attalia he presumably went along this road to Perga, and he presumably went back the same way when he returned to Attalia. In the case of his initial landing, however, Acts does not mention Attalia, and Paul may have gone to Perga more directly. In fact the navigable River Kestros flowed only 5 mi (8 km) to the east of Perga, and Paul might have sailed up the river to a port not far from the city. Strabo (XIV 4, 2) indicates the possibility of reaching Perga in such a manner when he describes Pamphylia and the city of Attalia and writes, "Then one

FIGURE 18. Portrait Statue of the Emperor Hadrian (A.D. 117–138), from Perga, in the Archaeological Museum in Antalya.

FIGURE 19. The Gate of Hadrian in Antalya.

comes to the Kestros river; and, sailing up this river, one comes to Perga, a city; and near Perga, on a lofty site, to the temple of Artemis Pergaia, where a general festival is celebrated every year."

Perga was believed by its inhabitants to have been founded by Greek heroes after the Trojan War. Two of these, named Mopsos and Kalchas, are mentioned as founders in inscriptions on statue bases found in the gateway of the older city. In 333 B.C. Alexander the Great passed through the city twice. From the second century B.C. there are coins of Perga that depict the cult statue of Artemis Pergaia standing in a temple, doubtless the temple spoken of by Strabo. In 80/79 B.C. this temple was plundered of its treasures by Verres, the same Roman official who was later prosecuted by Cicero for his misgovernment of Sicily. In general, however, Perga prospered in the Roman period, especially in the first three centuries of the present era.

Today the ruins of Perga are near the village of Murtana, and they have been undergoing excavation by Turkish archeologists since 1967. As one approaches Perga from the south and the sea, there is a hill on the left known as Koca Belen, built into which is a Greco-Roman theater with seats for 15,000 spectators. The stage building erected in the second century A.D. still stands to a considerable height, has two tiers and is richly

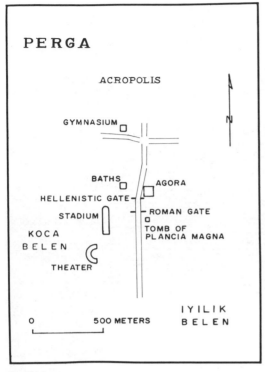

PERGA

ACROPOLIS

GYMNASIUM

BATHS

AGORA

HELLENISTIC GATE

STADIUM

ROMAN GATE

KOCA
BELEN

TOMB OF
PLANCIA MAGNA

THEATER

IYILIK
BELEN

0   500 METERS

PLAN 8.

FIGURE 20. Portrait Statue of Plancia Magna, from Perga, in the Archaeological Museum in Antalya.

decorated with reliefs representing mythological scenes and featuring Dionysos and the local river god, Kestros. In the late Roman period, like many other theaters of the ancient world, this theater was used for gladiatorial shows and fights with wild beasts, and an extra parapet was built onto the lower seats to protect the spectators. Some 330 ft (100 m) ahead on the right is a stadium, one of the best preserved of antiquity, second only to the stadium of Aphrodisias. The date of the stadium at Perga is probably the second century A.D., and the stadium could accommodate 12,000 spectators. Farther to the right and just outside the city wall is the Tomb of Plancia Magna (second century A.D.), a rich benefactress of the city and a priestess of Artemis.

The city is entered through a Roman gate of the fourth century A.D., and a little farther along is a Hellenistic gate, a large horseshoe-shaped courtyard flanked by two large round towers. The walls of the Hellenistic structure

FIGURE 21. Roman Theater at Aspendos (Modern Belkis) Between Perga and Side. Built, according to inscriptions, by the architect Zenon in the middle or latter half of the second century A.D., the theater could seat 20,000 spectators. It is one of the best-preserved ancient buildings in all Asia Minor.

were faced with marble and contained niches and statues. The courtyard was rebuilt in the second century A.D. by Plancia Magna, and further building was done by Septimius Severus (A.D. 193–211). The city wall on the south side dates from the fourth century A.D., but on the east and west sides the city wall is of Hellenistic date and is well preserved, with some of the towers on the east side still almost their original height.

Inside the Hellenistic gate the main streets of the city run north and south and east and west, and they were colonnaded. The agora was a square, 215 ft (65 m) on each side, surrounded by colonnades and lined with shops and rooms. To the west of the main north-south street are the ruins of Roman baths, and north of the main east-west street there is a gymnasium (palaestra, literally a wrestling

place) that was dedicated to the emperor Claudius (A.D. 41–54) by a certain C. Julius Cornutus and his wife and children. To the northwest, outside the city wall, is a street lined with tombs. To the north a flat hill was the acropolis of the city and probably the site of the original colony. At the foot of the acropolis was a handsome fountain (nymphaeum, literally a place of the nymphs), and it was adorned with a reclining statue of Kestros, the god of the river. On the acropolis the only ruins to be seen are Byzantine, and there are also ruins of two Byzantine churches in the main part of the ancient city and of one Byzantine church on a hill, southeast of the city, called Iyilik Belen. The famous Temple of Artemis Pergaia has not been located, but it may be guessed that it was on either the acropolis hill or the Iyilik Belen. Statues and

FIGURE 22. Relief Sculpture of a Chariot Driver, in the Side Museum.

inscriptions show that Aphrodite, Apollo, Hermes, Heracles, and other Greek deities were also worshiped.

With much of the Hellenistic wall still standing and with such buildings still to be seen as the Greco-Roman theater and the gymnasium—the latter dedicated to the very emperor who was reigning when Paul must have gone to Perga—Perga is one of the most impressive of the sites (second only to Ephesus) in which to see something of a Pauline city of Asia Minor as it was in the time of the apostle.[6]

The only thing we are told in the Book of Acts about Paul and his party with respect to Perga is that at that point John Mark left and went back to Jerusalem (Ac 13:13). Why he left we are not told and can only surmise. On Cyprus, Barnabas, who was John Mark's cousin (Col 4:10), appeared to be the leader of the group, but at Paphos, in the Roman world,

Paul as a Roman citizen took the lead; perhaps John Mark did not approve of his relative's apparent relegation to second place. Perhaps, too, going to Perga and proposing to go on into inner Asia Minor represented a change and an extension of the original plans, and the way ahead was also no doubt difficult and even dangerous. The mountains were forbidding, Alexander the Great had combated brigands in the area, and Augustus had found it necessary to establish a series of military posts, including posts at Antioch and Lystra. Perhaps it was in the region lying ahead of them now that Paul would experience some of the "danger from robbers," of which he speaks in II Cor 11:26. There is yet another possible explanation. The coastal region near Perga was low and damp and was known at that time for its unhealthful climate, malaria being particularly prevalent. Later Paul wrote to the Galatians (4:13), "You know it was because of a bodily

FIGURE 23. Relief Sculpture at the Greco-Roman Theater at Perga, Showing (Left to Right) Pan, Dionysos, and a Maenad (Priestess or Votary of Dionysos).

ailment that I preached the gospel to you at first," and on the basis of this statement it is possible to surmise that it was illness contracted in the lowlands that led Paul to move on up into the higher country inland (although the reference to "eyes" in 4:15 is difficult to fit with this theory). At any rate John Mark went back from Perga, and Paul and Barnabas went on to Antioch.

From Perga to Pisidian Antioch three routes would appear to have been possible. One Roman road swung quite far to the west, and it would probably not have been taken. A second way might have been to go more or less straight north, up the Kestros River and past Egridir Lake, on the east side of which there is a chapel dedicated to St. Paul. Perhaps most likely would have been a route along the Roman road to Side and then along another Roman road that went north, passing Lake Beysehir on the east side. At all events Paul

and Barnabas must have climbed through the mountains to the inner plateau of Asia Minor, 3,000 ft (915 m) and more in elevation, and gone a distance of at least 80 mi (130 km) from Perga, a journey of perhaps six days' duration, considering the terrain.

Like Antioch of Syria, Pisidian Antioch was founded by Seleucus I Nicator (312–281 B.C.) and named in the same fashion as the Syrian city. The Romans made it a free city in 189 B.C. and a Roman colony in the Roman province of Galatia in 25 B.C. The population was Phrygian, Greek, Jewish, and Roman. The chief god was Men, a fact mentioned by Strabo and confirmed by coins and inscriptions. Men was evidently a complex deity, identified by the Greeks with Dionysos, Apollo, and Asklepios and therefore associated with wine, with prophecy, and with healing. Probably the Phrygian goddess Cybele was also an important object of worship.

The ruins of this ancient Antioch are about 1 mi (1.6 km) from the modern village called Yalvaş. The site extends over a number of hills, about 3,500–3,800 ft (1,067–1,158 m) above sea level, near the Anthios River, and the Sultan Dagh mountain range rises to the east and north. An aqueduct brought water from those mountains and is still preserved to the north of the city. At the northwest corner of the site a portion of the city wall still exists. In the city there were two forums, one named for Augustus and one for Tiberius, and it is possible to trace the course of the main street and to recognize the theater. A semicircular rock-cutting with a square mass of stone in the center may be the remains of the Temple of Men, and the ruins of a Byzantine church are also to be seen. Smaller monuments and coins can be seen in several different museums, including the museum at Yalvaş.

Iconium, where Paul and Barnabas went from Pisidian Antioch, is the modern Konya, the capital of the province of Konya in south central Turkey, 170 mi (275 km) south of Ankara; from Antioch it was a journey of 80 mi (130 km) to the southeast. The site is in an oasis at an elevation of 3,770 ft (1,150 m) on the edge of a large plain, the Orondian Mountains and the nearby twin conical peaks of St. Philip and St. Thecla rise to the west, and the Kara Dagh (Black Mountain) rises 50 mi (80 km) to the southeast. There was certainly settlement in the region at a very early time, for Çatal Hüyük, dating from before 6000 B.C., is only 25 mi (40 km) to the southeast.

In Greek mythology Iconium figures as the place where Perseus cut off the head of Medusa. In its later history Iconium was first under the rule of Seleucid and Pergamene kings and then, in 25 B.C., incorporated into the Roman Empire and the Roman province of Galatia. Within the province it was in the region of Phrygia, and the inhabitants spoke the Phrygian language and thought of themselves as Phrygians. Under Claudius (A.D. 41–54) the city was given the honorary name of Claudiconium, and under Hadrian (117–138) it was made a Roman colony. Of the Roman city there remain only pieces of sculpture and inscriptions built into the Turkish walls and, in the Konya Museum, antiquities from the whole region, including fine sarcophagi and grave stelas of the third century A.D. In the thirteenth century Iconium was the home of Maulana Jalal-uddin Rumi (1207–1273), one of the greatest mystics of Islam and the founder of the order of the whirling dervishes.

In Christian tradition Iconium was the chief setting for the events narrated in the apocryphal *Acts of Paul and Thecla*. According to that work, when Paul goes to Iconium his fame has preceded him, and Onesiphorus goes out to meet him. The latter has never seen Paul, but Titus has given him a description and he recognizes the apostle when he sees "a man small of stature, with a bald head and crooked legs, in a good state of body, with eyebrows meeting and nose somewhat hooked, full of friendliness; for now he appeared like a man, and now he had the face of an angel." Paul preaches in the house of Onesiphorus (cf. II Tim 1:16; 4:19), and a young woman named Thecla listens from a nearby window. Under the influence of what she hears Thecla renounces the betrothal that her parents have arranged, and persecutions ensue both for her and for Paul. After various experiences and miraculous deliverances Thecla withdraws to Seleucia in Cilicia, where she enlightens many with the Word of God and finally dies in peace. At one point in his career (about A.D. 375), Gregory of Nazianzus devoted himself to the contemplative life in the same city of Seleucia, and he speaks in his writings (*Oration* XXI; *Poemata historica* I 11) of Seleucia already being a place of pilgrimage in honor of Thecla. This Seleucia was founded by Seleucus I Nicator at the beginning of the third century, and it lay on the bank of the Kalykadnos River near the sea. It is the modern Silifke, and its Roman ruins include a theater, a temple, and a large necropolis. About 0.6 mi (1 km) south of Silifke is the Christian site called Meryemlik where there is a Church of St. Thecla dating from the fifth century A.D. Underneath that church the apse of an earlier church has been found, and beneath that is the cave in which Thecla lived.[7]

From Iconium to Lystra was a distance of about 25 mi (40 km) on the Roman road, which led on yet further to Derbe and to the Cilician Gates. In terms of the administrative regions within the province of Galatia, when Paul and Barnabas proceeded from Iconium to Lystra, they crossed the frontier between Phrygia and Lycaonia.[8] The site of Lystra is now a tell known as Zordula Hüyük, north of the present town of Hatunsaray, and it was identified positively in 1885 when an altar was found, still in place, with a Latin inscription that gave the name of the city in its Roman form as Lustra (LVSTRA) and indicated that it was a Roman colony.

Although the tell has not been excavated, surface finds suggest settlement in the third and second millenniums B.C. In due time the city must have been under Persian and Hellenistic rule, and Augustus made it a Roman colony (Julia Felix Gemina Lustra) around 6 B.C. as a stronghold against the dangerous mountain tribes of the area. Thus Roman settlers and military forces were there, along with the native Lycaonian inhabitants. From the account in Ac 14:8–11 of the experiences of Paul and Barnabas in Lystra, we learn that the native Lycaonian language was still being spoken there and that there was a Temple of Zeus in front of the city. Timothy, the good friend and associate of Paul, was from Lystra (Ac 16:1), and he may well have been won to the Christian faith by Paul during Paul's first visit to Lystra.

Derbe, the last of the four cities in the province of Galatia that Paul and Barnabas visited at this time, lay yet farther to the south and east, and it is identified with Devri Sehri, which is 2.5 mi (4 km) south-southeast of Kerti Hüyük (the latter is about 15 mi [24 km] west and north of the Roman city of Laranda, which is now called by the name of the Seljuk prince Karaman). This identification rests upon a discovery in 1956 of an inscription at Kerti Hüyük, in which the council and people of Derbe made a dedication to Antoninus Pius in A.D. 157, and on the discovery in 1958 of an epitaph, said to have come from Devri Sehri, that names a certain Bishop Michael of Derbe.[9] This location of Derbe is more than a day's journey from Lystra, but when Ac 14:20 states that Paul and Barnabas went on from Lystra "on the next day" and proceeded to Derbe, it probably only means that they started out on the next day to go on the journey to Derbe.

At Kerti Hüyük and Devri Sehri there is evidence of settlement in the Iron Age and in the Hellenistic and Roman periods, but not much is known of the history of Derbe, save that Cicero and Strabo mention a chieftain by the name of Antipater who ruled a small kingdom that included Derbe, Lystra, and Laranda. Paul and Barnabas made many disciples there (Ac 14:21), and Gaius, who was Paul's companion on a later journey (Ac 20:4), was from Derbe.

From Derbe a relatively direct route would have been to travel to Tarsus through the Cilician Gates, some 150 mi (240 km) distant, and on to Syrian Antioch, but Derbe was the last city in the Roman province of Galatia, and at that point, Paul and Barnabas went back through the same province to the cities previously visited in order to strengthen "the souls of the disciples" (Ac 14:22). On his second missionary journey Paul went through the same area again, and the record of that trip in Ac 16 mentions Derbe, Lystra, and Iconium. At that time Timothy, who lived at Lystra, went on with Paul. Paul also passed "through the region of Galatia and Phrygia" on his third missionary journey (Ac 18:23).

5
SECOND MISSIONARY JOURNEY
(A.D. 49–51)

On his second missionary journey Paul, now with Silas as his companion (Ac 15:40) and with Timothy joining them at Lystra (Ac 16:3), went all the way through Asia Minor to Troas and then crossed to Macedonia. The famous city of Troy, scene of the Trojan War— dated by Eratosthenes in 1184 or 1194 B.C. — and still a large and prosperous town in Hellenistic-Roman times (Troy IX in terms of the archeological strata), was located at the western end of the Hellespont (the straits now known as the Dardanelles), and from Troy the surrounding district was known as the Troad. In this district, some 10 mi (16 km) south of Troy, Antigonus founded a city and Lysimachus refounded it and gave it the name of Alexandria Troas, the latter part of the name referring to the area and serving to distinguish the city from other Alexandrias. Soon, however, it was most simply designated as Troas (Ac 16:8).

Augustus made Troas a Roman colony, and it was an important seaport for travel from the northwestern part of the Roman province of Asia to Macedonia and the west. The site is now deserted, but the ruins of a theater, an aqueduct, and city walls 6 mi (10 km) in circumference give some idea of the prosperity and magnitude of the ancient city.

Between Troas and Macedonia Paul's ship made an overnight stop at Samothrace (Ac 16:11). This is a mountainous island that offers no harbor, only an anchorage for ships. From the highest peak (5,200 ft [1,586 m]) a view is possible both back to the Troad and ahead to the mainland of Macedonia. A town named Samothrace was on the north side of the island, and adjacent to it was a famous sanctuary of the Great Gods, who were worshiped in the Samothracian mysteries and were the special patrons of persons at sea. The deities included a Great Mother and her spouse, and attendant demons called the Kabeiroi. Among those who were initiated into these mysteries were Philip II of Macedonia and his wife Olympias. Of the many archeological finds from Samothrace, the most famous is the Winged Victory, erected by Demetrius Poliorcetes of Macedonia to celebrate a naval victory over the Egyptians in 306 B.C.

MACEDONIA

Geographically Macedonia consists of a relatively narrow plain on the northwestern border of the Aegean and rough hill country in the interior. As early as the Paleolithic and Neolithic ages there are evidences of human life in the region, and in historic times the people of Macedonia were originally Greeks, probably mixed with Illyrian and Thracian elements. The Greeks in the south, however, regarded the Macedonians as barbarians, with only a veneer of Hellenism and speaking a dialect of the true Greek language. In the inland valleys there were various tribes, each under its own chief, while on the long plain below there

PROVINCIA
MACEDONIA
Pella
Thessalonica
Beroea
Amphipolis
Philippi
Neapolis
THASOS
SAMOTHRACE
THESSALIA
Troas
PROVINCIA
ACHAIA
EUBOEA
Delphi
BOEOTIA
ATTICA
Athens
Piraeus
Corinth
Mycenae
Epidauros
C. SOUNION
Ephesus
PELOPONNESOS
PATMOS
C. MALEA
CRETE
Knossos
MT. IDA
Fair Havens
CLAUDA
Gortyn
Phaistos

GREECE
0   100 KM

MAP 4.

was a king to whom they owed allegiance but
against whom they were often in revolt. The
kingship prevailed, however, and in contrast
with the Greeks in the south who thought of
themselves primarily as citizens of a given city,
the Macedonians considered themselves to be
one people, and they formed, it has been said,

the first nation in European history.[1]

The early capital of Macedonia was at Aigai
(Aegae), and Pliny (*Nat. Hist.* IV 10, 33) tells us
that it was the customary burial place of the
Macedonian kings. It was previously thought
that Aigai could be identified with the modern
Edessa (55 mi [88 km] west of modern Thes-

MAP 5.

saloniki), but Pliny (*Nat. Hist.* IV 10, 33, and VI 39, 216), Plutarch (*Life of Pyrrhus* x 2; XII 6; and XXVI 6), and Ptolemy (*Geography* III 13, 39, and Map x of Europe) all name Aigai and Edessa separately and show that they were not the same. Other ancient references and recent excavations combine to make it probable that Aigai was in the vicinity of the two closely related villages of Palatitsia and Vergina, 60 mi (94 km) southwest of Thessaloniki and 7 mi (11 km) southeast of Verria or Veroia (New Testament Beroea).[2]

At Palatitsia in the 1850s the French archeologist Léon Heuzey found the ruins of a large colonnaded building, which is known as the Palace of Palatitsia and is dated in the third century B.C., probably in the reign of Antigonos II Gonatas (278–240 B.C.). Also of third-century date is a remarkable Mace-

donian tomb in the form of a temple with Ionic columns on the facade and a sphinx-adorned marble throne in the interior. Later work, by Konstantine A. Rhomaios and Manolis Andronicos of the University of Thessaloniki, on the palace and in a vast nearby necropolis of more than 200 graves dating from 1000 to 600 B.C. led to interest in a very large mound close to Vergina. Within the large mound, in 1976 and later, Professor Andronicos found a smaller mound and, in that, uncovered two ancient tombs. The smaller of the two tombs had been broken into and looted in antiquity, but some wall paintings were still preserved, including one of Pluto carrying off Persephone to the under-world. The large tomb consisted of a small antechamber and a main barrel-vaulted chamber, and this tomb was intact, never having been broken into before. In it were such rich objects of gold and silver as to make it probable that it was a royal tomb, probably the first unplundered tomb of ancient Macedonian royalty ever found. The date appears to be in the third quarter of the fourth century B.C., and although there are no inscriptions to provide indisputable evidence, the excavator believes that the burial remains found in two golden caskets are none other than those of Philip II of Macedonia (359–336 B.C.) who was assassinated at Aigai, and of his last wife, Cleopatra. The splendid objects from the tomb are now in the beautiful Thessaloniki Museum.

Although the old capital of Aigai thus continued to be the royal burial place for a long time, King Archelaus (413–399) left Aigai in 413 B.C. and moved the capital to Pella, where he built a fine palace for himself. He also attracted famous artists and writers to Pella.

The painter Zeuxis came to decorate the palace, and the poet Timotheus and the dramatist Euripides also came. Thus Hellenic civilization was strongly fostered in Macedonia, and in the slightly later reign of Amyntas III (390–369 B.C.) the unification of Macedonia around this later capital was much advanced. It was at Pella that Philip II, son of Amyntas III and himself king of Macedonia, and Philip II's son, Alexander the Great (born 356, died 323), were born.

The site of Pella is 24 mi (38 km) west of Thessaloniki, in the vicinity of two villages still called Palaia Pella and Nea Pella. Stephanos of Byzantium (Antonius Westermann, ed., *Stephani Byzantii* ΕΘΝΙΚΩΝ *quae supersunt* [Leipzig: Teubner, 1839], p. 229) says that Pella of Macedonia was formerly called Bounomos (literally, "grazed by cattle" and therefore "pasture" or "meadow"), and Livy (XLIV 46, 4–8) describes Pella as consisting of a city defended

FIGURE 24. Floor Mosaic at Pella Showing Alexander and Krateros on a Deer Hunt.

FIGURE 25. Marble Head of Alexander the Great Recovered from the Sea at Abukir, in the Greco-Roman Museum in Alexandria.

by an enclosing wall and a fortress, where the kings kept their treasure, on the island of Phakos overlooking the surrounding marshes. Excavations have revealed a prehistoric settlement on Phakos and remains of the Classical and Hellenistic periods over the whole area between the island and Palaia Pella and Nea Pella. The acropolis has been identified on twin hills and also the royal treasury. In the central part of the town, north of the Thessaloniki-Edessa road, there were blocks of buildings and paved streets 33 ft (10 m) wide. Reservoirs with immense jars served for the storage of water, and water pipes and drains are still extant. At least some of the buildings had two stories and the ground floors of the large houses were paved with mosaics made of river pebbles. Among the striking mosaic pictures that have been recovered, one shows Dionysos riding on a panther, and another depicts a lion hunt—perhaps the hunt near Susa in which Alexander was saved by his friend Krateros. The buildings with the mosaic floors date around the end of the fourth cen-

tury or the beginning of the third century B.C. Architectural fragments include tiles stamped with the name of Pella; thus the identification of the site is positive.

It was Philip II who for the first time united Macedonia and Greece and proposed a Panhellenic war against the Persians, an enterprise that was interrupted by his murder but was taken up again by his son. The amazing accomplishments of the latter, Alexander the Great, carried the Greek language and culture to the edge of India, established the vision of the οἰκουμένη, the whole inhabited world as a unity, and introduced the Hellenistic Age in which that vision was at least partially fulfilled.

After Alexander, Macedonia was heavily involved in the struggles of his successors, and prominent among them was Cassander (died 298/297), who was the founder of Thessalonica. Eventually Antigonos II Gonatas (278-240) mastered almost all of what had once been Philip's Macedonia and ruled as king—a contemporary of Antiochus I Soter (281-261) of the Seleucid kingdom and of Ptolemy II Philadelphus (285-246) of Egypt. His rule was continued by the Antigonid line (278-168) until the coming of the Romans.

The conquest of Macedonia by the Romans was consummated in the Battle of Pydna (on the coast south of Thessalonica) in 168 B.C. They divided the land into four districts (167 B.C.): the first was between the Nestos and Strymon rivers with Amphipolis as the capital; the second, from the Strymon to the Axios River with Thessalonica as the capital; the third, from the Axios to the Peneios River with Pella as the capital; and the fourth extending from the Peneios to the borders of Illyria and Epirus with Pelagonia as the capital. In 148 B.C. the whole of Macedonia was made a Roman province, ruled by a proconsul with his seat of administration at Thessalonica.

Following routes that for the most part had already been in existence for centuries, the Romans constructed across Macedonia from west to east the famous military and commercial road, the Via Egnatia. It is mentioned

(*Histories* xxiv 12) by Polybius (who died around 125 B.C.) and is described (vii 7, 4) by Strabo (c. 63 B.C.—after A.D. 21) as being marked by Roman milestones from Apollonia on the west coast to Kypsela beyond the Hebros River (now the Maritza, opposite Samothrace) in Thrace, a distance of 535 Roman miles (493 English mi [793 km]). Actually there were two beginning points on the Adriatic, namely, from Dyrrachium (Durazzo) as well as from Apollonia, and the two roads converged at Clodiana and then went on through Edessa and Pella to reach the sea at Thessalonica. From there the road continued through another Apollonia (of Ac 17:1) to Amphipolis, Philippi, and Neapolis, and with the full conquest of Thrace in A.D. 46, the highway was carried on to Byzantium.

From Neapolis to Philippi, Amphipolis, Apollonia, and Thessalonica the apostle Paul must have traveled on the Via Egnatia, and it was to Christian communities that he founded in two of those cities (Philippi and Thessalonica) that he later wrote letters that are a part of the New Testament. Thus it was in Macedonia, as well as in Rome, that Christianity first arose in Europe.

In about A.D. 300 the Roman ruler Galerius (named Caesar in 293, emperor 305–311) settled in Thessalonica. In 303, largely at the instigation of Galerius, he and the emperor Diocletian initiated a general persecution of Christianity, the longest and most severe of the attacks upon the faith. Diocletian retired from office soon afterward, but Galerius as emperor continued the violence, chiefly in the eastern provinces, until on his deathbed in 311 he issued an edict of toleration.

In 313 the emperor Constantine and his eastern colleague Licinius (who succeeded Galerius in 311) issued the Edict of Milan, which granted Christianity the same full legal standing as all other religions in the empire. After defeating and executing Licinius (324) Constantine, as the sole ruler, lived almost continuously in the East and in 330 officially founded at the former Byzantium the New Rome (Constantinople), thus transferring the center of the empire from Latin to Greek territory. With Theodosius I the Great (379–395) the religious and political trends were confirmed. He outlawed the public and private practice of paganism, making Christianity henceforth the only legal religion of the empire (392), and after him the division of the empire into separate eastern and western parts was permanent (395). In less than one hundred years the West fell to the barbarians (476), but the East continued as the Byzantine Empire, held together by the Greek language and the Orthodox Christian faith.

In the earlier Byzantine period, from the fifth to the seventh centuries, there were invasions of Goths, Huns, Avars, Bulgars, Slavs, and Neo-Persians. Justinian I the Great (527–565), however, expanded the boundaries of the empire from Spain and North Africa to deep into Asia, and Heraclius (610–642) succeeded in repelling the Persians, although it was in his reign that the Hegira of Muhammad took place (622), the Prophet whose followers, first Arabs and later Turks, were to become the greatest danger to and eventually the overthrowers of the empire.

In the later Byzantine period, from the eighth to the fifteenth centuries, there was controversy in the church over the worship of images (726–843), conversion of the Slavs by Constantine (Cyril) and Methodius of Thessalonica (862), conversion of the Bulgars soon afterward (864), and final schism between the Church of Constantinople and the Church of Rome (1054). In this period the typical Byzantine architectural church form evolved, namely, the cruciform domed church, in which the dome, symbolizing the boundlessness of the universe, is combined with the shape of the cross of Christ. The mosaic decoration of churches also reached its height in this period, to be succeeded in less prosperous times by painted decorations. In 1204 the Crusaders of the Fourth Crusade conquered Constantinople and founded several small states; thus there was now for a time a Latin empire of Constantinople and a Latin kingdom of Thessalonica. In turn the emperor

FIGURE 26. Theodosius I the Great (A.D. 379–395) with His Wife and Two Sons, Arcadius and Honorius, on the Base Supporting the Obelisk of Thutmose III, Brought to Constantinople in A.D. 390.

Michael VIII Palaeologos (1258–1282) reconquered Constantinople and reestablished Byzantine rule, but in less than 200 years this rule was finally ended by the Ottoman Turks.

Shortly after the middle of the fourteenth century the Ottoman Turks pressed on from Asia Minor into Europe, and they soon surrounded the chief centers of the Byzantine Empire. They took Thessalonica in 1387, a second time in 1391, and finally in 1430. In 1453 they attacked Constantinople. On Tuesday May 29 of that year, Constantine XI (1449–1453) died fighting on the ramparts, the Turkish sultan Muhammad II was the victor, and the Byzantine Empire ceased to exist.

In the Byzantine Empire Macedonia remained an important province, and under favorable circumstances, the chief cities were filled with fine church buildings. In the first period of Turkish rule there was an economic, intellectual, and artistic decline, and most of the churches were made into mosques. Yet the older monasteries of Mt. Athos and the newer ones of Meteora provided refuge, the Orthodox clergy continued to function, and the majority of the population remained Christian. In the second period of Turkish rule, from the eighteenth century on, there was a Greek renaissance. The Greek War of Independence from the Turks took place in 1821, and in 1912 Bulgarian, Serbian, and Greek armies combined to drive the Turks out of Macedonia. Then the onetime mosques were restored as churches. Afterward the allies quarreled among themselves, and in 1913 Macedonia was divided among Bulgaria, Serbia (now Yugoslavia), and Greece—the distribution of territory that, in spite of many more struggles, still obtains.

FIGURE 27. The Church of St. Paul at Kavalla (Ancient Neapolis), Marking the Spot Where Paul Supposedly Stepped Ashore.

Neapolis

When the apostle Paul went to Macedonia he landed at Neapolis (Ac 16:11). Neapolis had been founded in the seventh century B.C. as a colony of the offshore island of Thasos. The location was strategic because it provided a harbor adjacent to the ancient coast road, which joined Asia and Europe and was eventually the route of the Via Egnatia. Around 350 B.C. Philip II of Macedonia took Neapolis and used it as a harbor for Philippi and for the road that led to the gold mines of Mt. Pangaion, which were so important to his own success. In 42 B.C. a famous battle was fought at Philippi between Antony and Octavian and Brutus and Cassius, and on that occasion Brutus and Cassius used the harbor at Neapolis as their base. In the Byzantine period Neapolis was called Christoupolis, and

the modern name Kavalla probably comes from the fact that the Turks used it as a station on their post road and called it *cavallo*, a vulgarization of the Latin word for horse.

Kavalla lies in a natural amphitheater of hills. In the Panaghia quarter there are remains of the ancient city wall and ruins of the sanctuary of Parthenos, the patron goddess of the city, which flourished from the seventh to the first century B.C. Finds from the sanctuary and from other archeological sites, including Amphipolis, are in the Kavalla Museum. An aqueduct extending across the valley is probably of Roman origin although it was rebuilt in the sixteenth century. A Byzantine castle (fourteenth century) crowns the hill to the east, and on the slope of the hill is the house in which Muhammad Ali, ruler of Egypt in 1805–1848, was born in 1769. Near the seashore, where many fishing boats tie up, is the

Greek Orthodox Church of St. Paul, built in 1928, behind which is a round stone that is supposed to mark the spot where Paul stepped ashore.

Philippi

Philippi is 9 mi (15 km) inland from Kavalla. Alongside the modern highway there are considerable stretches of an ancient road, bordered by large stone blocks and surfaced with smaller irregular stones, perhaps a later surface of the Via Egnatia. In Philippi itself the ancient Via Egnatia is plainly recognizable on the north side of the forum, as the road is paved with large marble slabs in which there are ruts worn by the wheels of carts and chariots.

The ruins of the ancient city are at the edge of a plain surrounded by Mts. Orbelos, Symbolon, and Pangaion. In the plain the main river is a tributary of the river Strymon, and in ancient times it was called the Gangites. In about 360 B.C. Greek colonists from Thasos settled at the foot of Mt. Orbelos and called the place Krenides (Springs) from the abundant springs at the foot of the hill. In 356 Philip II took the city, increased its size with a large number of inhabitants, fortified it with a strong wall, and changed its name to Philippi to refer to himself. The battle of 42 B.C., in which Antony and Octavian defeated Brutus and Cassius, was fought on the plain west of the city near the river Gangites. Afterward many Roman settlers were established at Philippi, and it was made a Roman colony, first known as Colonia Victrix Philippensium, in celebration of the victory, and later as Colonia Augusta Julia Philippensis, in honor of Octavian Augustus of the Julian line.

In the Roman organization of Macedonia, Philippi was in the first district, of which Amphipolis was the capital, and Thessalonica

FIGURE 28. Ancient Via Egnatia (in the Foreground), Leading Toward Philippi.

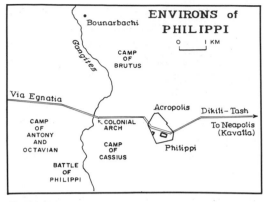

PLAN 9.

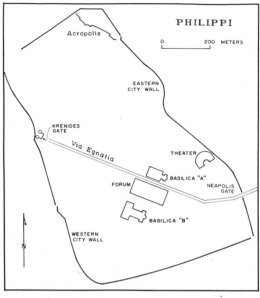

PLAN 10.

was the capital of the entire province. The usual text of Ac 16:12 appears to be incorrect as it describes Philippi as "the leading city of the district of Macedonia, and a Roman colony," but the Greek is such that this reading could be the result of a copyist's error. The original text actually said, entirely correctly, "a city of the first district of Macedonia, and a colony."

At the site of Philippi, portions of the city wall constructed by Philip II are still to be seen, chiefly on the slopes and summit of the acropolis hill (where there are also a Byzantine castle and walls), but other portions have been traced on the lower side of the city. In all, the total length of the wall was nearly 12,000 ft (3,600 m). On the slopes of the same hill are open-air shrines with more than 140 bas-reliefs of the gods, including the Thracian deity Bendis (who was equated with the Greek Artemis) as well as Cybele and Bacchus, and a sanctuary of the Egyptian Gods (Isis, Serapis, Harpokrates). Built into the foot of the hill is a Greek theater, probably from the time of Philip II in its original form but with new rows of seats constructed in the upper part and the orchestra changed into an arena for wild-beast contests in the later Roman period (second and third centuries A.D.)

The Via Egnatia entered Philippi through the Neapolis Gate (Gate "A" on the archeologists' plan) on the east, provided the main axis (the *decumanus maximus*) of the city, and

departed through the Krenides Gate (Gate "B") on the west. In the heart of the city on the south side of the Via Egnatia was the Roman forum, a rectangle 330 by 165 ft (100 by 50 m) in size, paved with marble. As excavated, the buildings of the forum are dated by inscriptions of the period of the Antonine emperors in the late second century A.D., but small finds confirm the occupation of the site as early as the Hellenistic period, so this was probably the position of the forum in Paul's day as well as later. At the northwest and northeast corners of the forum are matching Corinthian temples, the former the Temple of Antoninus Pius, the latter the Temple of Fausta, his wife. On the east end of the forum there are the buildings of a library, on the west end there are government buildings, and on the south side there is a stoa and, back of it, shops. Near the center of the north side of the forum are four stone steps that probably led up to the *bema* (Bῆμα), a judgment seat or speaker's platform (New Testament, "tribunal"). Therefore this is probably the place where Paul and Silas stood when they were brought before the magistrates of the city (Ac 16:20). On either side of the *bema* are large water reservoirs, and the gutters on the

FIGURE 29. Seats in the Theater at Philippi.

FIGURE 30. Via Egnatia, with Deep Ruts from Ancient Traffic, Beside the Forum at Philippi.

edges of the forum still carry water. On a paving stone in front of the *bema* is outlined a gaming board. To the south of the forum excavations have uncovered a large gymnasium (palaestra), baths, and lavatory.

From the forum the Via Egnatia continued straight for some 1,300 ft (400 m) to pass through a gate in the western city wall, outside of which flowed a small river coming down from the Krenides at the foot of the hills further to the north. In the investigation of the lower city wall of Philippi this gate has been located and excavated, and it is called Gate "B" or the Krenides Gate.[3] At this point the Via Egnatia turned northward and ran along the east side of the Krenides stream until a swampy area was avoided, then it turned westward across the stream and ran straight out across the plain to the banks of the much larger Gangites River and the area where the famous battle of Philippi (42 B.C.) was fought. At this point, on the east side of the Gangites, the Via Egnatia was surmounted by a Roman arch, probably built in the first half of the first century A.D. In the nineteenth century the foundations of this arch were still to be seen, and the probable appearance of the arch could be reconstructed, but now it has disappeared completely.

In Ac 16:13f. Paul and his party "went outside the gate to the riverside" and found a place of prayer, with Jewish women assembled, from among whom Lydia became the first believer. It has been thought that the river in question might be the Gangites and the "gate" the Roman arch just described.[4] The arch, however, was more than 1.5 mi (2.5 km) from Philippi, and the distance alone would make it unlikely that the women would have come so far for their place of prayer. A second possibility for the "gate" of Ac 16:13 would be the Krenides Gate in the western city wall, and the river in question could have been the Krenides stream.[5] At that place the paving blocks of a Roman road run to the bank of the stream, and the way is lined with some tomb monuments of Roman officials. Beside the road there is also the foundation of a circular building, but the original nature of it is not known. Locally the stream at this place is known as the River of Lydia.

There is, however, yet one more location to consider as the possible place where Paul preached and Lydia was baptized. A short distance outside the Neapolis Gate (Gate "A") in the east wall of Philippi and beside a small stream that flows there, a Christian basilica has been discovered and excavated (by S. Pelekanides in 1956 and 1957), which dates from the first half of the fourth century and is

FIGURE 31. Columns of the Temple of Fausta, Wife of Antoninus Pius (A.D. 138–161).

probably as early as the reign of Constantine. In its original form this basilica "outside the walls" was entered through an atrium and a narthex, had a broad nave and two narrow side aisles and a semicircular apse, and was surrounded by a number of subsidiary rooms. The floors of the nave and narthex were of mosaic, of which considerable portions are preserved in the narthex showing four-leaved crosses, rosettes, birds, etc. Under the floor were tombs with Greek inscriptions, and these—and some coins—are the chief basis for the dating of the church. There is evidence of damage by fire and restoration of the basilica with some interior changes about a century or two after the original construction, and in the medieval period a much smaller and simpler church was erected in the midst of the ruins of its predecessors. The original basilica itself was not large—the nave measured 90 ft (27.5 m) in length—and it is surmised that it may have been built soon after Constantine ended per-

secution and brought peace to the Christians with the Edict of Milan (A.D. 313). That the church was built at this relatively early date in this particular location could be because the site was remembered as the place of Paul's initial ministry in Philippi and of Lydia's baptism. No evidence of a baptistery has been discovered, perhaps because baptism was still conducted in the running stream—as Paul had presumably baptized Lydia and her family, and even as Jesus was originally baptized by John the Baptist.[6]

In the city above the forum and on the north side of the present highway, which parallels the ancient Via Egnatia, there is a small crypt in the side of the acropolis hill. This is judged to have been originally a cistern, and it is the traditional site of the prison of Paul and Silas. The crypt was first discovered in 1876, and at that time it still contained paintings that depicted the imprisonment of Paul and Silas and other events that befell them in Philippi.

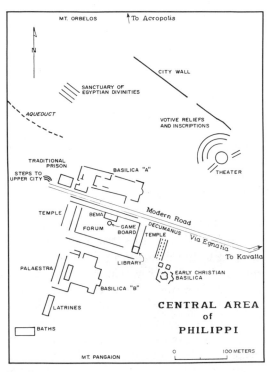

PLAN 11.

had a nave, two side aisles, a transept, and a semicircular apse. The floor and walls of the nave were of white marble and so too were the columns, except in some positions of special importance where green marble was used. Beside the nave on the north side was a room with a well-preserved mosaic floor, which has been thought to be a baptistery but, in the absence of any water piping, may instead have been a service room (*diaconicon*). The interior length of the nave was 136 ft (41.6 m), the width of the transept was 130 ft (39.5), and the entire complex was nearly 400 ft (120 m) in length and 160 ft (48 m) in breadth.[7]

Basilica "A" was apparently destroyed by some catastrophe, perhaps by a powerful earthquake known to have taken place in the area in A.D. 518. Probably toward the end of the first half of the sixth century Basilica "B" was constructed, perhaps as a replacement for Basilica "A." The location of the new basilica was on the plain south of the forum, where its massive, still-standing brick-and-stone piers and walls can be seen from afar. The ruin, on this account, has long been known by the Turkish word for walls and towers, Direkler.

A group of Roman buildings was leveled to make a place, and the basilica was built into the east side of what had been the Roman palaestra. From west to east the basilica had an atrium, a narthex, a broad nave and two broad side aisles, a large rectangular area, and a large apse. Including the narthex and the apse the basilica was 184 ft (56 m) in length. The nave and aisles terminated at two massive stone piers, and two similar piers stood on either side of the apse. Together the four piers were intended to carry a large dome rising over the large rectangular space, in which was to be the altar. On either side of the large rectangular area was an annexed room with an apse at the east and with a smaller room adjoining it on the west. The smaller room on the north side of the church was a baptistery, which contained a rectangular baptismal basin in its center. The walls of the basilica were of alternating courses of brick and stone. The columns of the nave were of green marble, and their

Only faint fragments of the paintings now remain, but they are believed to be of the seventh century A.D. The location of the crypt as the possible place of imprisonment of Paul and Silas fits with a statement by Vitruvius, a Roman writer on architecture, to the effect that prisons were usually beside or near the forum of a city (*On Architecture* v 2, 1).

Probably not later than the middle of the fifth century a great Christian basilica was erected on a terrace cut into the slope of the hill and in architectural relationship to the crypt just described. From the excavations of the French Archaeological School of Athens this is known as Basilica "A," or the Terrace Basilica. As the architectural remains show, a propylaeum or monumental entryway led up from the Via Egnatia on the edge of the forum below, giving access to a colonnaded courtyard that surrounded the traditional prison. East of this courtyard was the atrium of the basilica, and the atrium in turn opened through three doorways into the narthex. The church itself

FIGURE 32. Broken Marble Column in Basilica "B" in Philippi.

capitals were decorated with acanthus leaves and stylized fish carved in high relief. Although the capitals were sculptured in local marble, their designs are much like the designs of the capitals in Haghia Sophia in Constantinople (dedicated in 563), and it may even be that artists came from Constantinople to participate in the work.

Before Basilica "B" was completed, however, it is evident that the great dome of the structure collapsed, and after that catastrophe, the building was left unfinished. Later, perhaps in the tenth or eleventh century, a small church was built in the previous narthex, with an apse reaching into the west end of the original nave.[8]

To the east of the forum there has also been excavated an octagon church, 108 ft (33 m) in length and 97 ft (29.7 m) in width. The exterior of the building is a square, and the octagon is inscribed within it, with an encircling ambulatory. Although the architectural remains are very damaged, it appears that the octagon was covered with a dome or a pyramidal wooden roof and that there was marble and mosaic decoration on the walls and a marble pavement. The building was approached from the Via Egnatia through a long portico, which was divided by colonnades into three aisles. Connected with the church are a number of compartments and a baptistery. The baptistery was evidently covered with a dome, and in the center of the room is a cross-shaped baptismal basin with two stairs leading down into it. Pieces of mosaic depicting figures (perhaps of apostles) and having inscriptions were found, and they suggest that the ceiling and walls were covered with mosaics. Adjacent to the baptistery was a complete Roman-type bath, and water was supplied to the baptistery from the *caldarium* of the baths. Coins found in one compartment date from the fourth century to the time of Justinian (527–565), which suggests that the entire church complex was used down into the sixth or seventh century. The excavator dates the original octagon at the end of the fourth or the beginning of the fifth century, and he has identified under it a small one-room building of the third century, perhaps a temple.[9]

Amphipolis

From Philippi Paul and his party proceeded along the Via Egnatia through Amphipolis and Apollonia to Thessalonica (Ac 17:1).

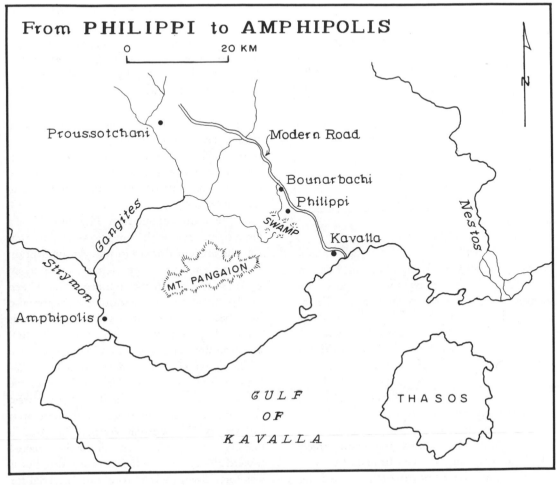

From PHILIPPI to AMPHIPOLIS

0   20 KM

Proussotchani

Modern Road

Bounarbachi

Philippi

Gangites

SWAMP

Kavalla

Nestos

Strymon

MT. PANGAION

Amphipolis

GULF
OF
KAVALLA

THASOS

MAP 6.

Amphipolis was originally named Ennea Ho-doi (Nine Ways) and was eventually colonized by the Athenians. It was taken by Philip II, and under the Romans it was the capital of the first district of Macedonia. The town was on a hill protected to the north, west, and south by the Strymon River, and the terrain rose in natural terraces to the east toward Mt. Pangaion. In the excavation of the ancient town a great marble lion was found, which was probably erected in the fourth century B.C. to commemorate the victory of Philip II, and the lion now stands beside the modern highway. Walls of the Classical and Hellenistic periods have been traced, and tombs of the fourth to the second centuries B.C. have been unearthed, from which gravestones and gold jewelry have been taken to the museum at Kavalla. Some foundations of basilican churches, with mosaic floors, have also been uncovered.

Thessalonica

Thessalonica, also called Salonika in the Middle Ages and Thessaloniki in modern Greek, was built at or near the earlier settlement of Therme, from which the Thermaic Gulf (or Gulf of Salonika) takes its name. As Strabo relates (VII 21), the city was founded by Cassander (315 B.C.), one of Alexander the

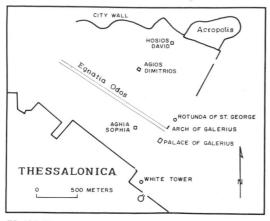

PLAN 12.

Great's generals who strengthened his hold on Macedonia by marrying the last surviving member of the former royal family, Thessalonica, daughter of Philip II and half sister of Alexander, and who named the new city after his wife. Under the Romans Thessalonica was the capital of the province of Macedonia; under the emperor Galerius (A.D. 305–311) it was the eastern capital of the empire; and in the Byzantine Empire it was the second city, after Constantinople.

In modern Thessaloniki the main street, which runs through the city from east to west (strictly, southeast to northwest), is called the Egnatia Odos, but it is not certain that the ancient Via Egnatia followed the same route. Rather, the discovery of two Roman milestones has suggested that the Via Egnatia came in from Pella through the Golden or Axios Gate (at the west end of the modern Egnatia Odos) and then left the city from the Letaea Gate (near the west end of the modern Dimitrios Street).[10] In the central city the streets are generally laid out on the grid pattern, and since such a regular city plan has close parallels with other early Hellenistic cities, such as Antioch on the Orontes, it is probable that this arrangement goes back to the foundation of Thessalonica by Cassander.

A harbor was constructed at Thessalonica by the emperor Constantine, and Theodosius I

(379–395), who lived there for a time, built fortification walls. As seen today, the existing walls and towers represent many additions and reconstructions, but they follow a natural line along the crest of the hills and to the acropolis in the northeast corner of the city, a line that may even be that of the earlier Hellenistic walls. Likewise, on the waterfront the so-called White Tower (Lefkos Pyrgos) probably preserves Hellenistic foundations, although in its present form it was finished in 1536 and is an excellent example of Ottoman military architecture.[11]

In the center of modern Thessaloniki is a large open area, with some extant ruins, that was the ancient Roman forum. An inscription of 60 B.C., found in the vicinity, refers to an agora, so the Hellenistic agora could have been in this location too, although it might also have been elsewhere. It is also known that as early as Hellenistic times there were a stadium, a gymnasium, and a serapeum in Thessalonica.

The Egnatia Odos was at one time known as Vardar Street (from the Vardar River as the Axios was at that time called), and at the west end of the street there was a Roman arch known as the Vardar Arch. This was a massive stone structure probably erected toward the end of the first century A.D., but it was torn down in 1867 to obtain material for the repair of the city wall. A broken inscription from the arch is preserved, however, in the British Museum and begins, "In the time of the politarchs." This is of importance because the same term (πολιτάρχης) is used in Ac 17:6 for the rulers of Thessalonica, but it is otherwise unknown in extant Greek literature.

At the east end of the Egnatia Odos is the Arch of Galerius, and laid out on a vertical axis with it, the ruins of the Palace of Galerius are less than 1,000 ft (300 m) to the southwest, and the Rotunda of St. George is 200 ft (60 m) to the northeast. The arch was erected to celebrate the victories of Galerius in his campaign of A.D. 297 against the Persians in Mesopotamia and Armenia. It is built of brick and faced with sculptured marble reliefs, which depict the battles of Galerius and show him, together with Diocletian, making a sacrifice of thanksgiving.

The palace was a rectangular construction with a central courtyard and porticoes on the four sides, and portions of a mosaic floor with geometric decoration are preserved. In connection with the whole structure was an octagonal building. A marble arch was also found in the area, with sculptured foliage and busts of Galerius and Tyche, the patron goddess of Thessalonica.

The rotunda, which was connected with the arch by a colonnaded street, is a great brick cylinder surmounted by a tiled dome. The interior is 79 ft (24 m) in diameter, the wall is 21 ft (6.3 m) thick at the base, and it is deeply indented with eight vaulted niches, with the original entrance from the outside through the niche at the south. This structure was probably intended by Galerius for his tomb, but he died and was buried elsewhere (311).

Probably in the reign of Theodosius I the Great (379–395) the rotunda was converted into a Christian church. The cylinder was surrounded by an ambulatory, a second entrance was made through the niche on the west, a deep apse was built out to the east, and magnificent mosaics were placed in the vaulted ceilings of the niches, in the apse, and in the dome.

The original apse mosaics have perished, but portions of those in the niches and the dome survive, and they are among the greatest extant examples of early Byzantine art. Two of the niches retain part of their mosaics, showing birds, fruits, and geometric patterns. The base of the dome is 215 ft (65.5 m) in circumference, and around the circle there were eight panels of mosaics, of which seven survive at least in part. Each panel shows two or three saints, standing as orants in the early Christian position of prayer with uplifted hands, in front of two-storied architectural facades, no doubt like contemporary Roman buildings and probably intended to suggest the heavenly places in which the saints minister.

FIGURE 33. Lion of Amphipolis.

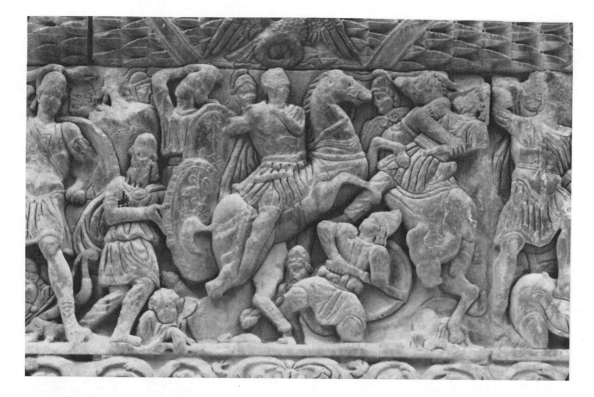

FIGURE 34 (top). Galerius in Battle, Relief on the Arch of Galerius in Thessaloniki. FIGURE 35 (bottom). The Sacrifice of Diocletian (on the Left in Rich Garments) and Galerius (on the Right in Battle Dress), Relief on the Arch of Galerius in Thessaloniki.

Greek inscriptions identify the saints by name and also give their professions—e.g., soldier, priest, doctor—and the months in which their festivals were celebrated. All can be identified as well-known early Christian martyrs; e.g., in the second panel to the right from the apse are Onesiphoros, who received Paul at Iconium, and his servant Porphyrios, and in the third panel are Damian and Cosmas, the "silverless" ones who healed the sick without charge and only asked their patients to accept the Christian faith. Above the dome circle of these saints was another zone of mosaics that portrayed twelve personages—presumably the twelve apostles—but only the feet survive. Finally, in the apex of the dome, and only partially preserved, is a large figure of Christ, encircled in a wreath of foliage and fruits held by four angels.

At some point in its history—whether originally or not is debated—the rotunda church was dedicated to St. George and is known as Agios Georgios. In 1591 it was made into a mosque, with a tall minaret beside it, and in 1912 it was restored as a church. The mosque minaret was allowed to stand, however, when all the other minarets in the city were torn down. Later the rotunda was secularized and made a national monument and museum of Christian art. Like many other churches in Thessaloniki, the rotunda was damaged by earthquake in 1978 and repaired afterward.[12]

During the persecution of Christianity instituted by Galerius in 303, two of the martyrs of whom there is record were Theodora, the only daughter of Galerius, and Demetrius, an officer. In a medieval account written by the monk Ignatius it is related that on an occasion when Galerius was absent on a military expedition, Theodora was baptized by Bishop Alexander. Theodora, the story goes, was walking along the seashore where the persecuted Christians were forced to dwell, and she was attracted by some hymns of worship she heard in a church. After receiving instruction from Alexander, she was baptized. In order to have a private place for her devotions, she pretended illness and asked her father to build a house and a bath for her in the northern part of the city, near some quarries. The so-called bath was secretly inaugurated as a church and decorated with a mosaic, which Ignatius describes as recognizably the same as the mosaic of Christ in the eastern apse of the church now known as Hosios David (Holy David). Theodora was betrayed by one of her slaves to her mother as being a Christian, and in order to gain time, she covered the mosaic in the church with leather, bricks, and mortar. Nevertheless, when she steadfastly refused to renounce her faith, she suffered martyrdom by her father's command.

In the continuation of his account, Ignatius tells us that the church became the chapel of a monastery known as Moni Latomos (Monastery of the Quarrymen) and that an aged monk named Senoufias came from Egypt and lived in the monastery. Just before his death, after praying alone in the chapel, he rediscovered the mosaic of Christ when the leather, brick, and mortar, which had hidden it for so long, were miraculously taken away.

According to tradition, Hosios David, whose name the church bears, was a saint who came from the East in the early sixth century, or perhaps already in the fifth, lived as a monk in a monastery called Kukulleoton outside the city, and died in Thessalonica around 530–540.[13] In its later history under Turkish rule, the church was converted into a mosque, and its interior walls were covered with plaster. When the building was restored as a church in 1921 it was cleaned, and the original mosaic in the east apse was discovered as well as other later wall paintings.

In its original form the church of Hosios David was square with four square chambers in its four corners, which left the rest of the interior in the form of a Greek cross of four equal arms. The eastern arm extended into a projecting semicircular apse, the center of the building was surmounted by a dome, and the corner chambers had domed ceilings. Today only about two-thirds of the original building

FIGURE 36. Rotunda and Minaret in Thessaloniki.

remains, for the square chamber at the south-western corner has been destroyed and the central dome is also missing. The eastern apse is largely intact, however, and the famous mosaic is relatively intact in the upper part of the apse.

According to Ignatius the mosaic represents the visions of Ezekiel and Habakkuk, and if that is correct, the figure in the lower left-hand corner may be recognized as Ezekiel, and that in the lower right-hand corner as Habakkuk. Between them, at the bottom of the picture, is a river, probably the Jordan, from which a pagan river-god half emerges and also from which flow the four rivers of Paradise. Above is Christ seated in the center of a great rainbow, the colors of which extend out to form a great circle. From behind the circle appear the four symbols of the evangelists (man, lion, ox, and eagle for Matthew, Mark, Luke, and John), each with a Gospel codex. Christ himself is shown as youthful and beardless, and there is a

halo with a jeweled cross behind his head. His right hand is raised, palm forward, in a gesture presumably of reassurance. His left hand holds a scroll with a Greek inscription, which can be translated as, "Behold our God in whom we hope and here rejoice in our salvation, for he will give us rest and hospitality in this house"—possibly a paraphrase of Is 25:9–10.[14]

It is related that Demetrius came from a noble Greek family in Thessalonica and that he became an officer in the Roman army. He so distinguished himself as to attract the attention of Galerius and receive an appointment as a prefect. He was converted to Christianity, however, and in the persecution was arrested for preaching the gospel. Galerius tried to persuade him to renounce his religion, but Demetrius refused, and Galerius, wishing to hasten on to some games in the stadium, had him held in the basement of some nearby baths.

In the stadium a prize was announced for

anyone able to defeat a champion gladiator name Lyaios. A young Christian named Nestor, who was a friend of Demetrius, asked the blessing of Demetrius for his undertaking and then fought and killed Lyaios. When Galerius learned that Nestor attributed his victory to the blessing of Demetrius, Galerius sent soldiers to the baths to kill Demetrius with their lances. That night the martyr's body was recovered by fellow Christians and buried in the basement of the baths.

When liberty of worship was attained, a small church building was constructed over the grave of Demetrius. This church became a shrine, and the water that flowed there was believed to possess miraculous powers of healing. In 412–413 Leontius, the prefect of Illyricum, was healed in this manner of paralysis and, in gratitude, replaced the small church with a large basilica dedicated to Demetrius. The basilica was damaged by fire and then rebuilt after the original plan in the seventh century, at which time it was also adorned with some fine mosaics. Made a mosque in 1493, it was restored as a church in 1912, burned by fire in 1917, and reconstructed once again in 1926–1948; it is the present church of Agios Dimitrios in the heart of Thessaloniki.

The Roman baths in which the martyrdom of the saint took place were originally on a level with a street situated to the east, but the ruins of the baths are now underground, in the crypt underneath the basilica. The remains of the baths consist of a number of longitudinal and transverse walls, and in one of the latter there are three semicircular and two rectangular recesses facing to the east. To the north and south of the last wall are also rectangular vaulted rooms, originally part of the baths. Remaining in the rectangular vaulted rooms to the north and south, originally a part of the baths, there is a series of recesses, which probably mark the burial places of special persons allowed to rest within these sacred precincts. Another small room to the south has an apse and looks like a tiny basilica. This was previously thought to be the original church of

FIGURE 37. Apse Mosaic of Christ in the Church of Hosios David in Thessaloniki.

Demetrius, erected by his followers after the peace of the church, but it has been shown (by G. and M. Sotiriou in 1952) that parts of the room belong to the structure of the Roman baths and that the rest, including the apse, date only from the fifth century A.D.

During the archeological excavation another apse was found immediately behind the recessed wall mentioned just above, and this apse is ascribed to the fourth century and believed to be a part of the original church. The apse is approximately 30 ft (9 m) across, extending on either side almost to two of the longitudinal walls of the Roman baths, and above those walls are the two inner lines of the colonnades of the upper and later church built by Leontius in the early fifth century and rebuilt in the seventh. It thus appears that the original fourth-century church of St. Demetrius was largely an adaptation of part of the Roman baths. Close to the center of the apse is a small cross-shaped crypt containing a flask of blood-soaked earth—presumably testimony to the martyrdom—and the altar of the later church is directly above this spot. To allow for this position of the altar, the apse of the later church was placed further to the east, and it is supported by an arc of massive piers, constructed from ancient materials including many pagan altars, that circles out from the recessed wall of the Roman baths.

The area enclosed between the Roman recessed wall and the arc of piers was, in the time of the later church, a cult center and a

FIGURE 38. Church of Agios Dimitrios in Thessaloniki.

martyrium of St. Demetrius—in the sense of "a place of witness," not in the sense of containing actual relics. Two staircases led down from the sanctuary above, and a pipe from a nearby well brought in water that was evidently believed to be holy water with properties of blessing and healing. A parapet of marble slabs was placed parallel to the recessed wall, and in the enclosed space that resulted, a marble fountain or basin received the water, which the clergy administered to the pilgrims who came. Later a semicircular enclosure or canopy (ciborium) with six columns was built around the fountain, and later still a circular pool was built between the ciborium and the arc of piers. There was also an ambulatory around this central cult area, with a portico on the east providing access from a street or courtyard outside.

The fifth-century church was a basilica with atrium, narthex, nave, four side aisles, transept, and apse. It will be remembered that Galerius left Demetrius imprisoned in the baths while he himself went on to the games in the stadium and that stadium was a short distance west of the baths, so in the building of the later, larger church the remains of the stadium were transformed into the atrium of the church, and some of its tiers of seats were reused as steps. The floor of the church in this form was of white marble. Some of the columns of colonnades were of white marble, some of green marble, and they were surmounted by handsome Corinthian capitals. Including the narthex, the length of the church was 187 ft (57 m).

In the church of Agios Dimitrios as its exists today, some of the columns and capitals of the fifth-century church are preserved, as are some sculptured fragments from the seventh-century rebuilding. Also notable are the mosaics, the oldest of which are probably from the seventh century and include the two following scenes.

First, on the north face of the pier at the southeast corner of the nave, Demetrius stands between two men, his hands placed protectingly around their shoulders. The inscription below reads, "You see the builders of this

FIGURE 39. Chalice with Cross (Fourth Century A.D.), in the Crypt Museum of Agios Dimitrios in Thessaloniki.

FIGURE 40. St. Demetrius with Little Children, Mosaic in Agios Dimitrios in Thessaloniki.

famous house on each side of the martyr Demetrius, who averts the barbarians' terrible naval might and saves the city." The personage on the right of Demetrius is a bishop carrying a large Bible, its cover ornamented with a large cross. He is probably Bishop John I of Thessalonica who led the defense of Thessalonica against an attack by the Avars and Slavs in 617–619, in which the city was saved, it was believed, when St. Demetrius invoked a storm to wreck the ships of the enemy. The bishop is also known as the author of the first of the books of legends about St. Demetrius (*Miracula sancti Demetrii*) and, according to the mosaic inscription, was in charge of the rebuilding of the church in the seventh century. The personage on the left of Demetrius in the mosaic is a secular official carrying a staff of office, and he may probably be identified as the prefect Leontius, the original founder of the church in the fourth century. A date for the mosaic in the second quarter of the seventh century is probable.

FIGURE 41. Portrait Statue of the Emperor Augustus (27 B.C.–A.D. 14), in the Archaeological Museum in Thessaloniki.

Second, on the west face of the pier at the northeast corner of the nave, Demetrius stands between two children, his left hand placed on the shoulder of one and his right hand raised, palm forward, presumably in a gesture of reassurance. Stylistic considerations suggest a date around the middle of the

seventh century, i.e., more or less contemporary with the mosaic of Demetrius and the builders just described and located just across from it at the other corner of the chancel. Together the two mosaics reflect two of the chief characteristics of St. Demetrius as the defender of his city and as a friend and helper of little children.[15]

At the height of the Byzantine period there are supposed to have been 365 churches in Thessalonica. Although only about twenty remain—and only Agios Georgios, Hosios David, and Agios Dimitrios have been here described—they constitute a great treasury of Byzantine art and architecture.

Beroea

From Thessalonica Paul and Silas proceeded to Beroea (Ac 17:10). The route was presumably along the Via Egnatia westward for about 20 mi (32 km) to a bridge over the Axios River, and then southwest on a side road for another 30 mi (48 km) to Beroea. The city was on a plain with many springs at the foot of Mt. Bermion, and its name signified a "place that has many waters." It was founded in the ninth century B.C. by the Dorian Greeks, and it was an important city in the Classical, Roman, and Byzantine periods. After it surrendered to the Romans (168 B.C.) it became a part of the third of the four districts into which Macedonia was divided. In Byzantine times it was fortified with walls and a citadel, some parts of which still remain. It reportedly once had seventy-one churches, but it suffered from various invasions. When the Turks took the city in 1430 many of the churches were changed into mosques, but some ten or fifteen Byzantine churches still remain. The church of Agios Christos has wall paintings dated in 1314 and signed by Kallerges, an outstanding artist of that time. Other churches are St. Nicolas,

FIGURE 42. Head of Serapis, Roman Copy from a Famous Work of Bryaxis (Fourth Century B.C.), in the Archaeological Museum in Thessaloniki.

FIGURE 43 (above). Memorial Tablet in the Form of a Clipeus, a Shield-Shaped Disk (Middle of the First Century A.D.), in the Archaeological Museum in Thessaloniki. FIGURE 44 (below). Ancient Bema Steps in Veroia.

which is of fine architecture and has rich interior decoration, and St. Spyridon, which has some fine Byzantine sculpture.

The city is now known as Verria or Veroia. Roman gravestones and other antiquities are preserved in its museum. In the heart of the city the steps of a bema have been reconstructed, and a modern structure has been built in front of them to commemorate the place where it is believed that the apostle Paul spoke.

GREEK WORLD

In proceeding from Beroea to Athens (Ac 17:14f.) Paul went from the Roman province of Macedonia to the Roman province of Achaia. In earlier times Achaia had been the district on the north coast of the large peninsula known as the Peloponnesos, where there was a confederation of twelve cities called the Achaian League. As a Roman province Achaia included not only the Peloponnesos but also Attica, a triangular district with Cape Sounion as its apex. According to Strabo (XVII 3, 25) Achaia extended "as far as Thessaly and Aetolia and Acarnania," in other words, it comprised most of ancient Greece south of Macedonia.

Together with the many adjacent islands, chiefly in the Aegean Sea, Achaia was the heart of the Greek world. Geographically Greece is a picturesque region. The mainland is mountainous with deeply indented shores. Mt. Olympus is 9,571 ft (2,917 m) in height, and Mt. Parnassus is 8,065 ft (2,457 m) high. The islands, legend has it, were a handful of rocks left over after the making of the earth, tossed over the Creator's shoulder, and fallen thus into the sea. At any rate there are so many that no island is ever completely out of sight of another, and the sea does not have the loneliness of utterly empty space.

As elsewhere, the first permanent settlements were established during the Neolithic Age. At Athens Neolithic pottery, dating probably around 4000 B.C., has been found on the north slope of the Acropolis hill, and the people who settled there dug wells not far from what was later known as the Klepsydra Spring. To the north, in Thessaly, there are important Neolithic sites at Sesklo and Dimini, the latter a fortified place even then. Both sites are near modern Volos, the third largest port of Greece, and the chief artifacts

FIGURE 45. Replica of Priest King Mural at Knossos.

from the two sites are in the Volos Museum. On Crete, the southernmost Greek island, there was a Neolithic settlement at Knossos, so early that at the outset pottery was unknown.

In the Bronze Age, beginning around 3000 B.C., metal-using societies developed rapidly, and the Minoan-Mycenaean civilization emerged. The Minoan is first recognizable on the island of Crete where, by around 3000 B.C., there was a highly organized society with famous palace towns. Of these towns the most important were Knossos, 3 mi (5 km) from Iraklion (Heraklion) on the north coast, and Phaistos, near the south coast. The legendary king of the time was Minos, but this word is now thought to have been not a personal name but a title, like Pharaoh and Caesar, hence the designation of the "Minoan" civilization.

The palace at Knossos, explored and reconstructed by Arthur Evans, and the palace at Phaistos, excavated by the Italian Archae-

FIGURE 46. Storage Jar in the Palace Warehouse at Phaistos.

ological School at Athens, were so elaborate that they probably gave rise to the legend of the labyrinth, in which the Minotaur, half man and half bull, was confined. The architecture of the palaces is indeed remarkable. A throne room and various apartments were arranged around a large central courtyard and built on several levels. Numerous windows provided light, and elaborate installations brought in spring water and carried off used water and rainwater. Very large storage jars were ranged in large storerooms. The interior decoration of the palaces was especially notable. Wall paintings, executed on stucco, depicted plants, animals, and people and showed dancers performing with bulls. As for their language, the Minoans spoke a non-Indo-European tongue, written in a script known as Linear A.

The Minoan civilization existed also on Santorini, actually the name of a group of five islands that are almost the southernmost islands of the Cyclades (Circle) in the center of the Aegean. Together with the large crescent-shaped Thera, two of the islands partially complete a circumference, and two more are in the center. On the island of Thera, the modern town of Phera is on top of the cliffs; ancient Thera, a Dorian Greek city of the ninth century B.C., is on the southeast side near Cape Mesa Vouno; and Akrotiri, the site of the most recent excavations, is on the narrower crescent out toward the southwest and Cape Akrotiri. At Akrotiri both pottery and frescoes have been found like those of Minoan Crete, but buried in deep layers of volcanic ash. Santorini was, in fact, destroyed by a tremendous volcanic eruption, and the circumferential islands surround the crater of the volcano, now filled by the sea to a great depth. The date of the disaster was probably around 1450 B.C. Volcanic ash and great sea waves probably carried as far as Crete and resulted in the destruction of the coastal settlements there too.

The Mycenaean civilization, taking its name from the site of Mycenae, emerged around

FIGURE 47. Steep Side of the Crater at Santorini.

1600 B.C. The decipherment of the Linear B script shows that these people, unlike the Minoans, spoke Greek. In the fifteenth century, and perhaps after the great natural disaster at Thera, many features of Mycenaean life were adopted in Crete, including the Greek language. For the next two centuries (the fourteenth and thirteenth) the two civilizations were essentially one – the Minoan-Mycenaean – and then all collapsed around 1200–1150 B.C. Because the Greek language is recognizably related to Sanskrit, Old Persian, Latin, German, and other such tongues, the Greek-speaking peoples are identified as Indo-European, a term essentially designating that particular family of languages. The Mycenaeans are probably also to be identified with the Achaians, who were mentioned in the Homeric poems and who settled in Thessaly as well as on the Peloponnesos. Around 1200 B.C. Agamemnon was on the throne of Mycenae, and a little later he led the Mycenaeans against Troy in Asia Minor, in the war that is the theme of the *Iliad*. Thus Agamemnon is probably a more or less historical person.

As for the more exact date of the fall of Troy, the most widely accepted approximation comes from the calculations of the Greek scholar Eratosthenes, who lived and worked chiefly in the latter part of the third century B.C. in Alexandria, and his work is quoted in respect to the present question by Clement of Alexandria (*Stromata* I 21, ANF II p. 331). By studying the genealogies of the Spartan kings and others Eratosthenes calculated that the Dorian invasion (to be mentioned just below) took place 328 years before the first year of the first Olympiad (776 B.C.) or in 1104 B.C. That invasion, in turn, was reckoned in Greek tradition as having occurred two generations after the Trojan War. With the allowance of a supposed forty years to a generation, that puts the fall of Troy back to 1184 B.C. (another reckoning gives 1194).

The site of Mycenae is in the Peloponnesos,

FIGURE 48. Gold Mask of an Achaian King from the Fifth Royal Tomb at Mycenae (Often Thought to be Agamemnon), in the National Archaeological Museum in Athens.

25 mi (40 km) southwest of Corinth where there is a great hill citadel with an acropolis and a lower town. Shaft graves, chamber tombs, and *tholos* or beehive tombs date from 1600 to 1100 B.C. The cyclopean city wall, a fortification of huge boulders without mortar, dates around 1350, and its chief feature is the Lion Gate. Among the beehive structures are the Treasury of Atreus (the father of Agamemnon), or the Tomb of Agamemnon (as it is variously called), and the Tomb of Clytemnestra (the wife of Agamemnon). From the tombs of Mycenae has come such a quantity of golden objects, which can be seen in the National Archaeological Museum in Athens, as to fully justify the Homeric epithet

for Mycenae as πολύχρυσος, "rich in gold." There are many other Mycenaean sites in Greece, among them Sesklo, already mentioned as a Neolithic site, where the remains of a large palace may mark the city of Aeson, father of Jason who went off with the Argonauts to obtain the Golden Fleece.

With the collapse of the Minoan-Mycenaean civilization around 1200–1150 B.C., and perhaps having to do with that collapse, another wave of Indo-Europeans came in, namely, the Dorian Greeks. They made a fierce, destructive conquest, but in time they came to feel a sense of unity with the other Greeks. Also in Attica the Achaians and the older indigenous people mingled, and from Attica, Attic emigrants went to the central coast of Asia Minor as the inhabitants of a region called Ionia. There they built an essentially Greek civilization around 1000 B.C., and there they adopted the Phoenician alphabet in which to write the Greek language.

Thus, by the long evolution sketched above, there emerged the real Greek civilization. This civilization assumed the characteristic form of the city-state with a king whose authority gradually declined, an aristocratic council, and a popular assembly. The chief centers were Athens in the plain of Attica, Thebes to the north in Boeotia, Corinth near the isthmus of the same name, and Sparta in the southern Peloponnesos. In Ionia, Miletus and Ephesus were especially important, and Greek mariners also carried Greek colonists as far afield as the Black Sea in the north, Libya in the south, Cyprus in the east, and Sicily and southern Italy in the west. In all these places, however, the people shared a common language, religion, political practice, and outlook on life. Their homeland they called Hellas, themselves Hellenes, and their civilization Hellenic.

As Hellenes they were descendants of a mythical ancestor, Hellen, son of Deucalion who, when Zeus resolved to destroy humankind with a flood, constructed an ark and drifted for nine days and nights until, with his wife, he landed on Mt. Parnassus. The Greeks were always individualistic and lovers of independence, and so they almost always remained diverse and disunited. In Sparta physical fitness and unquestioning obedience were emphasized. In Ionia and Attica intellectual initiative was encouraged. At Miletus around 600 B.C. Anaximander drew a map of the world, and Thales predicted an eclipse of the sun. At Ephesus around 500 Heraclitus taught that fire is the source of all things and that all things are in flux. At Athens around 600 Solon introduced a more humane law code, and Pisistratus, a beneficent tyrant,[16] popularized art and literature; around 500, Cleisthenes made an assembly of citizens the most important political force.

Then came the foreign threat. In the middle of the sixth century B.C. Croesus, the famous king of Lydia, conquered the Greek cities of Ionia, and then Cyrus captured Croesus and brought the Ionian cities under Persian sway. Thereafter Darius sent an army against Athens but was defeated at Marathon (490 B.C.), and Xerxes renewed the attack by both land and sea but was stopped at Thermopylae by the Spartans and defeated on the sea at Salamis near Athens (480 B.C.)

The golden age ensued. In 448 B.C. the Athenian statesman Pericles concluded a peace with Persia and had already embarked on an architectural program calculated to make Athens the finest city in Greece. In 438 the Parthenon, dedicated to Athena, was completed and adorned with the sculptures of Phidias. As a student of philosophy Pericles also attracted the teacher Anaxagoras to Athens from Ionia, and soon the Sophists were widely promulgating their "wisdom," and Aeschylus, Sophocles, and Euripides were writing their dramas.

When the old rivalry between Athens and Sparta revived and the Peloponnesian War broke out (431 B.C.), the end result was that Greece never recovered its strength but became weak and disunited. Yet Socrates (469–399) and Plato (427–347) lived in this time, and it has been said, "In Greek history little that happened mattered much; it was what the Greeks thought that counted."[17]

That thought would spread throughout the empires of Alexander the Great and of the Romans and would be influential in the intellectual formulation of the doctrines of Christianity.

It remained for a Macedonian king—Philip II—to take over and unite the Greeks under his own rule and for his son—Alexander the Great—to lead the united forces of Macedonia and Greece in the Asian expedition the father had planned. Although the empire Alexander won disintegrated quickly into several kingdoms, the East continued to be administered by Greeks until the Romans took over, and Greek civilization mingled with that of the East in the new Hellenistic Age.

At this point Greece was dominated by Macedonian kings, the Antigonids, descendants of Antigonus the One-Eyed, one of Alexander's generals. Then in three Macedonian wars the Romans intervened against the Antigonids. Macedonia was annexed in 168 B.C. and made a Roman province in 148, and the Achaian League was defeated and Corinth was destroyed in 146, the same year that Carthage was overcome. Greece was placed first under the proconsul of Macedonia; under Augustus (27 B.C.) it was made into the Roman province of Achaia; and from A.D. 44, under Claudius, it was a senatorial province governed by a proconsul with his seat of administration at Corinth. This was the world of Greece when, at the end of the year 49, the brethren at Beroea sent Paul off on his way to the sea and those who conducted him took him as far as Athens (Ac 17:14f.).

Athens

As we follow Paul into the heart of the ancient Greek world information can be derived from two other ancient travelers. Apollonius of Tyana was a wandering Neo-Pythagorean philosopher, who was born at Tyana in Cappadocia around the beginning of the Christian era and died at Ephesus probably in A.D. 98. He studied in Tarsus and in the Temple of Asklepios at Aigai on the Gulf of Iskenderun, and then traveled into all parts of the known world. At one time he endured trial and imprisonment in Rome, and he spent the last ten years of his life in Greece. His was a remarkable career, in some respects parallel to that of Paul. The biography of Apollonius was written by Flavius Philostratus at the request of Julia Domna, wife of the emperor Severus, but it was not published until after her death in A.D. 217. For the biography Philostratus drew upon a collection of letters by Apollonius and upon a travel journal by the Assyrian Damis, a disciple and companion of Apollonius. These sources provide a striking parallel to Paul, his letters, and the travel diary of a companion in the "we" sections of the Book of Acts. Although the *Life of Apollonius* by Philostratus contains legendary and miraculous material and must be used with discrimination, it is an important source of knowledge about the times and places in the first century A.D.

Pausanias was a Greek traveler and geographer of the second century A.D. He was born in Lydia and went to Greece after visiting Palestine and Egypt. His work, which we know as the *Description of Greece*, deals with events from A.D. 143 to 176, so it was probably written about the latter date. It is in ten books; the first book is on Attica including Athens, the second book is on the Corinthian land including Corinth and Mycenae, and so on. It is a very detailed narrative of where Pausanias went and what he saw. Although it contains a few unimportant mistakes, in many parts of Greece the accuracy of the descriptions has been proved by the finding of remains of the buildings mentioned. It was in fact Pausanias's accurate notice of Mycenae that led to the discovery of that site by Heinrich Schliemann, and the work of Pausanias has also been used constantly in connection with the excavations in the Agora at Athens. Concerning the work of Pausanias J. G. Frazer wrote, "Of no other part of the ancient world has a description at once so minute and so trustworthy survived. . . . In all parts of the country the truthfulness of his descriptions has been attested by remains of the buildings which he describes. . . . Without him the ruins of Greece would for the most part be a labyrinth without a clue, a riddle without an answer. His book furnishes the clue to the labyrinth, the answer to many riddles."[18]

Since Paul went from Beroea "to the sea" (Ac 17:14) and then on to Athens, we may assume a sea voyage. Such a voyage would presumably have taken him down the Gulf of Salonika, with Mt. Olympus off to starboard, past the Northern Sporades (the "scattered" islands), and into the channel between the island of Euboea and the mainland. Euboea is the largest island of Greece proper, and at Chalkis, the Straits of Euripos are only about 210 ft (35 m) wide, and Mt. Parnassus is off to starboard. Then the route would have continued around Cape Sounion, the easternmost projection of the mainland where the seas were often contrary. Appropriately, therefore, on the very summit of the promontory there was a temple to Poseidon, of which fifteen white marble columns still stand. The temple was built in the second half of the fifth century B.C.

on the site of a still older temple built of tufa, and a fortress wall enclosed the sanctuary area. From Sounion to Athens is a distance of 42 mi (68 km), and Pausanias, who visited Athens between A.D. 143 and 159, says that as soon as Sounion is passed those sailing to Athens could see already the spear and helmet of the statue of Athena on the Acropolis.

At Athens there were many harbors. The oldest was the Phaleron, on the south side of Athens where the sea comes closest to the city, today 5 mi (8 km) from the Syndagma or Constitution Square in the heart of the city (from which it is customary to measure distances). Pausanias says that the Phaleron Harbor was the one the legendary kings of Athens sailed from—Theseus to kill the Minotaur on Crete and Menestheus to lead the fleet to Troy. One local tradition says that Paul landed there.

The largest harbor is at Piraeus, 6 mi (10 km) from the city. Themistocles (527–460 B.C.), the Athenian general and statesman who created the Athenian navy, thought that this place was more convenient since it actually consisted

FIGURE 49. Small Harbor on Phaleron Bay, Athens.

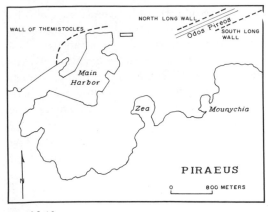

PLAN 13.

of three harbors as compared with only one at Phaleron, so he made it the Athenian port, and Pausanias says that the grave of Themistocles was near it. In addition to the main harbor at Piraeus the other two harbors were the old port of Zea (now the Pacha Limani), where the Athenians sheltered a large part of the naval fleet that was victorious over the Persians at Salamis (480 B.C.), and the ancient Mounychia Harbor (now Tourko Limano), also mentioned by name by Pausanias.

In the *Life of Apollonius of Tyana* by Philostratus it is reported that "having come to anchor in the Piraeus, he went up from the harbor to the city" (IV 17), and Pausanias (I 2, 2) says, "As you go up from the Piraeus," so evidently both landed and went into Athens from there. Probably, therefore, since it was the main port, this is also where Paul landed. However, farther out along the peninsula that projects toward Cape Sounion, beyond the Ellinikon Airport at Glyphada (10 mi [16 km] from the city), there is a large beach, and nearby there are the ruins of an early Christian basilica, and some local tradition maintains that the ruins mark the spot of Paul's landing.

Athens is on the fertile Attic Plain, which slopes gently toward the Saronic Gulf. The plain is overlooked by Mt. Hymettus (3,369 ft [1,027 m] high) on the east, a source of marble of a bluish hue; Mt. Pentelicus (3,635 ft [1,108 m]) on the northeast, a source of fine white,

blue-veined Pentelic marble; Mt. Parnes (4,636 ft [1,413 m]) on the northwest; and Mt. Aegaleus (1,532 ft [467 m]) on the west. Pausanias mentions the first three of these mountains: "The Attic mountains are Pentelicus, where there are quarries, Parnes, where there is hunting of wild boars and of bears, and Hymettus, which grows the most suitable pasture for bees." (I 32, 1).

Athens itself is more immediately overhung by Mt. Lycabettus (1,112 ft [339 m]) to the northeast, the sharp point of which is now called Hagios Georgios from a monastery on the summit. The mountain is not included within the walls of the city, but the river Eridanus flows from Mt. Lycabettus through the city, and the river Ilissus flows from the same region to the south of the city.

In the city is the Acropolis hill, an oblong rocky mass (512 ft [156 m] high) that is precipitous on all sides except the west. Close to it and below it is the Areopagus rock (377 ft [115 m]). Farther west are the Pnyx (351 ft [107 m]) and the Hill of the Nymphs (341 ft [104 m]), and there is a modern observatory on the latter. Southwest, outside the old city wall, is the Mouseion Hill (482 ft [147 m]).[19]

If Paul walked into the city from Piraeus, as it appears both Apollonius and Pausanias did, and if he took the route described by Pausanias, he would probably have followed something like the route of the modern Piraeus highway. Themistocles had built walls to fortify Piraeus Harbor, and in the Classical period there had been long walls from Piraeus to Athens, but they were already in ruins by Paul's time. Approaching the city from the northwest, one came to a district called the Outer Kerameikos, which was a quarter inhabited by potters (as its name indicates) and by metalworkers. There the main city wall was reached. This wall was built by Themistocles (around 480 B.C.), strengthened by Conon (394), and doubled by a second wall in the time of Lykourgos (336–328). At the present time the line of these walls is still traceable for a distance of about 600 ft (185 m).

Outside the city wall there was an extensive

FIGURE 50. In the Harbor at Piraeus, the Main Harbor of Athens.

PLAN 14.

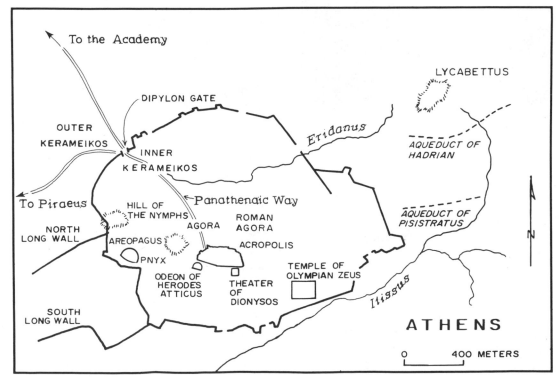

To the Academy

LYCABETTUS

DIPYLON GATE

OUTER
KERAMEIKOS

INNER
KERAMEIKOS

Eridanus

AQUEDUCT OF
HADRIAN

To Piraeus

Panathenaic Way

HILL OF
THE NYMPHS

NORTH
LONG WALL

AGORA

ROMAN
AGORA

AQUEDUCT OF
PISISTRATUS

AREOPAGUS

ACROPOLIS

PNYX

ODEON OF
HERODES
ATTICUS

THEATER
OF
DIONYSOS

TEMPLE OF
OLYMPIAN ZEUS

Ilissus

SOUTH
LONG WALL

ATHENS

0   400 METERS

FIGURE 51. Grave Stela from the Kerameikos (Fourth Century B.C.), in the National Archaeological Museum in Athens. The deceased is the seated figure. The inscription on the architrave reads, "Here lies Polyxena, leaving behind a grieving young husband, a mother, and the father who begat her."

cemetery, since as in many other places, the custom was to bury people outside the walls and alongside principal roads. Here, according to Pausanias, was the grave of Menander (343–329 B.C.), the Greek comic dramatist and the cenotaph of Euripides, but Menander's actual burial place was in Macedonia where he had gone to lecture at the court of Archelaus.

At this point two roads converged, one from

Piraeus and the other from the Academy (where Plato taught), 2 mi (3.5 km) to the west and, more distantly, from Corinth in the south and Boeotia in the north. In the wall there were two gates, the Sacred Gate to the southwest and the Dipylon Gate, the Double Gate, to the northeast. The Eridanus River, which originated on the slope of Mt. Lycabettus, flowed out of the city through the Sacred Gate. Between the gates the Pompeion —a Greek structure of the fourth century B.C. rebuilt by Hadrian in the second century A.D. —was a storehouse for equipment for religious processions and a starting point for the Panathenaic parade, a feature of the most ancient and important festival of Athens, which was celebrated in honor of Athena and involved a march to the Acropolis.

From the Dipylon Gate, built by Lykourgos (338–326), a wide street simply called the Dromos (the Road) ran into the city. It crossed the Inner Kerameikos and led to the Agora, where one continued on foot on the Panathenaic Way to the base of the Acropolis.

The agora (corresponding to the Latin *forum* and often translated as the marketplace, Ac 17:17) was the characteristic feature of any Greek city. To the Greeks a city without an agora was barbarian, and the Agora at Athens was the most famous of all. The Athenian Agora was the center of the public and business life of the city, and people met there every day to learn the latest news and to discuss all manner of subjects (cf. Ac 17:21). Temples and government buildings, shops and offices, and altars and statuary filled the Agora, and stoas and colonnades gave protection against the summer sun and the winter rain and cold.

Coming in from the Kerameikos to the Agora, Pausanias (I 3, 1) says, "First on the right is what is called the Royal Portico (στοὰ Βασιλείος), where the king [the annually appointed king-archon] sits when holding the yearly office called the kingship." This Stoa Basileios, also known as the Stoa of Zeus Eleutherios and built in 430 or 421 B.C., was one place where Socrates discussed philosophy

FIGURE 52. Looking Across the Athenian Agora to the Stoa of Attalos and Mt. Lycabettus.

with his friends, and it was sometimes a meeting place of the Areopagus court; almost nothing of it remains. Next to it was the Temple of Apollo Patroös, Apollo being called by this epithet as the father of Ion, the mythical ancestor of the Athenians and Ionians. This temple was completed in the fourth century B.C., and it contained a gigantic statue of Apollo, which is now in the Agora Museum.

Back of these buildings on a rocky plateau called Kolonos Agoraios, with a panoramic view of the Agora, was the Hephaisteion. This sanctuary, built between 449 and 444, was dedicated to Hephaistos (Vulcan), the god of fire and volcanoes. He was also god of the arts dependent on fire, especially metalworking, and hence was the god of the industrial workers and artisans in the nearby Kerameikos. Since the building was ornamented with many sculptures depicting the exploits of Theseus, it is sometimes called the Theseion. Today it is the least damaged of any ancient

Greek temple, and it is surrounded by a garden, planted as in ancient times with pomegranates, myrtle, and grape vines.

The Metroon in the Agora was the Temple of Cybele, mother of the gods, whose cult was introduced into Athens soon after 430 B.C., and the temple was completed in the second century B.C. The Bouleuterion or Council House was the meeting place of the assembly known as the Βουλή (Latin concilium). An old Bouleuterion was built in the fifth century B.C., and later a new Bouleuterion was built beside it. The Tholos, a circular building with a pyramidal roof put up in 470 B.C. on the site of an earlier building that was destroyed by the Persians, was the official seat of the prytanes who administered the official government of Athens. These three structures were the principal buildings of state, and they were near each other at the southwest corner of the Agora. For the most part only their foundations have been preserved.

FIGURE 53. Hephaisteion on Kolonos Agoraios.

Further along the Panathenaic Way, east of the Stoa of Zeus but still on the right and near the junction of the Panathenaic Way and other important streets of the Agora, is the Altar of the Twelve Gods. Dating from the sixth century, this was the point from which distances from ancient Athens were measured. The sacred area was surrounded by a wall, called the Peribolos of the Twelve Gods, and in Roman times the altar was called the Altar of Mercy, since it provided asylum for the poor, for suppliants, and for strangers seeking the protection of the city. Pausanias wrote (I 17, 1), "In the Athenian Agora among the objects not generally known is an altar to Mercy, of all divinities the most useful in the life of mortals and in the vicissitudes of fortune, but honored by the Athenians alone among the Greeks. And they are conspicuous not only for their humanity but also for their devotion to religion. They have an altar to Modesty, to Rumor, and to Effort. It is quite obvious that those who excel in piety are correspondingly rewarded by good fortune."

Still further along, a raised platform of earth marks the position of the Temple of Ares (Mars). Originally built on the some other site in 440–436 B.C., perhaps on the Areopagus hill, the temple was moved stone by stone to this site in the time of Augustus. Nearby was the Odeon, a music hall, which was the gift of M. Vipsanius Agrippa, minister of Augustus (about 15 B.C.). Behind that was the Middle Stoa, which dated from the second century B.C. and stretched across the Agora for 500 ft (150 m). At the west end of the stoa there was a group of buildings, probably office buildings and shops and, near them, a sixth-century boundary stone inscribed, "I am the boundary of the Agora." Among these buildings was one shop that may have been the shop of the cobbler Simon, with whom Socrates was accustomed to stop and talk.

At the extreme south end of the Agora was

FIGURE 54. Combat of Greek and Trojan Heros on a Krater, a Vessel Resembling an Amphora (c. 530 B.C.), in the Agora Museum in Athens.

another long stoa of the second century B.C., and at the west end of it was the Heliaca. This building housed a popular court organized in the sixth century B.C. by Solon, which at the beginning met in the open at sunrise and hence took its name from Helios, the sun. Adjacent to it was the Klepsydra, a water clock of the fourth century B.C.

On the left of the Panathenaic Way as one comes from the entrance to the Agora, there is first the probable site of the Stoa Poikile (Painted Porch), the first of the great stoas built in the Agora (460 B.C.) and the place where Zeno taught in the next century—and from which his followers were called the Stoics. Next on the left was the Northeast Stoa and then the Stoa of Attalos. The latter was built in the second century B.C. by Attalos II, king of Pergamon, who was a student of the Athenian philosopher Carneades, the founder of the so-called New Academy. This stoa has

been reconstructed and houses the Agora Museum. In front of it, on the west end, was a *bema* and, to the south, the Library of Pantainos, which was built about A.D. 100. Everywhere throughout the Agora there was a multitude of statues of gods and humans, many of which are enumerated by Pausanias.

Further to the east and almost due north of the Acropolis was the Roman Agora. A large court, with some of its marble paving still to be seen, dates from the end of the Hellenistic or the beginning of the Roman period; a monumental gate on the west side is from the second half of the first century B.C.; and the interior colonnade and the east gate are from the first half of the second century A.D., perhaps from the time of Hadrian. Nearby were Hadrian's Library and the Tower of the Winds, the latter an octagonal tower oriented toward the eight points that were considered to be the directions of the winds, the names and symbols

FIGURE 55. Portrait Bust of the Emperor Trajan (A.D. 96–117), in the Agora Museum in Athens.

of which were carved on the tower. With it was also a water clock.

The Athenian Agora was the center of the civic life of the city, but the Acropolis was the center of the religious life, and on it was built the most remarkable assemblage of monuments ever produced by the ancient Greek civilization. In contrast with the Agora, where for the most part only the foundations of the buildings now remain, some of the ancient structures on the Acropolis are relatively intact in spite of the vicissitudes of time and war.

A rocky hill and a true natural fortress, it was here that the first inhabitants settled, probably as early as 3000 B.C. or before. During the Mycenaean period, perhaps around 1500, the Acropolis was fortified for the first time

with a strong wall built of boulders, and the entrance at the west was in the approximate location of the later Propylaia. The first Temple of Athena was probably built about 1000 B.C., and other shrines and treasuries had been built by the time of the Persian invasion as they were badly damaged at that time. It was after the Persian invasion and in the golden age under Pericles (495–429) that the greatest monuments were constructed and adorned with the sculptures of Phidias and his associates. Other temples and monuments were built still later in the whole Classical period of the fifth and fourth centuries.

As one ascends to the Acropolis through the Propylaia there is access to the right to the Temple of Athena Nike, ahead and to the left is the Erechtheion, and ahead and to the right is the Parthenon. Between the two latter buildings there once stood the great bronze statue of Athena Promachos, more than 29 ft (9 m) high and made, according to Demosthenes, by Phidias from the spoils of the Persian wars and consecrated in 454 B.C. This statue was carried off to Constantinople, probably under Justinian in the sixth century A.D., and in 1203 it was broken up by a superstitious populace.

The Parthenon is a Doric temple, built entirely of Pentelic marble on a limestone base. An outer colonnade of forty-six columns was encircled by a frieze showing the great Panathenaic procession, which took place every four years, and above the frieze, on the pediments, were representations of the war of the gods and giants, the war of the Greeks with the Amazons, and other subjects. Inside was a gold and ivory statue of Athena by Phidias, 40 ft (12 m) in height. According to ancient descriptions, on the robe, breastplate, and crested helmet of the goddess were sculptures; in her right hand was a figure of Victory; in her left hand, a lance; and leaning against her knee, a shield. The Parthenon remained

FIGURE 56. Portrait Bust of the Emperor Antoninus Pius (A.D. 138–161), in the Agora Museum in Athens.

FIGURE 57. Portrait Bust of a Young Man (Early First Century A.D.), in the Agora Museum in Athens.

FIGURE 58. Portrait Bust of a Young Woman (Period of Tiberius, A.D. 14-37), in the Agora Museum in Athens.

intact until the end of the Roman Empire, was transformed into a Christian church in the Byzantine period, was called the Church of St. Mary of Athens during the Crusades, was converted into a mosque in 1460, and was being used as a Turkish powder magazine in 1687 when a Venetian shell struck and caused a damaging explosion. In the early nineteenth century Lord Elgin obtained permission from the Turks to take the sculptures of the Parthenon, as well as many from the Erechtheion and the Nike Temple, to England.

Of the famous Parthenon J. P. Mahaffy wrote: "There is no ruin all the world over which combines so much striking beauty, so distinct a type, so vast a volume of history, so great a pageant of immortal memories. . . . All the Old World's culture culminated in Greece—all Greece in Athens—all Athens in its Acropolis—all the Acropolis in the Parthenon."[20]

The Erechtheion is famous for its Porch of the Maidens, and the Temple of Athena Nike is decorated with a frieze of bas reliefs showing the assembly of the gods, the battles of the Greeks and Persians, and other subjects. Elsewhere on the Acropolis are the cuttings and foundations for many other buildings, and in the southeast corner, erected on the site of

FIGURE 59 (top). The Erechtheion on the Acropolis. *FIGURE 60 (bottom)*. Seats in the Theater of Dionysos.

FIGURE 61. The Temple of the Olympian Zeus, Looking Toward the Acropolis.

other ancient buildings, is the Acropolis Museum.

On the south slope of the Acropolis is the Odeon of Herodes Atticus, built in A.D. 161 as a theater and concert hall, and the Theater of Dionysos, dating from the sixth century B.C. although its earlier wooden seats were replaced by stone in the fourth century B.C. Below the Acropolis, on the level ground to the east and south, is the colossal Temple of the Olympian Zeus, begun under Antiochus IV Epiphanes in the second century B.C. and completed by Hadrian in the second century A.D. The base is 354 ft (108 m) by 135 ft (41 m), and the height is more than 90 ft (27 m). Of an original 104 Corinthian columns, sixteen remain. Of the work of Antiochus IV Epiphanes, Livy wrote (XLI 20, 8), "The temple of Olympian Jupiter (Zeus) is the only one in the world which has been conceived on a plan which is proportionate to the majesty of the god."

The Areopagus, below the Acropolis to the west and north and overlooking the Agora, is now little more than a barren rock ascended from the south by sixteen steep steps. Pausanias (I 28, 5–6) states that this Hill of Ares was so named because Ares was the first to be tried there, and Pausanias describes a Stone of Outrage and a Stone of Ruthlessness on which stood, respectively, the defendants and the prosecutors in legal proceedings. Pausanias

also speaks of a nearby sanctuary of the goddesses called Erinyes or Furies, who avenged the crime of murder, and says that persons acquitted in trials on the hill went there to make sacrifice. The same goddesses were also called Arai or Curses, because they fulfilled curses, and euphemistically, they were called Semnai or August.

The court that met on the rock was also called the Areopagus, as well as the "council in the Areopagus" and the "council of the Areopagites." Although the court dealt with capital crime in the early days, its functions varied and by the time of Paul it probably had authority over religious affairs as well. The usual expression for appearing before the tribunal was "to go up into the Areopagus," so the traditional meeting place of the court was no doubt on the hill. But a fourth-century B.C. inscription found under the Stoa of Attalos mentions an entrance to the Areopagus at the Bouleuterion, and a fourth-century B.C. speech attributed to Demosthenes describes the Areopagus as sitting in the Stoa Basileios, so on occasion the court also met in those places in the Agora.

As to the experience of Paul in Athens, he is said to have seen that the city was full of idols (Ac 17:16), as was undoubtedly the case. Livy (XLV 27, 11), for example, says that Athens is replete with ancient glory and has many

FIGURE 62. The Areopagus (the Rocky Hill at the Bottom of the Picture).

notable sights, including "the statues of gods and men—statues notable for every sort of material and artistry." In the city Paul spoke first in the synagogue, as was his usual custom, and also talked in the marketplace with those who chanced to be there. In the Agora some of the Epicurean and Stoic philosophers met him, and they took him to the Areopagus. In his address to the members of the Areopagus, most likely delivered at the traditional meeting place of the council on the rock, Paul began in a complimentary way, remarking that the Athenians were very religious and saying, in that connection, that he had observed an altar dedicated "to an unknown god" (Ac 17:23). His remark about the piety of the people is paralleled by Pausanias's comment about the Athenians that "they are conspicuous not only for their humanity but also for their devotion to religion," and by a remark of Josephus (*Against Apion* II 11, §130) to the effect that the

Athenians are the most pious of all the Greeks. As for the altar Paul spoke about, Pausanias (I 1, 4; cf. v 14, 8) mentions various temples in the vicinity of the harbor at Phaleron Bay "and altars of the gods named Unknown, and of heroes," and in the *Life of Apollonius* (VI 3), Apollonius remarks that it is a proof of wisdom "to speak well of all the gods, especially at Athens, where altars are set up in honor even of unknown gods."

The saying used by Paul in his address, "For we are indeed his offspring" (Ac 17:28), is a quotation from *Phenomena* by Aratus (third century B.C.). The poet was a native of Soli in Cilicia, and his works were probably studied with pride in the schools of nearby Tarsus, so the use of the quotation seems most natural on the lips of Paul of Tarsus. In the climax of his address Paul refers to the Resurrection, and one wonders whether Paul thought of the vast cemetery he had passed through outside the

FIGURE 63. Bronze Statue of Athena (Fourth Century B.C.), from Piraeus, in the National Archaeological Museum, in Athens.

Dipylon Gate as he came into Athens, or whether he remembered *The Eumenides* by Aeschylus (525–456 B.C.)—a play about the goddesses of that name and about the origin of the Areopagus court—in which Apollo says, "Whenever the dust of the earth drinks up the blood of a man who has died, there is no resurrection" (*Eumenides* 647–648). Such a statement represented a widely held opinion, which was also reflected in many of the inscriptions in the cemeteries of that time. But it is significant to see how the Christians could look upon even the cemetery in light of their knowledge of the Resurrection as Paul declared it to the Athenians. The Greek word from which the English word "cemetery" is derived meant both a sleeping room and a burial place, and Paul would soon use the figure of "sleep" as he wrote to the Thessalonian church about the death of some of their members: "But we would not have you ignorant, brethren, concerning those who are asleep, that you may not grieve as others do who have no hope" (I Th 4:13). Several centuries later Chrysostom delivered a homily "On the Word Cemetery" and said: "Before the coming of Christ, death was called death. Since Christ has come and died for the life of the world, no longer is death called death; now it is called sleep; and for that reason, the place where we bury our loved ones is called a *κοιμητήριον* (sleeping-place)."

In response to what Paul had to say, some of his listeners were scornful, some were interested, and some were persuaded. Those who believed are named as Dionysius the Areopagite and a woman named Damaris (Ac 17:37). Of Damaris we know no more, but from the way in which he is designated, Dionysius must have been a member of the council, and according to several later sources, he became the head of the church in Athens. In his honor a Church of St. Dionysius was later built on the north slope of the Areopagus hill, probably near the sanctuary of the pagan Furies mentioned by Pausanias, but the site is now marked only by some enormous pieces of fallen rock. In the approximate vicinity, over-

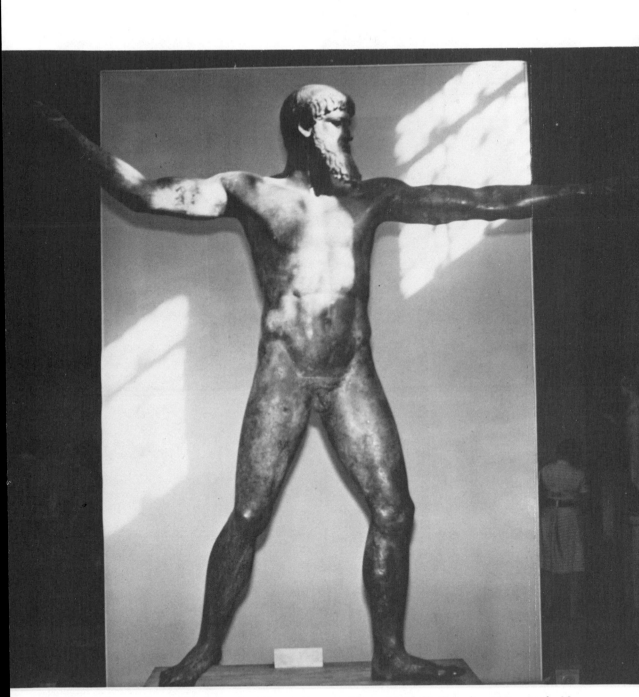

FIGURE 64. Bronze Statue of Poseidon (c. 460 B.C.), Recovered from the Sea by Cape Artemision, in the National Archaeological Museum in Athens.

FIGURE 65. Aphrodite Threatens Pan with Her Slipper While a Small Eros (Cupid) Grasps the Horn of Pan (c. 100 B.C.), in the National Archaeological Museum in Athens.

looking the extreme southeast corner of the Agora, is the Byzantine Church of the Twelve Apostles.

There are other probable indications of the continuing influence of Paul in Athens. Aristides was an Athenian philosopher who wrote in defense of Christianity, perhaps as early as A.D. 125. The first full copy of his writings was a Syriac version found in 1891 by J. Rendel Harris at the Mt. Sinai Monastery, and there is also a Greek text. It is plain that Aristides knew about Paul, and he also speaks of Dionysius. He presents a powerful argument in favor of faith in Christ, and parts of it read like Paul's address at the Areopagus. Aristides

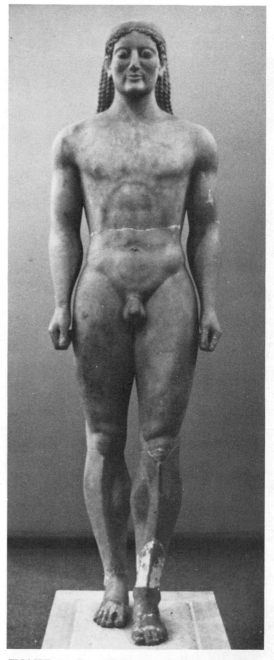

FIGURE 66. Funeral Statue of a Youth Named Kroisos, in the National Archaeological Museum in Athens. Such a statue is called a Kouros, meaning a sculptured representation of a youth, often nude, suggesting the harmony of mind and body. The inscription gives the name and bids the passerby, "Stop and lament. . . ."

FIGURE 67. Mosaic Icon of Mary and the Baby (Fourteenth Century A.D.), from Asia Minor, in the Byzantine Museum in Athens.

proclaims the true idea of God, and with respect to the Resurrection, he says about the Christians, "If any righteous man among them passes from this world, they rejoice and thank God and they escort his body as if he were setting out on a journey from one place to another" (*Apology* 16).

Athenagoras, a native of Athens and a philosopher, also wrote in the second century. At the outset he searched the Scriptures for arguments against Christianity, then he suddenly was converted and addressed a defense of Christianity to the emperors Marcus Aurelius and Commodus. Athenagorus also wrote a treatise on the Resurrection, and as he approaches the climax of his argument, the modern editor of his work writes, "The calm sublimity of this paragraph excels all that ever came from an Athenian before." The same editor comments on the concluding chapter of

Athenagoras's treatise and points out the continuity with Paul: "This chapter is of itself a masterpiece. . . . Blest be Athenagoras for completing what St. Paul began on the Areopagus, and for giving us 'beauty for ashes' out of the gardens of Plato. Now we find what power there was in the apostle's word, when he preached to the Athenians 'Jesus and the resurrection.'"[21]

Corinth

Paul left Athens and went to Corinth (Ac 18:1). From Athens to Corinth is a distance of 53 mi (85 km), and Paul no doubt went overland on foot. At a distance of 2 mi (3.5 km) from Athens was the Academy where Plato taught and was buried and where his successors continued to teach, the ruins of which are around the present church of Hagios

MAP 7.

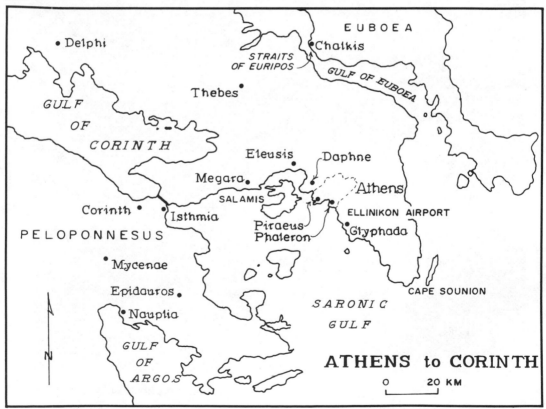

Triphon. Farther to the west, at a distance of 3 mi (5 km), is Daphne, which took its name from the laurel trees—sacred to Apollo—that grew there. A Temple of Apollo was destroyed in A.D. 395, and a monastery dedicated to the Dormition of the Virgin was founded in the fifth or sixth century. In the church at Daphne there are beautiful mosaics of Christ and Mary from the eleventh century.

Eleusis, 14 mi (22.5 km) farther, is one of the oldest cities in Attica, and for a long time, it rivaled Athens. According to mythology, in the time of King Keleos, Demeter came here seeking her daughter Persephone who had been carried off by Hades (Pluto). The king gave Demeter hospitality, and in gratitude she presented his son Triptolemus with the first grain of corn and taught him how to till the soil. Although Persephone was restored to her mother, she had eaten a pomegranate in Hades and had to return there for six months each year. The grief of Demeter over the abduction of her daughter symbolizes the mourning of nature over the death of plants in winter, and the return of Persephone symbolizes the springing up of growing things after the months of death. This myth embodied the thought of the relation of human destiny to natural phenomena and thoughts of life and death and life after death.

This configuration of ideas was the basis of the Eleusinian mysteries, which it was said were founded by the king-priest Eumolpos ("he who sings in tune") at the command of Demeter. The emperor Hadrian was initiated into these mysteries in A.D. 124, and they were renowned until the end of the fourth century when they were banned by Theodosius. The festivals of the Eleusinian mysteries were celebrated twice a year, the Greater Eleusinia in the month of Boedromion (Sept./Oct.) and the Lesser Eleusinia in the month of Anthesterion (Feb./Mar.). The Greater Eleusinia lasted for ten days and involved a journey to Eleusis, the carrying of veiled sacred objects to the Eleusinion in Athens, an assembly at the Stoa Poikile, ritual bathing at Phaleron Bay, fasting and purification, a pro-

FIGURE 68. Votive Relief from Eleusis (c. 430 B.C.), in the National Archaeological Museum in Athens. Demeter gives Triptolemus an ear of corn to spread its cultivation to humankind, while her daughter Kore or Persephone crowns the youth.

cession from Athens to Eleusis with arrival during the night, sacrifices, an enactment of the mysteries, initiation, vigils in the Telesterion, and a final return from Eleusis to Athens. In the mysteries it is probable that the torchlight excursions and sacred dramas enacted events involving Demeter and Persephone and thereby showed how the soul would make its journey in the underworld. With respect to the mysteries the Homeric *Hymn to Demeter* said: "Happy among the inhabitants of the earth is he who has gazed upon these things. But he who is not initiated does not have a like fate to the initiates when he has died and is below in darkness."

In connection with such initiations it may be noted that when Paul says in Phil 4:12, "I have learned the secret of facing plenty and hunger, abundance and want," he uses the same word (μυέω) that was employed in classical Greek to mean "to initiate (into the mysteries)," so Paul's statement could be translated, "I have been initiated." Also one may wonder if the teachings in the Eleusinian mysteries about the death and life of plants being symbolic of the death and life of human beings had anything to do with Paul's phraseology when he wrote about the Resurrection in 1 Cor 15:36–38: "What you sow does not come to life unless it

FIGURE 69. The Corinth Canal.

dies. And what you sow is not the body which is to be, but a bare kernel. . . . But God gives it a body as he has chosen."

As to archeological remains at Eleusis, there are ruins of a king's palace on the acropolis hill and, on a terrace at the southwest end of the hill, a sanctuary of the Great Goddesses, i.e., of Demeter and Persephone. In a cliff are two caves, which represented the entrance to Hades through which Persephone was carried away and later came back, and these constituted the Ploutonion or sanctuary of Pluto. Further on are the remains of the Telesterion in which the Telete or service of initiation into the mysteries was completed.

As one proceeds beyond Eleusis there is to be seen to the left across the Bay of Eleusis the island of Salamis, where the Athenians defeated the Persians in the famous naval engagement of 480 B.C. Then one comes to Megara, presently a large market town with its main square probably on the site of the ancient agora. At one time Megara was an important city of ancient Greece, with caves sacred to Demeter, and with long walls linking it to its port of Nisaia. Sailors from Megara founded colonies as far away as Sicily.

Beyond Megara the Isthmus of Corinth links the mainland of Greece to the peninsula known as the Peloponnesos (Peloponnesus) or Island of Pelops, a legendary personage said to be the son of Tantalus, an ancestor of Agamemnon. At its narrowest the isthmus is less than 4 mi (6 km) wide, with the Saronic Gulf of the Aegean Sea on the east and the Gulf of Corinth of the Ionian Sea on the west. Instead of sailing all the way around the stormy Peloponnesian Cape Malea—of which Strabo (VIII 6, 20) reports the saying, "But when you double Malea, forget your home" —the idea arose of crossing the isthmus directly. As early as the sixth or seventh century a paved track (a δίολκος or "haul-across") was built that was capable of carrying ships loaded onto cradles. The limestone blocks of this tramway are still to be seen in some places, and they show that the road was 10–12 ft (3–4 m) wide, with two grooves 5 ft

FIGURE 70. The Lechaion Road Leading into Ancient Corinth, with Acrocorinth in the Background.

(1.5 m) apart and small curbs at bends in the road to guide the vehicles. Proposals to cut a canal across the isthmus were made by a number of people, from Periander, the tyrant of Corinth from 625–585 B.C., to Nero and Hadrian. Nero actually attempted the project on his visit to Greece in A.D. 67, digging the first dirt with a gold shovel, and Vespasian sent 6,000 Jewish prisoners from Judea as laborers. But it was not until 1893 that a canal was actually completed by a French company, and it shortens the route from Piraeus to the Adriatic by 185 nautical miles.

On the Bay of Corinth at the west end of the canal the ancient port was Lechaion, 2 mi (3 km) north of ancient Corinth and connected with the city by long walls and a broad paved road. The site of Lechaion is now marked by the ruins of a Christian basilica, which was probably built in the middle of the fifth century, restored in the early sixth century, and destroyed by an earthquake in the middle of the sixth century. The basilica was dedicated

to the martyr Leonides and his companions, who were drowned at Corinth.

On the Saronic Gulf the site now called Isthmia was at the east end of the present canal on the south side. A Temple of Poseidon was erected there about 700 B.C. and rebuilt in the fifth century and again in the fourth, and it remained standing until early Christian times. It was at Isthmia that the Isthmian Games

PLAN 15.

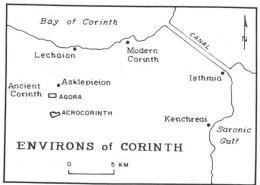

Bay of Corinth

CANAL

Lechaion • • Modern Corinth

• Asklepieion

Ancient Corinth □ AGORA

Isthmia •

ACROCORINTH

Kenchreai •

Saronic Gulf

ENVIRONS of CORINTH

0   5 KM

were held in the spring of every second year, beginning in 582 B.C. and continued in even years B.C. and odd A.D. This was the most famous festival in Greece after the Olympic Games, which were held at Olympia in the western Peloponnesos beginning in 776 B.C. (the beginning of the official era of the Olympiads) and conducted every four years. The original stadium at Isthmia was near the Temple of Poseidon, but in Hellenistic times a new stadium was placed in a natural depression some 800 ft (250 m) away.²² There was also a theater only about 165 ft (50 m) northeast of the precinct of Poseidon, and along with other rebuilding, the theater was probably reconstructed for the visit of Nero in A.D. 67. The fact that the famous Isthmian Games were held at this place, so close to Corinth, may provide background for the language concerning athletics that Paul uses in I Cor 9:24–26: "Do you not know that in a race all the runners compete, but only one receives

the prize? So run that you may obtain it. Every athlete exercises self-control in all things. They do it to receive a perishable wreath, but we an imperishable. Well, I do not run aimlessly, I do not box as one beating the air."

About 2.5 mi (4 km) south of the Isthmian sanctuary of Poseidon and 7 mi (11 km) east of ancient Corinth was the port of Kenchreai (New Testament Cenchreae, Ac 18:18; Rom 16:1), now the village of Kechriais. Thucydides (IV 44, 4) mentions Kenchreai in connection with the attack of the Athenians on Corinth in 425 B.C. Strabo (VIII 6, 4 and 22) describes the place as a village and harbor, 70 stadia (8 mi [13 km]) from Corinth, and says it was the easternmost naval station of the Corinthians and their port for trade with Asia. Pausanias (II 2, 3) says there was a Temple of Aphrodite on one side of the harbor and sanctuaries of Asklepios and Isis on the other, as well as a bronze image of Poseidon on a mole running out to sea. The remains of two moles are still to

FIGURE 71. North Shops and Temple of Apollo in Ancient Corinth.

be seen at the site, as well as the ruins of various commercial buildings and the ruins of what are thought to have been the sanctuaries of Aphrodite and Isis—all from the Roman period. In the fourth century and later an ecclesiastical complex developed on top of the ruins of the Isis sanctuary. Within historical times there appears to have been considerable rise and fall of the land in relation to the sea, and the present shoreline is probably as much as 7 ft (2 m) lower than it was in the time of Christ.

Ancient Corinth lay inland from its two ports of Lechaion and Kenchreai at the foot of Acrocorinth, an imposing hill 1,886 ft (575 m) in elevation. Stone implements and pottery vessels attest occupation of the area in the Neolithic period, and tools of metal show the transition to the Bronze Age around 3000 B.C. About 2000 B.C. the settlement seems to have been devastated, and at the beginning of the first millennium it was occupied by the Dorian Greeks. By the eighth century Corinth had founded colonies at Corfu and Syracuse. In the seventh century Kypselos made himself tyrant of the city, and he was followed by his famous son Periander (625–583), under whom Corinth reached great power and prosperity. The city was famed for pottery and bronze work, and its products were carried abroad by extensive shipping. Corinth survived the vicissitudes of the Peloponnesian War (431–404) and the Corinthian War (393–387), and later in the fourth century Alexander the Great went there to summon the Greeks to join in the united campaign against the Persians. As the leader of the Achaian League, Corinth came into conflict with Rome in the third century B.C. In 146 B.C. a Roman army commanded by the Consul L. Mummius sacked the city, killed or enslaved its citizens, and largely demolished its buildings. Corinth lay desolate for a century and then was refounded as a Roman colony in accordance with a decree Julius Caesar issued in 44 B.C., only shortly before his death. Earlier the city was known as Ephyra ("lookout" or "guard"), but then it was called Colonia Laus Julia

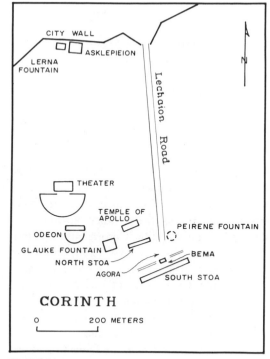

PLAN 16.

Corinthiensis, in honor of its new founder, a name that has been found in an inscription at Corinth. The new settlers seem to have been freedmen from Italy, with whom Greeks and people from the East, including many Jews, were mingled. Commercial prosperity soon returned, and the city also became the administrative center of the senatorial province of Achaia and thus the seat of the proconsul.

In the first quarter of the first century A.D. there was an extensive building program at Corinth. Some structures of the earlier Greek city were rebuilt (the Temple of Apollo, South Stoa, the fountains of Peirene and Glauke, the theater, and the Asklepieion), but for the most part a new Roman city arose. In fact, after 44 B.C. and until the latter part of the second century A.D., the datable inscriptions are chiefly in Latin rather than in Greek.

Strabo (VIII 6, 21) states that Corinth was surrounded by a wall, except where it was protected by Acrocorinth, and that the wall was 40 stadia (4.5 mi [7.5 km]) long. The ancient wall has, in fact, been traced in a circuit of more than 6 mi (10 km), which is actually in excess of Strabo's figure since 6 mi is equivalent to some 55 Greek stadia. Just inside the northern city wall and 1,300 ft (400 m) north of the theater, were the Fountain of Lerna and the Asklepieion, which constituted a great center for the sick who were seeking cures from the healing god, Asklepios.

According to the legend as related by Pausanias (II 26, 1-8), the cult of Asklepios originated at Epidauros, 25 mi (40 km) southeast of Corinth. King Phlegyas came from Boeotia to conquer the territory, and—so the story goes—his daughter Coronis and the god Apollo became the parents of a son, born on a hill not far from Epidauros. The mother died, but the infant was nourished by a goat, and Apollo sent the Centaur Chiron to educate the boy, and he taught him the secrets of healing herbs. One day a shepherd saw a golden halo around the boy's head, and in time the boy gained the reputation of a god who could cure disease and even raise the dead. This boy was Asklepios, and Epidauros became his most famous sanctuary. There was a temple of Apollo on the hill above, and excavations in Epidauros have revealed buildings mostly of the fourth century B.C., including a Temple of Asklepios, a theater with exceptional acoustics seating 14,000, a structure of six concentric circles (tholos) perhaps intended for cult practices involving sacred snakes, and a long north stoa with inscriptions mentioning the abaton ("untrodden") or secret holy place and the enkoimeterion or room where the patients slept in the hope of receiving healing dreams.

After Epidauros, the Asklepieion at Corinth was probably the most famous of the centers, although there were many other such sanctuaries at Pergamon in Asia Minor and elsewhere. At Corinth the Temple of Asklepios was built in the fourth century B.C., replacing an earlier sanctuary of the sixth century. The location was on a natural terrace. To the west was a vast hall, probably the place where the sick slept. The Fountain of Lerna was closely associated with the sanctuary. At the fountain there was a large rectangular central court with colonnades on four sides, and off the east colonnade there were three dining rooms. In the dining rooms stone couches were built along the walls, with bolsters to support the diner's left elbow while food was taken with the right hand. There were tables for food near the couches, and a square block in the center of the dining room was probably where the food was prepared. The practice of having cultic meals in such places is well attested in the early Roman period and illustrates eating "at table in an idol's temple" discussed by Paul in I Cor 8.

The Lechaion Road from the north led directly to the forum of Corinth. As it approached the forum the road was 20-25 ft (6-7 m) in width and flanked by raised sidewalks on either side, and both road and sidewalks were paved with hard limestone. Steps built into the road suggest that it was not intended for wheeled traffic near the forum, and the street was lined with colonnades and shops on either side. Above these shops on the west side of the road was a large basilica, a great rectangular hall divided by two rows of columns with rooms at either end. Beyond the basilica on an eminence to the west was the great Temple of Apollo (sixth century B.C.), of which seven of the original thirty-eight columns still stand, nearly 24 ft (7 m) in height and 6 ft (almost 2 m) in diameter. Behind the shops on the east side of the Lechaion Road was a large open court, probably the Peribolos or sacred enclosure mentioned by Pausanias as dedicated to Apollo. South of this enclosure was another structure enclosing a copious natural spring, the famous Fountain of Peirene, which reputedly first flowed when Pegasus stamped his foot.

At the end of the Lechaion Road, access to the forum was provided by an ornamental Roman arch. The forum, a large rectangular area, was divided into two parts, the northern or lower and the southern or upper part. Colonnades, shops, basilicas, and other monuments surrounded the forum. The dividing

FIGURE 72 (top). Roman Period Temple of Octavia at Ancient Corinth, with Acrocorinth in the Background.
FIGURE 73 (bottom). Marble Slab with Cross, Rosettes, and Peacocks, from the Church (Late Fourth or Fifth Century A.D.) on the Bema in Ancient Corinth.

FIGURE 74. Head of the Young Nero, in the Ancient Corinth Museum. *(Photo Courtesy Corinth Excavations, American School of Classical Studies, Athens)*

line between the lower and upper areas was marked by a long east-west row of one-story shops with a platform for public speaking (*bema*) at its midpoint. The southern edge of the forum was marked by the colonnades of the South Stoa, which gave access to another row of shops and buildings. Many of these shops had deep wells that were connected with the Peirene water system. The pottery found in this area includes many drinking vessels inscribed with such names and words as Dionysos, Zeus, health, security, and love—which suggests that these shops served chiefly as taverns.

The road leading to Kenchreai left from the south edge of the forum. On a sloping hill northwest of the forum was the theater, built in the fifth century B.C. and rebuilt several times in the Greek and Roman periods. About 1 mi (1.6 km) west of the forum was the Potters' Quarter, where the craftsmen produced the wares that contributed to the fame of their city. On the road leading up to Acrocorinth Pausanias saw ten sanctuaries, and one of them, a sanctuary of Demeter, has been found high on the slope of the hill. Dating from the seventh century B.C. to Roman times, it fea-

FIGURE 75. Statuette of the Good Shepherd (Fourth Century A.D.), from Ancient Corinth, in the Byzantine Museum in Athens.

tures an open-air meeting place with seats cut as steps in the rock, and several dining rooms are lined with couches and places for washing and cooking, presumably providing for cultic eating as at the Lerna-Asklepieion complex.

The Acrocorinth was probably fortified as early as the seventh and sixth centuries B.C., but for the most part the remains of the

FIGURE 76. "Synagogue of the Hebrews" Inscription, in the Ancient Corinth Museum. *(Photo Courtesy Corinth Excavations, American School of Classical Studies, Athens)*

ancient walls on the hill date back only to the fourth century B.C., and the ramparts were restored by Justinian in the sixth century A.D. On the top of the mountain was the famous Temple of Aphrodite, the goddess whose worship Strabo (VIII 6, 20) says brought many people and much wealth to Corinth. The scanty architectural remains of the temple are on the northern and the higher of the two summits, and a subterranean chamber gave access to a natural spring; on the citadel and on the walls of the chamber many Roman visitors inscribed their names.

The speaker's platform in the center of the middle row of shops in the forum is of special interest in connection with the presence of Paul in the city. This structure consisted of a high broad platform raised on two steps with raised benches at the back and part way along the sides. Below on either side were rectangular enclosures with benches, and beside these, passageways gave access from the lower to the upper areas of the forum. The construction was of white and blue marble, and the platform must have presented an impressive appearance and served very well as a place for public addresses because a large crowd could assemble in front of it. The date of the construction is believed to be in the first half of the

first century A.D., perhaps about A.D. 44.[23] It is doubtless this platform that is referred to in a Corinthian inscription stating that a certain text was read "from the rostra."[24] The Latin word *rostra* corresponds with the Greek word *bema* (Βῆμα, New Testament "tribunal"), so this must be where Paul was brought "before the tribunal" as recorded in Ac 18:12–17. In memory of this event an early Christian church with three apses was erected upon the platform, probably in the fourth or fifth century.

In the vicinity of the theater at Corinth was a plaza, some 60 ft (18 m) square, that was paved with limestone blocks and dated probably in the middle of the first century A.D. On one of the blocks from this plaza is the inscription, ERASTVS.PRO.AED/ S.P.STRAVIT, which means that in return for his aedileship Erastus laid the pavement at his own expense.[25] The Latin word *aedilis* ("aedile") was the title of a Roman city official who was in charge of various public works. In Rom 16:23, which was doubtless written in Corinth, Paul mentions an Erastus whom he calls "the city treasurer." Here he uses the Greek word οἰκονόμος, which has the broad meanings of treasurer, steward, manager, and administrator, and it seems quite likely that

Paul is referring to the very man whose name appears in the theater plaza inscription.

In another inscription found in the vicinity of the Lechaion Road near the forum, dating probably in the last years of Augustus or in the reign of Tiberius, there is mention of a shop or market with the same word in Latin (*macellum*) that Paul uses in Greek (μάκελλον) in 1 Cor 10:25 when he refers to the "meat market."[26] Yet another inscription found on a block of white marble on the Lechaion Road near the Roman arch at the entrance to the forum is roughly cut and only partially preserved, but it unmistakably reads, "Synagogue of the Hebrews," and therefore probably stood over the doorway of a Jewish synagogue somewhere in the vicinity.[27] Although the style of lettering is considered to indicate a date later than the time of Paul, the synagogue was presumably the successor to the one in which, according to Ac 18:4, the apostle preached when he first went to Corinth.

6
THIRD MISSIONARY JOURNEY
(A.D. 51–54)

After his appearance before Gallio Paul stayed on in Corinth for some time, then returned by way of Kenchreai, Ephesus, and Caesarea to Antioch in Syria (Ac 18:18–22). At Ephesus he promised to return (Ac 18:21), so when he started out again on his third missionary journey he went through Galatia, Phrygia, and the "upper country" to Ephesus (Ac 19:1). There he spoke for three months in the synagogue, then for two years in the hall of Tyrannus. After a riot instigated by the worshipers of "Artemis of the Ephesians" (Ac 19:28), he proceeded to Macedonia and Greece and returned by way of Philippi, Troas, Miletus, and other points to Jerusalem, hastening to be there, if possible, on the day of Pentecost (Ac 20:16).

WESTERN ASIA MINOR

On the west coast of Asia Minor four main rivers run down to the Aegean Sea, and even in ancient times they provided natural routes of travel and favorable locations for cities. From north to south the rivers and their main cities are the Caicus, with Pergamum on two of its tributaries; the Hermus, with Smyrna (modern Izmir); the Cayster, with Ephesus; and the Maeander, with Miletus. At each river mouth the sea formerly came in much farther than at present, but much silting up has taken place, and the sea is now much farther away.

There were no doubt indigenous people liv-

ing in the area at an early time. As a westward projection of *Asia*, the region was involved in the larger history of Asia. Thus two monuments of the Hittites—whose main center was further east and whose power broke up about 1200 B.C.—have been found near Smyrna. As a *westward* projection of Asia the region was also involved in the history of Europe. Thus Mycenaean pottery has been found in a grave at Ephesus, dating around 1400–1300 B.C. As far as Greek literature is concerned, history began in this area with the Trojan War (1184 or 1194 B.C. according to the date given by Eratosthenes), and it was Homer, a Greek poet probably born in Smyrna 300–400 years later, who recorded the siege of Troy (Ilion) in the *Iliad* and the wanderings of Ulysses on the way home in the *Odyssey.*

Perhaps a century after the Trojan War, Greeks began to settle on the west coast, the Aeolians between Troy and the Gulf of Smyrna (Aeolis), the Ionians from there as far as the River Maeander (Ionia), and the Dorians south of the Maeander and on the islands of Rhodes and Kos. Ionia developed the main cities, twelve of which—Ephesus, Miletus, and others—formed a Panionic League, to which Smyrna was added later as a thirteenth member. The remarkable development of science and philosophy in these cities has already been alluded to with the earlier references to the work of Anaximander and Thales at Miletus and of Heraclitus at Ephesus.

To the east was Lydia, with its capital at Sardis, of which Croesus (560–546 B.C.) was the most famous king. It was in Lydia that coinage is supposed to have been invented, and lumps of silver found at Sardis, stamped with symbols of Lydian kings of the seventh century B.C., are the earliest known coins. When Croesus moved to resist the rising power of Persia, Cyrus II the Great defeated him at Sardis (547 B.C.), and the whole of Asia Minor was soon incorporated into the Persian Empire, with Sardis becoming the western terminus of Darius I the Great's royal post road from Susa. In 334 B.C. Alexander the Great crossed the Hellespont. At Troy he dedicated his armor to Athena, at Sigeum in the Troad he placed a crown on the Tomb of Achilles, the bravest of Agamemnon's warriors whom Alexander regarded as his own ancestor, and thus he marked his own war against Persia as a sequel to the Trojan War.

In the ensuing Hellenistic period Alexander's successors in Macedonia, the Ptolemies of Egypt, and the Seleucids of Syria all contended for Asia Minor. Assisted by his son Demetrius Poliorcetes, Antigonus of Macedonia tried to hold all of Asia, but Lysimachus from Thrace, Seleucus I from Babylonia, and Cassander from Macedonia combined to defeat and kill him at the Battle of Ipsus in Asia Minor (301 B.C.); thereafter Lysimachus received the greater part of Asia Minor. In turn Lysimachus was defeated and slain by Seleucus I (281 B.C.) who gave the holdings of Lysimachus to his own son Antiochus I, and the Seleucids ruled Asia Minor. Then in 180 B.C. the Romans, assisted by Eumenes III of Pergamum, defeated Antiochus III the Great at Magnesia near Sipylus and, thereafter, gave Eumenes III most of the contested territory. At the end of his life (133 B.C.) Attalus III of Pergamum bequeathed his kingdom to Rome, and with Pompey's defeat of Mithradates VI Eupator of Pontus and his son-in-law Tigranes of Armenia and with the taking of Syria and Palestine (64–63 B.C.), the circle of the Roman Empire was extended around the eastern end of the Mediterranean.

By the middle of the first century A.D. the whole of Asia Minor was organized into Roman provinces. Most of them were imperial and governed by a legate appointed by the emperor, but Asia (the area on the west coast) and Bithynia were senatorial and governed by a proconsul who was appointed annually. The population continued to be mainly Greek in the old Greek cities and Anatolian in the inland parts, Romans were there as officials and businessmen, and Jews were there as a result of the Dispersion. The language was generally Koine Greek, in which nearly all the inscriptions are written; Latin was used officially; and the old Anatolian languages persisted inland. The peace imposed by the Romans lasted for 300 years and brought wealth and prosperity. Everywhere small but handsome Hellenistic buildings were replaced by larger structures of Roman type—temples, theaters, and markets—so except where excavation has brought earlier levels to light, what is to be seen at the various sites are usually buildings of the Roman imperial age.[1]

In A.D. 330 Constantine founded Constantinople (formerly Byzantium), and the Byzantine Empire endured for eleven centuries until the final fall of Constantinople to the Ottoman Turks in 1453. Even in the seventh century, however, Arab invasions penetrated the Anatolian plateau, and most of Asia Minor was lost to the Seljuk Turks in the eleventh century (particularly with the defeat of Romanus IV in 1071).

MILETUS

In 499 B.C. Miletus was involved in a revolt of the Ionians against the Persians, and after the Persians won a naval battle in 494 at the island of Lade (off Miletus), they plundered the city. In 479, however, the Persians were defeated at Mykale (north of Miletus), and Miletus was liberated and rebuilt. This rebuilding was under the direction of Hippodamus, the famous Greek architect of Miletus who introduced there and at other places a system of town planning in which a series of broad, straight streets intersect each other at right angles. After coming again under Persian control, Miletus was taken and freed by Alexander the Great in 334. In the Hellenistic and Roman periods great works of building were done there.

Miletus had no fewer than four harbors and three markets. Of these the so-called South Market was the largest of all the known agoras in the entire Greek world, and its splendid Market Gate has been reerected in the Pergamum Museum in Berlin. On the slope of the acropolis hill was a Roman theater, seating 15,000 spectators. The oldest sanctuary was a Temple of Athena, but Apollo was actually the principal divinity of Miletus, and he was worshiped in an open colonnaded court in front of the northernmost and best of the four harbors. His sanctuary was called the Delphinion, because Apollo was identified with the Cretan Delphinios, who was supposed to have shown the way to Delphi in the form of a dolphin and was therefore the protector of seafarers. In the Delphinion each spring sacrifice was made and a procession gathered to go from Miletus to a great Temple of Apollo at Didyma south of Miletus.

The Didyma temple was the seat of a famous oracle, who figures in the *Church History* (i 7) of Sozomen. Licinius, brother-in-law of Constantine and his colleague in the East, had joined Constantine in issuing the Edict of Milan (A.D. 313), which granted full legal standing to Christianity, but because of a disagreement with Constantine, Licinius was about to persecute the Christian churches under his control and about to engage in a war with Constantine—in which Licinius was defeated (323) so that Constantine emerged as the sole ruler of the Roman Empire. At this juncture Licinius consulted the oracle of Apollo at Didyma and received in answer a quotation from Homer (*Iliad* viii 102–103), "Old sir, of a surety young warriors press you sorely; whereas your might is broken and grievous old age is upon you." Thus the oracle evidently foretold both the defeat of Licinius and the victory of Christianity. By the time

of Julian the Apostate (361–363) Christian chapels had evidently been built near the temple at Didyma, for Sozomen (v 20) relates that that emperor ordered several houses of prayer in that location to be torn down. Finally, with the suppression of paganism by Theodosius I in his edict of A.D. 385, the oracle at Didyma was silenced, and a Christian basilica was built within the temple and stood, in spite of several earthquakes and a fire, until late in the Middle Ages.

EPHESUS

Of the several cities on the west coast of Asia Minor Ephesus had the most favorable location, with its place on the Cayster River and with access also to the valleys of the Hermus and the Maeander on either side, and it became the largest and greatest city. Its site is delimited by the Cayster (now the Küçük Menderes, which flows through the now silted-up plain) on the north and by three hills that form a curve on the east and south. To the northeast is the acropolis or citadel hill, called Ayasoluk (285 ft [87 m] high), which is crowned with the ruins of the Basilica of St. John and which has the town of Selçuk at its base to the east and south; in the middle to the east is Mt. Pion (now Panayir Dagh, 430 ft [131 m]), with the famous theater of Ephesus on its western slope; and to the south is the longer ridge of Mt. Koressos (now Bülbül Dagh, 1,175 ft [358 m]). In ancient times the sea came in not far from the foot of these hills—in the Ionian period it extended almost back to the acropolis and in the Roman period to a harbor at the foot of the street that leads down from the theater—but silting up was progressive and the shoreline is now more than 4 mi (7 km) to the west.

At this site there has been a succession of six cities. First there was a settlement of presumably native people, whom Strabo (xiv 1, 21) calls Lelegians and Carians; other ancient sources speak of the women known as Amazons. These early inhabitants already worshiped a great Anatolian mother goddess, probably the same as the one known later as Cybele. Her sanctuary was at the north foot of Mt. Pion, with niches in the mountainside and votive reliefs.

Second a colony of Ionian Greeks was established at Ephesus. The leader of the colonists, who came from the mainland of Greece, was said to have been King Androklos, son of the legendary King Kodros of Athens, and he was reported to have chosen the site in accordance with clues that he had received from the oracle at Delphi. The date was probably soon after 1000 B.C., and from the Greek point of view, Androklos was regarded as the founder of Ephesus.

The location of the city of the Ionian Greeks was on the north slopes of Mt. Pion and above the ancient Koressos Harbor, some 4,000 ft (1,200 m) west of the later Artemision. The colonists erected a shrine to Apollo and built the first fortifications of the city, but little remains from that time except a small portion of a wall built of polygonal masonry.

The immigrant Greeks also adopted the worship of the Anatolian mother goddess, and they gave her the name of their own goddess Artemis (the Roman Diana). Thus Pausanias (VII 2, 6) speaks of the coming of the Greeks to Ephesus and says that "the cult of Ephesian Artemis is far more ancient than their coming." Although the Greek Artemis was primarily a huntress, the Ephesian Artemis was primarily a deity of fertility, and in this capacity, her symbol was the egg. It was her shrine that became the famous Artemision. The location of the Artemision is on the plain between Mt. Pion and the Ayasoluk Hill, and in ancient times, the sea probably extended this far inland and the temple was probably on the water's edge. In its earliest identifiable form the Artemision consisted of two platforms, one to the west with an altar and one to the east with the cult image of the deity, and the date of the temple is about the beginning of the sixth century B.C.

This second city of Ephesus endured for some 400 years until a new period and a third

city began in the time of Croesus. This famous ruler came to the throne of Lydia in 560 B.C. and began the conquest of most of Asia Minor west of the Halys River. The first Greeks he attacked on the coast were the Ephesians. In the siege of Ephesus by Croesus, Herodotus (I 26) relates that the people dedicated their city to Artemis and signified the same by attaching a rope between the city wall and the temple of the goddess 7 stadia (.8 mi [1.3 km]) away. When Croesus took the city he began the rebuilding of the temple and donated columns for it himself, some of which, with his name on them, are now in the British Museum. The work was under the supervision of a famous Cretan architect named Chersiphron, together with his son Metagenes. As completed around 500 B.C. the temple was a very large and handsome building. It stood on a base 375 ft (115 m) by 180 ft (55 m) in size, and it was adorned with marble columns 60 ft (18 m) in height, marble architraves, and roof beams of cedar, with the image of the goddess in the interior. Pliny (Nat. Hist. XXXVI 96–97) explains that the temple was deliberately built on marshy soil that it might not be threatened by earthquakes, and he tells how Chersiphron lifted the massive architraves on bags of sand and then gradually emptied the lowest layer of bags so that the fabric settled gently into its correct position. Admiringly Pliny calls the temple a remarkable example of the Greek conception of grandeur.

Croesus also moved the earlier city to the level ground south of the temple, where soundings prove that this city existed even though excavation is not possible because it lies below the water level of today. A necropolis of this time (550–450 B.C.) has been found, however, in the saddle between Mt. Pion and Mt. Koressos, with a dozen quite plain sarcophagi of clay and stone, and this necropolis lay on either side of a street that was at least earlier than the city of Lysimachus.

When Cyrus defeated Croesus (547 B.C.) Ephesus came under Persian rule; then in the time of Alexander the Great a number of events occurred. According to Plutarch (*Life of Alexander* III 3), on the very night of Alexander's birth (356 B.C.) the Temple of Artemis at Ephesus was burned. Strabo (XIV 1, 22) says that the fire was set by Herostratos, and Aristotle (*Meteorologica* III 1, 371a, 32–34) discusses the spectacular evidence of the behavior of the flame and wind caused by the conflagration. When Alexander came to Ephesus in 334 B.C. the citizens had begun to rebuild the temple with Dinocrates as the architect, the man who later built Alexandria and proposed to carve Mt. Athos into a statue of Alexander. Alexander offered to pay all the expenses of the temple, if he might make the dedicatory inscription in his own name, but the Ephesians declined, saying in a politic way that it was not fitting for a god (Alexander) to make a dedication to another god (Artemis). The new building was completed toward the middle of the third century B.C. and was of much the same dimensions as its predecessor. The foundation of a great altar (about 130 ft [40 m] wide) has recently been discovered, lying in front of the western facade of the temple and on an axis with it. This was the temple that, according to the list drawn up in Hellenistic times, was one of the Seven Wonders of the World (Temple of Artemis, Pyramids of Egypt, Colossus of Rhodes, statue of Zeus at Olympia, Hanging Gardens of Babylon, lighthouse at Alexandria, mausoleum at Halikarnassos). The temple stood until A.D. 263, when it was burned by the Goths and afterward plundered for materials that were reused in constructions in Selçuk (Basilica of St. John) and Istanbul (Hagia Sophia).

The fourth city at Ephesus was that of Lysimachus, a general and one of the successors of Alexander the Great. Like Alexander he was a citizen of Pella. After the Battle of Ipsus in 301 B.C., Lysimachus ruled most of Asia Minor until his death in 281. Because of the subsidence of the land where the preceding city and the Artemision lay, in 287 Lysimachus moved the city to higher ground in the area between Mt. Pion and Mt. Koressos. According to Strabo (XIV 1, 21) Lysimachus only

FIGURE 77. Restored Column of the Temple of Artemis in Ephesus.

persuaded the reluctant people to move from the low ground around the temple by waiting for a downpour of rain, then blocking the sewers and flooding the old city, whereupon the people were glad to make the change. Also, Pausanias (I 9, 7; VIII 3, 4–5) says, Lysimachus brought additional settlers from Lebedos and Colophon. Lysimachus now fortified the city with a wall with towers and gates running for more than 5 mi (9 km) on a strategic line over the tops of Mt. Pion and Mt. Koressos, where well-preserved sections of the wall can still be seen. Below Mt. Pion and to the west a new harbor was established at the point where the sea came at that time. The city itself was laid out on the regular Hippodamian plan of streets intersecting at right angles, except for the so-called Kouretes Street, which followed an older winding path. Lysimachus called the new city Arsinoeia in honor of his wife Arsinoe, daughter of Ptolemy I, but the name lasted little longer than the lifetime of the king.

After Lysimachus Ephesus was under the Ptolemies, then the Seleucids, and then the kings of Pergamum. King Attalos II of Pergamum saw the Ephesian harbor still being silted up and thought it would be deepened if the entrance were made narrower, but the mole he built had the opposite result; the mole increased the deposits of silt and made the whole harbor more shallow. When Attalos III bequeathed the kingdom of Pergamum to the Romans (133 B.C.) Ephesus came under Roman rule. The Ephesians rebelled in 88 B.C., but lost. Under Augustus they enjoyed the benefits of a general peace and dedicated a sacred precinct to Rome and the emperor. Dio (LI 20, 6) says Ephesus was now the chief city in Asia, Strabo (XIV 1, 24) describes it as the largest emporium in Asia this side of the Taurus, and Pausanias (I 9, 7) calls it "the modern city of Ephesus." In A.D. 17 there was a terrible earthquake, but Tiberius and Hadrian helped with restorations, and the surviving ruins in the main area are almost all from the Roman period and the first and second centuries A.D., which was the time of the greatest prosperity of Ephesus.

During the Byzantine period the city grew smaller. Some people were still living on the west slope of Mt. Pion, but others settled on the Ayasoluk Hill, where the Tomb and Church of St. John became the center of the fifth and Christian city of Ephesus. Walls were constructed on the hill in early Christian times and were extensively reconstructed in the Byzantine and Seljuk periods, and the hill is surmounted by a Byzantine citadel, which has been restored by the Turks. The main gateway was built in the sixth century A.D., using stones from Ephesian buildings of the Roman period, particularly from the stadium. The gate was decorated with reliefs showing scenes from the lives of Achilles and Hector, whom Achilles killed, and these reliefs were later thought to represent Christian martyrs, so it was called the Persecution Gate.

Finally, the sixth city at Ephesus is the Turkish town of Selçuk. There was an Arab raid in A.D. 700, Seljuk Turkish occupation for the first time in 1090, and permanent conquest by the Ottoman Turks in 1426. A Seljuk Turk named Isa Bey built the relatively well-preserved Isa Bey Mosque (completed in 1375) on the western slope of the Ayasoluk Hill, using columns from the Roman ruins of Ephesus. The Turkish town spread to the east and south at the base of the hill, and in 1914, the town took the name of Selçuk.

According to an inscription found on the east wall of the south entrance to the theater, the annual festival procession of Artemis in Ephesus began at the Artemision, entered the city at the Magnesian Gate, continued to the theater, and went out by the Koressos Gate and back to the Artemision. The Magnesian Gate is partly preserved, the only Ephesian city gate to survive. It lies on the southeastern side of the city, on the road to Magnesia, between surviving portions of the third-century wall of Lysimachus on Mt. Pion and Mt. Koressos. The gate was flanked by fortification towers on either side, and it consisted of three entrances, the central one for wheeled traffic. According to fragments of an inscription the gate was probably completed in the

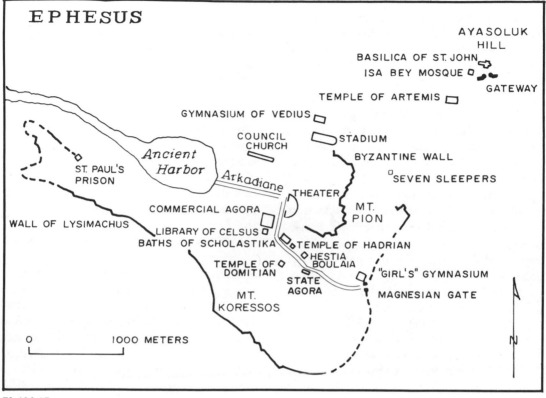

PLAN 17.

time of Vespasian (A.D. 69–79).

In its first section the Processional Way, which leads into the city from the Magnesian Gate, is now called Kouretes Street. The Kouretes were initiates associated with the mother goddess (cf. Strabo x 3, 7), and lists with their names have been found on this street, hence, the name. Proceeding along the route of this street, on the right side immediately beside the Magnesian Gate is the East Gymnasium (palaestra), where portrait statues of the Sophist Flavius Damianus and his wife Vedia Phaedrina were found, suggesting that this couple was responsible for the construction of the gymnasium, probably in the second half of the third century A.D. Because numerous statues of women were also found, this has been called the Girls' Gymnasium. Nearby are the ruins of an aqueduct that brought water to the city from the Marnas River in the Dervend Mountains 4 mi (6 km) to the southeast.

On the left side of the street, a little further along, is a round building faced with marble with sixteen niches on the exterior, probably a former Greek temple but turned into a church in the Byzantine period and said to be the Tomb of St. Luke (probably incorrectly, because the so-called anti-Marcionite Prologue to the Third Gospel says that Luke died in Bithynia and Jerome (*Illustrious Men* 7) states that his remains were buried at Constantinople). Farther along the street are the State Agora, the Bouleuterion, and the Prytaneion. The Bouleuterion is a building with a semicircular auditorium on two levels, seating 1,400 persons, the gift at least in part, according to a building inscription, of P. Vedius Antoninus and his wife Flavia Papiana in the middle of the second century A.D. The

Prytaneion was both the political and the religious center of the city, for it was the meeting place of the governing magistrates known as prytanes, and it contained the sanctuary of Hestia Boulaia (the Roman Vesta), the goddess of the hearth fire of the city. The base of the hearth, on which the sacred flame was never allowed to go out, dates from the period of Augustus, and that emperor also built two small temples nearby, in 29 B.C., for Divus Julius and Dea Roma. In the Prytaneion complex three statues of Artemis of Ephesus were found, which are now in the Selçuk and Izmir museums. The goddess is represented as a tall figure wearing a breast-covering wth many eggs, her symbol, and a long fitted skirt adorned with many figures of animals, of which she was the mistress. East of the State Agora is the so-called Bath of Varius (second century A.D.), on both sides of some steps leading up Mt. Pion to the north are the remains of luxurious private homes with mosaics and frescoes, and across Kouretes Street to the south is the Great East Nymphaeum, a fountain built in the second century A.D. and restored in the fourth century. It was also at the east end of the State Agora that the ancient necropolis was discovered, with its clay-and-stone sarcophagi of the mid-sixth to mid-fifth centuries B.C.

Beyond the State Agora Domitian Street, which runs up Mt. Koressos, goes left off of Kouretes Street. There on a terrace on the west side of the street are the huge vaulted substructures that supported the Temple of Domitian. In the ruins were found a part of the temple altar with relief scenes of trophies and sacrifice (now in the Selçuk Museum) and the head and arm of a colossal statue of Domitian (now in the Izmir Museum). This was the first temple in Ephesus erected especially for the cult of an emperor, and as such, it was known as a *neokorie* (i.e., a provincial sanctuary recognized as an imperial temple), and the city in which it stood was given the honorable title of Neokoros (properly, one who sweeps a temple and, therefore, temple warden).

Beyond its junction with Domitian Street,

Kouretes Street bends slightly to the right and runs on northwestward. On the right are the Fountain of Trajan, dedicated before A.D. 114, and the Temple of Hadrian (A.D. 117–138), the latter being the second sanctuary in Ephesus (after the Temple of Domitian) built especially for the cult of an emperor. Opposite the Temple of Hadrian, on the left side of Kouretes Street, are two fine private houses built on several terraces on the hillside. They were erected in the first century A.D., occupied for centuries, and destroyed in the early seventh century. They were decorated with paintings and mosaics of different dates; one fresco of the first century A.D. is a picture, with an inscription, of Socrates (now in the Selçuk Museum).

Behind the Temple of Hadrian at the southwestern foot of Mt. Pion are the so-called Baths of Scholastika. They were constructed originally about the beginning of the second century A.D. and included a brothel section, identified as such by an inscription. Around A.D. 400 the baths were reconstructed by a Christian lady named Scholastika, whose name is now attached to the ruins and whose headless statue, with an inscription, stands in the entrance room.

At this point the Processional Way turns to the north, and from here on it is known as Marble Street. The marble paving slabs still to be seen were laid by a man named Eutropios, probably in the fifth century A.D. Along the west side of the street is the base of a stoa from the time of Nero (A.D. 54–68), and along the east side are extensive remains of a late Roman colonnade.

At the beginning of Marble Street there is an entrance on the right to the north section of the Baths of Scholastika, and on the left is the Library of Celsus, one of the principal and best-preserved buildings of ancient Ephesus. According to inscriptions in Latin and Greek it was erected in A.D. 110 by a Roman consul named Aquila in honor of his father, Celsus, the latter having been consul in A.D. 92 and a Roman governor of Asia. The building was adorned with an elaborate architectural

FIGURE 78. Temple of Hadrian in Ephesus.

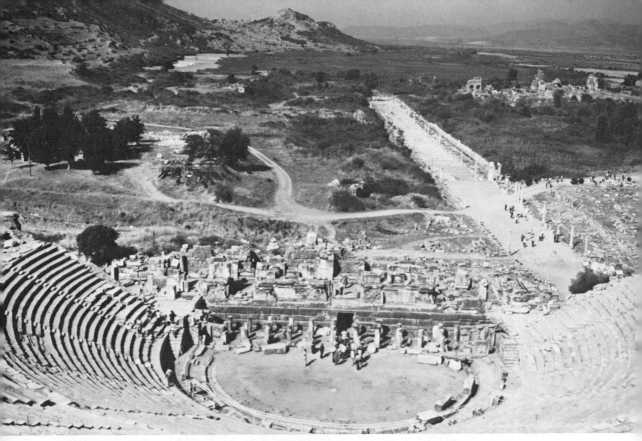

FIGURE 79. Theater and Street (the Arkadiane) Leading to the Harbor in Ephesus.

facade, now reconstructed, and the lofty interior hall had two galleries and three tiers of niches for scrolls and volumes. In a tomb chamber a marble sarcophagus contains an unopened lead coffin in which the remains of Celsus are presumably still preserved.

Just beyond the Library of Celsus the Commercial Agora lies to the west of Marble Street. This was the Hellenistic marketplace of the city, and additions were made in the Roman period under Augustus, Nero, and Caracalla (A.D. 211–217). The area was a square, 360 ft (110 m) on a side, surrounded by stoas with shops back of them, and in the center was a horologe or a water clock and sundial combined. Also there were hundreds of statues on all sides, of which only the bases remain, with inscriptions showing that they represented philosophers, rhetoricians, athletes, and government officials. From the southwest corner of the agora there was access to the Temple of Serapis, probably erected in the second century A.D. by Egyptian colonists. In the Christian era the temple was converted into a church, and there is a baptistery at the east corner.

From the Commercial Agora, Marble Street leads on to the theater, the largest and most impressive of all the structures of ancient Ephesus and, at the same time, a site of special interest in connection with Paul since at the time of the riot that was occasioned by his work the protesting worshipers of Artemis "rushed together into the theater" (Ac 19:29). The theater is built into the steep western slope of Mt. Pion, and from the top there is a splendid view over the city and down the street that in ancient times led to the harbor and the sea. The structure was begun in Hellenistic times, enlarged under Claudius (A.D. 41–54), and completed under Trajan (98–117). The seating capacity was 24,000, with three tiers of twenty-two rows each.

From the theater a main street led westward straight down to the harbor. Since the remains visible today are from a restoration by the emperor Arcadius (A.D. 383–408) it is known as the Arkadiane, but there is little doubt that

FIGURE 80. Columns of the Arkadiane Street in Ephesus.

the street existed in Hellenistic times, and the foundations of the harbor gateway, on exactly the same axis as the western end of the Arkadiane, are of Hellenistic date. The street was more than 1,700 ft (500 m) long, the central lane for wheeled traffic was 36 ft (11 m) wide, and there were colonnades 16 ft (5 m) deep on either side, with shops behind them. An inscription that credits the colonnades to Arcadius also states that the street was lighted.

At the lower end of the Arkadiane, on the north side, huge ruins represent the Harbor Baths and Harbor Gymnasium, and the site was evidently intended for these purposes as early as Lysimachus's time. Beside these structures and to the north was a very long Roman basilica, 853 ft (260 m) in length and 98 ft (30 m) in width. It was divided by two rows of columns into three aisles, was probably a building for business and exchange, and was probably constructed in the first half of the second century A.D. and later abandoned. At the beginning of the fourth century a Christian church, with square atrium and

mosaic-paved narthex, was built in the western part of this building, and later a double church and (in the eastern section) a bishop's palace occupied the structure, and a baptistery was constructed on the north side of the atrium. The baptistery, dating from the fourth century, is well preserved, and large cross signs adorn its marble walls. The church was named for the Virgin Mary, and in A.D. 431 the Third Ecumenical Council met in these facilities and affirmed with Cyril of Alexandria, against Nestorius, that Mary was Theotokos (Mother of God); hence, the church is also known as the Council Church.[2]

As the processional street continued northward from the theater there were a stadium and a combined gymnasium and bath on the right. The stadium was built into the northwest slope of Mt. Pion and was extensively reconstructed under Nero (A.D. 54–68). The gymnasium and bath (a common combination) were dedicated by a wealthy Ephesian named Vedius to Artemis, Antoninus Pius (A.D. 138–161), and the city of Ephesus. In this

FIGURE 81. Marble Slab with Cross, at the Baptistery in the Council Church in Ephesus.

There is, however, a cave chapel on the steep slope of Mt. Koressos above the city to the south, discovered in 1955 and called the Grotto of St. Paul. This was a natural cave that was enlarged to be a cult place in early Christian times. Numerous invocations are scratched on the walls, and three inscriptions are addressed to the apostle Paul. One inscription, for example, written by a person whose name is only partially preserved, reads, "Holy Paul aid thy servant." Another inscription, accompanying a cross sign, uses the language of the soldier of the cross who fights the good fight of the faith, reminiscent of I Tim 6:12 and II Tim 4:7.[3] Thus the remembrance of Paul was alive at Ephesus in the minds of later Christian generations. As for the conflict with the worship of Artemis, there is testimony to the victory of Christianity in an inscription found at Ephesus on a rectangular stone, which was evidently once the base for a statue of the goddess. In perhaps the fifth century an otherwise unknown Christian named Demeas took down the figure and put up a cross instead. The inscription reads, "Demeas has removed the deceitful image of the demon Artemis and in its place put this sign which drives away the idols, to the praise of God and of the cross, the victorious, imperishable symbol of Christ."[4]

John and Mary at Ephesus

To recapitulate the complex questions associated with John at Ephesus discussed earlier, the early Christian tradition generally understood that the apostle stayed at one time in the house of Andronicus and Drusiana, and assembled the believers there, but had his own simple dwelling on the hill above the Temple of Artemis. There he lived to old age, then fell asleep and was buried on the hill. His tomb was well known, like those of Peter and Paul at Rome, and like those as well, his tomb was later surmounted by a great basilica. At Ephesus there was also a tradition concerning Mary the mother of Jesus, whom Jesus at the Crucifixion entrusted to the care of the disciple whom he loved (Jn 19:26–27).

vicinity Marble Street reached the north edge of the city, and near here must have been the Koressos Gate from which the Processional Way returned to the Artemision.

With respect to the apostle Paul, there is a large square tower overlooking the ancient harbor, at the end of the wall built by Lysimachus, that local tradition calls St. Paul's Prison. Actually this structure was probably an item of harbor defense, although conceivably it had other uses too. An Ephesian imprisonment of Paul is only theoretical, and is based chiefly on his reference to fighting with wild beasts at Ephesus (I Cor 15:32), a remark that could have been only figurative rather than literal. Of course it is also possible that Paul might have been given protective custody by the Romans after the riot in the theater, which conceivably could account for the local tradition in question.

FIGURE 82 (top). The Basilica of St. John in Ephesus. FIGURE 83 (bottom). Area over the Tomb of St. John in the Basilica of St. John in Ephesus.

FIGURE 84 (top). Restored Baptistery in the Basilica of St. John in Ephesus. FIGURE 85 (bottom). A Sarcophagus Plaque at the Basilica of St. John in Ephesus, with Rosettes and Crosses (After the Time of Justinian).

At Jerusalem the tradition was that Mary died on Mt. Zion, where the Dormition Church commemorates the event, and was laid to rest—prior to her assumption—in the Tomb of Mary in the Kidron Valley near the Garden of Gethsemane. This view is presented in a number of apocryphal works that go generally under the title of *The Assumption of the Virgin* and are probably fifth century and later in date.[5] Also Theodosius (A.D. 530) mentions a Church of Mary the Mother of the Lord in the Valley of Jehoshaphat (*De situ terrae sanctae* [CCSL CLXXV, p. 137]), and Arculf (A.D. 670) says that the church on Mount Zion was where Mary died (*Adamnai de locis sanctis libri tres* [CCSL CLXXV, p. 197]).

At Ephesus, however, the Third Ecumenical Council met in the Church of the Virgin Mary and proclaimed the doctrine of Mary as Theotokos (Mother of God). This church probably dates in its earliest form from the beginning of the fourth century. In connection with the council it is mentioned repeatedly as the great church of the city, and in a sermon (*Homily* IV) preached against Nestorius at the time of the council, Cyril of Alexandria spoke of the "Church of Mary, Mother of God," into which the Holy Spirit "had gathered us all together." Therefore the church evidently bore the name of Mary prior to the council, and it may have been at least in part because Ephesus was already a center of veneration of Mary that the council met there to discuss her status.[6] In a letter from the fathers of the council to the clergy and faithful in Constantinople it is remarked that Nestorius arrived earlier than the others "in Ephesus, where [are] John the Theologian and the Theotokos Virgin, the holy Mary." Since John was evidently thought of as being present in Ephesus in the sense that he had lived and died there and was especially remembered there by virtue of his honored tomb, the statement must mean that Mary was also thought of as having lived and been laid to rest at Ephesus.[7]

In Germany an invalid nun, Katharina von Emmerich (1774–1824), who had not left her bed in twelve years and had received the

FIGURE 86. Marble Statue of the Ephesian Artemis (Time of Domitian, A.D. 81–96), in the Ephesus (Selçuk) Museum.

stigmata, described in detail the house of Mary at Ephesus, a place the nun had never been, in a series of visions written down by Clemens von Brentano. According to the description the house was on a mountain three or three and one-half hours south of Ephesus, from which the city, the sea, and the islands could be seen, and the Tomb of Mary was about 1 mi (1.6 km) from the house. In 1891 M. Poulin, Superior of the Lazarists of Smyrna, identified a ruined house at a site called Panaya Kapulü in the hills 5 mi (8 km) south of Ephesus and 1 mi (1.6 km) northwest of the peak of Ala Dagh as identical in location and plan with what Katharina von Emmerich had described, and the ruin is now known as the House of the Virgin Mary (Meryem Ana). Excavations at the site by Italian archeologists under the leadership of A. Prandi seem to indicate that the foundations of the house are indeed from the first century A.D. and that the chapel above is probably to be ascribed to the sixth century. Although the evidence is not conclusive and the supposed tomb has not been located, the site was visited by Pope Paul VI in 1967, and it has become a place of pilgrimage in honor and remembrance of Mary.[8]

Timothy at Ephesus

According to Eusebius (*Ch. Hist.* III 4), Timothy, the disciple of Paul, was the first head of the church in Ephesus (cf. 1 Tim 1:3). The apocryphal *Acts of St. Timothy* (which may come from a history of the Ephesian church composed by an unknown author in the first half of the fourth century) reports that Timothy was appointed to that position by Paul in the reign of Nero (A.D. 54–68) and that Timothy suffered martyrdom in the reign of Nerva (96–98). According to this source the occasion of Timothy's martyrdom was his taking a stand against the shameless proceedings of a pagan festival. The festival is designated by the word Katagogia (καταγώγια), which is a term referring to the epiphany (i.e., the coming or the return) of a deity, and the deity in question is probably Dionysos, whose similarly named festival is also attested by inscriptions at Miletus and Priene. The place where the fatal confrontation took place is called in the apocryphal source the Embolos (ἔμβολος). Confirmation of the probable

FIGURE 87. Broken Statue of Aphrodite, in the Ephesus Museum.

FIGURE 88 (*on facing page*). Statue of Dionysos from the Fountain of Trajan in Ephesus, in the Ephesus Museum.

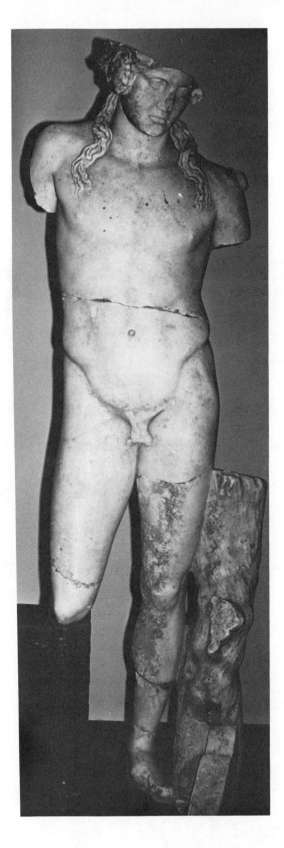

accuracy of these references is found in an Ephesian inscription of the second century A.D. that mentions "the day of the Katagogiae" and in several Ephesian inscriptions that refer to a quarter of the city—perhaps between Mt. Koressos and Mt. Pion—called Embolos. According to the apocryphal *Acts* the body of Timothy was taken by his friends and laid away in the quarter of the city that was across from the harbor, and his martyrium was there on Mt. Pion and therefore perhaps somewhere in the vicinity of the Catacomb of the Seven Sleepers, although it has never been found.[9]

Seven Sleepers

The Catacomb of the Seven Sleepers is on the northeastern slope of Mt. Pion where there are steep rock walls and natural caves, and the area may have been an early gathering place for the Christians of Ephesus as well as a place of refuge and a place of burial. According to legend, seven Christian youths of Ephesus hid in a cave there at the time of the persecution under Decius (A.D. 250), were sealed in the cavern by the emperor's command, and fell into a sleep from which they only awakened 200 years later when some stones happened to be removed from the entrance. This event occurred under the Christian emperor Theodosius II (A.D. 408–450) and Bishop Maximus, and it provided evidence of the bodily resurrection. At the site, the oldest part of the entire complex is a catacomb with ten burial chambers, over which a church was erected, probably in the early or middle part of the fifth century. This church is 82 ft (25 m) in length, with an apse in the east, and the breadth of the church is divided into three parts marked by differences in ground level. West of the church is a burial hall 50 ft (15 m) in length, with many burial niches, and a quadrangular mausoleum with a cross-shaped inner room. Probably by the end of the fifth century, a long crypt was constructed to the north of the church and, still later, a burial chapel, with

many more burial places, was added to the southeast. Finally, perhaps at the end of the sixth century, a large cross-shaped mausoleum of a certain Flavius Abradas was begun south of the church, but left uncompleted. In addition to the buildings some 2,000 clay lamps have been found, and there are numerous graffiti on the walls that were left by pilgrims from many lands who visited the site down into the fifteenth century.[10]

SEVEN CITIES OF
THE REVELATION

In addition to Ephesus the Book of Revelation (2–3) addresses letters to the churches of six more cities of Asia; the total number of seven was certainly not all the churches of the province, but no doubt they were symbolically representative of the whole church. In addition the particular seven appear to have been on a natural circuit of travel for the messenger who carried the communications, namely from Ephesus north 40 mi (65 km) to Smyrna and another 68 mi (110 km) to Pergamum, then southeast 45 mi (72 km) to Thyatira, 30 mi (48 km) more on to Sardis, 30 mi (48 km) farther to Philadelphia, and 40 mi (65 km) more to Laodicea.[11]

Smyrna

Smyrna, the present Izmir, lies on the large indentation of the Aegean Sea known as the Gulf of Smyrna or the Gulf of Izmir. Archaeological excavation has revealed that the earliest settlement, dating from the first half of the third millennium B.C., was on a small peninsula on a hill just east of the present suburban town of Bayrakli, 2.5 mi (4 km) north of Izmir. By the end of the seventh century B.C. there was a fine temple there, dedicated to the goddess Athena and adorned

FIGURE 89. Head of Zeus, in the Ephesus Museum.

with lions' heads—the lion being the symbol of the ancient city. In about 600 B.C., as Herodotus (I 16) relates, King Alyattes of Lydia captured the city and destroyed the temple; although the temple was rebuilt, it was completely ruined by the Persians in about 545 B.C.

In the time of Alexander the Great a new and larger city was founded on the slopes of Mt. Pagos, which rises above modern Izmir. According to Pausanias (VII 5, 1–2), Alexander was hunting on the mountain, fell asleep under a plane tree in front of a temple of two Nemeses, and in a dream was told by the two goddesses to build a city at the place. Smyrna was reportedly the finest of the Ionian cities. Strabo (XIV 1, 37) says that the streets were laid out in straight lines as far as possible, and paved with stone; and the orator Aelius Aristides (A.D. 117 or 129–189), who lived there, describes the parallel streets running from west to east as so oriented as to be open both to the sea breezes from the harbor and to the sunshine as well (PWRE ser. 2, vol. 3:1, col. 758). After the city was damaged by a severe earthquake in A.D. 178, the emperor Marcus Aurelius and his wife Faustina assisted in the rebuilding.

Smyrna was one of the cities considered to have been the birthplace of Homer, and Strabo (XIV 1, 37) mentions a stoa in the city that was called the Homereion, a place of worship of the deified poet. On the flat land by the harbor were a gymnasium and a temple of the mother goddess, and on the slopes of Mt. Pagos were a theater and a stadium. A commercial agora near the harbor has not been located, but the state agora, somewhat further inland, has been excavated. From the agora have come sculptures in high relief, notably marble statues of Poseidon and Demeter standing side by side. Since Poseidon was the god of the sea and Demeter the goddess of the harvest and the earth, the collocation of the two may have been intended to suggest the importance of Smyrna to trade by both land and sea.[12] In later Christian history Smyrna was the scene of the martyrdom of Polycarp in about A.D. 156.

FIGURE 90. Izmir (Ancient Smyrna); the Ancient Agora Is the Open Area Below.

Pergamum

Pergamum is represented by the modern town Bergama, which is on the north edge of the plain of the Caicus River, 15 mi (24 km) inland from the Aegean Sea. Ancient Pergamum was built on the summit and south slope of a mountain ridge (1,165 ft (355 m] above sea level), that lies between two branches of the Caicus—the Selinus (Bergama-Çay) to the west and the Cetius (Kastel-Çay) to the east.

The natural acropolis on the summit of the hill was probably fortified at least as early as the fourth century B.C., for Lysimachus, ruler of Anatolia from 301 on, made Philetaerus commander of Pergamum and entrusted to him the keeping of a large sum for war expenses. Philetaerus, however, abandoned his allegiance to Lysimachus (282), seized the treasure for himself, and founded the Attalid dynasty (282–133), in which his successors were Eumenes I (263–241), Attalus I, the first to take the title of king (241–197), Eumenes II (197–159), Attalus II (159–138), and Attalus III (138–133). Between the rival powers of the Seleucids and the Macedonians the Attalids maintained a successful and brilliant kingdom, partly because of an alliance with Rome, and at his death Attalus III bequeathed the kingdom to the Romans, who incorporated it in their province of Asia.

During the reign of Eumenes II the upper, middle, and lower districts of Pergamum were surrounded by their respective fortification walls, and the same king was responsible for many of the buildings on the upper acropolis, for which he used the Acropolis at Athens as a model. Entering the upper acropolis through the main gate, the palace of Eumenes II lies ahead, and to the left is the sacred precinct (*temenos*) of Athena, with its monumental entrance (*propylon*) on the steep edge of the hill to the west. Adjacent to the temple on the north side are the ruins of the famous library of Pergamum, which reportedly contained 200,000 volumes and was eventually given by Mark Antony to Cleopatra. Further north and of later date is the Traianeum, a temple erected to Trajan by his successor Hadrian (A.D. 117–138).

Dramatically located on the steep western slope of the acropolis hill is the Hellenistic theater. Eighty rows of seats, accommodating 10,000 spectators, descend 118 ft (36 m) to the level of the stage and the level of a long colonnaded terrace, at the north end of which is a Temple of Dionysos. On the southern slope of the acropolis hill, a short distance below the Temple of Athena, is the site of the great square altar of Zeus, probably built by Eumenes II. It was adorned with the famous frieze (reerected in the Berlin Museum) that represents the battle of the gods and giants and symbolizes the victory of the Pergamene people over the Galatians. Immediately below this altar is the area of the upper agora of the city, and to the east of the altar are the remains of a building identified as a Heroon that was probably dedicated to the worship of the kings Attalus I and Eumenes II.

On the lower southern slopes of the hill are the buildings of the middle city of Pergamum. These include the sanctuaries of Hera and of Demeter, a Temple of Asklepios, a magnificent gymnasium built on three separate terraces, the city fountain, and the lower agora. Below the lower agora a main street continued to the south gate of the city, which was a large courtyard fortified by towers on three sides. To the west is the so-called Red Courtyard (Kizil Avlu). This is a large architectural complex built of red brick, but once faced with marble. The central building is a basilica (about 200 x 80 ft [60 x 25m]) with a nave, two aisles, and an apse, and it is flanked by two circular buildings (about 60 ft [18 m] in diameter), and there are courtyards to the west of them. In front of the whole, to the west, is a large courtyard, beneath which the Selinus River flows in two vaulted canals. Found in the complex are fragments of colossal double statues (each carved on one side as an atlantes or male figure and on the other side as a caryatid or female figure), with Egyptian-type coiffures, and it is believed that the whole complex was a temple

FIGURE 91. Snakes as Symbols of Asklepios, at the Asklepieion in Pergamum.

of Egyptian deities—perhaps Serapis, Isis, and Harpokrates. The construction is ascribed to the reign of Hadrian. In the Byzantine period the main building was converted into a church and dedicated to St. John the Apostle.

The region on to the west of the Selinus River was settled in Roman times, and there are ruins of a Roman stadium, a Roman amphitheater, and a Roman theater. From the Roman theater an ancient road leads west to the Asklepieion, the healing sanctuary of Asklepios, which is on a southward-facing slope on the north edge of the Caicus River. The sanctuary was founded around 400 B.C. and attained its greatest importance in the second century A.D., at which time it was described by Aelius Aristides, who stayed there for thirteen years around the middle of the century (PWRE vol. 2, cols. 886–894; vol. 19:1, cols. 1261–1262). Most of the buildings presently visible also come from that time. At its height the Asklepieion of Pergamum ranked with similar healing centers of Asklepios at Epidauros and Kos.

Coming from the east, the road that leads to the Asklepieion was, in Roman times, colonnaded. The sanctuary area proper is some 360 x 425 ft (110 x 130 m), and there were colonnades on the north, west, and south sides. Entering through a propylon on the east, there is a cylindrical Temple of Asklepios to the left and an almost square stoa to the right at the northeast corner of the area; the stoa is identified by an inscription as a library dedicated by a certain Flavia Melitene. Inside the stoa was found a colossal statue (now in the Bergama Museum) of Hadrian, depicted naked as a deified emperor. Running to the west from the library is the well-preserved north colonnade, and it leads to the Roman theater, which was built into the steep slope of the hill and was able to accommodate 3,500 people. In the central area of the sanctuary are sleeping rooms—probably providing for incubation and autosuggestion—and fountains

and pools—probably providing water from a sacred spring for drinking, bathing, and mud baths, all of which were features of the treatment of the ill. Running diagonally through the eastern half of this area is a subterranean tunnel (260 ft [80 m] long), which leads to a two-storied cylindrical structure (87 ft [26.5 m] in diameter) at the southeast corner of the entire complex. On its lower level the interior periphery of this round building is marked by six apses, and the walls and floor were covered with marble mosaics. This is supposed to have been a main place for medical treatment.[13]

Thyatira

Thyatira occupied a favorable location, commercially speaking, in the valley of the Lycus River between the Caicus valley to the north and the Hermus valley to the south. The city belonged to the kingdom of Pergamum and,

FIGURE 92. North Colonnade Leading to the Theater in the Asklepieion in Pergamum.

later, to the Roman province of Asia. The site is occupied by the modern town of Akhisar, and there is relatively little to be seen from ancient times. Some architectural fragments of the Roman period have been brought to light, and inscriptions and coins make known the tutelary god of the city called, by a mixture of Hellenic and Anatolian names, Helios Tyrimnaios Pythios Apollo.

Sardis

The site of Sardis is in the valley of the Hermus River, 58 mi (94 km) from the Aegean coast, and it lies beside the Pactolus River, which flows into the Hermus from the south. South of the Hermus and east of the Pactolus is the Tmolus range, on a very sharp peak of which was the acropolis of the ancient city. The modern Izmir-Ankara highway and the railway parallel the Hermus and run through the center of the ancient city, and the railway station just east of the Pactolus is known as Sart.

Human settlement in the region is attested from at least as early as 3000 B.C., and Herodotus (I 7, 13, 15, 26) says that Greek warriors, who were "sons of Herakles," seized Sardis and founded a dynasty around 1185 B.C. Around 680 B.C. Gyges, a king mentioned in the annals of Ashurbanipal of Assyria, took Sardis and founded the Mermnad dynasty, in which he was followed by Ardys, Sadyattes, Alyattes, and the famous Croesus (561–547). With the victory of Cyrus over Croesus, Sardis became the western capital of the Persian Empire and the capital of the satrapy called Sfarda (Hebrew Sepharad); it was also the western terminus of the Persian royal road from Iran to the Mediterranean. Both Xenophon and Alexander the Great went to Sardis, and eventually it was ruled by the kings of Pergamum and then by the Romans. In A.D. 17 the city was leveled by an earthquake, and rebuilding was assisted by the emperors Tiberius and Claudius, after which the population may have increased to more than 100,000. In A.D. 616 the Persian king Chosroes

FIGURE 93. Ionic Capital of a Roman Basilica (First Century B.C.) That Was Converted into a Christian Church, in Thyatira (Modern Akhisar).

II destroyed Sardis, and around 1300 the city was occupied by the Turks.

In the excavations at Sardis the remains of the Lydian marketplace, dating from about 700 to 300 B.C., have been found on the south side of the modern highway and below the north side of the acropolis. There are also huge burial mounds of the Lydian period in a large necropolis at Bin Tepe (Thousand Hills), 4 mi (6.5 km) north of the city area, across the Hermus River and south of the Gygean Lake (Marmara Gölü). There are three mounds at the eastern end of the cemetery that are larger than all the rest, and one is believed to be the burial place of Gyges, and a second, the burial place of Alyattes. At the foot of the acropolis hill is the great Temple of Artemis, constructed through three phases from around 300 B.C. to around A.D. 150, and a small Byzantine church was built into its southeastern corner around A.D. 400.

The main street of the city ran from east to west, and its remains are underneath the modern highway and alongside it on the north side. The street was paved with slabs of marble and lined on both sides with arcades and shops. Just north of the road a huge gymnasium and a large synagogue have been excavated and partially restored. The gymnasium

FIGURE 94. Columns of the Temple of Artemis, Looking Toward the Acropolis in Sardis.

FIGURE 95 *(top)*. Byzantine Church Built into the Temple of Artemis in Sardis. FIGURE 96 *(bottom)*. Restored Roman Gymnasium (Second Century A.D.) in Sardis.

contains both a palaestra on the east and large baths on the west. Inscriptions date its central unit in A.D. 166 and its ornate eastern facade in A.D. 211, in the time of Caracalla, Geta, and Julia Domna. The synagogue, in use as such from around A.D. 200 to 616, is a basilican structure with an entrance porch, a forecourt, and a long main hall ending in an apse. In the forecourt and main hall there are geometric floor mosaics of the fourth century A.D., the walls were covered with marble, and among the finds was a large stone menorah. Both Hebrew and Greek inscriptions were also found, and they provide information about the Jewish community, which is likewise mentioned by Josephus (*Ant.* xiv 10, 14, 17, 24 §§232, 235, 259; xvi 6, 6 §171). The Jewish community has been estimated to have numbered 5,000–10,000, and judging from the prominent location of the synagogue adjacent to the gymnasium, the Jews must have occupied an important place in the life of the city.[14]

Of the Christians of the city, Bishop Melito of Sardis (c. A.D. 140–190) is well known and was an early pilgrim to Palestine.

Philadelphia

The city of Philadelphia (a name frequent in the ancient world) was founded by Attalus II of Pergamum (159–138 B.C.), and his love for his brother and predecessor, Eumenes II (197–159), was expressed in his own epithet Philadelphus—from which came the name of the city. The site is in the valley of the Cogamus River (Koca Çay), a tributary of the Hermus, and it is on the road between Sardis and Laodicea.

Like Sardis, Philadelphia was greatly damaged by the earthquake of A.D. 17, and Tiberius assisted in its recovery, on account of which the city took for a time the name of Neocaesarea (New City of Caesar). In the time of Vespasian (A.D. 70–79) the name was

FIGURE 97. Entrance Hall of the Jewish Synagogue (Third and Fourth Centuries A.D.) in Sardis.

changed to Flavia, the emperor's family name, but thereafter the name of Philadelphia was used again.

The ancient city is now represented by the town Alaşehir. To the south are three small hills, which were the site of the acropolis, and the location of a theater can be recognized there. To the north some of the Byzantine city walls are preserved for a length of more than 3,600 ft (1,110 m). To the east are the ruins of a basilica, still containing traces of frescoes dating from the eleventh century.

Laodicea, Colossae, Hierapolis

The city of Laodicea, known as Laodicea ad Lycum to distinguish it from other ancient cities of the same name, was founded between 261 and 253 B.C. by Antiochus II, king of Syria, and it was named in honor of his wife Laodice. Pliny (*Nat. Hist.* v 105) states that the place was previously called Diospolis (City of Zeus), and Zeus remained the chief deity of Laodicea.

The site, known locally as Eski Hisar, is on a small plateau on the south side of the Lycus River valley. On the northeastern slope of the hill are the ruins of two theaters; the larger of Greek type faces across the Lycus Valley to the northeast, and the smaller of Roman date faces northwest. At the opposite end of the plateau is a large stadium, dedicated, according to an inscription, to the emperor Vespasian in A.D. 79. Near the center of the plateau is a nymphaeum, a monumental fountain consisting of a square water basin flanked on two sides by colonnades and semicircular fountains. Water was supplied to a water tower on the south side of the city and to the nymphaeum by an aqueduct coming from springs at the site of the modern city Denizli, 4 mi (7 km) to the south. Among other finds at the nymphaeum was a life-size statue of the goddess Isis. Later, presumably in the Byzantine period, the basin of the nymphaeum was walled off and made into a closed room, approached by steps on one side, and this room was used for Christian purposes as

FIGURE 98. Portion of an Arch of the Ruined Church at Philadelphia (Modern Alaşehir).

crosses carved on various blocks show.

The most immediate neighbors of ancient Laodicea were Colossae and Hierapolis. Colossae is mentioned by Herodotus and Xenophon, but it evidently declined in importance after Laodicea and Hierapolis were founded. The site of Colossae is 12 mi (19 km) southeast of Laodicea, and it also is on the south bank of the Lycus River. Although unexcavated, the place of a large theater is recognizable, as well as the area of a necropolis.

Hierapolis is thought to have been founded by King Eumenes II of Pergamum (197–159 B.C.), since the earliest inscription found there is a decree in honor of his mother Apollonis. The site is across the Lycus 6 mi (10 km) north-northeast of Laodicea, and it is plainly visible from Laodicea.

The ruins of the city occupy a plateau that drops off steeply in white cliffs formed of lime deposits from hot springs above. From a later

FIGURE 99 *(top)*. Ruins of the Nymphaeum at Laodicea. FIGURE 100 *(bottom)*. Looking from Laodicea to Hierapolis (the White Terraces Across the Valley).

FIGURE 101 (top). White Terraces of the Hot Springs at Hierapolis. FIGURE 102 (bottom). Octagonal Martyrium of St. Philip at Hierapolis. (Photo Courtesy Biblical Illustrator/David Rogers)

fortress on the edge of the cliffs, the Turks called the place Pamukkale or Cotton Castle. Close to the edge of the plateau are the ruins of large baths, probably constructed in the second century A.D. Further up the slope is the Temple of Apollo, the principal deity of Hierapolis, and adjacent to the temple to the southeast was the Plutoneion, a shrine of the god of the underworld. Strabo (XIII 4, 14) and other ancient writers tell of the fatal mist that came forth from the ground there, and there is still a chamber in the hillside with a cleft in the rock where hot water flows and chemical smells emerge. Near the Temple of Apollo are the ruins of a large nymphaeum of the fourth century and of a Christian basilica of the sixth century; higher up the hill is a well-preserved theater of the second century A.D.

Running from north to south through the city is a straight main street, more than 1 mi (1.6 km) long, adorned at least in part with colonnades and gateways. Lining the street on both sides outside the city to the north is a very extensive necropolis—with tumuli, sarcophagi, and house-shaped tombs—and there is also a necropolis area on the hillside outside the city wall to the east. In the latter area, in a dominating position overlooking the city, there is a square building, approached by a broad flight of steps, with an octagonal chamber in the center and many small chambers around it. This dates from the beginning of the fifth century A.D., and it is identified as a martyrium associated with the name of Philip. The Philip in question is supposed to have been the apostle, who was martyred there in

A.D. 80, but there is a possibility of confusion with Philip the evangelist (Ac 21:8) who was also buried at Hierapolis (Eusebius, *Ch. Hist.* III 31).[15]

The Christian faith was evidently introduced in these three cities of the Lycus Valley by Epaphras, who Paul says in writing to the Colossians had worked hard for them and for those in Laodicea and in Hierapolis (Col 4:12–13). From the same passage we learn that Epaphras was a native of Colossae, and from Col 1:7 and 2:1 we gather that Epaphras worked on behalf of Paul (who had not visited the cities himself), probably during the more than two years Paul spent in Ephesus on his third missionary journey (Ac 19:8–10). According to Col 4:16 Paul wrote a letter that was to go to Laodicea, as well as the letter to the Colossians, and the two letters were to be interchanged. Since Marcion (the second-century Christian Gnostic) apparently knew the "letter to the Laodiceans" as the New Testament Ephesians, it is not unlikely that the letter we know as Ephesians was actually an encyclical that went first to Ephesus and then around the circuit to Laodicea, from where it was to go to Colossae in the interchange with the Colossian letter. As for the description in Rev 3:16 of the church at Laodicea as "lukewarm, and neither cold nor hot," it can be imagined that this comment is a play on words, contrasting what may have been the tepid water of the aqueduct at Laodicea with the possibly fresher and colder water at Colossae and with the very hot water of the cascades at Hierapolis.

7
SHIPWRECK JOURNEY
(A.D. 56–57)

As described in the Book of Acts the missionary journeys of Paul follow a well-marked geographical route, and, in addition to the Jews to whom he regularly spoke first, they brought him into contact with the other major peoples of the time. On the first missionary journey, when he worked in Antioch, Cyprus, and central Asia Minor, his theater of action was Asia and the people were largely the indigenous people of the regions—at Lystra, for example, those people who spoke the Lycaonian language (Ac 14:11). On the second and third missionary journeys when he was in Macedonia, Athens, Corinth, and Ephesus, his environment was that of the Aegean, and the majority of the people spoke Greek, to whom all people who spoke any other language were barbarians (Rom 1:14). After those journeys, one more great area was Paul's objective, namely, Rome and the West—the Latin world.

At this point in the Book of Acts Paul is going from Ephesus through Macedonia and Achaia and back to Jerusalem, saying, "After I have been there, I must also see Rome" (Ac 19:21). He is at the same point as he writes his Letter to the Romans. As he writes he is probably in Corinth (since in Rom 16:1 he commends Phoebe, a deaconess of the church in Kenchreai, Corinth's easternmost port city), and he is on the verge of departing for Jerusalem. But by this time he has preached all the way from Jerusalem to Illyricum (modern Albania), and there is no more room for him to work in those regions (since his task was always to take the gospel to new territories), so he hopes to see the Romans as he goes on even all the way to Spain (Rom 15:19, 23–24).

Paul went to Rome, indeed, but hardly in the way he originally envisioned. En route to Jerusalem there were intimations of trouble ahead (Ac 20:22–23; 21:11), and in Jerusalem, the events of Ac 21:17–23:35 unfolded, which brought Paul into custody in Caesarea. There he remained in prison for two years (Ac 24:27), when upon appeal to Caesar he was sent to Rome (Ac 25:11–12). For the long journey Paul's escort was a Roman centurion of the Augustan band, who was taking some other prisoners to Italy too. In addition, Paul had several companions who went with him and probably traveled freely and at their own expense. These companions included the one who narrates the journey in the first person plural—"we"—probably Luke himself; Aristarchus, a Macedonian from Thessalonica who had been involved with Paul in the riot in Ephesus (Ac 19:29) and was later a fellow prisoner with him, probably in Rome (Col 4:10); and, according to the Western text of Ac 27:2, Secundus, also a Thessalonian (Ac 20:4). Both because the journey was the climax of the narrative concerning Paul in the Book of Acts—and indeed a climax in the fulfillment, in its own strange way, of the ambition of Paul —and because it could be told on the basis of Luke's own personal experience of all that happened, the account is full.

CAESAREA

South of the Bay of Haifa there were practically no good natural harbors on the coast of Palestine, but in the third century B.C. and later, the Phoenicians had a small harbor at a place called the Tower of Strato, from the name of a king of Sidon, and there, probably in the years from 22 to 10/9 B.C., Herod the Great built a new city and port. The city was named Caesarea in honor of Caesar Augustus, and it was commonly called Caesarea Maritima to distinguish it from Caesarea Philippi (Paneas) in the north of Palestine. The harbor was called Limen Sebastos, Sebastos being the Greek equivalent of the Latin Augustus.

Josephus (*Ant.* xv 9, 6 §§331ff.) describes the harbor as larger than that of Piraeus. Herod, he says, lowered great blocks of stone into 20

PLAN 18.

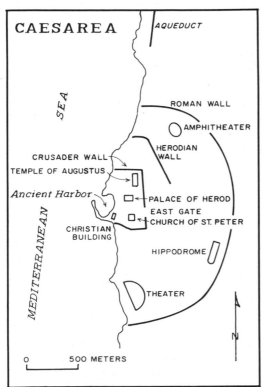

fathoms (120 ft [37 m]) of water and built a breakwater. The wall encircling the harbor was protected with massive towers. The entrance faced to the north, for at Caesarea the north wind was the most favorable, the south and southwest winds the most dangerous. On an eminence facing the mouth of the harbor was a Temple of Caesar (as Josephus calls it, strictly˙ speaking, a temple to Rome and Augustus), with a colossal statue of the emperor and another of Rome (perhaps the goddess Roma). Other buildings included a theater, an amphitheater, and various other public structures.

After Herod and Archelaus, the Roman procurators established their headquarters at Caesarea, and it remained the Roman administrative and military center in Palestine from A.D. 6 for several hundred years—except during the reign of Herod Agrippa I (A.D. 41–44). Tacitus (II 78) calls Caesarea the capital of Judea, and Vespasian raised it to the rank of Colonia Prima Flavia Augusta. Herod the Great undoubtedly had a fine palace in Caesarea, and the Roman procurators undoubtedly took that building for their official residence, as they did with Herod's Antonia and western palace in Jerusalem. The official residence of a Roman governor was a praetorium, a Latin word that originally signified a general's tent in a military camp. According to Ac 23:35 Paul was guarded in Caesarea in "Herod's praetorium," and this must have been Herod's palace, which had been made the headquarters of the Roman procurator of Judea.

Although Herod Agrippa I chose to demonstrate his harmony with Jewish priestly officialdom by residing at Jerusalem, he was in Caesarea upon occasion and died there, shortly after appearing in the theater in such royal splendor that the people acclaimed him as a god, an event recorded both in Ac 12:22 and in Josephus. In Late Roman and Byzantine times Caesarea was a center of both Jewish and Christian learning, and it was the residence in particular of the great Christian scholars and writers Origen and Eusebius.

FIGURE 103. Crusader Tower and Mediterranean Seashore at Caesarea.

After conquest by the Muslims in A.D. 640 Caesarea experienced a long decline. In 1101 it was taken by the Crusaders, and they built a wall and moat around a small central section of what had been the very much larger ancient city. Only in the nineteenth century was Caesarea resettled by Muslims, and then by Jews who established a small agricultural and fishing village called Sedot Yam, or Sea Meadows. These settlers began to find antiquities in the sand dunes that heap the coast and Roman jars on the sea bottom, and modern archeological work began. Israeli archeologists examined a synagogue north of the port in 1945, and thereafter Italian archeologists began clearing the theater in 1959 and following. Edwin Link made an underwater exploration of the harbor in 1960, and the representatives of various institutions in Israel and the United States were active in the 1970s.

Near the synagogue a fragment of a marble plaque was found in 1962, inscribed in Hebrew of probably the end of the third or the beginning of the fourth century with a list of the towns in Galilee in which the twenty-four divi-

sions of priests (I Ch 25:9–31) were then settled. In line 2 there is the name of Nazareth, and in line 4, the name of [M]igdal or Magdala. This is the first known occurrence of the name of Nazareth in an inscription, and the earliest occurrence of the name in Hebrew.

The theater was built by Herod the Great at the southern edge of the central section of the city in a fine hillside location facing the sea. In its original form it is the earliest Roman theater known in Palestine. In the second century A.D. it was rebuilt and yet later, in the third and fourth centuries, adapted for water spectacles. It seated 4,500 spectators. In the reconstruction of the theater a stone was reused as an ordinary building stone on which has been found the earliest known inscriptional occurrence of the name of Pontius Pilate. The inscription states that Pontius Pilate, prefect of Judea, dedicated (to the people of Caesarea?) a Tiberium, i.e., a temple to the emperor Tiberius.

The outline of the harbor can be seen from the air, and according to underwater study, its two breakwaters were 820 ft (250 m) and 1,970 ft (600 m) in length, respectively, and were built of great limestone blocks as much as 50 ft (15 m) long and 18 ft (5.5 m) wide. The amphitheater has been located, and it has an arena larger than that of the Colosseum in Rome. A hippodrome was built in the second century A.D., and it was more than a quarter of a mile (400 m) long and 330 ft (100 m) wide, and it seated 30,000 people.

In the central area, facing the ancient harbor, are the remains of a very large podium, and this probably supported the Temple of Augustus and Rome. A white marble foot, 3 ft (1 m) long, has been found, probably from one of the colossal statues of these deities. A subterranean Mithraeum of the third century A.D. has also been discovered, the first found in Palestine.

The provision of an adequate water supply for Caesarea was probably the work of Herod the Great, since he must have been concerned about this matter for his new city. A high aqueduct brought water from springs at the foot of Mt. Carmel, 7.5 mi (12 km) to the northeast. The first half of the water passage is a rock-hewn tunnel 2.5 ft (0.75 m) wide and 3 ft (0.9 m) high, the second half is a conduit carried on high arches. Roman soldiers also worked on the aqueduct later, and several Latin inscriptions of the Roman Tenth Legion, called Fretensis, have been found. A second lower-level aqueduct brought water from the Crocodile River, about 6 mi (10 km) north of the city. Also Herod the Great constructed a sewer system for the city, which Josephus (*Ant.* xv 9, 6 §340) says was cleaned out by the surge of the sea, and one of these sewers, 10.5 ft (3 m) high, has been found.

On the terrace in the central section of the city are the ruins of a Byzantine church with three apses. This may be a Church of St. Peter erected over the house of Cornelius, for as noted earlier, Jerome says that the house of Cornelius was turned into a Christian church. The central location in the city would be not unlikely for the residence of a high Roman officer, which Cornelius was.

Just south of the Crusader enclosure an important Christian building has been uncovered. In a mosaic of this building there is a quotation of Rom 13:3, and in the debris a statue of the Good Shepherd was found. It is tempting to speculate that this building might have been connected with the ecclesiastical school and library of Origen and Eusebius, but proof is lacking.

When the time came for Julius the centurion to sail from Caesarea with his prisoners, they embarked in a ship of Adramyttium, which was to sail to ports along the coast of Asia (Ac 27:2). In general the Romans were people of the land and builders of the great land roads, and the Greeks were people of the sea, so this ship was probably a Greek ship. Adramyttium was a seaport in the northwestern part of the Roman province of Asia, on the gulf east of Troas. The ship sailed past Ptolemais and Tyre and, the next day, put in at Sidon (Ac 27:3). Sidon (27 m [44 km] south of modern Beirut) was a Phoenician city with two harbors that were protected by small islands, and today it is dominated by a Crusader castle. The city was celebrated by Homer and was an important port under the Romans. The ancient town occupied what is now a huge mound, covered by the medieval and the modern cities of Sidon.

The next port was Myra in Lycia on the south coast of Asia Minor. To reach Myra the direct route would have been an almost straight course just south of Cyprus. Coming back on his third missionary journey Paul sailed from Patara[1] (also in Lycia just west of Myra) to Tyre, with Cyprus on the left (Ac 21:3), therefore taking this straight course. Now, however, "the winds were against us" (Ac 27:4), that is, they were blowing from the west or northwest. Ancient ships were square-rigged and could not sail into the wind or tack easily. Therefore "we sailed under the lee of Cyprus" and "across the sea which is off Cilicia and Pamphylia" (Ac 27:4–5), that is, they must have come up in the more-protected waters east of Cyprus and then sailed west along the coast. Here the Western text adds a note of time, "And when we had sailed . . . off Cilicia

187

FIGURE 104 (top). Ancient Tyre, Looking Toward the South Harbor. FIGURE 105 (bottom). Crusader Castle by the Sea (Twelfth Century A.D.) at Sidon.

FIGURE 106. Hellenistic Stoa in the Agora on Kos, an Island Touched by Paul en route to Jerusalem (Ac 21:1).

and Pamphylia for fifteen days we came to Myra." So it was a long and roundabout passage.

Myra was an important port and a recognized haven from the prevailing west winds. Strabo (xiv 3, 7) describes Myra as being located 20 stadia (2.3 mi (3.7 km]) from the sea on a high crest of land, and the ancient ruins, known as Kocademre, are some 3 mi (5 km) inland. The modern village in the vicinity is called Demre, and the present landing place is south of the town, but the ancient harbor, called Andriake, is 2.5 mi (4 km) to the west. Behind the town is a steep acropolis hill, ascended by an ancient road with steps. At the south foot of the hill is a well-preserved Roman theater with forty-seven tiers of seats. In the steep face of the hill just west of the theater, and also on the east side facing the Myrus River (now the Demre Çayi), are many rock-hewn tombs with inscriptions, for the most part in Lycian, and some reliefs in color. At the Andriake Harbor are a number of Roman buildings, including a large granary with busts of Hadrian and Faustina in the front wall.

In the time of the persecution by Diocletian (A.D. 303) the bishop of Myra was Nicolaus, and many stories were told about him as the patron of children and of sailors. In the Western church he became St. Nicholas, the bearer of gifts to children at Christmas. In the Eastern church he took the place of Poseidon, and on one island (Eleussa), a Temple of Poseidon was changed into a Church of St. Nicholas. In his honor Justinian built a church at Constantinople, which is mentioned by Procopius (*Buildings* i 6, 4), and at Myra there is also a Byzantine Church of St. Nicholas. The latter church was restored in the eleventh century, and the only part that may date from the time of the saint is the subterranean crypt. In the crypt is an early Christian sarcophagus, believed to the Tomb of St. Nicholas, although in the Middle Ages his relics were taken to Bari in Italy.

From Myra the ship of Adramyttium was presumably on its way to its home port, so

FIGURE 107. Statue Believed to be Hippocrates (Born on Kos c. 460 B.C.), in the Archaeological Museum on Kos.

FIGURE 108. Statue of Artemis as a Huntress, Ready to Shoot an Arrow, with a Dog at Her Feet (Second Century A.D.), in the Archaeological Museum on Kos.

Julius found a ship of Alexandria, sailing for Italy, on which to proceed (Ac 27:6). This was presumably a grain ship from Egypt, engaged in the very important grain trade with Rome. On this vessel "we sailed slowly," evidently working west along the coast with Rhodes off to port, and so "arrived with difficulty off Cnidus" (Ac 27:7). Cnidus (Knidos) was on a long promontory on the southwest coast of Asia Minor. Strabo (xiv 2, 15) describes it as a double city, part on the mainland and part on an island, connected by moles. This arrangement created two harbors—a commercial harbor and a naval harbor that could receive twenty ships. With Kos, Halikarnassos, and the three cities of Rhodes—Lindos, Kamiros, and Ialysos—Knidos formed the Dorian Hexapolis, and every four years the Dorian Games were held at Knidos.

The ancient ruins of Knidos include a theater constructed in the Hellenistic period and modified in the Roman period, a sanctuary of Aphrodite in which a famous cult statue executed by Praxiteles once stood, a Doric Temple of Apollo, and an Ionic temple on top of which was built a large fifth-century Byzantine church. Notable citizens of Knidos were the mathematician Eudoxus, who was a pupil of Plato, and the physician Ktesias, who served under Artaxerxes II Mnemon (404–359 B.C.) and wrote *Assyrica* and *Persica*, but the astronomical observatory and the medical school in Knidos have not yet been located.

CRETE

Since the wind did not allow the Alexandrian ship to proceed directly to the west, "we sailed under the lee of Crete off Salmone"; then sailing along near the coast of Crete and that only with difficulty, "we came to a place called Fair Havens, near which was the city of Lasea" (Ac 27:7–8). Pliny (*Nat. Hist.* iv 12, 58) describes this great island:

Crete itself stretches east and west with one side facing south and the other north; it is celebrated

FIGURE 109. Grave Statue of an Athlete Holding the Wreath of Victory, in the Archaeological Museum on Kos.

for the renown of its 100 cities. . . . Its Greek appellation, "the Island of the Blest," is thought by some to be due to the mildness of its climate. Its breadth nowhere exceeds 50 miles, its widest part being about the middle; its length is fully 270 miles and its circumference 589 miles. . . . Its easternmost projection (is) Cape Samonium [probably Capo San Sidero], pointing toward Rhodes, and its westernmost the Ram's Forehead [the Greek name of which survives in modern Capo Crio], towards Cyrene.[2]

Pliny also names many important cities on Crete, including Gortyna (Gortyn), Phaestus (Phaistos), and Cnossus (Knossos), and gives the distance from the Ram's Forehead to the promontory of Cyrene named Phycus (now Ras el-Sem) as 125 miles.

Fair Havens

From Ac 27:8 it is evident that Fair Havens was a locality in the territory of the city of Lasea. At the widest part of Crete, across the island south-southwest from Herakleion (Iraklion), the main projection of land is Cape Lithinon. To the east of the cape is a bay still known as Kaloi Limenes, which is the Greek name of Fair Havens (Καλοὶ Λιμένες). The bay forms a triangle and is protected by several small offshore islands. Of those islands even the largest is scarcely one quarter of a mile (1.6 km) long, and it is named Megalonisi; a second is named St. Paul's Island. At the apex of the triangle of the bay is a narrow valley between two lofty hills. On the western hill is a Church of St. Paul, supposedly located where Paul preached, and potsherds found there attest occupation in Roman and late Roman times.

To the east at a distance of 1.25 mi (2 km), on a small headland opposite an offshore island called Nissos Traphos and with two small bays on either side, is the site of Lasea (Lasaia). Two early Minoan cemeteries show settlement in that period, and there was continuous occupation from the late fifth century B.C. until the late Roman period, the city being most prosperous and extensive in

the Roman time. An aqueduct brought water from a spring about a half mile (1 km) away. There were cemeteries to the west of the city, with Roman burials in barrel-vaulted tombs. A mole, possibly of Roman date, ran almost out to the offshore island and provided protected water on one side or the other, depending upon the direction of the wind.

From Fair Havens it is 7.5 mi (12 km) almost straight inland to Phaistos, which like Knossos near the north coast, was a famous palace city of the Minoan civilization. From Phaistos it is another 9 mi (15 km) east along the main road to Gortyn. This part of Crete is called Messara, and Phaistos was the ancient capital, but by the third century B.C. Gortyn had conquered Phaistos and engaged in hostilities with Knossos for supremacy over the whole island. After the Roman conquest of Crete in 68 B.C. Gortyn became the first city of Crete and the capital of the island and of Cyrene together, which were for the time united in one province. In the fourth century A.D. Constantine separated Cyrene, but Gortyn remained the capital of Crete and was an important Christian center, finally to be destroyed by the Saracens in A.D. 824.

Gortyn had two ports, Matala on the Gulf of Messara to the west, 5 mi (8 km) north of Cape Lithinon, and Lebena on the coast to the south, 5 mi (8 km) east of Lasea. According to local tradition Paul preached at Gortyn while his ship was at Fair Havens. From Fair Havens to Lebena (6 mi, 10 km) and then up what must have been a main road to Gortyn would not have been a great distance for the apostle to go.

Titus at Gortyn

According to Titus 1:5 Paul at a later time left his disciple Titus on Crete to order affairs in the churches. According to Eusebius (Ch. Hist. III 4) Titus was the first head of the churches in Crete, and the apocryphal Acts of Titus states that he was bishop of Gortyn. In Gortyn he is commemorated in the Basilica of

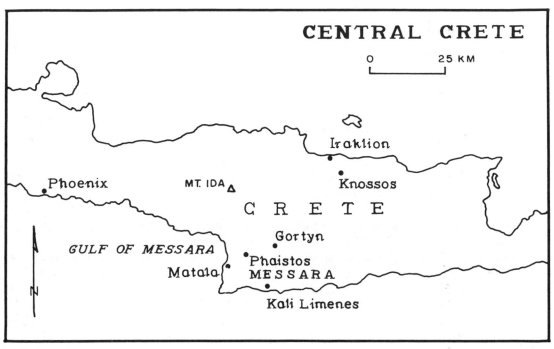

MAP 8.

FIGURE 110. Columns of the Hellenistic Temple on the Promontory at Lindos on the Island of Rhodes.

St. Titus, a building archeologically attributed to the fourth-sixth centuries A.D., with later repairs and additions (seventh-eighth centuries).

Gortyn was built on either side of the Lethaios River, now called the Mitropolitanos, and the extensive ruins of the ancient city are near the present village of Haghii Deka (Ten Saints) and north of Mitropolis where there is some evidence of Neolithic and Minoan occupation. On the west side of the Lethaios River is the acropolis of Gortyn, with traces of an early wall, an early temple, and at the foot of the hill, the remains of a theater. On the east side of the river are found an odeon of the first century B.C. restored by Trajan, the agora, and a Temple of Asklepios; south of the modern east-west road are a Temple of the Pythian Apollo, a Temple of Isis, Serapis, and Anubis, an amphitheater, and a building known as the Praetorium and identified as the residence of the governor of the province. The Basilica of St. Titus is on the north side of the modern road, just below the ancient agora,

and another Byzantine basilica, dedicated to the Ten Saints, is among the buildings on the south side.

With the hard sailing encountered from the very outset of their voyage much time had been lost, and by the time Paul's ship lay in Fair Havens, "the fast" had gone by and further sea travel was dangerous. The fast (Ac 27:9) was the Day of Atonement on the tenth day of Tishri, which in A.D. 56 probably fell on Oct. 9, and it marked the approach of winter, which made sailing dangerous. Pliny (*Nat. Hist.* II 47) tells about the sailing seasons: "The spring opens the seas to voyagers; at its beginning the West winds soften the wintry heaven . . . the date of this is February 8." He goes on to say that the rise of the Pleiades on May 10 brings summer, which is a period of south wind; then with the autumnal equinox the northeast wind begins, and this marks the beginning of autumn. "About 44 days after the autumnal equinox the setting of the Pleiades marks the beginning of winter, which it is customary to date on November 11; this is the

FIGURE 111. St. Paul's Bay (with Small Chapel) at Lindos on the Island of Rhodes.

FIGURE 112. Ruins of the Basilica of St. Titus (Fourth–Eighth Centuries A.D.) at Gortyn on the Island of Crete.

period of the winter Aquilo (wind); it is opposite to the Southwest wind [therefore the Aquilo is a Northeast wind]."

It is plain therefore that the normal sailing season began with spring on Feb. 8 and closed with the onset of winter on Nov. 11. Only two things, says Pliny, made people go to sea in the winter, namely, pirates and avarice. Whether he means pirates were the first to be bold enough to venture out in the winter, or whether he means that other people thought they were less likely to encounter pirates in the winter and so undertook to go out then themselves, is not clear. The mention of avarice is plain, however, for commercial ventures were no doubt pushed to the limit for the sake of gain.

At this juncture Paul, being quite familiar with Mediterranean conditions and having already suffered three shipwrecks (II Cor 11:25), advised against going further. The captain and the owner of the ship and the majority on board, however, wished to push on, and the centurion sided with them. Although Fair Havens or nearby Lasea would seem to have offered sufficiently protected anchorages for the ship to have remained there safely, the argument was that Fair Havens was not a suitable wintering place and that Phoenix, a harbor further along the coast of Crete, would be preferable. Perhaps, as Pliny's reference to the effect of avarice on sailing endeavors can suggest, the commercial aspects of the matter were of weight, for the further the ship could be brought before a halt was made for the winter, the earlier it could be

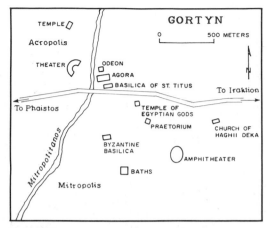

PLAN 19.

hoped to reach the markets of Italy in the spring.

Phoenix

A city named Phoenix (Phoinix or Phoinika) and a harbor called Phoinikous are listed by Ptolemy (*Geography* III 15, 3) with a longitude that would put them approximately at Cape Mouros on the south coast of Crete. This cape is a rocky promontory that extends out nearly 1 mi (1.6 km) from the coast. The modern village of Loutro is on the east side of the peninsula, on a deep harbor that faces to the southeast. On the other (west) side of the promontory is Phoinika Bay, which faces to the southwest. Minoan shards found on the peninsula attest a prehistoric settlement, and there are remains of the Roman and Byzantine periods as well as a Turkish fort on the height.

In the Revised Standard Version of Ac 27: 12 the harbor the voyagers desired to reach is described as "looking northeast and southeast." This statement agrees with the assumption that the harbor in question is that of the village of Loutro on the east side of the peninsula, which is the harbor presently in use, since this harbor does in fact correspond with this description. The Greek text of Ac 27:12, however, says literally that the harbor mentioned was facing toward the wind from Libya (i.e., from the southwest) and toward the northwest. So, unless an involved interpretation is entertained that reverses the apparently plain meaning of the text, it would appear proper to translate the text as in the margin of the Revised Standard Version and read that the harbor was "looking southwest and northwest." This, then, corresponds in general with the outlook of the Phoinika Bay on the west side of Cape Mouros, which opens out to the southwest. Although this bay has a depth of some 25 fathoms (150 ft [46 m]) and is free of reefs, it is not now used for a harbor, but in ancient times the situation was probably different. Along the shore there were actually two inlets from this bay. At the upper corner of the bay there is an inlet that is still 7–8 fathoms (42–48 ft [13–15 m]) deep close inshore, and it faces southwest. Toward the lower corner of the bay there was another inlet, facing northwest, but it is now largely filled up. There is a line of seashells around the bay, however, 14 ft (4 m) above the present sea level, so the coast seems to have risen that much since antiquity. Accordingly both inlets were probably satisfactory places for ships in ancient times. It is surmised that earthquake activity was respon-

MAP 9.

sible for this raising of the coast, and it is also believed that either earthquakes or the action of the sea greatly diminished a rocky spit at the bottom end of the bay, which at one time extended 165–335 ft (50–100 m) further out and thus provided that much more protection for the whole bay and its harbors.

On the west side of Cape Mouros then, the situation probably corresponded exactly with the correct reading of Ac 27:12, i.e., the two inlets from Phoinika Bay looked toward the southwest (toward Libya) and toward the northwest, which was the correct outlook for the desired protection. As Pliny said in the quotation about the sailing seasons, the winter wind called Aquilo was opposite to the southwest wind, i.e., it was the northeast wind. In fact the winter winds at Cape Mouros are still reported as northeast winds, and the boatmen of Loutro are said to regard the harbor on the Loutro side as unsafe from November to February. So it is well possible that the people of ancient Phoenix used the harbors on both sides of the peninsula (cf. the two harbors at Sidon, Tyre, and other ancient ports), but the west side was probably the more important. In fact in Ptolemy's list the places are named from west to east, and the sequence is the Phoinikous Harbor and then the city Phoenix, i.e., the harbor was west of the city. The western bay and the little chapel at its head are still called Phoinika, and it was probably that place that the captain of Paul's ship was thinking about for winter protection, and it is that place that is precisely described in Ac 27:12.[3]

So when "the south wind blew gently" (literally, when a light breeze from the south sprang up, i.e., a wind just like that of the summertime according to Pliny's description of the sailing seasons), advance to Phoenix seemed feasible, and against Paul's wiser advice, they weighed anchor and sailed along Crete, close inshore (Ac 27:13). But it was late in the season, since the Day of Atonement (probably Oct. 9) was past, the time was probably well on toward Pliny's date for the beginning of winter on Nov. 11, and the south wind proved to have been deceptive. Soon a different wind swept down from the land, which the Greek of Ac 27:14 describes literally as being of typhoon quality (τυφωνικός). In Codex Vaticanus and other of the oldest Greek manuscripts, the wind is named Eurakylon (Εὐρακύλων) and in the old Latin, Euroaquilo. The Euros (Εὖρος) is the east wind, the Aquilo is the northeast wind, as Pliny said; therefore this was a "northeaster" as the name is translated in the RSV or, more precisely, an east-northeast wind. The name does not occur elsewhere, and it is perhaps not surprising that it is written in several different ways in later New Testament manuscripts, most often in the form Euroclydon (Εὐροκλύδων, KJV), in which the latter part of the name can be the Greek word for "wave," and the meaning can be the east wind that stirs up the waves. The strong cold wind that blows across the Mediterranean in the winter from a general northeasterly direction is explained meteorologically as being associated with the occurrence of a depression ("low") over Libya, which induces a strong flow of air from Greece; on Malta, this wind is called "gregale," from greco or Greek.

As to where the voyagers were when the Eurakylon struck, it is said (Ac 27:14) that it came upon them "soon" after they left Fair Havens. Only 5 mi (8 km) west of Kali Limenes the coast of Cape Lithinon turns sharply north (toward Matala, the port of Gortyn on the Gulf of Messara), and there the ship, trying to proceed westward, lost the protection of the shore, and the wind that tore down upon them so hard from the land came off the loftiest mountain on Crete, Mt. Ida (Mt. Psiloriti), 8,056 ft (2,456 m) in elevation. At that juncture the ship was "seized and carried off," as the Greek of Ac 27:15 says literally, and being unable to "hold its own" against the wind, "we gave way to the wind and were being driven." Here the Western text says slightly more fully, and entirely correctly as far as sailing procedure is concerned, "we gave way to the wind which was blowing and, having furled the sails, were being driven."

Running thus under bare poles before the storm, the first temporary and partial relief was found when the ship came under the lee of a small island called Cauda (in Codex Vaticanus, Kauda; in Sinaiticus, Klauda; in another manuscript, Gauden). The form of the name with the "l" appears to have been preferred by the Greek writers, Kauda may have been the Latin form, and Pliny, naming the islands around Crete, lists Gaudos (*Nat. Hist.* IV 12, 61). In modern Greek the island is called Gaudonesi (νῆσος, "island"), and it is also known as Gavdhos and Gozzo. It is 23 mi (37 km) off Crete. There in relatively calmer water they were able to take some measures for safety, but it was not easy. First they were barely able to gain control of the skiff (Ac 27:16). Evidently the ship's boat or dinghy was over the side or under tow and in danger of being smashed against the hull, and it took all the strength they could muster to get it aboard and secure. Then after hauling up the skiff, they used "helps" (this is the literal meaning of the Greek word Βοήϑεια, probably used in Ac 27:17 as a nautical term for a cable) to undergird the ship to keep its timbers from splitting apart.

Beyond Cauda the danger was that they should be driven on across the Mediterranean and should run onto the Syrtis (Ac 27:17). This name means "a sandbank," and it is the Greek name for two shallow gulfs on the north coast of Africa; the larger, Syrtis Major, now the Gulf of Sidra west of Cyrenaica (which must be the one meant here) and the much smaller one further west, Syrtis Minor, now the Gulf of Gabes. The Syrtis would mean shallow water, treacherous sand—possibly quicksand—and beyond that, only the desert. So to slow their drift in the dangerous direction in which the wind was driving them they "lowered the gear" (Ac 27:17), which must mean that they put out a sea anchor.

These were the events of the first day of the storm. On the next day they were so violently storm tossed that they began to throw their cargo overboard (Ac 27:18). This we have assumed was primarily grain in the case of an Alexandrian ship, but some of it was kept for food, for later they ate bread (Ac 27:35) and

FIGURE 113. Mt. Ida (Mt. Psiloriti) Seen from Phaistos on the Island of Crete.

only at the very end threw the balance of the wheat into the sea (Ac 27:38). On the third day they took the only measure that still remained to them. Already they had furled the sails when they came out from behind Cape Lithinon, at Cauda they had gotten the skiff onboard and undergirded the ship, and thereafter they had put out the sea anchor and jettisoned the cargo. Now on this third day "they cast out with their own hands the tackle of the ship" (Ac 27:19). In this case the "tackle" (σκευή) may mean the rigging of the ship, sacrificed to reduce windage. In the Koine and some other manuscripts the text states that "we" did this with our own hands, so perhaps Luke himself assisted, and the Western text adds that the tackle was cast "into the sea."

They had done all that they could, and they were being driven helplessly onward. Neither sun nor stars were visible for many a day, so no navigational sights could be taken in order to know their position. In a magnificent understatement the narrative says that "no small tempest [χειμών, literally, winter storm] lay on us" (Ac 27:20). In suspense (27:33) or entirely hopeless (27:20), and perhaps sick, they went without food. But finally Paul assured them that there would be no loss of life, only loss of the ship in running on some island (Ac 27:21–26).

On the fourteenth night they were drifting across the Sea of Adria, a name that was first applied to the gulf at the head of the Adriatic Sea (between Greece and Italy) but was later applied to the whole central Mediterranean. About midnight the sailors suspected that land was near. Was it some seaman's sixth sense that told them this, or the cry of a land bird, or could they already hear the surf pounding on the rocks? Soundings found 20 fathoms, then 15 (120 ft [37 m], then 90 ft [27 m]), as the bottom shoaled. In fear of running on the rocks in the black of night, four anchors were put out from the stern. Then they prayed for day to come; the Western text adds, "that we might know whether we could be saved." With thought only for themselves the sailors sought to escape, lowering the skiff under pretense of

putting out bow anchors. Paul bade the centurion and his soldiers stop this attempt, and they cut the dinghy loose and let it go (Ac 27:27–32).

At dawn Paul urged all to eat, for they would need their strength, and then they threw the remainder of the wheat into the sea to lighten the ship that much more (Ac 27:33–38). He also assured them again that "not a hair is to perish from the head of any of you"—or according to the Western text he said, "for I hope in my God that not a hair is to perish." When he had said this he took bread, gave thanks, broke it, and began to eat, and the Western text adds, "having given also to us," which suggests that Paul saw to it that the food was distributed to the others before he himself began to eat. In the same passage the number of souls on board is recorded as 276, but there are manuscript variants that give the figure as low as 76, probably because of copyists' errors in dealing with numerals written in the form of Greek letters.

When it was day they could see a bay with a beach, and they planned to bring the ship ashore at that place (Ac 27:39). The Greek word used in Codex Sinaiticus (ἐξῶσαι) regularly means to "drive (a ship) ashore," i.e., to beach it, which is doubtless the technically correct description of exactly what the sailors intended. In Codex Vaticanus a very similar word is used—only one letter is different (ἐκσῶσαι), probably from an error in hearing—which means to bring a ship "safe" to shore, which of course they would have hoped to accomplish if it were possible.

Instead of trying to retrieve the four anchors, they cast them off and left them in the sea, and they freed the rudders, which had evidently been lashed. To gain way for steering they hoisted the foresail, which had evidently been saved, and made for the beach. But they fell upon a place with sea on two sides (as the Greek διθάλασσος means literally; cf. "place of two seas" in the RSV marginal gloss) and ran aground (Ac 27:41). The bow stuck fast, and the stern was being smashed by the surf. The soldiers thought to kill the prisoners, lest they escape, but the centurion wished to save Paul and did not allow it. So swimming or floating on planks all reached shore, and so ended the most famous shipwreck journey of history (Ac 27:40–44).

MALTA

Malta, where Paul and his party now found themselves (Ac 28:1), is a small island 17.5 mi (28 km) long from southeast to northwest and 9.5 mi (15 km) wide. It is located 60 mi (96 km) from Cape Passero at the southeastern tip of Sicily and 220 mi (355 km) from Tripoli on the coast of North Africa. Closely associated with the island of Malta is the island of Gozo to the northwest, and the tiny island of Comino is between the two. Malta is largely composed of limestone, and its long southwestern side for the most part drops off into the sea in steep cliffs. On the long northeastern side of the island the slope toward the sea is more gradual, and there are more inlets and bays. At the southeastern end of the island there is a large bay called Marsascirocco (Marsaxlokk), with the fishing village of Marsaxlokk at the head of its northern arm and the Delimara promontory protecting it on the eastern side. On the northeastern side of the island a series of bays and inlets are so arranged as to make two harbors, known as Marsamxett Harbor and

MAP 10.

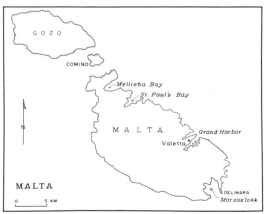

Grand Harbor, and the modern city of Valletta (or Valetta, capital of Malta since 1570) is on the long promontory between the two. Some 7.5 mi (12 km) further along the coast to the northwest is St. Paul's Bay.

The island was already occupied in the Neolithic and Bronze ages; the first settlers are believed to have come from Sicily around 5000 B.C. At a date presently estimated at 2900–2300 there was a remarkable Hypogeum, as it is called, at Hal Saflieni, a district southwest of Valletta. This was an agglomeration of curving underground halls and chambers, the larger rooms adorned with carvings and paintings, in which were found the remains of 6,000 or more persons, together with the ornaments, amulets, and pottery that had been buried with them. At Tarxien, only 1,300 ft (400 m) to the east of the Hypogeum, is a group of megalithic temples of the same period. In these, huge upright stones are joined by means of slightly sinuous joints cut with extraordinary precision, and spherical stones remain nearby that were used as rollers for maneuvering the enormous blocks—the earliest known use, it has been remarked, of ball bearings. Remaining in the south temple of this group is the lower portion of a gigantic statue of a goddess, which when complete, must have stood about 9 ft (2.75 m) high.

It was proably not long after 1000 B.C. that Malta was reached by the Phoenicians. Diodorus (v 12, 2–3) says that they planted a colony there because as they extended their trade to the western ocean (i.e., at least as far as Spain), they found the island a place of safe retreat, with good harbors in the otherwise open sea. In fact the name Malta may come from the Phoenician *malat*, meaning a port of refuge. The Phoenicians also established a very important colony at Carthage, and after their homeland was taken by the Assyrians and the Babylonians in the sixth century B.C., the Carthaginians came to control the Phoenician colonies and trading settlements in the West. In Latin the Phoenicians were called *Poeni*, and in Latin literature the noun *Poenus* designated a Carthaginian, with *Punicus* the corresponding adjectival form. In order, therefore, to mark the change from the earlier Phoenician period, the period of Carthaginian domination is commonly called the Punic period. Thus it can be said that from the sixth to the third centuries B.C. Malta was a part of the Punic Empire.

On Malta the original Phoenician trading post and a later Carthaginian port were on the Marsascirocco Bay at the southeastern end of the island. From chance finds in the area it is known that there were temples there to the Phoenician deities Melqart (identified with the Greek Heracles) and Astarte (identified with the Greek Hera, the Roman Juno). The Temple of Astarte has been located and excavated at a site called Tas-Silġ, on the Delimara promontory east of the village of Marsaxlokk. This temple was constructed over a prehistoric sanctuary and flourished from the sixth century B.C. into the first century A.D. In the fourth century a Christian basilica was built within its colonnaded court.

In later times the main port was at the so-called Grand Harbor on the northeastern side of the island. Although the entire harbor area is now occupied by Valletta and surrounding towns, there are prehistoric temple ruins on the Corradino or Kordin Heights overlooking the Grand Harbor on its eastern side, as well as somewhat further away at the Hypogeum and Tarxien as already described, and there are tombs of the Punic and Roman periods all the way from Maida in the west to Zabbar in the east. The Carthaginians also founded new capital cities on high inland points on both of the main Maltese islands. On Malta this was the ancient city of Melita, which is now Medina, with a suburb called Rabat; on Gozo it was the town of Gaulos, the modern Victoria, also called Rabat. In the Roman period and afterward until A.D. 1570, Medina/Rabat remained the capital of Malta.

In 218 B.C., at the beginning of the Second Punic War, the Romans took Malta. Under their administration the island was incorporated into the province of Sicily, and it was ruled by the governor of Sicily. This governor-

ship was held by Gaius Verres for three years just preceding 70 B.C., at which time Cicero prosecuted Verres for misgovernment and extortion. In his speeches Cicero told how Verres had plundered an ancient Temple of Juno that stood on a headland not far from the town of Melita (perhaps the temple now excavated at Tas-Silġ), and Cicero also referred to the hordes of pirates who infested the neighboring waters in those days and spent their winters on Malta. When he himself went into exile in 58 B.C. Cicero would have liked to have gone to Malta. With the reorganization of the empire under Augustus, Malta was placed directly under a Roman procurator, and under the procurator the leading local official of the island had the title "the first" (ὁ πρῶτος, primus), as is found in Greek and Latin inscriptions and as is used with precise exactitude in Ac 28:7.

In spite of Roman rule Malta remained essentially Punic in its culture for two centuries or more. In Ac 28:2 the people are called literally "barbarians" (βάρβαροι), but this word in its original sense simply means those who did not know Greek; thus the native inhabitants were probably neither Hellenized nor Romanized but were still speaking a Phoenician dialect. Presumably this was similar enough to Aramaic that Paul might have spoken with them in that language.

In A.D. 870 Malta was conquered by the Abbasid caliphs, who had already taken the greater part of Spain, the southern part of France, Italy, and Sicily. As a heritage of this period the Maltese language remains even yet a blend of North African Arabic and Sicilian Italian. In 1090 Christian control of the island was reestablished by Count Roger of Normandy, after he had also taken Sicily from the Arabs. The Normans were succeeded by other European dynasties, among them that of the Aragonese, and in 1427 Alfonso V of Aragon called the capital city, the Roman Melita, by the name of Città Notabile. In 1530 the Knights of St. John established themselves on Malta, after having been driven from Rhodes (in 1522) by Suleiman I the Mag-

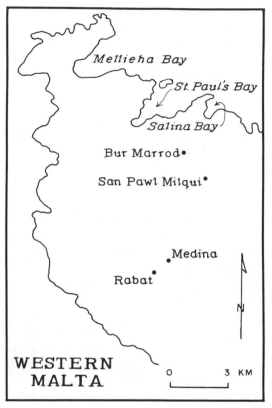

MAP 11.

nificent, and in 1565 Suleiman I sent Turkish forces against the Knights on Malta. The Turks landed at Marsaxlokk unopposed, then fought their main battles before the fortifications at Grand Harbor. The Knights, led by Jean Parisot de La Valette, held out through a long siege, and the name of the city of Valletta, founded immediately thereafter and the capital of the island from 1570 onward, commemorates their victory, which checked the advance of Muslim power in all of southern and western Europe.

It was the Saracens, as the Christians commonly called the Muslims, who applied the name Medina, meaning *the* city, to the Roman Melita, but with the foundation of their new city of Valletta the Knights called Medina the Città Vecchia. There a short section of heavy Roman masonry, perhaps part of the town walls, is preserved, and the

remains of a large house dating from the third and second centuries B.C. and enlarged in the Augustan period have been made into a "Roman Villa" Museum, which contains the chief Carthaginian and Roman antiquities that have been found on the island. In the vicinity of the city are also numerous rock-hewn tombs and catacombs, both pagan and Christian.

The traditional place where Paul came ashore, St. Paul's Bay, is one of three relatively large bays on the northern shore of Malta toward the northwestern end of the island; the first is Salina Bay, the second, St. Paul's Bay, and the third, Mellieha Bay. Although there is some evidence for a rise of 3–5 ft (1–1.5 m) in the level of the sea at some points on the shore, the approaches to St. Paul's Bay fit generally well with the soundings reported in Ac 27:28. A flat strand on the southwestern side of the bay could be the point where the sailors hoped to beach the ship, and a sandbank just inside the entrance, locally called St. Paul's Bank, could be where the ship went aground. West of this sandbank are several rocks that are known as St. Paul's Islands. On the largest, named Selmunett, there is a statue of Paul that was erected in 1845 to mark the spot where he and the others supposedly landed. The village that extends for nearly 1 mi (1.6 km) along the south side of the bay is also called St. Paul's Bay (San Pawl il-Bahar).[4]

According to Ac 28:7–9 "the first" or chief man of the island was Publius, and he had lands in the neighborhood of the place of the shipwreck, received Paul and his companions hospitably, and entertained "us" for three days. Paul healed Publius's father of fever and dysentery, and many other people of the island were also cured. According to Chrysostom (*Hom. LIV*), Paul's stay resulted in the conversion of the Maltese to Christianity.

FIGURE 114. St. Paul's Grotto Under the Church of St. Paul in Medina/Rabat, Malta. (*Photo Courtesy the Rev. Chapter, St. Paul's Grotto, Collegiate Church, Rabat, Malta*)

Extending inland from St. Paul's Bay and Salina Bay is the plain of Bur Marrod, and above it, on the slope of a hill called Gebel Ghawzara about 1.25 mi (2 km) from the nearest point of St. Paul's Bay, is a seventeenth-century church called San Pawl Milqi (St. Paul Welcomed), which is traditionally the place where Paul first met with Publius. Excavations by the Italian Missione Archeologica in Malta have shown that this place was in fact the site of a Roman villa. The architectural remains are those of a complex intended both for residence and for agriculture, in particular the making of olive oil. The foundation of the establishment was in the second century B.C., there was damage by fire in the early first century A.D., and in the rebuilding that ensued, the living quarters were extended to the west and walls were decorated with painted wall plaster. In perhaps the third century A.D. a double defensive wall was put around the villa, and it continued to flourish in the fourth and fifth centuries.

The tradition associating this site with Paul appears to be a relatively early one, shown by the fact that as early as the later Roman period one room of the villa was given special treatment and provided with several entrances and a small antechamber to the west. At some point the name PAULUS was inscribed on a wellhead, and a graffito depicted a wrecked ship. By the seventh century at the latest the site was plainly a place of pilgrimage definitely associated with Paul. Although the present chapel was only built between 1616 and 1622 there is a documentary record of a building in 1488, and the excavations have uncovered the remains of no fewer than three previous churches on the site.[5]

In addition to the Roman villa at San Pawl Milqi there is also a site in the northeastern corner of Medina that is traditionally associated with Publius and with Paul, namely, the site marked by the Church of St. Paul. This place is supposed to have been the official residence of Publius in the capital city, and under the church there is a grotto in which Paul is supposed to have dwelt and gathered the first believers. Publius is supposed to have made the house into a place of Christian worship, and he himself is regarded as the first bishop of Malta. The first church on the site was destroyed by the Arabs in A.D. 870, rebuilt in 1090 by the Norman Count Roger, and destroyed by earthquake in 1693. After the earthquake the present cathedral was erected in 1697–1702. Connected with the grotto under the cathedral are rock-cut catacombs, partly pre-Christian but also containing evidence of early Christian burials.

As we have learned from Pliny, the sailing season on the Mediterranean closed with the onset of winter on Nov. 11 and opened with the beginning of spring on Feb. 8, and the period between these two dates must have corresponded very approximately with the three months Paul and his party remained on Malta (Ac 28:11). Although their own ship had broken up on the bar where they ran aground, another Alexandrian ship, doubtless another grain ship, had gotten in safely and had waited out the winter, probably in one of the larger harbors. This ship was distinguished by the sign of the Dioscuri, the twin sons of Zeus, Castor and Pollux. According to Greek mythology Poseidon had rewarded the brotherly love of these two by giving them power over wind and waves, and they were the patron deities of sailors. Their sign in the Zodiac, that of the Gemini (Latin "twins"), was thought to bring good fortune at sea, and there were temples dedicated to them at Naples and in the Forum at Rome. The centurion arranged passage on this ship for his party, and they sailed to Sicily, put in at Syracuse, and "we stayed there for three days" (Ac 28:12).

SICILY

Sicily is considered to be the most beautiful of the Mediterranean islands. It is triangular in shape (150 mi [240 km] from east to west, 100 mi [160 km] from north to south at the broadest point), and it has been called Trinacria with reference to its three promontories. The

MAP 12.

highest point is the volcano Mt. Etna (10,758 ft [3,279 m]).

Sicily was already inhabited in the Upper Paleolithic, Neolithic, and succeeding ages. Diodorus, himself a native of Sicily (first century B.C.), says that the first inhabitants were the Sikani and, after them, the Sikeli, from whom the name of the island was derived (v 2, 4; 6, 1–6). In later times, like other islands in the western Mediterranean, Sicily was in turn Phoenician, Greek, Carthaginian, and Roman. In the fifth century A.D. it was raided by the Goths and Vandals, in the ninth century dominated by the Arabs, in the twelfth century controlled by the Normans, in the thirteenth century ruled by the Spaniards, and, finally, integrated with southern Italy.

Palermo (ancient Panormus), on the northwest coast, was a Punic colony, and it is now the capital of the island. Not far away are the Grotta di Addaura, with Upper Paleolithic incised rock drawings of human beings and animals, and Segesta, with a Greek temple and a Greek theater that are among the most impressive structures of ancient Sicily.

Syracuse

Syracuse (Siracusa), on the southeast coast, was in ancient times the most important city of Sicily, and indeed, it came to rival Athens and Carthage. The city was situated both on the mainland and on a low rocky island called Ortygia. The island was later connected with the mainland by a causeway, and the two are now separated only by a narrow canal, Darsena. On the south side of Syracuse is a fine natural harbor (the Porto Grande), and on the north there is a small one (the Porto Piccolo).

At Syracuse the Sikeli inhabitants were displaced by Greek immigrants who founded a Greek colony on Ortygia in 734 B.C. The leader of the Greeks was Archias of Corinth. The story is that he went to the oracle at Delphi and was asked whether he chose wealth or health. When he chose wealth, he was sent to found Syracuse, which became famously wealthy. At Syracuse there is a river named Alpheus and on the island a fountain called Arethusa. Pausanias refers to these and writes (*Description of Greece* v, "Elis" 1 7, 3), "For when he [the god at Delphi] dispatched Archias the Corinthian to found Syracuse he uttered this oracle":

An isle, Ortygia, lies on the misty ocean
Over against Trinacria, where the mouth
   of Alpheus bubbles,
Mingling with the springs of broad Arethusa.

In the course of its history Syracuse has been involved in wars with Carthage and Athens, ruled by a series of tyrants—beginning with Dionysius I (405–367 B.C.) and including Hieron I (478–467) and Hieron II (275–216)—and finally taken by the Romans in 212 B.C. Hieron I invited to his court famous men of letters, and among these was the Greek poet

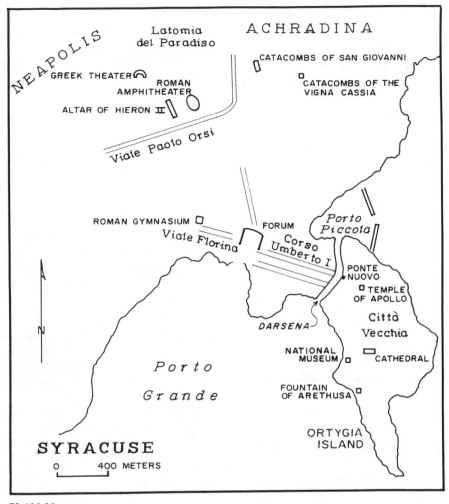

PLAN 20.

Aeschylus (525–456 B.C.), who presented some of his plays in Syracuse. In the time of Hieron II and Gelon his son, Archimedes (287–212) lived and worked in Syracuse. When the Romans besieged Syracuse for three years Archimedes devised war engines for Hieron and, it was said, constructed a system of mirrors and lenses that focused the sun's rays and set the Roman ships on fire when they were within a bowshot of the wall. In the capture of Syracuse Archimedes was killed by a Roman soldier, although the Roman general Marcellus had given orders to spare him and his house. Under the Romans Syracuse was

the residence of the Roman governor of Sicily, was given the rank of a colony by Augustus in 21 B.C., and was especially famed for fishing, shipbuilding, and bronze work.

In the ancient city there were five districts—Ortygia, Achradina, Tyche, Neapolis, and Epipolai. On the island of Ortygia there is a Temple of Apollo (sixth century B.C.) at the north end, and below the center, there is a Temple of Athena (fifth century B.C.). The latter was transformed into a Christian church in the seventh century A.D. and is now a cathedral, which still contains a stately row of Doric columns in the interior. Farther south, on the west side of the island, the famous Fountain of Arethusa is still to be seen.

Crossing the Darsena Canal by the Ponte Nuovo to the mainland and the Achradina district, and proceeding along Corso Umberto I, one comes to the Foro Siracusano, a vast square with gardens on the site of the ancient forum. Beyond, beside the Viale Florina, is a small Roman theater (inaccurately called the Roman gymnasium), which was probably built in the first century A.D. To the north the Corso Gelone leads toward the Neapolis quarter and the principal ancient monuments still to be seen. The Greek theater is probably where Aeschylus presented his plays; in its present form it is probably from the third century B.C., with later Hellenistic and Roman modifications. At least the remaining part is mostly cut into the rock of the hill, and the theater is a beautiful example of this type of structure—and also provides a fine view out over the city and the great harbor. Not far to the southeast of the theater is the Altar of Hieron II, an enormous rock-hewn podium 650 ft (198 m) long that was intended for public animal sacrifices. Again not far to the north-

east is the Roman amphitheater, probably dating from the third century A.D., and it is one of the largest structures of this sort known, measuring externally 460 ft (140 m) by 653 ft (199 m). To the north of these structures, there are some very extensive quarries, from which much building stone was taken for the ancient city, and these quarries were also used as prisons for captives of war. Using the Greek word for a stone quarry ($\lambda \alpha \tau o \mu i \alpha$), this area is called Latomia del Paradiso. One artificial cavern, which narrows toward the top and can be thought to have the shape of a human ear, is called the Ear of Dionysius, and legend has it that the tyrant Dionysius I employed it to listen in secret to his prisoners.

The Epipolai district extends northwestward along a rocky plateau to the Euryalus Fort, about 4.5 mi (7 km) distant. The walls around the area and the fort were built originally by Dionysius I between 402 and 397 B.C. against the threat of a Carthaginian invasion, and they were further modified in the next two centuries. It is from the Euryalus Fort that Archimedes is supposed to have set fire to the Roman fleet (just before 212 B.C.) with his

FIGURE 115. Marble Sarcophagus (Mid-Fourth Century A.D.) Decorated with Biblical Scenes, from the Catacombs of San Giovanni, in the National Archaeological Museum, Syracuse, Sicily (Photo Courtesy the Soprintendenza Archeologica, Siracusa)

mirrors and lenses. The fortification wall is 17 mi (27 km) in extent, is provided from place to place with gates and towers, and is protected by rock-cut ditches. In all, the complex of fort and walls is one of the most impressive systems of defense surviving from antiquity.

Across the Corso Gelone to the east of the Greek and Roman monuments of Neapolis, there is an area of early Christian catacombs. The most extensive and important are reached off the Viale Teocrito to the left, and they are called the Catacombs of San Giovanni since they are near a monastery of the same name. Partly because the catacombs are cut in hard limestone rather than in volcanic tufa as at Rome, they are different from the Roman catacombs in that they have larger galleries with round chapels at points of junction. The date of the Catacombs of San Giovanni is in the fourth, fifth, and sixth centuries, but the crypt of San Marziano near the exit is dated in the first century. There there is an underground church, and if the date is correct, it is indeed a very early church. Supposedly there are to be seen here the place where Paul preached, the original baptistery, and the pillar on which Marcianus (St. Marcian)—Paul's first convert and the first bishop of Syracuse—was martyred. There are other catacombs further east, particularly the Catacombs of the Vigna Cassia, which has some galleries that date from the third and fourth centuries.[6]

ITALY

From Syracuse Paul's ship presumably followed a somewhat curving course up and along the east coast of Sicily into the Strait of Messina to the city of Rhegium (Ac 28:13). The strait is a narrow and beautiful passage, 8 mi (13 km) wide at its southern extremity and 2 mi (3 km) wide at the north, between the northeastern tip of Sicily and the mainland of southern Italy. The city of Messina is on the Sicilian side, and it was a Greek colony established in the eighth century B.C. with the name of Zankle. The city of Rhegium (Reggio di Calabria) is on the Italian side, and it was also founded about the same time as a Greek colony. Strabo (VI 1, 6) cites Aeschylus to the effect that Sicily was once rent (ἀπορραγῆναι) from the continent by earthquakes, and so, with reference to this fact, the town was called Rhegium.

To the north of Rhegium was the famous rock of Scylla, in mythology supposedly inhabited by a female monster of partly human form, and to the north of Messina was the famous whirlpool of Charybdis, also personified as a female monster. In Greek legend Odysseus and Jason successfully passed between the twin dangers, and so too, in biblical history, did Paul's ship. With a favorable south wind the ship sailed up the Tyrrhenian Sea to Puteoli (Ac 28:13) on the Gulf of Naples in the district of Italy known as Campania, and there the sea voyage came to an end.

Gulf of Naples

Entering the Gulf of Naples from the sea, the island of Ischia (Aenaris) is on the left, Capri (Capreae) is on the right, and Mt. Vesuvius is ahead, rising to a height of about 4,000 ft (1,220 m). The Greeks went to both Ischia and Capri in the eighth century B.C., and Capri was especially favored by the Roman emperors as a resort. Augustus visited Capri in 29 B.C., and Tiberius resided there from A.D. 26 or 27 until his death in 37, and according to Tacitus, Tiberius had twelve villas there. Of Capri, Tacitus writes (Annals IV 67), "In winter, the climate is gentle, owing to the mountain barrier which intercepts the cold sweep of the winds; its summers catch the western breeze and are made a delight by the circling expanse of open sea; while it overlooked the most beautiful of bays, until the activity of Vesuvius began to change the face of the landscape."

On shore, all around the sweep of the gulf from Cape Miseno opposite Ischia on the north to the Sorrento Peninsula opposite Capri on the south was a series of towns, with Naples (Neapolis or Napoli), Herculaneum (Ercolano), and Pompeii closest to the foot of

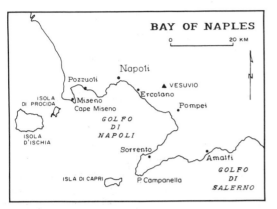

BAY OF NAPLES

0   20 KM

Napoli

Pozzuoli

ISOLA DI PROCIDA

Miseno
Cape Miseno

VESUVIO

Ercolano

Pompei

GOLFO DI NAPOLI

Sorrento

ISOLA D'ISCHIA

Amalfi

GOLFO DI SALERNO

ISLA DI CAPRI   P. Campanella

MAP 13.

Mt. Vesuvius, the latter two to be buried in the eruption of A.D. 79.

Naples was founded in the middle of the seventh century B.C. from Cumae just to the west, and Naples was originally named for the Siren Parthenope, who according to mythology, was washed ashore there after failing to capture Odysseus and whose monument was still there in the time of Strabo (I 2, 13; v 4, 7). The old city (called Palaepolis) was in the southwest part of the modern city along the modern harbor area, and it included Megaris, a small island (Castel dell'Ovo) in the harbor where the Rhodians probably had an early trading colony (Strabo XIV 2, 10). The later city developed to the northeast and was called Neapolis, from which comes the modern name of Naples. In Italy Naples is now the third largest city (after Rome and Milan), and its harbor is second only to that of Genoa in importance. In ancient Naples there was a Temple of the Dioscuri, the patron deities of seafarers, and the building materials of the temple were reused in the church of S. Paolo Maggiore (built between 1591 and 1603).

In ancient times, however, it was the region to the west of Naples, extending around the gulf to Cumae, that was the more important. This is an area of volcanic hills, craters, lakes, and springs, with beautiful views out over the Bay of Pozzuoli. The Greek settlers of the fifth century B.C. used the word Phlegra for the region, which was the name of a plain in Thrace famous for underground fire and said to be where the giants were struck with lightning when they were fighting with the gods—therefore, the name of any place exposed to volcanic action. Hence the area in Italy became known as the Campi Phlegraei, the Phlegraean Fields (Pliny, *Nat. Hist.* III 5, 61), and it is the modern Solfatara. Four cities were important in the area; Cumae the political center, Misenum the Roman naval base, Baiae the pleasure resort, and Puteoli the commercial port.

The site of Cumae was on the seacoast about 12 mi (19 km) west of Naples. The center of the city was the acropolis, originally part of a volcanic crater. There are still traces of the Greek walls (fifth century B.C.) and two natural terraces on which stand the ruins of two temples of comparable date, modified in later times. On the upper terrace is the Temple of Jupiter, on the lower terrace, the Temple of Apollo—the latter converted into a Christian basilica in the sixth century A.D. with an octagonal bowl on the outside of the building for a baptistery. From the Temple of Apollo steps lead down to the Grotto of the Sibyl of Cumae. This prophetess was the most famous of all those called sibyls in the ancient world, and her grotto was discovered in the course of excavations in 1932. A long corridor (431 ft [131.5 m] long, 8 ft [2.4 m] wide, 16 ft [5 m] high) is hollowed out in the tufa ridge and lighted by six lateral galleries facing onto the sea. The corridor leads to a vast rectangular hall, also carved out of the tufa, with a vaulted roof and niches, and there are three ceremonial baths and smaller innermost chambers where the sibyl lived and uttered her prophecies. The stone cutting is attributed to the fifth century B.C., with alterations in the fourth to third centuries. Vergil (70–19 B.C.) probably saw the sibyl in person, and he describes the frenzy of her utterance as he pictures Aeneas coming to her for consultation (*Aeneid* VI 98–101). "In such words the Cumaean Sibyl chants from the shrine her dread enigmas and echoes from the cavern, wrapping truth in darkness—so does Apollo shake the reins as she rages, and ply the spur beneath her breast." During the Roman Empire the cult of the sibyl was condemned, and the grotto was converted into a cistern; later it was used for a Christian cemetery.

Misenum is now the small village of Miseno, near the end of Cape Miseno on the west side of the Bay of Pozzuoli. Misenum served as the harbor of Cumae for centuries, and under Augustus it was made the main base of the Roman fleet in the West—the ships that defeated Antony and Cleopatra at Actium (31 B.C.) were based there. Pliny the Elder (author of the *Natural History*) was admiral of the fleet at this place when Mt. Vesuvius erupted, and he lost his life (A.D. 79) in the effort to aid Pompeii.

North of Misenum on a long hillside sloping down to the west side of the Bay of Pozzuoli is the site of Baiae, still occupied by a small town (Baia). There hot and mineral springs and a gentle climate provided an environment in which the Romans developed a most luxurious and fashionable pleasure resort. Julius Caesar, Pompey, Cicero, and other famous Romans had villas there, and many ruins of baths and temples are still to be seen.

Puteoli

The site of Puteoli (the modern city of Pozzuoli) is on a promontory at the north end of the Bay of Pozzuoli in the heart of the Phlegraean Fields, 3 mi (5 km) from Baiae and 8 mi (13 km) from Naples. Puteoli was settled around 520 B.C. by political refugees from the Greek island of Samos, and it was originally named Dikaearchia. In 215 B.C., when Hannibal was invading Italy, the Romans put a garrison at the place, and in 194 B.C. it was made a Roman colony with the name of Puteoli. Strabo (v 4, 6) reports two possible derivations of this name from Latin, either from *putei* with reference to the wells found there, or from *puteo* with reference to the strong sulphurous smells of the district. Under Augustus, Nero, and Vespasian Puteoli continued to rank as a Roman colony.

By the time it was made a colony, Puteoli had already surpassed Neapolis (Naples) in importance as a port, and this was due in part to its proximity to the Via Appia, which was reached at Capua (only 20 mi [32 km] away) and led to Rome. Around 125 B.C. Lucilius placed Puteoli second only to Delos in commercial importance—Delos (the smallest and most famous of the Cyclades) then being considered the greatest harbor of the ancient world. Delos, however, was sacked by Mithradates VI of Pontus in 87 B.C. and never recovered; by the first and second centuries A.D. it was quite deserted. So at least from the time of Augustus, Puteoli was considered the supreme port, and Strabo calls it the "greatest port in the whole world." Puteoli was also equipped with a famous lighthouse, and its importance of course lay primarily in the connection it provided with Rome. In A.D. 50 Claudius established a port nearer to Rome at Ostia at the mouth of the Tiber, and built a lighthouse there, but that harbor silted up badly and the importance of Puteoli continued to the extent that Nero considered digging a canal from there to the Tiber. Finally, however, Trajan (A.D. 98–117) made an adequate harbor at Ostia, and from the second century onward Puteoli declined and was finally abandoned as a port in the sixth century.

Exports from Puteoli were sulphur, objects of iron including military armor and farm implements, pottery, mosaics, and pozzolana (which took its name from the place)—a mortar mixed of lime and volcanic ash. Strabo explains that with pozzolana it was possible to construct very strong jetties at Puteoli, thus making the wide-open shores curve into bays so that the largest merchant vessels could moor there in safety.

Imports were even more important. The Alexandrian grain ships went there, and Seneca (*Epistle* 77) tells how the inhabitants of Puteoli watched eagerly for the Alexandrian ships to approach, ships of the very type Paul was on. The very large vessels that brought obelisks from Egypt also came to this port. Many travelers embarked and disembarked at

FIGURE 116. Ancient Marble Lion on the Island of Delos.

Puteoli. Josephus (*Life* 16) speaks of landing there on his way to Rome, and Suetonius (*Titus* v 3) tells that Titus, hastening to Rome after the destruction of Jerusalem, put in at Rhegium, then disembarked at Puteoli.

Although little of the ancient port of Puteoli is accessible—its piers and arches being covered by the modern solid breakwater—some of the town's ancient monuments are identifiable. The Macellum or town market (erroneously called the Temple of Serapis because a statue of that deity was found there in 1750) was a large rectangle (about 125 ft [38 m] by 118 ft [36 m]) surrounded by porticoes and shops. Because of variation in the ground level caused by volcanic action (a phenomenon known as bradyseism) the Macellum has been partially submerged in the sea and raised again. A small amphitheater (427 ft [130 m] by 312 ft [95 m]) of the Augustan period has been found under the Naples-Rome express railway line. A large

amphitheater (489 ft [149 m] by 380 ft [116 m]) nearby was built in the Flavian period, probably under Vespasian (A.D. 69–79), and it was the third largest such structure in Italy, seating 40,000 spectators and surpassed only by the amphitheaters in Rome (616 ft [188 m] by 512 ft [156 m]) and Capua (548 ft [167 m] by 449 ft [137m]). On a low acropolis was a Temple of Augustus, built over an earlier temple. On the same site a Christian church was built in the eleventh century and modified in the seventeenth and eighteenth centuries, and it is the present cathedral (Duomo), but on the right side six Corinthian columns and the architrave of the Augustan temple are still preserved.

In A.D. 305 five Christians were condemned to be thrown to the beasts in the Flavian amphitheater, but they were finally beheaded instead near a volcano now called the Solfatara, 1 mi (1.6 km) northeast of Puteoli. One

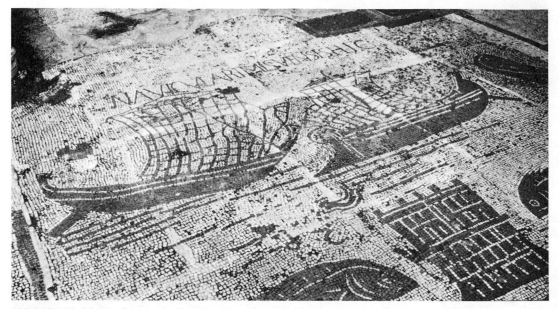

FIGURE 117. Mosaic Pavement Showing Two Ships, in Ostia.

of these was Proculus, a deacon of the church in Puteoli, and the cathedral just mentioned bears his name (San Proculo). Another was Januarius, bishop of Beneventum, and a church was built in the sixteenth century on the site of his death (San Gennaro), but it is in the cathedral in Naples that the annual lique-factions of the blood of the saint, supposedly preserved by his nurse Eusebia, are said to take place.

When Paul got to Puteoli, "we found brethren, and were invited to stay with them for seven days" (Ac 28:14). As in Rome so also in Puteoli, Christianity had been introduced prior to the coming of Paul. The reference to staying with the brethren for seven days makes it probable that Julius the centurion—perhaps thinking more highly of Paul than ever after the experiences of the shipwreck journey —allowed Paul and his companions to move about the city with some freedom and to visit the believers. How Christianity had come there we do not know, but it may be supposed that Paul spoke to gatherings of the brethren while he stayed with them.

Brooding over the area was Vesuvius, and lying peacefully at its immediate base were Herculaneum and Pompeii. Less than twenty-five years later, after centuries of inactivity, the volcano erupted on Aug. 24, A.D. 79, with great violence and buried both cities. Since 1861 systematic excavations have brought to light again the streets and houses, the mosaics and wall paintings, which vividly show the world of that time.

In 1938 there was found on the wall of an upper room of a modest Roman house in Herculaneum (the Casa del Bicentenaio or Bicentenary House) a rectangle with an indentation in the form of a cross. Nail marks could be from where a wooden cross had been fixed and removed before A.D. 79. Under the cross mark—if that is what it is—and some-what to the right where the lava could have pushed it, was a wooden object that could have been a house altar. Had some humble Christian prayed there? Had he even heard Paul speak of the cross? Did that humble Christian die under Nero and some pagan house owner later tear the cross down? These questions suggest intriguing hypotheses, but they are questions to which positive answers cannot be given. Very possibly, however, the mark on the wall of the house is the sign of the cross, a very early example of the same.[7]

Via Appia

From Puteoli Paul and his party presumably went on to Capua, 20 mi (32 km) away, the nearest point at which to reach the Via Appia, the main highway to Rome.[8] The Roman Capua is now Santa Maria di Capua Vetere (not modern Capua, 3 mi [5 km] further toward Rome, which was the Roman Casilinum and the port on the river Volturno for ancient Capua). The chief remaining monuments in Santa Maria di Capua Vetere are the enormous amphitheater, second only to the Colosseum in Rome and built in the second century A.D., and a Mithraeum of the second to third centuries, decorated with panels showing the rites of initiation into the cult of Mithras.

"The worn and well-known track of Appia, queen of the long roads" as the highway was described by Statius (A.D. 45–96) in *Silvae* (II 2, 12), was built from Rome to Capua by the censor Appius Claudius Caecus in 312 B.C., extended to Beneventum, Venusia, and Tarentum in the early third century B.C., and finally continued to Brundisium on the southeastern coast soon after 248 B.C.

The distance from ancient Capua to Rome is 131 mi (211 km). Strabo (V 3, 6) says that "the only cities on the coast that the Via Appia touches are Terracina, Formia, and Sinuessa." From Capua, then, the probable course of the highway followed the contour of the hills westward to touch the coast at Sinuessa (modern Mondragone), then turned inland again to Minturnae (near modern Minturno, 1.2 mi [2 km] from the sea), came again to the sea at Formiae (where monumental tombs still line the Via Appia, the largest, 79 ft [24 m] high, known as the Tomba di Cicerone, since

Formiae is where Cicero died in 43 B.C.), went inland by way of Fundi (modern Fondi, where monumental tombs again line the way), and went down to the coast once more at Tarracina.

Tarracina (modern Terracina) was originally known as Anxur until it was taken by the Romans in 406 B.C. and given the name Tarracina. The site is on and at the foot of Monte San Angelo, a high hill with a splendid view over the Gulf of Gaeta. The ancient acropolis was on top of the cliff above the present city, and it was surrounded by massive walls built by Sulla in the early first century B.C. Within these walls is the Temple of Jupiter Anxur, which also dates from the time of Sulla. The Via Appia originally climbed over the hill and provided the main longitudinal street of the city (*decumanus*). Later Trajan (A.D. 98–117) cut through the cliff below the citadel along the coast and brought the highway down to the sea level, and the lower town developed (mostly in the second and third centuries A.D.) between the sea and the lower Via Appia.

Tarracina marked approximately the halfway point on the way from Capua to Rome, and there remained 64 mi (103 km) to go. The intermediate points between Tarracina and Rome mentioned in Ac 28:15 are the Forum of Appius and the Three Taverns. For the first 19 mi (30 km) onward from Tarracina the route was straight across the Pontine Marshes (the Agro Pontino), then a vast swampy area on the coastal plain. The road here had only a gravel surface, and it was not paved until the times of Nerva (A.D. 96–98) and Trajan (98–117). There was, however, a canal alongside the road, constructed by Augustus, which represented an attempt to drain the marshes and also provided an alternate means of travel on mule-drawn barges. The Forum of Appius (Forum Appii) is not precisely located, but it is mentioned by Horace (*Satires* I 5, 3–6) as the usual halt at the end of the first day's journey out from Rome and as a place "crammed with boatmen and stingy tavern-keepers," and it was at the northern terminus of the boat canal through the Pontine Marshes. Whether Paul and his party were on a canalboat from Tarracina to the Forum of Appius or on foot, there is no way to know, but perhaps foot travel was the more likely as that form of travel may be presumed for most of Paul's land journeys. The Three Taverns (Tres Tabernae) was probably a little nearer Rome (near the modern Cisterna), and it is mentioned by Cicero (*Letters to Atticus* II 12) as the point where a branch road from the coastal city of Antium (the Roman city northeast of the present Anzio) joined the Via Appia.

The rest of the way was over the Alban Hills, probably passing through Lanuvium (modern Lanuvio, the hometown of Quirinius of Lk 2:2) and Alba Longa (modern Castel Gondolfo on Lake Albano), and then across the Campagna di Roma, the vast plain surrounding Rome that was the ancient Latium, the traditional home of the Latin race founded by Aeneas.

Environs of Rome

On the Campagna, not far from the Via Appia, was the Aqueduct Claudia, which came from the Alban Hills and was carried on arches 110 ft (34 m) high. Completed by Claudius in A.D. 50, it brought water to Rome from more than 40 mi (64 km) away. On either side of the highway as it approached the city were monumental tombs, as was so often the case on the outskirts of a city. Burial had to be outside the city limits, but places along the main roads were preferred, and the Via Appia was the most important road coming into Rome so many important Roman families chose burial locations there.

This stretch of the ancient road is now known as the Via Appia Antica to distinguish it from the Via Appia Nuova, the modern highway that parallels it at some distance to the east. From the point where the Via Appia Antica leaves the junction with the modern road to the Porta San Sebastiano in the

Aurelian Wall is a distance of some 7.5 mi (12 km), and all along the way tombs and foundations of tombs and statues and fragments of statues are still to be seen, and portions of the ancient pavement remain in place as well. The tombs include the Casal Rotondo, a circular monument on a square base from the time of Augustus, the largest tomb on the Via Appia (at the fifth milestone); the Tomb of Seneca, who was minister of state to Nero (near the fourth milestone); and the Tomb of Cecilia Metella, daughter-in-law of Marcus Crassus (115–53 B.C.), a very wealthy Roman under the dictator Sulla, and wife of Crassus the Younger, one of Caesar's generals in Gaul (at the third milestone). Not far from the Tomb of Cecilia Metella is the Circus of Maxentius, built in A.D. 309 with a seating capacity of 20,000 by the emperor Maxentius in honor of his son Romulus, traces of whose circular tomb are at the left of the circus.

Walls of Rome

With respect to the walls of Rome, the so-called Servian Wall bears the name of King Servius Tullius (578–534 B.C.), but it may have only been built or at least completed in its full extent around 390 B.C. When completed it had a circuit of nearly 7 mi (11 km). After the Punic wars of the third and second centuries B.C. Rome was for the most part secure from hostile aggression, and the Servian Wall was allowed to fall into decay as the city spread far beyond the wall. By the latter part of the third century A.D., however, the threat of barbarian invasions led to the building of a new wall. This was begun by Aurelian between 270 and 272, and it was completed by Probus (A.D. 276–282). The new wall not only enclosed the seven hills on a larger periphery than the Servian Wall, but it also took in the Campus Martius on the east side of the Tiber and the region on the west side of the river including part of the Janiculum Hill. The greater part of the Aurelian Wall is still preserved and can be seen around the city. In the building of the new wall some of the older tombs were demolished, and some were enclosed inside the wall —for example, the family Tomb of the Scipios (third century B.C.) on the ancient Via Appia, which is now to be found inside the Porta San Sebastiano.

The Porta San Sebastiano was the ancient Porta Appia in the Aurelian Wall, and it was rebuilt by Honorius in the fifth century and restored in the sixth century. Inside the Porta San Sebastiano the ancient Via Appia continues as the Via di Porta San Sebastiano and is soon joined by the Via Latina, which comes in diagonally from the right through the Porta Latina in the Aurelian Wall. At the junction of the two streets is a small plaza (Piazzale Numa Pompilio), and to the left are the Baths of Caracalla (Terme di Caracalla), which were begun in A.D. 212 and completed in 217. A colossal brick structure, 1,105 ft (337 m) on each side, and once adorned with marble walls, mosaic floors, granite columns, and bronze doors, the Baths of Caracalla were the most grand and luxurious of all the ancient Roman baths, although of all the many such structures in Rome the very largest were the Baths of Diocletian (A.D. 306) near the modern railway station. The baths had three principal parts—*frigidarium*, *tepidarium*, and *calidarium*—

but they also contained gymnasiums for physical exercise, libraries, art galleries, conference rooms, and places for conversation and debate. Thus they were important meeting places for the people of the great city. Today the Baths of Caracalla are used for summer opera and concerts, and the Baths of Diocletian were altered by Michelangelo on the order of Pius IV in 1563; one part became the Church of St. Mary of the Angels, and the other part houses the National Museum of Rome.

From the plaza beside the Baths of Caracalla the street continues as the Via delle Terme di Caracalla to the Piazza di Porta Capena. There the line of the Servian Wall was rediscovered in the nineteenth century, and there also was the location of the Porta Capena, the gate in the Servian Wall through which the ancient Via Appia entered the main part of Rome. Today an obelisk of the third or fourth century brought from Axum in Ethiopia stands there, and nearby is a park named Parco Porta Capena, with a modern sport stadium. At the Porta Capena the long march on the Via Appia reached its climax, and presumably it was at this place that Paul at last entered the central area of Rome.

8
IN ROME
(A.D. 57–59)

The site of ancient Rome was marked by seven hills in the plain beside the Tiber River. This river, the largest in central Italy, reached the sea (at Ostia) about 12.5 mi (20 km) away, a distance that is now some 15 mi (24 km) due to silting, which has extended the coastline seaward. At the site of Rome an island in the Tiber (Isola Tiberina) provided the easiest place in a long distance to cross the river, and the favorable geographical situation contributed to the importance that the city early attained.

HISTORY

There is evidence of human habitation on the site of Rome from the second millennium B.C. onward, and Latin tribes probably settled on the several hills from the tenth century B.C. onward. As recorded by Livy and Plutarch, the traditional founding of the city was by Romulus and Remus in 753 B.C. Romulus, whose name is equivalent to Romanus (Roman), supposedly dug a furrow with a plow around a rectangular area on the Palatine Hill and thus traced the first boundary of the city. As the community developed, the seven hills were plainly its natural strongholds, and we hear of an early religious festival that was called Septimontium (Seven Hills), and Varro (*On the Latin Language* v 41) states that Septimontium was the name of the city before it was called Rome.

In all there were seven legendary kings of Rome: Romulus (753–715 B.C.), Numa Pompilius (715–672), Tullus Hostilius (672–640), Ancus Marcius (640–616), Lucius Tarquinius Priscus (616–578), Servius Tullius (578–534), and Lucius Tarquinius Superbus (534–510). Romulus, Hostilius, and Ancus Marcius were Latins, Numa Pompilius was of the closely related Sabine tribe, and the last three kings were Etruscans.

Although the traditions concerning the Etruscans are far from clear, this people may have come into central Italy from the eastern Mediterranean, and their language was non-Indo-European. In the earliest literary reference to them by Hesiod (*Theogony*, 1011–1016) they are called Tyrsenoi, later Greek authors called them Tyrrhenoi, and the Romans named them Etrusci or Etruscans. The part of Italy they inhabited was Etruria, which was to the north of Latium, between the Tiber and the Arno rivers, on the western slope of the Apennines and looking toward the sea that was named after them, the Tyrrhenian Sea.

Under Tarquinius Priscus, as Dionysius of Halikarnassos (III 47 ff.) and Livy (I 34 ff.) tell us, the Latin town of Rome was transformed into an Etruscan city, with an organized urban life and the establishment of military and political power. This first Tarquin, it is said, began to build walls around the city, founded the Circus Maximus, drained the marshy valley between the Palatine and the Capitoline hills with the great sewer called the Cloaca Maxima, laid out what became the Forum Romanum, and at least planned and perhaps began the Temple of Jupiter on the Capitoline Hill, the most famous of all Roman temples. In this temple, according to a report preserved by Pliny (*Nat. Hist.* xxxv 45, 157), Tarquinius Priscus also put up a painted clay statue of Jupiter, made by an Etruscan artist. Since Augustine (*City of God* IV 31) says that for more than 170 years the ancient Romans worshiped the gods without an image (reckoned from the founding of Rome in 753 B.C. this date would fall in the reign of Tarquinius Priscus), this would have been the first cult statue of a deity at Rome.

It has already been noted that the name of Servius Tullius is associated with the main ancient wall of Rome prior to the Aurelian Wall. As for Tarquinius Superbus (Tarquin the Proud), he is supposed to have built or at least completed the Temple of Jupiter Capitolinus, and it is he of whom the story was told that the Cumaean sibyl offered him nine books of the sibylline oracles for a price that he declined to pay. The sibyl burned three books, then three more, and finally sold him the remaining three for the price originally asked for all. These books were kept in the Capitoline Temple.

In 509 B.C. the discontent of the common people with the hard tasks of the construction to which they were set in addition to their military service under the Etruscan kings led to revolt. Tarquinius Superbus was driven out, and the Roman Republic was established.[1] The new government was aristocratic in that it was led by two consuls (Livy I 60), but it became more democratic when two tribunes of the people were designated. Latin was the predominant language. Authority was signified by the famous initials S.P.Q.R., *senatus populusque romanus* (the Senate and People of Rome).

Before long Rome dominated its whole world. The chief rival was the Phoenician colony at Carthage, which led to the Punic wars that ended with the destruction of Carthage in 146 B.C. The circle of control was extended around the eastern Mediterranean with the conquest of Jerusalem by Pompey in 63 B.C. Northern Europe was conquered by Julius Caesar by 51 B.C.

Pompey, Julius Caesar, and Crassus had formed a triumvirate; in civil wars Julius Caesar defeated Pompey (49–48 B.C.) and emerged as dictator; in 44 B.C. he was assassinated. Mark Antony, a relative of Julius Caesar, took command and became associated with Cleopatra, the last of the Ptolemies in Egypt. But Octavian, another relative, was the designated heir of Julius Caesar. In the naval battle of Actium in 31 B.C. Octavian defeated Antony and went on, in the next year, to take Alexandria, where Antony and Cleopatra took their own lives. So Octavian was victorious, and in 27 B.C. the Senate conferred upon him the title of Augustus, and he ruled as the first Roman emperor until A.D. 14, to be followed by Tiberius (14–37), Caligula (37–41), Claudius (41–54), and Nero (54–68); during Nero's reign Paul arrived in Rome.

MONUMENTS

At the Porta Capena, where we assume Paul entered the main part of the city of Rome, the seven hills were ahead; on the left the Aventine, on the right the Caelian, directly ahead the Palatine, beyond it the Capitoline, and on to the north the Esquiline, Viminal, and Quirinal. Sweeping past the hills in three great curves was the Tiber River, and across it, on the west side, was the Vatican region and, south of the Vatican, the Janiculum Hill.

From the Piazza di Porta Capena two streets run west to border the site of the Circus Maximus, lying between the Aventine and Palatine hills and extending well toward the second great eastward curve of the Tiber. This circus was the oldest and largest of this type of structure, a long rectangle rounded off at the end in a semicircle with a low wall (*spina*) running lengthwise in the center, designed primarily for the chariot races of which the Romans were especially fond. The Circus

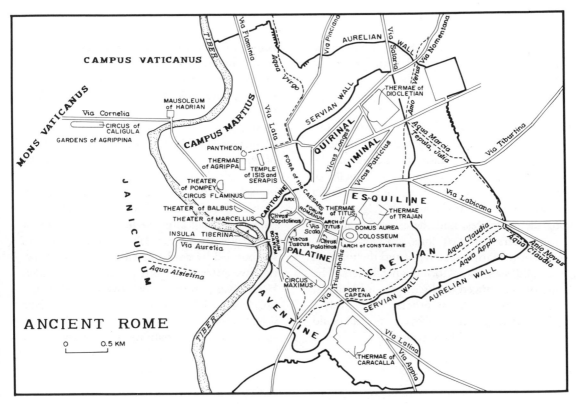

CAMPUS VATICANUS

MONS VATICANUS

Via Cornelia

MAUSOLEUM
of HADRIAN

CIRCUS of
CALIGULA
GARDENS of AGRIPPINA

CAMPUS MARTIUS

AURELIAN

THERMAE of
DIOCLETIAN

SERVIAN WALL

QUIRINAL

VIMINAL

PANTHEON

THERMAE
of AGRIPPA

TEMPLE
of ISIS and
SERAPIS

THEATER
of POMPEY

CIRCUS FLAMINUS

THEATER of BALBUS

THEATER of MARCELLUS

INSULA TIBERINA

Via Aurelia

ESQUILINE

THERMAE
of TITUS

THERMAE
of TRAJAN

Via Labicana

ARCH of
TITUS

DOMUS AUREA

COLOSSEUM

ARCH of CONSTANTINE

Aqua Claudia

Aqua Alsietina

PALATINE

CAELIAN

AURELIAN WALL

CIRCUS
MAXIMUS

PORTA
CAPENA

SERVIAN WALL

AVENTINE

Via Latina

Via Appia

THERMAE of
CARACALLA

ANCIENT ROME

0   0.5 KM

PLAN 21.

Maximus was begun by Tarquinius Priscus in the period of the kings, constructed of wood at the end of the period of the Republic, and enlarged by Julius Caesar in 46 B.C. Thus it was no doubt seen by Paul. It seated 300,000 spectators, and the imperial palaces were on the Palatine Hill above where an enormous podium allowed the court to observe the spectacles. On the *spina* of the circus Augustus erected an obelisk of Ramses II from Heliopolis, which was 79 ft (24 m) high. Today the circus is buried—perhaps nearly intact—under a cover of earth that is not feasible to excavate, the more so because there is an underground river nearby. Only the higher tiers of seats are recognizable, and the whole was made into a garden in 1958—the Valle Murcia—which reproduces with vegetation the plan of the structures underground. The obelisk was moved in 1587 by order of Sixtus V and erected in the Piazza del Popolo, with a cross on top.

From the Piazza di Porta Capena a wide street called the Via di San Gregorio runs north to the Arch of Constantine and the Colosseum. The Arch of Constantine was erected in A.D. 315 by the Senate and people of Rome to commemorate the important victory of Constantine over Maxentius (A.D. 312) in a battle that began at Saxa Rubra (9 mi [14.5 km] north of Rome on the ancient Via Flaminia where the modern village of Prima Porta takes its name from a brick arch of perhaps the Constantinian period) and concluded at the nearby Milvian Bridge over the Tiber. It was prior to this battle, Eusebius relates in his *Life of Constantine* (28 ff.), that Constantine saw in a vision in the sky at noonday and in a dream in the following night a flaming cross with the legend, "by this (sign) conquer," which led to his conversion to Christianity and to his use on his imperial standard (*labarum*) of the sacred monogram composed of the first two letters of the name of Christ. The Arch of Constantine is of white marble (69 ft [21 m] high, 85 ft [26 m] wide), has three openings, and is decorated with bas-reliefs, some of them taken from earlier monuments of Trajan and others.

The Colosseum was begun by Vespasian in A.D. 72 and completed by his son Titus in A.D. 80. It was designed for gladiatorial combats and fights with wild beasts, but it could also be flooded for naval battles. It was built of travertine and is 614 ft (187 m) long, 509 ft (155 m) wide, and 187 ft (57 m) high. Eight arches provide entrances, and the exterior wall rises in four tiers—the first three are Doric, Ionic, and Corinthian, respectively, and the topmost is a solid wall with Corinthian pilasters. The interior is arranged in three tiers—for knights, citizens, and common people, respectively—with standing room above, and it could accommodate 50,000 spectators. Under the floor of the arena was a kind of fortress with places for gladiators and wild animals. In the course of time the Colosseum was used as a stone quarry and damaged by earthquake, neglect, and traffic, but it is still the largest existing monument from ancient Roman times.

Across from the Colosseum on the small Oppian Hill (Colle Oppio) are the large ruins of the Baths of Titus (A.D. 79–81) and the Baths of Trajan (98–117), and this was previously the site of the famous Golden House (Domus Aurea) of Nero (54–68). This palace was built after the fire of A.D. 64, and it was evidently a vast labyrinthine structure, surrounded by gardens, with an artificial lake nearby. After the death of Nero the Golden House was destroyed or covered up by the building works of his successors, and the lake was drained to make room for the Colosseum, so only some foundations of the palace now

FIGURE 118. The Colosseum in Rome.

remain. The vestibule of the palace extended to the west where Hadrian (A.D. 136 or 137) built the Temple of Venus and Roma (north of the Arch of Titus). A colossal statue of Nero stood there, but it was moved to a site opposite the Colosseum and is thought to have been the source of the name Colosseum. The statue is no longer in existence, and even the last remains of its base were destroyed in 1936.

From the area of the Colosseum the Sacred Way (Via Sacra) ran westward to the base of the Capitoline Hill. Moving along this way, as one may suppose Paul did as he went to the very center of ancient Rome, on a small hill to the right is Hadrian's Temple of Venus and Roma. This was a double temple, with two apses back to back, the Temple of Roma looking west toward the Forum Romanum, and the Temple of Venus looking east toward the Colosseum. Built into this temple at its west end is the Church of St. Frances of Rome, built in the tenth century and often restored. In the right transept behind an iron gate are two stones from the Via Sacra. Imprints in the stone are accompanied by a legend affirming that they were left by St. Peter when he knelt to pray for the divine punishment of Simon Magus, who supposedly fell at the spot where the church was built. From the front of the church there is an excellent view westward toward the Forum.

Opposite the church to the left and on a small rise called the Velia is the Arch of Titus, which spanned the Via Sacra. This was erected in A.D. 81 after the death of Titus to commemorate his victory in Palestine in A.D. 70. The arch is faced with Pentelic marble, has a single opening, and contains reliefs on its interior panels. On one side a woman (Roma), who is the deified Rome, drives the imperial quadriga (a chariot drawn by four horses abreast) that carries Titus while Victory crowns him. On the other side Roman soldiers, laurel crowned, march in a triumphal procession carrying the spoils of war from Jerusalem—the seven-branched candelabrum, the table of shewbread, the sacred trumpets, and tablets fastened on staves. Under the vault overhead is the apotheosis of Titus, carried to heaven by an eagle. Under this arch no Jew ever passes.

Next on the right of the Via Sacra is the largest building in the area, a basilica begun by Maxentius in A.D. 306 and finished by Constantine. Built of brick, it is 328 ft (100 m) long and 249 ft (76 m) wide, with a broad central aisle and two side aisles. Three enormous arcades still stand, 67 ft (20.5 m) wide, 80 ft (24 m) high, and 57 ft (17 m) deep. The bulky pillars in the middle enclosed Corinthian columns, one of which was recovered intact and placed in front of the church of Santa Maria Maggiore. In one apse was a colossal statue of Constantine, of which only fragments survive. Michelangelo is said to have studied this basilica for his plans for St. Peter's Basilica, and the Basilica of Constantine is still used for open-air concerts in the summer.

Between that basilica and the Temple of Antoninus and Faustina further to the west is the probable location of the Temple of Romulus, adjacent to the Church of the Saints Cosmas and Damian. The temple was founded in A.D. 309 by Maxentius in memory of his deified son M. Valerius Romulus (named after the founder of the city), and according to representations on coins, it was probably a circular structure. The Church of Cosmas and Damian was built in A.D. 527 by Pope Felix IV and was renovated in the seventeenth century. It contains fine sixth-century mosaics, and in the apse, Peter and Paul are presenting the two saints before Christ. Cosmas and Damian were legendary martyrs of perhaps the last quarter of the third century. Twin brothers, and physicians, they were known as "silverless" because they took no fees and counted it their reward that those they benefited should believe in Christ.

The Temple of Antoninus and Faustina was erected by Antoninus Pius in A.D. 141 in honor of his deified wife Faustina, and when he died in 161 the Senate dedicated the temple to him as well. Six marble columns of the front porch (50 ft [15 m] high) are still standing, and above is the inscription, Divo Antonio et Divae

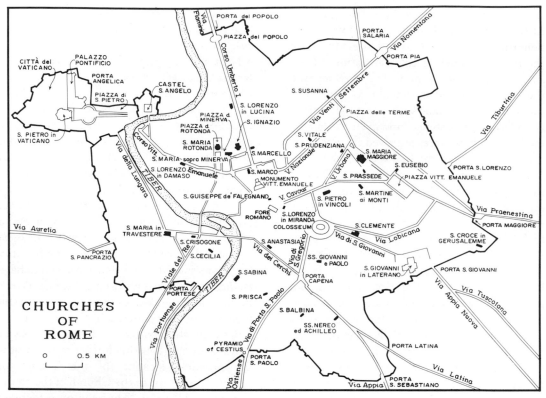

PLAN 22.

Faustinae ex S.C. (i.e., *senatus consultum*, "by decree of the Senate"). In the eleventh century this temple was converted into the Church of San Lorenzo in Miranda. St. Laurence was a deacon of the Roman church and was martyred under Valerian on Aug. 10, A.D. 258, four days after the martyrdom (on Aug. 6) of Xystus, the bishop of Rome. The church at this site supposedly marks the place where Laurence was judged and condemned to die by slow fire, and several other churches in Rome memorialize other events in his life.

Adjacent to the Temple of Antoninus and Faustina is a small ancient necropolis with tombs dating from the ninth century B.C. to about 700 B.C.; thus the cemetery was contemporary with the foundation of Rome. At that time there was a settlement of huts in the area, but about the middle of the seventh century the cemetery was abandoned and the

hut settlement disappeared to make room for a general common square or marketplace. This became the Forum Romanum. The eastern boundary of this square was marked by a stone platform, which must have supported some kind of religious monument, and by the beginning of the Republic this place became the Regia, the sanctuary where the official sacrifices of state were performed. In turn, the sanctuary became the residence of the Pontifex Maximus, who presided over the Pontifical College, the highest priestly organization of ancient Rome. There, where the Via Sacra descended from the Velia to the Forum, there was also a Temple of Vesta and, later, the House of the Vestal Virgins. Vesta was the goddess of the hearth fire in the home, and her temple symbolized the hearth of the city, conceived as a larger family. In the temple there was no image of the goddess, but only the fire. The Vestal Virgins were the priestesses of the goddess, they were chosen from among the daughters of the patrician families, and their duty was to watch over the sacred fire in the temple.

In his time Julius Caesar resided in the Regia and did much for the Forum, and afterward Augustus carried out many of Caesar's plans. At the southeast corner of the Forum, Augustus made the buildings into a complex in honor of Caesar, and in 29 B.C. Augustus erected the Temple of Divus Julius Caesar in front of the Regia on the spot where the body of Caesar was cremated. Also at the southeast corner of the Forum was the Temple of the Dioscuri (Castor and Pollux), which was built in 484 B.C. and restored several times. Three tall white marble Corinthian columns still support an architrave of the temple and date from the time of Augustus. Beside this temple to the south are the foundations of what is thought to have been the library of a Temple of Augustus, and in the fourth century A.D. this was transformed into the church of Santa Maria Antiqua, the oldest Christian monument in the Forum. In the church frescoes (in some cases superimposed upon each other) date from the sixth to the eighth centuries.

Next, on either side of the Forum, are the remains of great basilicas. On the north side was the Basilica Aemilia, erected in 179 B.C. and rebuilt in 55–34 B.C. by two Roman officials, L. Aemilius Paulus and his son L. Aemilius Lepidus Paulus. This was a vast rectangular building with a main hall (295 ft [90 m] long and 89 ft [27 m] wide), divided into central and side aisles and lighted by a clerestory. On the south side of the Forum, immediately paralleling the Via Sacra, was the Basilica Julia. This occupied a space 331 ft (101 m) long and 161 ft (49 m) wide and contained a central court (269 ft [82 m] long and 52 ft [16 m] wide), surrounded on all sides by two aisles with galleries in a second story. The Basilica Julia was known as a great center of Roman law, and it contained four law courts. It is very likely that it was here that the apostle Paul eventually heard the sentence of death pronounced upon himself.[2] From the Basilica Aemilia in A.D. 386 the Roman prefect Probianus took twenty-four beautiful columns of Phrygian marble to adorn the Church of St. Paul Outside the Walls, which was at that time under construction.

The area to the west of the Basilica Aemilia and at the west end of the Forum Romanum was the Comitium, the meeting place of the Comitia Curiata, the most ancient assembly of the people of Rome. On a high point was the Curia or Senate House. According to tradition the Curia was built originally by the third king Tullus Hostilius (672–640 B.C.), but a new Curia was begun by Julius Caesar in 47 B.C. and completed by Augustus. In A.D. 638 this building was transformed into a church of San Adriano, but in 1931–37 the church was demolished and the Curia restored. The Curia had several annexes, one of which was the Secretarium Senatus. Over this the Church of St. Luke and St. Martina was built in about the eighth century and rebuilt in 1635. This is a double church, the upper part dedicated to St. Luke and the lower church dedicated to St. Martina, and in the lower church two colonnades of the Secretarium are preserved.

To the south, facing the Curia, was a tribunal that, from 338 B.C., had the name of Rostra from the beaks of captured ships with which it was embellished (the Latin rostrum meaning the curved, often ornamental, end of a ship's prow, especially the beak or ram of a war galley). This speaker's platform was reconstructed by Julius Caesar, and it is believed to be the place from which Mark Antony appealed to the Romans for vengeance on the murderers of Caesar. Beside the Rostra were several archaic monuments, over which a black marble pavement, the so-called Lapis Niger, was laid in the first century B.C., and the remains of these monuments include the stump of a conical tufa column and a four-sided stela with inscriptions on all four sides. The writing on the stela is the oldest known in the Latin language, believed to be of the sixth century B.C., and it is probably a decree against profanation of a sacred site. In the immediate area is also the Column of Phocas, the latest Roman monument in the Forum in date, erected in A.D. 608 in honor of the Byzantine emperor Phocas.

At the south end of the Rostra, Augustus erected the Milliarium Aureum (Golden Milestone) in 20 B.C., on which were the names and distances of the chief cities of the empire from London to Jerusalem and elsewhere. At the north end of the Rostra the Umbilicus Romae marked the ideal center of the city, and therewith also of the Roman world. Close by rises the Arch of Septimius Severus, built by that emperor in A.D. 203 on the tenth anniversary of his accession and in honor of the victory of his sons Caracalla and Geta over the Parthians and Arabians. The arch, with three openings, is 75 ft (23 m) high and 81 ft (15.5 m) wide, and it was originally surmounted by a bronze chariot in which the emperor was seated between his sons. To the left and to the rear, west of the Basilica Julia, are eight granite columns of the Temple of Saturn, the Roman harvest god. Originally this temple housed the public treasury, called the *aerarium*.

West of the Forum Romanum rises the Capitoline Hill, the base of which is now bounded by the Via del Foro Romano. Along this street, from south to north, are the Arcade of the Gods Assembled (Porticus Deorum Consentium), built originally in the third or second century B.C. and restored in A.D. 367 and dedicated to the twelve Olympian gods (Juno, Vesta, Minerva, Ceres, Diana, Venus, Mars, Mercury, Jupiter, Neptune, Vulcan, and Apollo); the Temple of Vespasian, built by Domitian (A.D. 81–96) in honor of Vespasian and his son Titus; and the Temple of Concord, built in 367 B.C. to commemorate peace between the patricians and the people and reconstructed by Tiberius in A.D. 7.

Not far from the Temple of Concord, at the foot of the Capitoline Hill, is the Mamertine Prison. The prison is on two levels, with an upper chamber and a lower subterranean chamber, the latter entered originally only by a hole in the roof. The upper chamber is a vaulted trapezoid, with sides from 12 ft (3.6 m) to 16 ft (5 m) in length. The lower chamber is for the most part circular, nearly 30 ft (7 m) in diameter. The walls were built of tufa blocks, of which only three courses (less than 6 ft (1.8 m] high) are now visible, although some courses may be hidden beneath the present floor. The subterranean part and sometimes the entire prison were called the Tullianum, a name that may derive from a small spring (Latin *tullus*) that still rises in the floor of the lower chamber. According to Livy (I 33, 8) the prison was constructed by Ancus Marcius (640–616 B.C.) in a time of growing lawlessness in the city. Other ancient sources attribute the lower part to Servius Tullius (578–534) and derive the name Tullianum from his name. Some modern studies date the lower chamber about 300 B.C. and the upper chamber about 100 B.C. In ancient times this was the state prison of Rome and was used as a place of detention, but executions also took place there—e.g., those of Jugurtha and Vercingetorix. After execution the bodies were supposedly cast through a door into the Cloaca Maxima. It is traditionally and not unreasonably believed that Peter and possibly also Paul were imprisoned there, and according to legend Peter baptized his jailers Processus and Martinian with the water of the spring in the prison. There are now two churches over the prison; at a lower level is the church of San Pietro in Carcere, and at street level is the church of San Giuseppe dei Falegnami, both built in the sixteenth century.

From the corner of the Basilica Julia in the Forum Romanum a path called the Clivus Capitolinus, which was in effect a continuation of the Via Sacra, led up to the top of the Capitoline Hill. On the south summit of the hill was the Temple of Jupiter, and in the hollow between the south and the north summit was the Tabularium, which contained the state archives of the Republic. On the north summit was the Arx or citadel of ancient Rome, and some traces of a primitive fortification of tufa blocks were found when the foundations of the great national monument to Victor Emmanuel were laid on the slope of the hill below to the northwest. There were also private residences on the citadel in early times; one of them, the house of a certain M. Manlius Capitolinus, was destroyed in 384 B.C., and the Temple of Juno Moneta was erected on the same site in 344 B.C. In this case the surname of the goddess ("mint") may have been derived from the fact that it was in her temple that money was coined in the last centuries of the Republic. No trace of this temple has been found, but it may have occupied the site where the church of Santa Maria in Aracoeli now stands. This church was built in the fifth or sixth century and was rebuilt by the Franciscans in 1250. The name and place of the church are due to the legend that Augustus erected an altar on the spot where the sibyl of Tivoli prophesied to him the coming of Christ. In 1536 Michelangelo was commissioned to design the layout of the buildings on the hill, and now there is a square (Piazza del Campidoglio) with three palaces facing on it. Opposite the great approach steps from the west is the Palace of the Senators built over the ancient Tabularium, to the right is the Palace of the Municipal Councilors, and to the left is the New Palace, which houses the Capitoline Museum. In the center of the square is a bronze equestrian statue of Marcus Aurelius (A.D. 161–180), believed in the Middle Ages to be a statue of Constantine and thus preserved and brought there in 1538.

Overlooking the Forum Romanum from the south is the Palatine Hill, the site of the principal city residences of the Roman emperors. An ancient path ascended the Palatine from the Via Sacra in the vicinity of the Arch of Titus, and it is now commonly called the Clivus Palatinus. On the hill to the west of this approach the modern Farnesian Gardens are built over the ruins of the Palace of Tiberius, which was enlarged by Trajan and Hadrian. Continuing along the hill to the south and east there are many more monuments. The Temple of the Magna Mater (Cybele) was erected in the second century B.C. and reconstructed by Augustus. In the vicinity

are some traces of primitive dwellings, and the supposed house of Romulus was here. The House of Augustus (probably the residence of the first emperor himself, but sometimes called the House of Livia, the mother of Tiberius and later wife of Augustus) is one of the best-preserved buildings on the Palatine. It was a typical Roman *domus* with an *atrium* or entrance room, a *peristylium* or central courtyard surrounded by columns, a *tabulinum* where family records were kept, and a *triclinium* or dining room. Adjacent to this house is the Cryptoporticus, a long vaulted gallery paved with mosaics, attributed to perhaps the time of Nero. The Palace of the Flavians was built by Domitian, and it contains a basilica in which the emperor presided over the law court, an *aula regia* or throne room, and a *lararium* or chapel of the tutelary deities known as lares. The Domus Augustiana (not to be confused with the Domus Augusti or House of Augustus described just above) is a huge imperial residence that was used for centuries by various emperors, probably beginning at least with Domitian. All those structures occupy the whole southeastern part of the hill overlooking the Circus Maximus.

Beside the palace to the southeast and oriented in the same direction is also the Hippodrome or stadium of Domitian. Beyond that, at the extreme southeast corner of the Palatine Hill, are the so-called Baths of Septimius Severus. The ancient references to this building call it Septizonium, a name that has been variously understood as meaning a building of seven stories or as containing a reference to the seven planets. At any rate it seems to have been a splendid edifice with columns and fountains. Since the site is opposite the point where the Via Appia reached the city, the whole configuration may have been intended to present a most impressive appearance to visitors arriving in Rome by the main highway from the south.

On the southwest slope of the Palatine Hill above the Circus Maximus is a portico of granite columns with a number of small rooms attached, a building presumably related

FIGURE 119. Portrait Head of Julius Caesar, in the Greco-Roman Museum in Alexandria.

FIGURE 120. Broken Head of Vespasian (A.D. 69–79), in the Greco-Roman Museum in Alexandria.

originally to the imperial palaces above. On the walls are numerous graffiti, including the word Paedagogium, by which term this building is commonly known. Whether the building was in fact a school for pages of the imperial household, as the word properly means, or a structure for some other use, is not certain. Among the graffiti is a drawing (now in the Thermae Museum in the Baths of Diocletian) of a crucified man with an ass's head, saluted by a smaller figure, and an inscription in Greek reading, "Alexamenos worships his god." Whether this is a crude caricature of the crucifixion of Christ or whether it has some other meaning—perhaps it represents a divinity of the Sethian Gnostics—is not certain. The date of the drawing is perhaps about the beginning of the third century A.D.

Even in the time of Julius Caesar and immediately before the founding of the empire the Forum Romanum no longer seemed sufficient for the public affairs of so large a city as Rome. Julius Caesar, therefore, laid out a new forum, and several of the later emperors did

FIGURE 121. Via della Conciliazione Leading to St. Peter's Church in Rome.

the same. All together these forums were arranged between the Forum Romanum and the slopes of the Quirinal and Viminal hills to the north. In the Middle Ages and afterward these forums were all used as quarries from which to obtain building materials, and dwellings were constructed above the remaining ruins. In 1924 and following the area was cleared and the forums brought back to light as far as possible, and now they are to be seen along the modern Via dei Fori Imperiali, which runs from the Piazza Venezia to the Colosseum. Each forum normally consisted of a central temple surrounded by various public buildings.

The Forum of Julius Caesar was built about 46 B.C. with the spoils of the war in which he defeated Pompey in 48 B.C. At the Battle of Pharsalus, in which the victory was won, Caesar vowed to build a temple to Venus as the mythical ancestress of the Julian line, and the Temple of Venus Genetrix (Venus the Mother) was accordingly erected at the center of his forum. The podium and three columns of this temple are still to be seen on the right

side of the Via dei Fori Imperiali as one proceeds toward the Colosseum. The Forum of Augustus joined the Forum of Julius Caesar on the northeast, but its remains are now on the other side of the modern street. This forum commemorated the Battle of Philippi (42 B.C.) and was intended to provide for more courts and other needs of the city's increasing population. It was a rectangle about 410 ft (125 m) long and 295 ft (90 m) wide, and in the center was the Temple of Mars Ultor ("the Avenger" of the murder of Caesar).

The forum of Vespasian is somewhat further along the Via dei Fori Imperiali in the direction of the Colosseum. In literature the name forum was only applied to this area after the time of Constantine. The original and central feature was the Temple of Peace (Pax), which was begun by Vespasian in A.D. 71 after the destruction of Jerusalem and dedicated in A.D. 75. In the temple, as Josephus (*War* VII 5, 7 §§158–162) reports, were placed the gold vessels from the temple in Jerusalem and also many ancient masterpieces of painting and sculpture. Pliny (*Nat. Hist.* XXXVI 102) regarded

FIGURE 122. Plaza of St. Peter's Church in Rome, with Obelisk from Nero's Circus.

the Basilica Aemilia in the Forum Romanum, the Forum of Augustus, and Vespasian's Temple of Peace as the three most beautiful buildings in the world. Between the Forum of Vespasian and the Forum of Augustus was the Forum of Nerva, which was built by Domitian but dedicated by Nerva in A.D. 97. There the central temple was of the goddess Minerva, to whose cult Domitian was especially devoted.

The Forum of Trajan (Marcus Ulpius Traianus), further to the west, was the last and the largest of the imperial forums. It contained a library with two buildings for Latin and Greek volumes, respectively, the Basilica Ulpia with a large central aisle and two aisles on either side (probably completed in A.D. 112), and the striking and still-standing Column of Trajan (erected in A.D. 113). The column is of marble and, together with its pedestal, is 125 ft (38 m) in height. A spiral staircase ascends the interior. The exterior is decorated with a spiral band of reliefs showing some of the campaigns of Trajan. On the summit of the column was a gilt bronze statue of the emperor, but it was lost and replaced in 1588 with a figure of St. Peter. In the original forum there was no central temple, but Hadrian later constructed a large Temple of Trajan on the northwest side of the library.[3]

Such are the major monuments in the central part of ancient Rome, some of which existed long before the time of Paul, some of which were newly erected in his time, and many of which were built yet later but are a part of what is to be seen and understood when visiting the place Paul wished to come to for so long—and where he arrived in a way strangely different from what he might originally have anticipated. What happened during Paul's imprisonment, at the end of his life, and at the end of the life of Peter and the monuments that memorialized the two apostles are discussed in Chapter 2.

Two persons traditionally associated with Paul and Peter in Rome are also remembered at two sites not far from the area discussed immediately above, namely, Clement and Pudens. The churches that bear their names

are among the parish churches of Rome that are known as "title churches," because they were anciently called by the term *titulus* followed by the name of the owner of the house that became a place of Christian assembly.

Concerning Clement, Irenaeus (*Against Heresies* III 3) states that Peter and Paul founded and organized the church at Rome, which was then led by Linus (cf. II Tim 4:21), Anacletus, and Clement, and Irenaeus says that Clement had seen and been conversant with the apostles and might be said to have their preaching still echoing in his ears and their traditions before his eyes. Irenaeus also refers to Clement's letter to the Corinthians, and this document is still extant and contains quotations from Paul's letters (Rom, I Cor, Eph). In the *Liber Pontificalis* Clement is described as a Roman from the district of the Caelian Hill.[4]

As described above, the Caelian Hill is to the right as one looks from the Porta Capena toward the Colosseum. In that district east of the Colosseum, on the north side of the present Via San Giovanni in Laterano (which leads to the Basilica of St. John Lateran), is San Clemente, the Church of St. Clement, anciently called the *titulus Clementis*. Underneath this church, as revealed by modern excavation, are the remains of two Roman buildings, one a market hall or warehouse and the other a private house from the end of the first century A.D. The house is believed to have been the house of Clement and a place of early Christian assembly. At the beginning of the second century a Mithraeum, a cult place for the worship of Mithras, was built just across a narrow lane from the building in which the Christians met, and the two religions were evidently practiced in propinquity to each other. After the triumph of Christianity under Constantine and later, the house of Mithras was deserted by its devotees, and the place of

FIGURE 123. St. Paul's Church Outside the Walls of Rome, with Statue of Paul.

FIGURE 124. Altar of Mithras, Under the Church of San Clemente in Rome.

Christian meeting was extended by an apse that projected into the former Mithraeum. The meeting place was also provided with an atrium and narthex and was arranged in the interior with a broad central aisle and two side aisles, i.e., it was made into a church of the basilican type. This must have been the church to which Jerome refers when, in the chapter on Clement in his *Lives of Illustrious Men* (written at Bethlehem in A.D. 392), he says that "a church built at Rome preserves the memory of his name unto this day."

The basilica underwent some restorations in the eighth and ninth centuries, was partially destroyed in 1084 when Rome was sacked by the soldiers of Robert Guiscard, and is partially preserved today as the lower church under the upper Church of St. Clement. The upper church was constructed in 1108. At that time the old lower basilica was buttressed and filled in with rubble to serve as a platform for the new church. The new church was built on the same basilican plan as its predecessor, but on a reduced scale, with narrower aisles and a smaller apse. With minor restorations in the eighteenth century, this is the present upper Church of St. Clement, and it still preserves the purity of form and classic dignity of an early Christian basilica. The archeological discoveries are congruent with the tradition that the house below was indeed the house of Clement of Rome and a meeting place of the early Christians.

Turning to Pudens, the church of Santa Pudenziana is on the present Via Urbana and was anciently called the *titulus Pudentis ecclesia Pudentiana*. The Via Urbana is in the region between the Viminal and the Esquiline hills near the ancient Vicus Patricius, where there were residences of patrician families as early as the time of the Roman Republic. The title of the church reflects the tradition that it occupies the site of the house of Pudens, presumably the Roman Christian mentioned in II Tim 4:21 as sending greetings to Timothy. It is believed that Pudens was a Roman senator who gave hospitality to Peter, and that the church was built in honor of his daughter Pudentiana. According to the tradition Pudens was the father of two sons named Novatus and Timothy and of two daughters named Pudentiana and Praxedis. In a passage found in certain late manuscripts of the *Liber Pontificalis* (probably drawn from the *Acts of Sts. Pudentiana and Praxedis*), it is stated of Pope Pius I (A.D. 146–161):

He by request of the blessed Praxedis dedicated a church in the baths of Novatus in the Vicus Patricius to the honor of her sister, the holy Pudentiana, where also he offered many gifts and frequently he ministered, offering sacrifice to the Lord. Moreover he erected a font of baptism and

FIGURE 125 (top). Early Christian Painting in the Flavian Area (c. A.D. 100) of the Catacomb of Domitilla in Rome. FIGURE 126 (bottom). Apse Mosaic in the Church of Santa Pudenziana in Rome.

with his own hand he blessed and dedicated it and many who gathered to the faith he baptized in the name of the Trinity.[5]

Thus the supposition is that the house of Pudens was a meeting place of the early Christians and that the church named for his daughter and the baptistery had been constructed in the adjacent Baths of Novatus by the middle of the second century A.D.

Archeologically, fragments of a mosaic pavement and of a wall have been found at a depth of 30 ft (9 m) under the present church of Santa Pudenziana, and the fragments are probably from patrician residences of the time of Augustus or even of the Republic. Also in the first part of the second century A.D. private baths were constructed on the site, and bricks have been found stamped with dates equivalent to A.D. 127–129 and with the name of Pudens. Later, in an epitaph of A.D. 384, there is mention of the church of Pudentiana, and other texts indicate that the church was rebuilt by two priests under Pope Siricius (A.D. 384–399). At that time it was transformed from a hall church into a three-aisled basilica, and almost certainly at the same time the great mosaic was made that, although later somewhat cut away and somewhat restored, still adorns the semidome of the apse. In the center of the scene Christ is arrayed in a tunic of gold, is seated upon a throne, and holds an open book with the inscription, "The Lord, Guardian (conservator) of the Church of Pudentiana." At his left hand is Peter, at his right hand is Paul, and each apostle is flanked by four more apostles, although the outermost one on either side was lost when the apse was narrowed. On either side also a robed woman holds a crown over the head of Peter and of Paul. In a fifth-century mosaic panel in the church of Santa Sabina similar figures are labeled Ecclesia ex Circumcisione and Ecclesia ex Gentibus, so here too we probably have the symbolic representative of the Jewish church and the Gentile church, each crowning the apostle especially associated with its church. Less likely is the identification of the two women with Pudentiana and Praxedis. The background of the mosaic is formed by a portico, above which in the center rises the rough rock of Calvary, surmounted by a large jeweled cross. At the viewer's left are the buildings of the Church of the Holy Sepulcher in Jerusalem (the martyrion or place of witness, partly hidden behind the rock of Calvary; the rotunda or Anastasis; and the baptistery), and at the viewer's right, the church of Hagia Sion and the Cenacle on Mount Zion and, above, the church of Eleona on the Mount of Olives. In the clouds above are the symbols of the four evangelists—from left to right as seen by the viewer, the man or angel, lion, ox, and eagle (cf. Ezk 10:14; Rev 4:7) representing, respectively, Matthew, Mark, Luke, and John.[6]

Thus in this early and immensely impressive mosaic is symbolized much of the history of early Christianity, and we have traversed much of that history as we have followed Paul, Peter, John, and some of the other apostles to archeological sites across the Mediterranean world.

NOTES

CHAPTER 1

1. R. G. Heard, "The Old Gospel Prologues," JTS New Series 6 (1955), p. 7.

2. Ferdinand Christian Baur, *Paul the Apostle of Jesus Christ*, 2 vols. (London, Edinburgh: Williams and Norgate, 2d ed., 1873–75), 1, p. 5–14.

3. Albert Schwegler, *Das nachapostolische Zeitalter*, 2 vols. (Tübingen: L. F. Fues, 1846), 2, p. 77.

4. Eduard Zeller, *The Contents and Origin of the Acts of the Apostles*, 2 vols. (London, Edinburgh: Williams and Norgate, 1875–76), 2, p. 283.

5. Adolf Jülicher, *An Introduction to the New Testament* (London: Smith, Elder, 1904), pp. 434f.

6. John Knox, *Chapters in a Life of Paul* (New York: Abingdon-Cokesbury, 1950), pp. 41, 81f.

7. Günther Bornkamm, *Paul, Paulus* (London: Hodder and Stoughton, 1971), pp. xi, xv–xx.

8. Ernst Haenchen, *The Acts of the Apostles, A Commentary* (Philadelphia: Westminster, 1971), p. 116.

9. E. M. Blaiklock, *The Archaeology of the New Testament* (Grand Rapids, Mich.: Zondervan, 1970), pp. 93–95.

10. William M. Ramsay, *St. Paul the Traveller and the Roman Citizen* (New York: G. P. Putnam's Sons; London: Hodder and Stoughton, 1896), pp. 7f., 9f., 14.

11. William M. Ramsay, *The Bearing of Recent Discovery on the Trustworthiness of the New Testament* (London, New York: Hodder and Stoughton, 2d ed., 1915), pp. 81, 85.

12. F. F. Bruce, *The Acts of the Apostles* (London: Tyndale, 2d ed., 1952), pp. 2–6, 15–18, 34–40.

13. Alfred Wikenhauser, *Die Apostelgeschichte und ihr Geschichtswert*, Neutestamentliche Abhandlungen, 8:3–5 (Münster in Westf.: Aschendorff, 1921), and *Die Apostelgeschichte*, Regensburger Neues Testament, 5 (Regensburg: F. Pustet, 4th ed., 1961), p. 16.

14. A. N. Sherwin-White, *Roman Society and Roman Law in the New Testament* (Oxford: Clarendon Press, 1963), pp. 63–69, 78ff., 172f.

15. R.P.C. Hanson, *The Acts*, New Clarendon Bible (Oxford: Clarendon Press, 1967), pp. 2f., 11.

16. Ward Gasque, *A History of the Criticism of the Acts of the Apostles*, Beiträge zur Geschichte der biblischen Exegese, 17 (Tübingen: Mohr, 1976), pp. 5, 309.

17. E. Jerry Vardaman, "Lysanias and Quirinius: A New Solution Through Micrographics" (Unpublished paper sent by its author to the present writer on Jan. 29, 1975). As to the death of Herod the Great, the king died prior to a Passover and shortly after a lunar eclipse (Josephus, *Ant.* XVII 6, 4 §167), which was probably either the partial lunar eclipse of Mar. 13, 4 B.C., or the total lunar eclipse of Jan. 10, 1 B.C. For Herod's death in 4 B.C. (with the birth of Jesus necessarily before that date), see Timothy D. Barnes, "The Date of Herod's Death," JTS 19 (1968), pp. 204–209; for his death in 1 B.C. (with the birth of Jesus in 3/2 B.C.), see W. E. Filmer, "The Chronology of the Reign of Herod the Great," JTS 17 (1966), pp. 283–298, and Ernest L. Martin, *The Birth of Christ Recalculated* (Pasadena, Calif.: Foundation for Biblical Research, 2d ed., 1980). See also Chap. 2 n.13.

18. Adolf Harnack, *The Date of the Acts and of the Synoptic Gospels*, Crown Theological Library, New Testament Studies, 4 (New York: G. P. Putnam's Sons, 1911), p. 99.

19. Bruce, *Acts of the Apostles*, pp. 11–13. For references to other similar views see Gasque, *History of the Criticism* p. 264 n.27, and John A. T. Robinson, *Redating the New Testament* (London: S.C.M. Press, 1976), pp. 91f.

20. Adolf Deissmann, *Paul, A Study in Social and Religious History* (London: Hodder and Stoughton, 2d ed., 1926), p. 18.

21. Robinson, *Redating the New Testament*, pp. 156–161.

22. William M. Ramsay, *The Church in the Roman Empire Before A.D. 170* (New York, London: G. P. Putnam's Sons, 1893), pp. 31–33, 382–391.

23. Adolf Harnack, *Geschichte der altchristlichen Literatur bis Eusebius*, 2 pts., 4 vols. (Leipzig: J. C. Hinrichs, 2d ed., 1958), 2:1, p. 505.

24. For the apocryphal New Testament see Edgar Hennecke, Wilhelm Schneemelcher, and R. McL. Wilson, eds., *New Testament Apocrypha*, 2 vols. (London: Lutterworth Press, 1963–65).

25. For the church fathers see Berthold Altaner, *Patrology* (New York: Herder and Herder, 1960), and Johannes Quasten, *Patrology*, 3 vols. (Utrecht: Spectrum, 1950–60).

CHAPTER 2

1. Richard A. Parker and Waldo H. Dubberstein, *Babylonian Chronology 626 B.C.-A.D. 75* (Providence: Brown University Press, 1956), p. 25.

2. Willy Liebenam, *Fasti Consulares Imperii Romani von 30 v. Chr. bis 565 n. Chr. mit Kaiserliste und Anhang*, KLT 41–43 (Bonn: A. Marcus and E. Weber, 1909); E. Mary Smallwood, *Documents Illustrating the Principates of Gaius, Claudius, and Nero* (London: Cambridge University Press, 1967).

3. M. J. Routh, *Reliquiae Sacrae*, 5 vols. (Oxford: Typographeo academico, 1846–48), 2, pp. 238–309, 357–509.

4. Rudolf Helm, *Die Chronik des Hieronymus*, GCS, Eusebius VII (Berlin: Akademie Verlag, 2d ed., 1956).

5. Josef Karst, *Die Chronik aus dem Armenischen übersetz mit textkritischem Commentar*, GCS, Eusebius V (Leipzig: J. C. Hinrichs, 1911).

6. Routh, *Reliquiae Sacrae*, p. 306, excerpt L.

7. Liebenam, *Fasti Consulares Imperii Romani*, p. 11.

8. Helm, *Die Chronik des Hieronymus*, p. 174.

9. Karst, *Die Chronik aus dem Armenischen übersetz*, p. 213.

10. F. F. Bruce, *New Testament History* (London: Nelson, 1971), p. 201 n.20. Konradin Ferrari D'Occhieppo, professor of theoretical astronomy at the University of Vienna, is reported (*Agence France-Presse*, Apr. 7, 1976) as confirming the two possible dates of April 7, 30, and Apr. 3, 33 – and likewise preferring the date in the year 30.

11. CAH 10 (1934), p. 638.

12. Bo Reicke, *The New Testament Era* (Philadelphia: Fortress Press, 1968), p. 183.

13. Lk 3:1 dates the opening of the work of John the Baptist in the fifteenth year of Tiberius, therefore most probably in the year from Aug. 19, A.D. 28, to Aug. 18, A.D. 29 (Table 1), and the baptism and the beginning of the ministry of Jesus followed, therefore, probably in the fall of 28 or the summer or fall of 29. Jn 2:13, 6:4, and 11:55 specifically name three Passovers. If Jn 2:13 and 11:55 refer to the same Passover (when the cleansing of the Temple took place, probably in the climactic action of the ministry), then there could have been a half year from the fall of 28 to the spring of 29 (Jn 6:4) and a full year on to the spring of 30 (Jn 2:13 and 11:55), a total ministry of about one and one-half years ending at Passover in the year 30. If Jn 2:13, 6:4, and 11:55 refer to three separate Passovers, and if there was another unmentioned Passover in the period before the mention of a feast in Jn 5:1 (perhaps the Feast of Tabernacles in the fall), there could have been a half year from the fall of 29 to the first Passover in 30 and three full years thereafter to the Passovers of 31, 32, and 33, thus an entire ministry of about three and one-half years ending at Passover in the year 33 (Harold W. Hoehner, *Chronological Aspects of the Life of Christ.* [Grand Rapids; Mich.: Zondervan, 1977]; Ernest L. Martin, *The Birth of Christ Recalculated* [Pasadena, Calif.: Foundation for Biblical Research, 1978], p. 51).

E. J. Vardaman's discovery of evidence for placing Quirinius's assumption of office in the East as early as 11 B.C. leads him, however, to assign the birth of Jesus to a date c. 11 B.C. and no later than 10 B.C.; along with this Vardaman would place the death of Jesus earlier also, and he suggests that an earlier date fits better with what Josephus says about Pilate, if what Josephus says is rightly understood. In the passage in question Josephus (*Ant.* XVIII 4, 3 §89) states that Vitellius sent his friend Marcellus to administer Judea and ordered Pilate to Rome to give an account of himself to the emperor; so Pilate, having spent ten years in Judea, hurried to Rome, but before he got there "Tiberius had already passed away" (in the usual translation). Since Tiberius died on Mar. 16, A.D. 37, the usual dates given for the procuratorship of Pilate are approximately A.D. 26–36. But the suggestion has been made that the verb used by Josephus (μεταστάς) should be translated so that the passage reads "Tiberius had already moved"–i.e. to Capri, which he did around A.D. 26–27–and the death of Jesus would have to have been prior to this earlier date of Pilate's departure from Judea (communications of E. J. Vardaman to the present writer on May 30 and Sept. 19, 1979).

14. Reicke, *New Testament Era*, p. 191.

15. Ibid., p. 193.

16. Ibid., pp. 218f.

17. Dale Moody, "A New Chronology for the Life and Letters of Paul" (Paper sent from Jerusalem by the author to the present writer on Mar. 9, 1976), p. 12.

18. S. Dockx, "Chronologie de la vie de Saint Paul depuis sa conversion jusqu'à son séjour a Rome," *Novum Testamentum* 13 (1971), p. 284.

19. Liebenam, *Fasti Consulares Imperii Romani*, p. 104.

20. Edmund Groag, *Die römischen Reichsbeamten von Achaia bis auf Diokletian*, Akademie der Wissenschaften in Wien, Schriften der Balkankommission, Antiquarische Abteilung, 9 (Vienna, Leipzig: Hölder-Pichler-Tempsky, 1939), pp. 33f.

21. Hans Lietzmann, "Ein neuer Fund zur Chronologie des Paulus," ZWT 53/n.s.18 (1911), pp. 348f; Adolf Deissmann, *Paul, A Study in Social and Religious History* (London: Hodder and Stoughton, 2d ed., 1926), p. 272; Dockx, "Chronologie de la vie de Saint Paul," pp. 277–279.

22. George Ogg, *The Chronology of the Life of Paul* (London: Epworth Press, 1968), pp. 102f.

23. Cf. Dockx, "Chronologie de la vie de Saint Paul," p. 303.

24. Reicke, *New Testament Era*, p. 205.

25. A. Reifenberg, *Ancient Jewish Coins* (Jerusalem: R. Mass, 3d ed., 1963), no. 136, pp. 27f., 57, pl. IX; Ya'akov Meshorer, *Jewish Coins of the Second Temple Period* (Tel Aviv: Am Hassefer, 1967), no. 234, p. 174, pl. XXX.

26. ΕΤΟΥΣ (ἔτους), "of the Year," was abbreviated to L as a fragmentary form of initial Ε (Lloyd R. Laing, *Coins and Archaeology* [New York: Schocken Books, 1969], p. 21).

27. E. Jerry Vardaman, "Lysanias and Quirinius: A New Solution Through Micrographics" (Unpublished paper sent by its author to the present writer on Jan. 29, 1975), p. 13, and personal letters from Vardaman to the present writer on Feb. 23, Apr. 23, and May 14, 1976.

28. Liebenam, *Fasti Consulares Imperii Romani*, p. 13; Smallwood, *Documents Illustrating the Principates of Gaius, Claudius, and Nero*, p. 5.

29. Helm, *Die Chronik des Hieronymus*, p. 182.

30. Edwin Smith in Tom Davin, ed., *The Rudder Treasury* (New York: Sheridan House, 1953), pp. 55–66; James Smith, *The Voyage and Shipwreck of St. Paul* (London: Longmans, Green, 4th ed., 1880), pp. 126f.

31. Adolf Harnack, *The Date of the Acts and of the Synoptic Gospels*, Crown Theological Library, New Testament Studies, 4 (New York: G. P. Putnam's Sons, 1911), p. 94.

32. Jean-Luc Vesco, *En Méditerranee avec l'Apôtre Paul* (Paris: Editions du Cerf, 1972), p. 202.

33. Theodor Zahn, *Introduction to the New Testament*, 3 vols. (Edinburgh: T. and T. Clark, 1909), 2, p. 12.

34. CAH 10 (1934), pp. 729f.

35. Moody, "A New Chronology for the Life and Letters of Paul," p. 16.

36. Zahn, *Introduction to the New Testament*, 2, pp. 9f.

37. Edgar Hennecke, Wilhelm Schneemelcher, and R. McL. Wilson, *New Testament Apocrypha*, 2 vols. (London: Lutterworth Press, 1963–65), 2, pp. 279f.

38. Hans Lietzmann, *Petrus und Paulus in Rom* (Berlin, Leipzig: W. de Gruyter, 2d ed., 1927), pp. 242–245; Otto F. A. Meinardus, "Paul's Missionary Journey to Spain: Tradition and Folklore," BA 41 (1978), pp. 61–63.

39. Lietzmann in ZWT 53/n.s. 18 (1911), p. 352.

40. Stewart Perowne, *The Later Herods* (London: Hodder and Stoughton, 1958), pp. 59, 74.

41. For Jewishness as determined by the mother rather than the father, see Ac 16:3, where Paul circumcised Timothy because he had a Jewish mother.

42. S. Dockx, "Essai de chronologie pétrinienne," RSR 62 (1974), p. 227.

43. Ibid., p. 223.

44. Victor A. Tcherikover and Alexander Fuks, *Corpus Papyrorum Judaicarum*, 3 vols. (Cambridge, Mass.: Published for the Magnes Press, Hebrew Uni-

versity by Harvard University Press, 1957–60), 2, p. 199, no. 419d; E. J. Vardaman in a communication to the present writer on Sept. 19, 1979.

45. Helm, *Die Chronik des Hieronymus*, p. 179.

46. Dockx, "Essai de chronologie pétrinienne," p. 228 and n.20.

47. Ibid., pp. 233f.

48. Helm, *Die Chronik des Hieronymus*, p. 186.

49. Zahn, *Introduction to the New Testament*, 2, p. 69.

50. For example, this date for Peter by Theodor Klauser, *Die römische Petrustradition im Lichte der neuen Ausgrabungen unter der Peterskirche* (Cologne, Opladen: Westdeutscher Verlag, 1956), p. 16; and for both Peter and Paul by F. W. Beare, *The First Epistle of Peter* (Oxford: Basil, Blackwell, 3d ed., 1970), pp. 29f.

51. Engelbert Kirschbaum, *The Tombs of St Peter and St Paul* (New York: St. Martin's Press, 1959), p. 122.

52. Dockx, "Essai de chronologie pétrinienne," p. 240.

53. Hennecke, Schneemelcher, and Wilson, *New Testament Apocrypha*, 2, p. 280.

54. Ibid., 2, p. 386.

55. R. A. Lipsius and M. Bonnet, *Acta Apostolorum Apocrypha*, 2 pts., 3 vols. (Hildesheim: Georg Olms, 1959), 1, pp. 11f.

56. Ibid., 1, pp. 172, 216.

57. Louise Ropes Loomis, *The Book of the Popes* (*Liber Pontificalis*), vol. 1, *To the Pontificate of Gregory I* (New York: Columbia University Press, 1916), p. 5.

58. Lipsius and Bonnet, *Acta Apostolorum Apocrypha*, 1, p. 214.

59. Pio V. Pinto, *The Pilgrim's Guide to Rome* (New York: Harper and Row, 1975), pp. 101f.

60. Kirschbaum, *Tombs of St Peter and St Paul*, p. 122.

61. Samuel B. Platner and Thomas Ashby, *A Topographical Dictionary of Ancient Rome* (London: Oxford University Press, 1929), p. 546.

62. Ibid., pp. 264f.

63. Ibid., pp. 325f., 340, 358; Margherita Guarducci, *The Tomb of St. Peter* (New York: Hawthorn Books, 1960), pp. 50f., 55f., fig. 9.

64. Guarducci, *Tomb of St. Peter*, pp. 46, 63.

65. B. M. Apollonj-Ghetti et al., *Esplorazioni sotto la confessione di San Pietro in Vaticano eseguite negli anni 1940–1949*, 2 vols. (Vatican City: Tipografia poliglotta vaticana, 1951); Guarducci, *Tomb of St. Peter*, p. 63.

66. Guarducci, *Tomb of St. Peter*, pp. 58f.

67. Ibid., pp. 80–88.

68. Ibid., pp. 132–135.

69. Jocelyn Toynbee and John Ward Perkins, *The Shrine of St. Peter and the Vatican Excavations* (London, New York: Longmans, Green, 1956), p. 154.

70. Ibid., p. 197.

71. Ibid., p. 199, fig. 19.

72. Loomis, *Book of the Popes*, 1, p. 53.

73. R. Lanciani, *Pagan and Christian Rome* (Boston, New York: Houghton Mifflin, 1892), p. 128; Arthur S. Barnes, *St. Peter in Rome and His Tomb on the Vatican Hill* (London: S. Sonnenschein, 1900), p. 97.

74. Pinto, *Pilgrim's Guide to Rome*, pp. 101f.

75. R. Lanciani, *Wanderings Through Ancient Roman Churches* (Boston, New York: Houghton Mifflin, 1924), p. 169.

76. Kirschbaum, *Tombs of St Peter and St Paul*, p. 181, citing the epigraphers G. B. de Rossi and A. Silvagni.

77. Lietzmann, *Petrus und Paulus in Rom*, p. 316, plan; Kirschbaum, *Tombs of St Peter and St Paul*, p. 184; Vesco, *En Méditerranee avec l'Apôtre Paul*, p. 209, plan 19.

78. Lietzmann, *Petrus und Paulus in Rom*, pp. 157f.

79. Hans Lietzmann, *The Three Oldest Martyrologies* (Bonn: A. Marcus and E. Weber, 1904), p. 4.

80. For this text see Lietzmann, *Petrus und Paulus in Rom*, p. 81.

81. Liebenam, *Fasti Consulares Imperii Romani*, p. 30.

82. Paul Styger, *Die römischen Katakomben* (Berlin: Verlag für Kunstwissenschaft, 1933), pp. 177–184; Guarducci, *Tomb of St. Peter*, pp. 168–171.

83. Styger, *Die römischen Katakomben*, p. 339.

84. Guarducci, *Tomb of St. Peter*, p. 169.

85. Ibid., p. 170.

86. Oscar Cullmann, *Peter: Disciple, Apostle, Martyr* (London: S.C.M. Press, 2d ed., 1962), p. 132.

87. Styger, *Die römischen Katakomben*, pp. 341–344, pls. 50, 51.

88. H. Leclercq, "Refrigerium," in DACL 14:2, cols. 2180f., 2189 (inscriptions of Aurelius Vitalio and Fl. Concordius).

89. Toynbee and Perkins, *Shrine of St. Peter and the Vatican Excavations*, p. 189 n.56.

90. Lietzmann, *Three Oldest Martyrologies*, p. 4.

91. Styger, *Die römischen Katakomben*, pp. 345f.

92. Ibid., p. 181.

93. Guarducci, *Tomb of St. Peter*, p. 171.

94. Lietzmann, *Petrus und Paulus in Rom*, p. 107.

95. Ibid., p. 136.

96. Loomis, *Book of the Popes*, 1, p. 26.

97. Styger, *Die römischen Katakomben*, p. 348.

98. Loomis, *Book of the Popes*, 1, p. 5.

99. Lietzmann, *Petrus und Paulus in Rom*, p. 89.

100. Cullmann, *Peter: Disciple, Apostle, Martyr*, p. 128.

101. Guarducci, *Tomb of St. Peter*, pp. 176f.

102. Loomis, *Book of the Popes*, 1, p. 31.

103. Guarducci, *Tomb of St. Peter*, pp. 174f.

104. Cullmann, *Peter: Disciple, Apostle, Martyr*, p. 129.

105. Loomis, *Book of the Popes*, 1, p. 5.

106. Kirschbaum, *Tombs of St Peter and St Paul*, p. 212.

107. Ibid., p. 121.

108. Moody, "A New Chronology for the Life and Letters of Paul", p. 23.

109. CAH 10 (1934), pp. 735, 738.

110. Helm, *Die Chronik des Hieronymus*, p. 185.

111. Karst, *Die Chronik aus dem Armenischen übersetz*, p. 216.

112. Zahn, *Introduction to the New Testament*, 2, pp. 77f.

113. Pinto, *Pilgrim's Guide to Rome*, p. 37.

114. A. C. McGiffert in NPNFSS I, p. 132 n.6.

115. Zahn, *Introduction to the New Testament*, 3, p. 180.

116. Ibid., 3, p. 432.

117. Isbon T. Beckwith, *The Apocalypse of John* (New York: Macmillan, 1919), p. 362 n.1.

118. Zahn, *Introduction to the New Testament*, 2, pp. 452f. n.13.

119. Bruce, *New Testament History*, p. 376 n.36.

120. Helm, *Die Chronik des Hieronymus*, pp. 192f. The Latin *hospitiolum* is the diminutive of *hospitium*, which basically means hospitality and therefore signifies a place of entertainment for persons to whom hospitality is offered; in his *Letter to Eustochium* (CVIII 12) Jerome uses *hospitium* for "the hospitable roof" of Mary and Martha at Bethany.

121. William Wright, *Apocryphal Acts of the Apostles* (1871; reprint ed., Amsterdam: Philo Press, 2 vols., 1968), 2, pp. 55-57.

122. For the *Acts of John* according to Prochorus see Theodor Zahn, *Acta Joannis* (Erlangen: Deichert, 1880), pp. 1-165; and Richard Adelbert Lipsius, *Die Apokryphen Apostelgeschichten und Apostellegenden*, 3 vols. (Braunschweig: C. A. Schwetschke, 1883–90), 1, pp. 366-397. In the Greek text in Zahn, *Acta Joannis*, see pp. 45f. for Trajan, p. 151 for the dif-

123. F. Lamar Cribbs, "A Reassessment of the Date of Origin and the Destination of the Gospel of John," JBL 89 (1970), pp. 38-55.

124. Wright, *Apocryphal Acts of the Apostles*, 2, pp. 58f.

125. The spelling of the name with a final Nun—Neron—and the spelling of the title are confirmed in an Aramaic document from Murabba'at dated to the "second year of the emperor Nero" (D. A. Hillers in BASOR 170 [Apr. 1963], p. 65), and the spelling of the name also corresponds with the Greek Νέρων. The spelling of the name without the final Nun—Nero—corresponds with the Latin (e.g., Tacitus, *Annals* XIII 7). Other solutions to the puzzle of the number 616 are of course also possible, e.g., this for Gaius Caligula:

Γ	3
A	1
I	10
O	70
Σ	200
K	20
A	1
I	10
Σ	200
A	1
P	100
	616

126. Bernhard W. Henderson, *The Life and Principate of the Emperor Nero* (Philadelphia: J. B. Lippincott, 1905), pp. 439-443; cf. George Edmundson, *The Church in Rome in the First Century*, Bampton Lectures (London, New York: Longmans, Green, 1913), pp. 167-178. For the date of the Book of Revelation in the period following the death of Nero in June of 68 and up to Jan. 15, 69, when Galba was killed—the tumultuous time known as the Year of the Four Emperors—see Albert A. Bell, Jr., "The Date of John's Apocalypse, The Evidence of Some Roman Historians Reconsidered," NTS 25 (1979), pp. 93-102.

127. John A. T. Robinson, *Redating the New Testament* (London: S.C.M. Press, 1976), pp. 13-30, 352.

128. Hennecke, Schneemelcher, and Wilson, *New Testament Apocrypha*, 2, pp. 254-258; Francesco Corsaro, *Le ΠΡΑΞΕΙΣ di Giovanni* (Catania: Uni-

versità di Catania, 1968), pp. 92–103.

129. Wright, *Apocryphal Acts of the Apostles*, 2, p. 64.

130. Zahn, *Acta Joannis*, p. CLII.

131. Ibid., pp. 162–165.

132. Wright, *Apocryphal Acts of the Apostles*, 2, pp. 43–59.

133. Virgilio Corbo, *The House of St. Peter at Capharnaum* (Jerusalem: Franciscan Press, 1969), and *New Memoirs of Saint Peter by the Sea of Galilee* (Jerusalem: Franciscan Press, 1969).

134. Josef Keil, "XVIII. Vorläufiger Bericht über die Ausgrabungen in Ephesos," *Jahreshefte des österreichischen archäologischen Institutes in Wien* XXIX (1934), cols. 146–148.

135. John Wilkinson, *Egeria's Travels* (London: S.P.C.K., 1971), p. 122 (original Latin text, chap. 23, sec. 10).

136. The Church of All the Apostles in Constantinople was built by Constantine to be his own burial place, was rebuilt by Justinian, and in 1453 upon the fall of Constantinople to the Turks, was torn down and replaced by the Mosque of Sultan Muhammad II the Conqueror.

137. Titus Tobler and Augustus Molinier, eds., *Itinera Hierosolymitana et Descriptiones Terrae Sanctae*, 2 vols. (Geneva: J.-G. Fick, 1879–85), 1, p. 256 (*Hodoeporicon*, sec. 11).

138. *Forschungen in Ephesos*, Veröffentlicht vom Österreichischen Archäologischen Institut, vol. 4, pt. 3, *Die Johanneskirche* (Vienna, 1951); Wilhelm Alzinger in PWRE Supplementband XII (1970), cols. 1681–1683.

139. *Forschungen in Ephesos*, vol. 4, pt. 3, p. 185; PWRE Supplementband XII (1970), col. 1681.

140. *Forschungen in Ephesos*, vol. 4, pt. 3, p. 225, fig. 59.

141. Franz Miltner, *Ephesos, Stadt der Artemis und des Johannes* (Vienna: F. Deuticke, 1958), p. 110.

142. *Forschungen in Ephesos*, vol. 4, pt. 3, p. 228, fig. 61.

143. Ibid., pl. LXVIII.

CHAPTER 3

1. W. C. van Unnik, *Tarsus or Jerusalem, The City of Paul's Youth* (London: Epworth Press, 1962), pp. 17–45, 59–72.

2. Adolf Deissmann, *Paul, A Study in Social and Religious History* (London: Hodder and Stoughton, 2d ed., 1926), p. 90.

3. George Adam Smith, *The Historical Geography of the Holy Land* (London: Hodder and Stoughton, 25th ed., 1931), pp. 672f.

4. Philip K. Hitti, *History of Syria* (New York: Macmillan, 1951), p. 472.

5. David Noel Freedman in BA 41 (1978), p. 152.

6. Stewart Perowne, *The Journeys of St Paul* (London, New York: Hamlyn, 1973), p. 18.

7. Hitti, *History of Syria*, p. 415.

8. J. Sauvaget, "Le plan antique de Damas," *Syria* 26 (1949), pp. 314–358.

9. Colin Thubron, *Mirror to Damascus* (London: Heinemann, 1967), pp. 49f.

10. For the history of Antioch see Glanville Downey, *A History of Antioch in Syria from Seleucus to the Arab Conquest* (Princeton: Princeton University Press, 1961), and *Ancient Antioch* (Princeton: Princeton University Press, 1963).

11. Erwin Preuschen and the quotations from Adolf von Harnack in *The New Schaff-Herzog Encyclopedia of Religious Knowledge*, 13 vols. (New York, London: Funk and Wagnalls, 1908–14), 3, pp. 74f.

12. J. Lassus in PECS, p. 62.

13. Downey, *Ancient Antioch*, p. 211, figs. 45–59.

14. Louis Jalabert and René Mouterde, *Inscriptions grecques et latines de la Syrie*, vol. 3, pt. 2, Bibliothèque Archéologique et Historique, 51 (Paris: P. Geuthner, 1953), no. 1131, pp. 615f.

15. Walther Eltester, "Die Kirchen Antiochias im IV. Jahrhundert," ZNW 36 (1937), p. 273 n.79.

16. Paul Jacquot, *Antioche, centre de tourisme*, 3 vols. (Antioch: Comité de Tourisme d'Antioche, 1931), 2, pp. 375–378; *La Grotte de S. Pierre à Antioche, Étude par un missionaire Capucin* (n.p.: Mission des Capucines en Syrie et en Mesopotamie, 1934); M. Van Gutsem in *Analecta Bollandiana* 54 (1936), p. 184.

17. Eltester, "Die Kirchen Antiochias," pp. 251–286; Downey, *History of Antioch in Syria*, pp. 656–659.

18. Eltester, "Die Kirchen Antiochias," p. 273.

19. H. Harvard Arnason in BA 4 (1941), pp. 49–64, and 5 (1942), pp. 10–16.

CHAPTER 4

1. Tony Spiteris, *The Art of Cyprus* (New York: Reynal and Co. in association with William Morrow, 1970), p. 7.

2. Dora Jane Hamblin, *The First Cities* (New

York: Time-Life Books, 1973), pp. 42–67.

3. Luciano Giovannini, ed., *Arts de Cappadoce*, with the collaboration of the Istituto Internazionale di Arte Liturgica (Rome, Chicago, Genève: Les Éditions Nagel, 1971).

4. For the regions in the province of Galatia see William M. Ramsay, *St. Paul the Traveller and the Roman Citizen* (New York: G. P. Putnam's Sons; London: Hodder and Stoughton, 1896), pp. 104, 111. For the cities see William M. Ramsay, *The Cities of St. Paul* (London: Hodder and Stoughton, 1907).

5. William M. Ramsay, *The Historical Geography of Asia Minor* (1890; reprint ed., Amsterdam: A. M. Hakkert, 1962), p. 24.

6. For sites on the southern coast of Asia Minor see George E. Bean, *Turkey's Southern Shore: An Archaeological Guide* (New York: Praeger, 1968). For the art treasures of Turkey in general see Ekrem Akurgal, Cyril Mango, and Richard Ettinghausen, *Die Türkei und ihre Kunstschätze* (Geneva: Skira, 1966).

7. For Thecla and her martyrium at Silifke see Ernst Lucius, *Die Anfänge des Heiligenkults in der christlichen Kirche* (Tübingen: Mohr, 1904), pp. 205–214; and John Wilkinson, *Egeria's Travels* (London: S.P.C.K., 1971), pp. 288–292.

8. William M. Ramsay, *The Bearing of Recent Discovery on the Trustworthiness of the New Testament* (London, New York: Hodder and Stoughton, 2d ed., 1915), pp. 53–63 and map on p. 64.

9. M. H. Ballance in *Anatolian Studies* 7 (1957), pp. 147–151, and 14 (1964), pp. 139f.

CHAPTER 5

1. George Willis Botsford and Charles Alexander Robinson, *Hellenic History* (New York: Macmillan, 4th ed., 1956), p. 288.

2. N.G.L. Hammond, *A History of Macedonia* (Oxford: Clarendon Press, 1972–), 1, pp. 157f.; Manolis Andronicos, "Regal Treasures from a Macedonian Tomb," *National Geographic Magazine* 154, 1 (July 1978), pp. 55–76; Manolis Andronikos, "The Royal Tomb of Philip II," *Archaeology* 31, 4 (Sept./Oct. 1978), pp. 33–41.

3. Jacques Roger, "L'enceinte basse de Philippes," BCH 62 (1938), pp. 31–35, pls. X, XII, XIII.

4. Paul Collart, *Philippes, ville de Macédoine* (Paris: E. de Boccard, 1937), pp. 319–323, 497.

5. Paul Lemerle, *Philippes et la Macédoine orientale* (Paris: E. de Boccard, 1945), pp. 24–27, pl. I.

6. R. F. Hoddinott, *Early Byzantine Churches in Macedonia and Southern Serbia* (London: Macmillan, 1963), pp. 99–106.

7. Ibid., pp. 169–173.

8. Ibid., pp. 188–193.

9. S. Pelekanidis, "Excavations in Philippi," *Balkan Studies* 8 (1967), pp. 123–126.

10. N. Papahadjis and William Sanford, *Monuments of Thessalonike* (Thessaloniki: S. Molho, reprint of 1957 ed.), p. 10.

11. M. Kiel, "A Note on the Exact Date of Construction of the White Tower of Thessaloniki" *Balkan Studies* 14 (1973), pp. 352–357.

12. Hoddinott, *Early Byzantine Churches in Macedonia and Southern Serbia*, pp. 108–123.

13. Hans-Georg Beck, *Kirche und theologische Literatur im byzantinischen Reich*, Handbuch der Altertumswissenschaft, Byzantinisches Handbuch, div. 12, pt. 2, vol. 1 (Munich: C. H. Beck'sche Verlagsbuchhandlung, 1959), pp. 177, 222, 464.

14. Hoddinott, *Early Byzantine Churches in Macedonia and Southern Serbia*, pp. 173–179.

15. Ibid., pp. 125–155; Dimitri Obolensky, "The Cult of St. Demetrius of Thessaloniki in the History of Byzantine-Slav Relations," *Balkan Studies* 15 (1974), pp. 5ff.

16. In Greek history a "tyrant" was ordinarily a ruler who obtained his position by some means other than hereditary descent.

17. Cyril Edward Robinson, *Hellas, A Short History of Ancient Greece* (Boston: Beacon Press, 1948), p. 7.

18. J. G. Frazer, *Pausanias's Description of Greece*, 6 vols. (London: Macmillan, 2d ed., 1913), 1, pp. xiii, xcv–xcvi.

19. The etymology of the name Mouseion is probably from the Muses, so that this is the Hill of the Muses. On the hill is the monumental tomb, erected between A.D. 114 and 116 in honor of Caius Julius Antiochus Philopappos, a member of the royal dynasty of Commagene in Asia Minor and a benefactor of Athens. In the niches of the buildings there once stood statues not only of Philopappos himself but also of his ancestors, among them, on his left, his grandfather Antiochus IV Epiphanes, last king of Commagene, who was deposed by Vespasian in A.D. 72.

20. J. P. Mahaffy, *Rambles and Studies in Greece* (London: Macmillan, 1878), p. 83.

21. B. P. Pratten in ANF, 2, pp. 155, 162.

22. The length of the track in a Greek stadium was 600 Greek ft (178 m).

23. *Corinth, Results of Excavations,* American School of Classical Studies at Athens (Cambridge, Mass.: Harvard University Press, 1929–), vol. 1, pt. 3, pp. 91–111, 128–132.

24. *Hesperia* 8 (1939), pp. 181–190.

25. *Erastus pro aedilitate sua pecunia stravit,* cf. C. C. McCown in AJA 50 (1946), p. 426.

26. Henry J. Cadbury, "The Macellum of Corinth," JBL 53 (1934), pp. 134–141.

27. Benjamin Powell, "Greek Inscriptions from Corinth," AJA 7 (1903), pp. 60f.

CHAPTER 6

1. For the sites on the western coast of Asia Minor see George E. Bean, *Aegean Turkey: An Archaeological Guide* (London: Benn, 1966).

2. Wilhelm Alzinger in PWRE Supplementband XII (1970), cols. 1678f.

3. Franz Miltner in *Jahreshefte des österreichischen archäologischen Institutes in Wien* XLIII Beiblatt (1956), cols. 54–58; Dieter Knibbe in PWRE Supplementband XII (1970), col. 296; Wilhelm Alzinger, ibid., cols. 1685–1686.

4. Franz Miltner, *Ephesos, Stadt der Artemis und des Johannes* (Vienna: F. Deuticke, 1958), p. 107.

5. Montague Rhodes James, *The Apocryphal New Testament* (Oxford: Clarendon Press, 1924), pp. 194–227.

6. Pierre-Thomas Camelot, *Ephesus und Chalcedon,* Geschichte der ökumenischen Konzilien, 2 (Mainz: M. Grünewald, 1963), p. 50 n.2.

7. Theodor Zahn, *Acta Joannis* (Erlangen: Deichert, 1880), p. xxx n.2, CLXIXf.; R.L.P. Milburn, *Early Christian Interpretations of History* (London: A. and C. Black, 1954), p. 177; Clemens Kopp, *Das Mariengrab, Jerusalem?–Ephesus?* (Paderborn: Ferdinand Schöningh, 1955), pp. 27f.; Walter J. Burghardt, *The Testimony of the Patristic Age Concerning Mary's Death,* Woodstock Papers, 2 (Westminster, Md.: Newman Press, 1957), pp. 38f.

8. Dieter Knibbe in PWRE Supplementband XII (1970), cols. 296f.

9. Zahn, *Acta Joannis,* p. CLIX n.1; Josef Keil, "Zum Martyrium des heiligen Timotheus in Ephesos," *Jahreshefte des österreichischen archäologischen Institutes in Wien* XXIX (1934), cols. 82–92. For the Katagogia see Dieter Knibbe, ibid. XLVII Beiblatt (1964–65), cols. 28–34; M. Nilsson in PWRE X 2, col. 2459.

10. H. Leclercq, "Sept dormants d'Éphèse," DACL 15:1, cols. 1251–1262; Alzinger in PWRE Supplementband XII (1970), cols. 1684f.

11. William M. Ramsay, *The Letters to the Seven Churches of Asia* (New York: A. C. Armstrong, 1904).

12. E. Akurgal in PECS, pp. 847f.

13. For Pergamum see the many volumes of *Altertümer von Pergamon* now published for the Deutsches Archäologisches Institut by Walter de Gruyter, Berlin; and also Arnold Schober, *Die Kunst von Pergamon* (Vienna: M. F. Rohrer, 1951); and Eva Maria Schmidt, *The Great Altar at Pergamon* (Leipzig: E. A. Seemann, 1962).

14. George M. A. Hanfmann, *Letters from Sardis* (Cambridge, Mass.: Harvard University Press, 1972).

15. George E. Bean, *Turkey Beyond the Maeander, An Archaeological Guide* (London: Ernest Benn, 1971), pp. 232–259.

CHAPTER 7

1. For archeological exploration at Patara see G. Kenneth Sams in *Archaeology* 28 (1975), pp. 202–205.

2. In Roman measures the foot (*pes*) was approximately equal to 11.64 in. (29.57 cm) and the mile (*mille*) to 4,860 ft (1,482 m).

3. R. M. Ogilvie in JTS New Series 9 (1958), pp. 308–314.

4. In Mellieha Bay, the next large bay along the coast, there is evidence of Roman shipwrecks, and one modern theory has suggested placing Paul's experience there rather than at St. Paul's Bay where it is traditionally placed.

5. Stuart Rossiter, *Malta,* The Blue Guides (London: E. Benn, 1968), p. 27 (J. D. Evans), pp. 110–111; D. H. Trump, *Malta: An Archaeological Guide* (London: Faber and Faber, 1972), pp. 133–134; A. Claridge in PECS, p. 569.

6. H. Leclercq in DACL 15:2, col. 1849; Margaret Guido, *Sicily: An Archaeological Guide* (London: Faber and Faber, 1967), p. 186.

7. Amadeo Maiuri in *Rendiconti della Pontificia Accademia Romana di Archeologia* 15 (1939), pp. 193–218.

8. For the Via Appia see R. F. Paget, *Central Italy: An Archaeological Guide* (London: Faber and Faber, 1973), pp. 93–95, 224–239, and map 6.

CHAPTER 8

1. Emeline Richardson, *The Etruscans* (Chicago: University of Chicago Press, 1964), pp. 1–9, 66–70.

2. Albert G. Mackinnon, *The Rome of the Early Church* (London: Lutterworth, 1933), p. 48.

3. For the monuments and sites of ancient Rome see Samuel B. Platner and Thomas Ashby, *A Topographical Dictionary of Ancient Rome* (London: Oxford University Press, 1929); Curtius-Nawrath, *Das antike Rom*, ed. Ernest Nash (Vienna, Munich: Anton Schroll, 4th ed., 1963); Ernest Nash, *Pictorial Dictionary of Ancient Rome* (New York: Praeger, 2d ed., 1968).

4. Louise Ropes Loomis, *The Book of the Popes (Liber Pontificalis)* vol. 1, *To the Pontificate of Gregory I* (New York: Columbia University Press, 1916), p. 7. Identification of this Clement with the Clement mentioned in Phil 4:3 is conjectural.

5. Loomis, *Book of the Popes*, 1, p. 15 n.3.

6. Richard M. Mackowski, *Jerusalem, City of Jesus* (Grand Rapids, Mich.: William B. Eerdmans, 1980), pls. 1, 125, 130, Fig. 24B. Santa Prassede, the Church of St. Praxedis, the sister of Pudentiana, is on the Esquiline Hill on a side street off the Via Merulana. Probably also an ancient foundation, it was reconstructed in A.D. 822 and contains very extensive ninth-century mosaics (see H. Leclercq in DACL 14:2, cols. 1691–1700, 1967–1973).

INDEX OF BIBLICAL REFERENCES

GENERAL INDEX